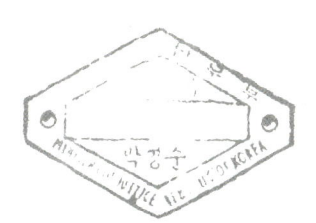

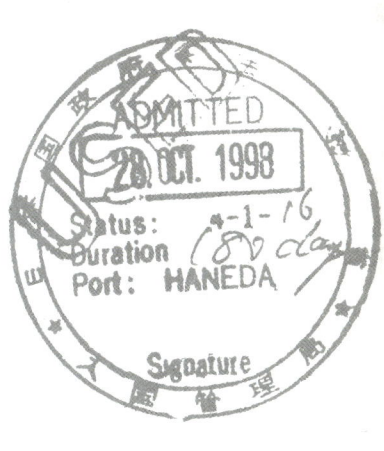

TRAVELER'S BALI COMPANION

The 2001–2002 Traveler's Companions
ARGENTINA • AUSTRALIA • BALI • CALIFORNIA • CANADA • CHILE • CHINA •
COSTA RICA • CUBA • EASTERN CANADA • ECUADOR • FLORIDA • HAWAII •
HONG KONG • INDIA • INDONESIA • IRELAND • JAPAN • KENYA •
MALAYSIA & SINGAPORE • MEDITERRANEAN FRANCE • MEXICO • NEPAL •
NEW ENGLAND • NEW ZEALAND • NORTHERN ITALY • PERU • PHILIPPINES •
PORTUGAL • RUSSIA • SOUTH AFRICA • SOUTHERN ENGLAND • SPAIN • THAILAND •
TURKEY • VENEZUELA • VIETNAM, LAOS AND CAMBODIA • WESTERN CANADA

Traveler's BALI Companion

First published 1998
Second Edition 2001
The Globe Pequot Press
246 Goose Lane, PO Box 480
Guilford, CT 06437 USA
www.globe-pequot.com

© 2001 by The Globe Pequot Press, Guilford CT, USA

ISBN: 0-7627-0951-0

Distributed in the European Union by
World Leisure Marketing Ltd, Unit 11
Newmarket Court, Newmarket Drive,
Derby, DE24 8NW, United Kingdom
www.map-guides.com

Created, edited and produced by
Allan Amsel Publishing, 53, rue Beaudouin
27700 Les Andelys, France.
E-mail: Allan.Amsel@wanadoo.fr
Editor in Chief: Allan Amsel
Editor: Anne Trager
Original design concept: Hon Bing-wah
Picture editor and designer: David Henry

All rights reserved. No part of this publication may be reproduced, stored in
a retrieval system, or transmitted in any form or by any means, electronic,
mechanical or otherwise without the prior permission of the publisher.
Requests for permission should be addressed to The Globe Pequot Press,
246 Goose Lane, PO Box 480, Guilford, CT 06437 USA.

Printed by Samwha Printing Co. Ltd., Seoul, South Korea

TRAVELER'S BALI COMPANION

by Jack Barker and Bradley Winterton

Photographed by Nik Wheeler

Second Edition

GUILFORD
CONNECTICUT

Contents

MAPS	
Bali	8–9
Denpasar	106
Southern Bali and the Bukit	108
Kuta Bay	111
Sanur	127
Nusa Dua	134
Ubud	150
The Heartlands	155
The Heights	173
The East	192
The Northern Coast	211
The West	221
The Offshore Islands	231

TOP SPOTS	11
Take Care of a Turtle	11
Wreck-dive a New Reef	12
Take in a Temple	13
Aspire to the Afterlife	14
Watch Tales Come to Life	16
Lay Back, Relax	20
Share a Shadow Drama	20
Watch Dolphins at Play	21
Climb a Volcano	23

YOUR CHOICE	25
The Great Outdoors	25
Sporting Spree	29
The Open Road	33
Backpacking	36
Living It Up	37
Family Fun	40
Cultural Kicks	43
Shop till You Drop	48
Short Breaks	52
Festive Flings	54
Galloping Gourmet	57
Special Interests	60
Taking a Tour	62

WELCOME TO BALI	69

THE COUNTRY AND ITS PEOPLE	77
From Java Man to an Island Empire	79
A Village Upbringing	86
Where Do You Sit? • Naming of Names • Sex Roles • Birth, Childhood, Love and Marriage • Tooth Filing	
Religion	96
Hotels for the Gods • The Affrighted Sun	

SOUTHERN BALI AND THE BUKIT — 105
Bali's Capital: Denpasar — 106
  General Information • What to See and Do • Shopping • Where to Stay • Where to Eat • How to Get There
Kuta and Around — 110
  General Information • Three Village Centers • Orientation • What to See and Do • Shopping • Where to Stay • Where to Eat • Nightlife • How to Get There • Excursions from Kuta
Sanur — 126
  General Information • Orientation • What to See and Do • Shopping • Where to Stay • Where to Eat • Nightlife • How to Get There • Excursions from Sanur
Nusa Dua — 134
  General Information • What to See and Do • Shopping • Where to Stay • Where to Eat • How to Get There • Excursions from Nusa Dua
Jimbaran Bay — 141
  General Information • What to See and Do • Where to Stay • Where to Eat • How to Get There

UBUD AND THE BALI HEARTLANDS — 147
Ubud — 148
  General Information • What to See and Do • Shopping • Where to Stay • Where to Eat • Nightlife • How to Get There
Excursions East from Ubud — 161
  Tegalalang, Pujung and Sebatu • Tirta Empul • Gunung Kawi • The Moon of Pejeng • Yeh Pulu • Goa Gajah: The Elephant Cave • Bangli
Excursions West of Ubud — 165
  Mengwi • Sangeh

THE HEIGHTS — 169
The Rolling Highlands — 171
  Bedugul • How to Get There
The Volcanic Peaks Route — 172
  Penelokan • Kedisan • Excursions from Kedisan • The Ascent of Mount Batur • Across Lake Batur to Trunyan • Climbing Mount Abang • Batur and Kintamani • Penulisan
The Eastern Highlands — 180
  Besakih and Mount Agung • Rendang to Klungkung

EAST BALI	**187**
Klungkung	189
Where to Stay • How to Get There • Excursions from Klungkung	
Padangbai	194
What to See and Do • Where to Stay • How to Get There	
Candi Dasa	195
General Information • What to See and Do • Where to Stay • Where to Eat and Nightlife • How to Get There • Excursions from Candi Dasa: Tenganan	
Amlapura (Karangasem)	199
The Palace • Where to Stay • How to Get There • Excursions from Amlapura	
Tirtagangga	201
Where to Stay and Eat • How to Get There	
Amed	203
What to See and Do • Where to Stay and Eat • How to Get There	
Tulamben	204
Where to Stay and Eat • How to Get There	

THE NORTHERN COAST	**207**
Singaraja	209
Lovina	210
General Information • What to See and Do • Where to Stay • Where to Eat • Nightlife • How to Get There	
Excursions from Lovina	213
The Hot Springs at Banjar • Pura Beji's Unheard Melodies • Sawan's Gongs • Yeh Sanih	

WEST BALI AND THE BALI BARAT NATIONAL PARK	**217**
West Bali	219
Gilimanuk	219
The Far West	220
The Bali Barat National Park • The Bali Barat Marine Park and the Northwest Coast • Where to Stay and Eat • How to Get There	
Pemuteran	222
Where to Stay and Eat • How to Get There	
The Southwest Coast	223
Negara • Medewi Beach	

THE OFFSHORE ISLANDS	**227**
Nusa Lembongan and Nusa Ceningan	229
Where to Stay and Eat • How to	
Get There	
Nusa Penida	230
General Information • What to See	
and Do • Where to Stay • How to	
Get There	
TRAVELERS' TIPS	**235**
Getting There	236
From the Airport	
Arriving	237
Visas and Red Tape •	
Customs Allowances	
Leaving	238
Departure Tax • Airline Offices •	
Beyond Bali	
Consulates and Embassies	240
Embassies and Consulates in Jakarta •	
Selected Indonesian Missions Abroad	
Tourist Information	241
Getting Around	242
Driving in Bali • Car Rental • Motorbike	
Rental • Bicycle Rental • Bemo Culture	

Accommodation	246
Eating Out	247
Basics	248
Time • Water • Weights and Measures	
Currency and Banking	248
Rate of Exchange	
Communications and Media	249
Telephone • Mail • Press and Radio	
Etiquette	250
What to Wear • Bargaining • Tipping	
Health	253
Water Safety • Sex • Drugs	
Security	255
When to Go	255
What to Take	256
Photography	256
Language	256
Web Sites	257
RECOMMENDED READING	258
QUICK REFERENCE A–Z GUIDE	**259**
to Places and Topics of Interest with	
Listed Accommodation, Restaurants and	
Useful Telephone Numbers	

BALI TOP SPOTS

Take Care of a Turtle

GINGERLY, I PLACED THE BABY TURTLE ON THE SAND. The tiny creature's shell was no more than 10 cm (four inches) across, and felt delicate, firm but brittle, as its flippers made contact with the sand and I released my gentle grip. It was a baby green turtle, among the most endangered of all the ocean's creatures, CITES 1 (Convention on International Trade of Endangered Species) registered, and would need all the help it could get. For a moment the turtle blinked, and then shuffled its flippers to turn through 360 degrees. "They usually do that rotating number," said Chris Brown of Reef Seen Aquatics, who runs the turtle-release program at Pemuteran on Bali's northwest coast. "They sort of set their gyroscopes before they move off."

Then the turtle headed diagonally off toward the waves.

But this wasn't the virgin beach the turtle had been expecting. There was a footprint and the turtle dived straight in, its head buried in the sand and its small back flippers flapping in the air. In 20 or 30 years this turtle would be a meter (over three feet) across, and although never at its best on land would still be able to crawl over boulders and potholes. Not at this age though: it was stuck. I picked it up and set straight. One eye veiled with sand, the turtle set off again, heading straight for the water. A high wave washed the turtle's face clean, and on the next, deeper wash it started to swim out in the clear water. It passed the fine gravel of the breaking waves and headed, safely, out to sea.

A turtle's life is strewn with dangers. From the time an adult female, age 20 or older, lays 100 or more eggs and buries them in the dry sand just above high tide, trouble begins. The turtle's first major predator is man, who digs up the nests for the valuable eggs. Left alone, the sun provides incubation heat and the baby turtles hatch and scrabble to the sea, dodging birds, ghost crabs, and fish keen to eat the tiny, soft-shelled and defenseless creatures. It is estimated that barely one in a thousand go on to reach reproductive age.

Turtles, in Balinese culture, are holy. They are seen as symbolizing fertility,

OPPOSITE: Catamarans cruise along the sheltered waters on the eastern side of the island. ABOVE: Turtles are holy animals to the Balinese.

productiveness, steadfastness and immortality. Unfortunately, in a society where religious observance is a part of daily life, being holy does not make a turtle safe: both eggs and adults are prime material for sacrifice. It is thought that in Bali alone up to 6,000 turtles every year are sacrificed at temple ceremonies and cremations, while more than 24,000 die to serve the restaurant and export market, with their shells being fashioned into tourist handicrafts.

Chris Brown's project aims to screen out all the early risks. Whenever a turtle lays its nest, the first to know are the local fishermen, who also know that Chris pays Rp1000 per egg, twice the going rate. They show him the nest and he reburies the eggs in a shallow sandpit next to his dive center. When they hatch, he transfers the baby turtles to growing pens, where they spend the next few months in sheltered, shallow seawater, munching through sardines, hardening their tiny shells and building up their flipping muscles. Then, when they are somewhere between three and six months old, visitors come and pay Rp50,000 to release a turtle of their own back into the wild.

It's an elegantly simple solution, and releasing a turtle is, it has to be said, a slightly emotional experience. As my turtle flapped off through the shallows toward the deep, I gave it a name and wished it good luck. And although it wouldn't have known or cared, I hoped that helping it through the most dangerous time of its life would give it a good chance to grow to maturity. Although the certificate I was given was soon lost, I still occasionally think about my turtly friend in the Bali Sea.

Wreck-dive a New Reef

IT WAS A BEACH-LAUNCH. I walked down to the waters' edge on the shore of the village of Tulamben and splashed into the warm shallows. The beach wasn't sand so much as round surf-polished stones derived from the heart of the world, laid down by past eruptions of Bali's highest volcano, Mount Agung. Early in the day the towering bulk of this huge volcano was clearly visible, dominating the eastern side of the island and dwarfing the humans who, ant-like, went about their business at the waters edge. Awkwardly, I slid on my fins, pulled my goggles into place, and clipped the regulator into my mouth. Dropping my head below the water surface I pulled myself along the dark discs of the shingle beach and floated out toward one of the world's most rewarding, and accessible, wreck-dives.

This wreck is so celebrated that nowadays there are divers' maps of it; detailed guides, painstakingly compiled, and freely photocopied in the lodges of Tulamben. Built in the United States in 1915 as a cargo steamship, the vessel is 120 m (400 ft) long and named (typically) the *Liberty*. She was torpedoed on January 11, 1942 by a Japanese submarine 15 km (nine miles) off Lombok, while carrying a cargo of raw rubber and railway parts. United States destroyers then towed her to Bali, but she was leaking badly. The crew was eventually evacuated and the *Liberty* was beached at Tulamben.

Over the next 20 years she was stripped of valuables. Then in 1963 Mount Agung erupted, with accompanying earthquakes. The sea received streams of molten lava, and the remains of the *Liberty* slid down into deeper and deeper water, the hull cracking in several places. With some of the superstructure lying a mere two meters under the surface (about seven feet), and much of the rest at around five meters (16 ft), it has become the most popular dive site in Bali, with over 100 divers visiting it on peak days.

The recognizable shape of a broken hull, rippled with color by the strong sun, loomed vastly into view when I'd flipped barely 20 m (70 ft) out to sea. Taking in its size, I paddled over the wreck, laid out in segments on the seabed, thronged with fish and streamed by the dotted exhalations of several divers.

On the seabord side, I emptied my jacket of air and sank down to explore further. Everywhere, life was colonizing rusty edges and encrusting smooth surfaces. There's nothing marine life loves so much as a wreck. Sponges, eels, anemone, gorgonian fans, coral gardens and some 400 species of brilliantly colored tropical fish were making their home in the lockers and corridors, holds and hatches.

Tulamben is notable, at least in part, because there's nothing else to do there except dive the wreck and snorkel. The row of little beach hotels that line the coast for a few hundred meters are all devoted to the cult of diving. There's plenty here for snorkelers too: the presence of the wreck and the attention of the dive industry has preserved this area from dynamite or cyanide fishermen, leaving the fish for divers to enjoy.

Local operators to Tulamben include the Ganda Mayu Bungalow ((0361) 730200 FAX (0361) 730385, on the beach; Tulamben Dive Center ((0363) 41032, Box 31, Amlapura; and Ena Dive Center ((0361) 287945 FAX (0361) 287945, Jalan Tirta Ening 1, Denpasar. The other most rewarding dives in Bali are in the marine park around Menjangan Island off the northwestern coast, and the waters off Lembongan Island in the south.

Take in a Temple

AT SUNSET, PINK LIGHT GLAZES SHEER CLIFFS THAT DROP 76 M (250 FT) INTO THE SEA, RINGING ULU WATU, one of the six holiest temples in this land of thousands of shrines. Dramatic, serene, the carved limestone of Ulu Watu sits on the tip of a short headland that juts out into the blue of the Indian Ocean, and is one of the most popular of all Bali's temples to visit.

The signs of tourism are immediately apparent in the serried ranks of buses, taxis and rented motorbikes. On arrival, visitors are requested to make a donation (of Rp1,100), for which they are lent a sarong and strip of cloth for a belt to enter the holy area appropriately attired. Even this is not enough to get visitors into the temple itself: in the face of such a steady stream of half-clad tourists, this is one temple that is definitely closed.

On the north coast, Pemuteran is a fine stepping-off point for diving or snorkeling the nearby reef.

The temple's history goes back at least 1,000 years and probably more. The sixteenth-century Buddhist sage Wawu Rauh is said to have achieved *moksa* (or attained Nirvana) here. These days the area is inhabited by a small band of mischievous monkeys — and vendors trying to persuade you to buy food to feed them. But though monkeys are well-respected by Hindus, they can and do steal cameras and wallets. Getting stolen goods back can be impossible, and temple attendants have plenty of tales of expensive equipment being dropped from monkey refuges on cliff-top trees into the sea far below.

Half a day is enough to see everything Ulu Watu has to offer. The easiest way to get to Ulu Watu is by taxi. Negotiate a round-trip fee (Rp80,000 is about right from the southern resorts though it can take some time to bargain down to this price). Visitors on a one-way fare should have no difficulty finding transport back to Kuta, Sanur or Nusa Dua until about 4 PM, though for many visitors the best moments are those around sunset. Ulu Watu is on the eastern tip of the Bukit, half an hour's drive east of Nusa Dua and 45 minutes south of Kuta or Sanur.

For many visitors Ulu Watu is the only temple they see, which is a real shame. The setting is spectacular, and it is a good place to watch the sunset and perhaps take in a display of traditional dancing after dark, but, like Tanah Lot to the east, Ulu Watu's spirituality has been eroded by tourism. Even Besakih, while still revered by the Balinese, is not best explored on a day-trip by minibus. The secret with Balinese temples is to visit them when something is happening, and the best way to do this is to keep your eyes open when traveling around for the telltale signs of an upcoming or ongoing ceremony. Women carrying offerings piled high on their heads or sudden crowds of men wearing headbands are unmistakable visual clues, and the gentle sound of *gamelan* music drifting across the breeze is a sure way of tracking down the center of activity.

In smaller temples the rules of etiquette are more important. Buttoned shirts are better than T-shirts, shorts are not good. There'll usually be time to go home and change, as most Balinese festivals go on for many hours and you're unlikely to miss too much. At the entrance someone will offer a sarong, to tie like a sash around your waist, and you'll probably be asked to make a small donation, but from then on you'll be able to experience the full color of this spectacular and ceremonial religion: offerings of fruit emblazoned occasionally with a plucked chicken; 20-man bands playing *gamelan* music for 20 hours at a time; and supplicants, praying to their gods in the ritual dress of the truly devout.

Aspire to the Afterlife

AT THE END OF A TRACK STOOD A HIGH BAMBOO TOWER AND, shining in the morning light, a stylized bull, intricately constructed out of bamboo and papier-mâché and richly adorned. Under a blue and orange canopy, a special *gamelan* group, the *gambong*, was playing bamboo-keyed instruments struck by players holding four hammers apiece. A young man approached to talk. The cremation ceremony was in honor of his grandfather, who had died 12 days earlier, at the age of 60.

Death is seen differently in Bali. It is perceived as a stage that, provided the full rituals of cremation are observed, returns the soul to the five vital elements — solid, liquid, energy, radiance and ether — before its future reincarnation. As much as a Western funeral is grave, solemn and private, the Balinese cremation is celebratory, cheerful and spectacularly public. It is, in fact, something like an English village fete: sociable, pleasant and relaxed.

The timing of this ceremony, and the details of its performance, are key to inclusion in the recycling loom of death and rebirth. This cremation, together with the ceremonies beforehand, was to cost

One of Bali's six holy temples, Ulu Watu, on arid Bukit Badung, presides over the best surf breaks in Bali.

the family the equivalent of US$3,000, a huge amount of money in rural Bali: they'd had to feed the whole village since the day of the grandfather's death. The grandson did not look depressed, though. Sadness, at cremations, makes it harder for the deceased soul to find release.

A man dressed elegantly in sarong, waistband, headdress and tennis shoes photographed the bull and, by means of an attached string, tweaked its extremely virile phallus. Great laughter burst from the *gambong* players. He proceeded to photograph the various groups of villagers present. Everyone was dressed in their best (even visitors should be clean, at least, with new-looking clothes, shirts with collars, and long trousers rather than shorts).

The papier-mâché bull was moved forward, and a bamboo ramp placed against the tower *(wadah)*. Bamboo funeral towers can have anything from one to eleven roofs, like the temple *meru* (tall, tiered towers). This one had seven. Always odd, the number depends on the caste of the deceased. Women climbed up the ramp to rub their hair on the bier. A procession of women carrying offerings on their heads lined in front of the bull.

Two live chicks were placed in the bamboo bull, which was then lifted off the ground and carried on the shoulders of some local youths, its bearers wildly bouncing it and circling round. The body of the deceased, wrapped in a white shroud, was brought out from a house and tied securely into the tower, which was lifted and carried into the lane, passing paddy fields reflecting the now dull sky, trailed by musicians with their cymbals, gongs and drums.

Finally it arrived at the place of burial and cremation: a rough field surrounded by high trees strewn with burned straw and bamboo shrines. The tower was set down and the body was moved into the papier-mâché bull, the ceremonial sarcophagus. After a sprinkling of holy water, the *gambong* struck up, and the lid was replaced in the bull's back. Kerosene (paraffin) was poured onto the bull. A match was struck.

The burning was strangely de-ritualized, as two men in yellow plastic safety helmets took care of the mechanics. Suddenly the musicians started up again, lively and even cheerful. The people relaxed, and my guide suggested we leave. After all, our dead host for the day had already departed for his new start in a new life.

Cremations take place months or even years after a death, on an auspicious date according to the famously complicated, 210-day Balinese calendar — and also when their heirs can afford to put on the ceremony. It's hard to plan to find one too far in advance, but most Balinese will know when, and where, the next will take place. Any tour operator will be able to help, but one specialist is Suta Tours ✆ (0361) 465249 FAX (0361) 288500, Jalan Bypass Tohpati Kusumba Tangtu 1, Denpasar. It is best to go with a guide, who will generally save visitors from inadvertently making social gaffes and spoiling what is, to the locals, a very important religious ceremony.

Watch Tales Come to Life

"THE WITCH OF BATUBULAN IS ONLY AN ILLUSION," said the man in the blue headdress and mauve sarong standing beside me in the temple forecourt. "But here it will be for real. There will be spirits."

Batubulan is where the famous Balinese *barong* dance is staged every morning for, frequently, a large crowd of tourists. But Balinese dance is sacred in origin, designed to be performed at festivals, known as *odalan*, for the rededication of a temple. And while at Batubulan dancers run through their routine for the benefit of visitors, at the temple festivals they do it for the gods, making a far more unpredictable, visually exciting and mystical experience. Spirits descend from the mountain, watching passively or

Heavily ritualized, Balinese cremation ceremonies are not mournful events. TOP: The shrouded body is lifted into the cremation tower. BOTTOM: Papier-mâché bulls lead the way to the cremation site.

Watch Tales Come to Life

Watch Tales Come to Life

"trancing" actors and members of the audience. This was what the man in the mauve sarong had meant — at the temples the magic is "for real."

In essence, Balinese dance is all religious. Its purpose is to adjust the balance between good and evil leaning it in favor of the good. The *barong* dance is the most dramatic of all. A witch, known as the *rangda*, is opposed by a shaggy dog, the *barong*. All the main actors in this dance are men: the *rangda* itself, the two men who act the *barong* — in a single costume like a British pantomime horse — and the would-be stalwart assistants of the *barong*, who try to attack the witch with short swords but are rendered powerless by a magical white cloth the *rangda* waves at them.

Arriving just a little after 9 PM, the sounds of *gamelan* music guided me to the temple, and over the outer wall I could see the blaze of light. At the door I wrapped on a sarong, sash, and headscarf to conform to the dress requirements, responded to some good-tempered strangers who wished me well on my visit, and stepped inside.

Seated on the floor, the local community was crowded into their temple, watching intently as the story they all knew so well

unfolded once more. A row of empty seats had been left for the gods, but I didn't rate a second glance as I slipped to the back and dropped to the ground. Lulled, I looked around at the vivid sculptures decorating the inside of the temple and listened to the music. Over and above a strong rhythm, intricate tunes soared, bronze keys above bamboo resonators, hide drums, wooden glockenspiels: a sound redolent with the sounds of crickets in the rice-fields and the spirits of the mountains.

On stage, the drama proceeded, slow and spectacular. The *rangda*, a bewigged, hunched monster, radiated evil with a sinister glee, his movements stilted and unpredictable. Infants and adults gazed wild-eyed at this visitation. Slow and theatrical, as ever, the acting increased intensity, exaggerated by the blackness of the sky and the bright costumes and colors below. The spirit's seats stayed empty — perhaps they were too busy taking over the actors and enchanting the audience. No one noticed as I slipped out; the ceremony itself would last until dawn.

It is well worth going to see a genuine Balinese temple festival. The Badung Tourist Office in Denpasar puts out a list of them every month and will fax it out on request, but it usually just takes asking around. All temple festivals demand weeks, if not months, of preparation, and everyone knows what's on and where in their own neighborhood.

When you go, dress appropriately. You'll need to purchase a sarong, sash and (for men) a simple headdress at any of the shops selling sarongs. Though there might be someone renting out correct dress by the door, it's not wise to rely on this, particularly in little-visited areas. It's probably best to rent a car to make sure you can, in the dark, find the festival, but get the driver to wait. Arrive around 9 PM or later.

ABOVE: The evil *rangda* mask from the barong dance. RIGHT: Entrance of the *rangda* mask for the temple dance. Almost all of Bali's dances are religious in origin, the only exceptions being those created in modern times for the benefit of foreign visitors.

Lay Back, Relax

LYING BELLY-DOWN ON A WOODEN BED, MY FACE LOOKED THROUGH AN OVAL OPENING ONTO A LUSH BLOOM OF BOUGAINVILLEA. Above, a masseuse worked quietly and firmly on my back: a high-pressure, systematic massage that patterned through my pressure points in a healing, relaxing treatment that removed all traces of back pain. In the background, the gentle sound of *gamelan* music soothed and relaxed, with the occasional crowing cock outside lending a special ambiance to the experience.

I hadn't booked one of the special massages such as *mandi lulur*, where a sandalwood oil massage is followed by a body scrub with Javanese herbs, a yogurt body mask and a final soak in a bath strewn with flowers. Nor had I requested a *mandi susu*, involving a lot of milk, nor a *mandi rempah* which uses enough spices to run an Indian restaurant for a month. It's wise not to wear expensive white underwear for this massage: it comes out a lot less white.

Massage is offered everywhere in Bali. At the finest resorts it is ceremonial, refined, and often very expensive. But there are plenty of small clinics that specialize in massage at prices that should make the more exclusive resorts blush in shame. A half-hour back massage by a professional masseur, followed by a do-it-yourself shower, commonly costs as little as Rp35,000 (US$5). Conventional massage centers will also offer manicures, pedicures, and often haircuts, but won't offer anything dodgy. If, on the other hand, you see somewhere offering massage and karaoke you might get both more — and less — than you'd planned for.

Further down the scale are the girls who give massages on the beach. Even though this alarms many visitors, there's not usually anything sexual about this. (Sexual propositions are usually delivered, much more seedily, by men offering "young girls.") Over recent years the price of beach massages has inflated alarmingly. Your massage table may vary from the patch of sand you're already lying on to communal bamboo benches built under a shady thatched roof. However, even a beachfront massage can provide a welcome break after a hard day's surfing, and the girls are enthusiastic if not, usually, particularly skilled.

Whichever option you choose, it would be a shame to leave Bali without trying a Balinese massage. Recommended massage studios are listed in the touring chapters of this book.

Share a Shadow Drama

THE "STAGE" WAS A CLOTH SCREEN ABOUT ONE METER BY THREE (THREE BY TEN FEET). The right of the stage, as viewed by the audience, was for the bug-eyed villains, the left for the ascetic features of the aristocratic heroes. A flaming lamp gave the flickering effect of early film. This was a *wayang kulit*, or shadow-puppet show.

Cross-legged and formally dressed, the *dalang*, or puppeteer, sat on a low wooden bench on the other side of the screen. Musicians dressed in sarong and headdress sat behind their xylophone-like instruments, tones struck by hammer and damped by the knuckles.

The performance began with an overture by the musicians, during which the puppeteer sprinkled holy water and made offerings to sanctify the show and "bring the puppets to life." A skeletal leaf representing the sacred Tree of Life swept down the middle of the screen, and the action began. It was an ancient story of good and evil from the Indian epic, *Ramayana*.

The puppeteer, telling the story and acting all the speaking parts, had sweat running down his face from the exertion and the heat of the lamp — a giant lidless kettle filled with kerosene, flames leaping from its stubby spout. Without pausing in his stream of jokes, chants and heroic invocations he beat the screen with his flimsy puppets, exiting some and grabbing others from his banana-wood puppet rest.

The puppets themselves were intricately shaped, and painted in great detail, with much gilt — quite unnecessarily for their function as casters of shadows, but appropriately for sacral adjuncts.

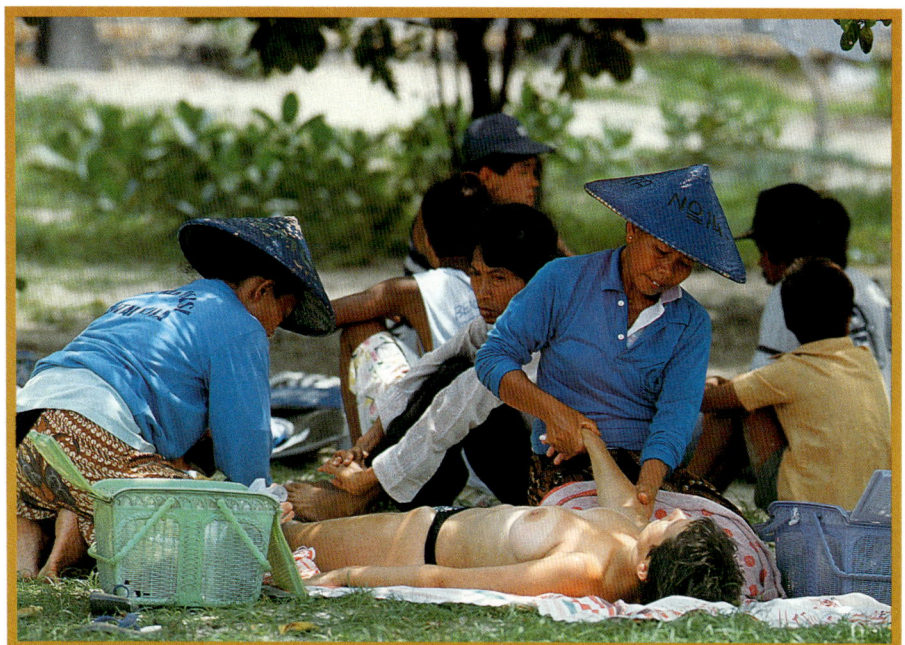

A string, worked by the *dalang*'s index finger, moved the puppet's jaw, while thin sticks manipulated the arms. The costumed musicians hammered away, interweaving their arpeggios and changing rhythm for every new scene and facet of the ancient story.

Every *wayang* play highlights and confirms the established social order and the interplay of this world with that of the gods, making life seem a small part of a greater enactment, over which it is foolish to think we have any measure of control.

It's an extraordinary scene, these stories from far-off India being reenacted in the tropical night and with such a combination of relish and formality. The eager, laughing faces of the audience, the constant reversing of the puppets, so that they appear first facing this way and then that, the old tackle, the flaring light, the relish of the exuberant puppeteer... it's akin to the Sicilian puppets of Palermo reenacting stories of the crusades based on the rhyming epics of Ariosto or Tasso.

As with most Balinese dance, *wayang kulit* displays are best when put on for the local community in informal settings. Of commercial shows, the greatest variety and quality is found in Ubud.

Watch Dolphins at Play

PEOPLE TELL TALES ABOUT DOLPHINS leaping and twisting into the air just beside the boat, only to dive deep into the waves and then come up again and repeat the performance.

This won't happen every day. But sightings happen most days off the coast of Lovina Beach in northern Bali, and there are plenty of fishermen keen to share the experience with visitors. The dolphins arrive at dawn before swimming off to chase fish in deeper waters, so a dolphin-watching day begins early, with your captain coming to wake you and lead you through the darkness before dawn to his boat.

The boats, the wooden *prahu* that are seen all over Indonesia, are small and brilliantly painted in white, red and blue. They can take four or five people, and they're extraordinarily stable. In fact, with their two solid bamboo poles attached by artfully constructed wooden arms on both sides, they must be some of the most stable vessels on earth.

Massage at Kuta Beach. Note the numbered sun hats. All masseurs must obtain a license. Half an hour's massage costs under US$5.

Watch Dolphins at Play

There will be a dozen or more such boats out on the average morning, with additional bona fide fishing vessels, who start earlier, a little further out to sea. When the dolphins appear, the skippers vie with each other to be first on the scene, revving up their engines and racing for the spot.

By the time the sun rises, dolphins are everywhere, in schools of 10 or 20, arching their backs above the element they live in, gray-blue curves above the water that is quietly lapping against the side of the boat. Then, at about 7:30 AM, the dolphins leave. The fishermen switch off their engines and hand you sweet tea and cold fried bananas. This is the "breakfast included" which will have probably formed a key part of price negotiations the previous day.

These trips to see the dolphins play should be inexpensive. Most fishermen will be prepared to take visitors out for Rp50,000 (around US$7).

It is possible to pay considerably more for a big marine sports company to take you to see dolphins in other locations, especially in southeastern Bali. Bali Diving Perdana ((0361) 286493, for instance, starts at the same early time from Sanur for the sail around to the Ulu Watu area for dolphin sighting. The cliffs are dramatic as a backdrop, but your chances of actually seeing the creatures leaping are actually less than in Lovina, where dolphins are practically guaranteed.

Climb a Volcano

IT WAS 4:30 AM AS I STARTED TO CLIMB. A guide helped me to follow the path and I quickly stopped using my flashlight. It was easier to get used to the darkness. Carefully I found footholds by shafts of moonlight and the gentle glow of stars dotting the clear, cloudless sky. I was climbing Bali's second-highest volcano — climbing is best started early, when the weather is cooler and the air clearer. Muscles weakened by weeks on the beach quickly began complaining as the path wound, steep and relentless, ahead.

Soon the sky began to lighten in the east and the sound of birds waking for the start of their day filtered up from the valley below. Distant sounds of cockerels in the villages ringing Lake Batur, stretching out toward the base of Mount Agung, squawked loud and assertive, and the first truck engines fired up for another early start to a long Balinese day.

High in the clear air, I struggled to the ridge and along a narrow path to a *warung* (semi-mobile eatery) serving cool drinks and, most importantly, hot tea. At 1,600 m (5,500 ft) above sea-level I settled down to watch dawn paint colors into this spectacular world. First the sky pinked about the glowering bulk of Mount Agung, silhouetting the thin trail of smoke from the summit of its perfect cone, a constant reminder that this is still one of the world's most active volcanoes. Then the sun itself inched above the horizon, hitting me with a blast of tropical warmth and picking out peaks stretching away to the east. The lightening sky illuminated the lake waters, striated with mist, the terraced farmlands, and the black, light-absorbing lava trails left by recent eruptions.

It's not surprising that the two volcanoes of Agung and Batur have a key role in the belief systems on the islands. And while Batur is an easy climb that, started early, takes a morning, Mount Agung is rather more of a challenge. Reaching an altitude of 2,743 m (9,000 ft), it can be climbed in one day but more usually takes two. Either way it's no easy matter. The surface is crumbly, and footsteps tend, in places, to go two steps forward and then gently slither at least one pace back. Nights on the top are cold, but it's the blazing sun during the day that makes the climb such heavy going. Note that the dry season, from April to October, is best for climbing either mountain.

Sacred Mount Agung at 2,743 m (9,000 ft) tempts climbers, but it is far from an easy ascent. It is essential to hire knowledgeable guides to ensure a safe trip.

BALI YOUR CHOICE

The Great Outdoors

It's a tragedy that some visitors never stray from their resort hotel, as Bali has a diversity of landscapes and ecosystems that belies it's relatively small size. Much of the west is preserved as a national park that encompasses rainforest, woodland, mountains and swamps, and is the last refuge of the highly endangered Rothschild's myna (or Balinese starling). In the south, the land climbs steadily from the main resort regions through terraced rice-paddies and small villages, perfect for exploring on foot or by mountain bike, as it rises toward the peaks of the island's greatest volcanoes, Batur and Agung. At 3,142 m (10,308 ft) Agung is the highest of all, a home of the gods and, like Batur, broodingly, dangerously active. Flows of lava from recent eruptions are still visible even in this lush, fertile environment.

Bali's fauna and flora are similar to those of Java. The roar of the old Balinese tiger has probably been silenced now forever, even in its last refuges in remote west Bali. Similarly, crocodiles are no longer on show in the Prancak River. Wild monkeys, though, are still common, as are various kinds of bats. Turtles are regularly caught and slaughtered for temple feasts. The domesticated Balinese pig can be seen in every village, and so can the beautiful faun-like Balinese cattle. Water buffalo can be seen lugging carts along the roads in the northern parts of the island.

Bali's forests consist of the spectacularly tall and skeletal coral tree, the erect and unbranching pala, teak, mahogany and, high on the mountains, pine. A sacred banyan tree stands somewhere in every village, and huge *kepuh* are frequently found growing around cemeteries. There are several species of palm — coconut, *lontar* (providing leaves for making books in the traditional style), *sago* (providing sap for palm beer and material for thatching) and *salak* (yielding the fruit of the same name). The waxy white and

---

OPPOSITE: Worth the effort of an early rise in cool conditions: the sunrise seen from Lake Batur.
ABOVE: Bougainvillea flourishes everywhere in Bali.

yellow flowers of the frangipani (*kamboja*) spread their sweet scent around many a temple precinct, and protect the buried sections of wooden building posts from rot.

HIKING
The fit can crown their stay with an ascent of Bali's highest mountain, the volcano **Mount Agung** (Gunung Agung). This is a serious proposition, and whether you start from Besakih or the upland village of Sebudi it takes two days. A guide is essential, as are camping equipment for a cold night aloft and, obviously, stout footwear.

The much easier climb up **Mount Batur** (Gunung Batur) is far more commonly hiked, though only in the dry season, from April to October. Although you can go up in the wet season it isn't very pleasant, with leeches everywhere and the view hidden by clouds. Of the four main craters Batur 1 is the easiest, and can be climbed without a guide. Access is from Toyah Bungkah or Pura Yati. The volcano tends to cloud over as the day heats up so an early start is recommended. You will need a guide to get there if, as many do, you start in the dark to catch sunrise: ask among the kids who carry bottled drinks up for sale and come to a private arrangement (see CLIMB A VOLCANO, page 23 in TOP SPOTS).

The central region of the island offers volcanic panoramas of every kind and it isn't essential to climb anything. On a clear day, from the crater rim at Penelokan (a village whose name actually means "nice view") or Kintamani you can get stupendous views of Mount Batur quietly steaming, and from just round the rim, you can see Agung, resplendent in its loftiness, not far away to the east. While on the rim, incidentally, you can easily climb to the modest, extinct volcanic summit of Mount Abang (Gunung Abang). If you need to contact a trekking guide, specialist companies here include **Jero Wijaya Lakeside Cottage** ((0366) 51249, Kintamani; **Lakeview** ((0366) 51464, Penelokan; and **Surya Hotel** ((0366) 51378, Kedisan.

PARKS AND RESERVES
As for national parks, Bali has one. It takes in much of the western side of the island, extending across the sea to Menjangan Island and the neighboring coast: together this area is known as the **West Bali National Park** (Bali Barat National Park). The park's attractions extend below the water too, on account of the incomparable coral and tropical fish.

The West Bali National Park has its headquarters at Cekik near Gilimanuk. This quiet place is where the now tragically extinct Balinese tiger was last seen. It's a good place to get away from the tourist jamboree and take a solitary walk. The park covers over 750 sq km (290 sq miles), and although much of this area is out of bounds to the public there are trails for hiking if accompanied by a park rangers. The authorities at the national park headquarters will suggest routes and tell you what you should take along with you. Permits are available at Cekik and Labuhan Lalang, or from the Forestry Department ((0361) 235679, Jalan Niti Mandala, Renon, Denpasar. The permits are free but you will have to pay the guide.

The Great Outdoors

There are no such restrictions for hiking outside the national park. Camping isn't popular in Bali — it's simply too hot and humid for it to be much pleasure. In any case, the small *losmens* (home-stays) are affordable and friendly, and staying in them absolves you of the need to carry camping equipment.

Hiking is demanding, also because of the heat. The place to do it is up in the hills where it's cooler, often quite cooler, with rain showers common in the middle of the day. There's a trail, for example, that branches off from the road that runs along the island's north coast and ends at the Bali Aga village of Trunyan. Watch out for a sign not far from Air Sanih that points to a "hiking trail to Trunyan," four hours away (or so they claim). It will be a steep ascent, but the air grows cooler as you climb. Don't try setting out on this trail in the late afternoon without a good and reliable flashlight. There may be no moon to light the way, or it may be clouded over in these mountainous parts. There certainly won't be any street lights.

RIDING

Riding isn't a mainstream activity in Bali, but it is possible to ride camels and elephants as well as conventional horses.

Camel "safaris" and moonlight camel treks are based at the Hotel Nikko on the edge of Nusa Dua. They've brought in camels from drier climes, and now you can ride them along Jimbaran Beach by day or night. You can wear anything except flip-flops (more often referred to in Bali by the Australian term, thongs), but a hat against the sun is recommended in daytime. If you're interested contact **Bali Camel Safaris** ((0361) 773377, extension 210; costs are US$29 per hour adult, US$15 per child.

You can also trek Bali by elephant. Twenty minutes north of Ubud, in the wooded Balinese interior near the village of Taro, **Elephant Trekking** ((0361) 286072 offers an adventure to remember. Elephants are not native to Bali, but at least, unlike the camels, they are used to the humidity.

Camel rides on Nusa Dua are proving popular with tourists looking for something a bit different.

There are elephants on Sumatra, for instance, and in climatically similar Burma and Thailand, not to mention India.

This is a peace-inducing experience, because the elephants are such calm beasts. When the ride is over you can help wash down the world's largest land mammal — probably the most enjoyable part of the experience.

Then there are horses. In the region north of Tanah Lot temple you can go on a day tour. Horses are a traditional means of transport in this part of Bali, and there aren't many other tourists around the area where they take you. Riding experience is not strictly necessary, though operators won't take anyone under 12, and 15 is the suggested minimum age for those entirely new to riding. You'll first be assessed for your riding ability and then allocated an appropriate steed. They have everything from ponies to full-sized horses (though "full-sized" in Bali may not be quite what you're used to back home if you're an experienced rider). Their horseback tour includes rice terraces, bush-land and the beach, where there is usually a stop for a swim (so pack a swimsuit). As with the camels, don't wear flip-flops since they catch in the stirrups. Rides are operated by **Bali Horse Riding** ((0361) 224603, Yeh Gangga Beach. The guides are expert, and will use a lead string for nervous riders.

In Kuta the place to contact for these trips is **Bali Jaran-Jaran Keneka** ((0361) 751672 FAX (0361) 755734 at the Logi Garden Hotel, Legian, and there are more horses available for riding on the remote northern coast operated by **Reef Seen** (/FAX (0362) 92339 E-MAIL reefseen@denpasar.wasantara.net.id, Desa Pemuteran, Gerokgak, Singaraja.

For most of these rides — camel, elephant and horseback — it is usual for the companies to pick up clients from any of the southern hotels as part of an organized day-trip. The exception is Reef Seen, whose location on the northwest coast makes it more appropriate for those already exploring this undiscovered area.

BEACHES

Bali has a huge variety of beaches. Those in the south generally have fine, golden sand, while those in the north tend to have coarser sand which, thanks to their volcanic origin, can be black or gray. Some are protected by offshore reefs, which make for calm waters at high tide but rule out swimming when the tide goes out.

The most visited beaches are in the south, around the airport and the Bukit Peninsula. The best known beach is at **Kuta** and is exposed to the southeast trade winds from April to October, rolling huge waves in from the Indian Ocean. This is not all good: the water that crashes in on ocean rollers has to go somewhere, and often drags back out to sea in ferocious riptides. It is best to swim in the small areas, one on Kuta and another on Legian, marked out with flags and watched by lifeguards. For the rest of the year the wind switches round, bringing the best surf to Nusa Dua and Sanur and leaving Kuta calmer.

An offshore reef protects the inner beaches at **Nusa Dua** and **Sanur**. Outside the reef currents are too strong for any but the most hardened surfer, while inside the reef the swimming is only good at high tide. Of the two beaches, Sanur is the quieter, while the water at Nusa Dua is constantly crowded with jet-skis, banana boats and other exuberant water sports — frankly, all rather tiring for those who just want to relax on the sand.

Kuta, Sanur and Nusa Dua are the major resorts, and these are where most visitors are likely to step into the sea. There are more beaches however. **Jimbaran Bay** is one of the best, in a sheltered position just to the north of the international airport. A long crescent of steeply shelving white sand is in sight of the airplanes landing and taking off and the bobbing wooden fishing boats of one of Bali's major harbors. Along the southeast coast, **Balina Beach** is sheltered in Amuk Bay, while the beachfront resort of **Candi Dasa** has had the misfortune to lose its beach after mining its offshore reef for building materials. Now all that remains are small patches of sand swept against concrete breakwaters. The southwest coast has a range of sturdy beaches, washed from April to October by huge crashing waves. If you're up to it, **Soka**, **Balian** and **Medewi** beaches can provide some heavy-duty excitement well off the beaten track, and the crashing waves drown out the sound of the main road rushing by just inland.

The north coast of the island provides a very different selection of beaches, much calmer through the high season from April to October, looking out over the Bali Sea and often made up of black volcanic sand. Dry, this is often no darker than a light gray, but once wet it glistens black in the sunlight. The northwestern beaches around **Pemuteran** are relatively narrow but fringed, generally, by palms; they have a laid-back atmosphere and no vendors. Just before Singaraja, **Lovina** is the only main resort on the north coast. It is good for budget travelers as prices are low and the beach pleasant, if not matching the fine white sand of the south. In the northeast **Amed** is the first of a line of black-and-gray sandy beaches that stretch around the shore, lined with endless wooden outrigger canoes. They're perfect for those who want to get away from the tourist industry, and there is a scatter of small, basic places to stay.

Sporting Spree

WATER SPORTS

Surfing is a world all of its own. It's a quasi-religious cult with its own language and sacred locations. And Bali is considered one of the world's ideal surfing venues because of the consistency of its waves, which break in exactly the same way for hours on end. It's also popular as, when conditions make the ocean on one beach flat, there are other beaches only a short drive away where the surfing is likely to be stupendous.

The classic place for surfing is Ulu Watu. Here the waves are world class — surf movies have been filmed here and it has been used for international competitions. Close by is Padang Padang. Neither venue is for the beginner. Both are well off the usual tourist routes but are worth seeking out for the chance of watching the masters of the art at play.

Sailboats line the beach in Jimbaran, waiting for early morning sailors.

At Kuta the waves are smaller (though they can still be too dangerous to surf). Here, the classic locations are Half Legian, Kuta Reef and Canggu and, further north up the beach, Medewi.

Be aware that there are dangers. The surf can be huge, and the currents can, in places, present fatal hazards. People die surfing at Kuta and Legian every year, despite the beach watch mounted by the Badung Surf Rescue. Do be careful.

Try out the waves first on a **boogie board**. These small, rectangular boards are easy to use — they take a morning to master — and can be rented by the hour everywhere along the beach. Rp10,000 an hour is the usual rate, less once you become a regular. Stay between the red and yellow flags, which are the only ones watched over by the Surf Rescue. (If you do get into trouble, hold your arm high in the air — this is the sign the rescue workers look for.)

Sailing and windsurfing are offered on the sheltered eastern side of the island during the dry season (April to October). Inquire at any of the larger hotels at Nusa Dua or Sanur. For more reasonable rates, ask along Sanur Beach or at the Rai Restaurant at Benoa. Sailing is on local outriggers or Hobie Cat catamarans.

In recent years, **whitewater rafting** has become quite popular in Bali, though it tends to be more of a pleasant outdoor activity than an outright adventure. The following outfits can set you afloat: Ayung River Rafting ((0361) 238759 FAX (0361) 224236, Jalan Diponegoro 150, Denpasar; Bali International Rafting ((0361) 281408 FAX (0361) 281409, Jalan Ngurah Rai (Bypass), Sanur; Bali Adventure Rafting ((0361) 721480, Jalan Ngurah Rai (Bypass), Sanur; or Sobek ((0361) 287059 FAX (0361) 289448 E-MAIL sobek@denpasar.wasantara.net.id, Jalan Tirta Ening 9, Jalan Ngurah Rai (Bypass), Sanur.

If you don't mind paying international rates, there is at least one company that combines most of these adventures — and more — into a single program. Bali **Adventure Tours** ((0361) 721480 FAX (0361) 721481 E-MAIL info@baliadventuretours.com WEB SITE www.baliadventuretours.com, Jalan Ngurah Rai (Bypass), Pesanggaran, offers whitewater rafting, whitewater kayaking, elephant safaris, mountain cycling, paragliding, off-road motorcycling, motorcross circuits and paddy trekking.

DIVING

Diving is one of the major specialist pursuits in Bali, and there are several places where seasoned practitioners take the plunge with enthusiasm. Indonesia's waters provide some of the least-known diving locations in the world, but although Bali's sites are well-dived these days, their splendor is none the less grand. Because it is relatively small, the dive operators from the southern resorts can reach even the most distant dive-sites, the best of which are generally in the north; the main diving centers are at Candi Dasa in the east and Sanur in the south. Fortunately, this is Bali so there are usually dive operators in business near the best dives themselves.

For new divers, Bali is one of the more economical places to learn, thanks to the receding international value of the rupiah.

A fine authority on these waters is *Kal Muller's Diving Indonesia*, optimistically subtitled *A Guide to the World's Greatest Diving*. With over 300 pages, it's a comprehensive and professional survey of diving in Balinese waters (the author has had over 20 years of diving experience), and all the guide companies specializing in water sports have copies lying around their offices.

Bali's top diving locations are spread around the island. The most popular dive is **Tulamben,** a beach dive which leads immediately to the spectacular wreck (see WRECK-DIVE A NEW REEF, page 12 in TOP SPOTS) of the USS *Liberty*, which was sunk by the Japanese during World War II. It's one of the world's greatest wreck dives, now colonized by corals and sheltering shoals of fish and their predators. If you want to get the place to yourself, stay overnight and get in early before the crowds from the southern resorts arrive.

Nusa Menjangan is 30 minutes from the mainland but unfortunately quite a long way from the main resorts. It is

suitable for diving in all seasons. Above ground the land is strictly protected as a breeding site for the Bali starling, and the shoaling corals are now part of the West Bali National Park. National park status, and the area's isolation, go to protect what is considered by many to be the most beautiful diving location in Bali.

Amed, on the northeast corner of the island, is nowadays intensively fished by the Javanese immigrants whose boats line the shore, but the coral still survives and the contrasting white and black sands ensure a dramatic dive. Beach-launches keep costs to a minimum, and there are a number of boat and shore-launch dives around Candi Dasa.

From the resorts of Nusa Dua and Sanur, boats cross to the little-visited islands of **Nusa Lembongan** (Lembongan Island) and its neighbor **Nusa Penida** (Penida Island): their isolation has helped protect their coral. Spectacular dives, with steep dropoffs, offer the chance to see large creatures such as the Napoleon wrasse and giant clams.

It must be emphasized that diving is a sport that requires training. Fortunately, learning to dive is relatively economical on Bali — tuition fees can be as low as US$250 for the five-day PADI course — and there are few better places to do it. There are dive schools at Candi Dasa, Lovina, Kuta and Sanur.

The biggest diving company in Bali is **Baruna** ((0361) 753820 FAX (0361) 753809, Jalan Ngurah Rai (Bypass), Denpasar. They will give you full instruction and take you on your first dives in the safe waters along the coral reef off Sanur and Nusa Dua.

Other companies are **Citra Bali Dive Center** ((0361) 286788 FAX (0361) 424324, Blanjong 5E 40, Sanur, and the **Ena Dive Center** (0361) 287945 FAX (0361) 287945, Jalan Tirta Ening 1, Denpasar. There are more, and often it is worth looking up dive schools in the area where you want to dive; be sure to check for newness of equipment and cleanliness.

For non-divers, there's always **snorkeling** to give you a glimpse of the underwater wonders. Most hotels will help you arrange this — the Bali Hai day-tours to Nusa Lembongan, for instance, provide the equipment plus a good lunch afterwards. Instruction takes a couple of

Rafting, one of Bali's newer sports, is at its best towards the end of the monsoon rains, late March, when the River Ayung is at its fullest.

Sporting Spree

minutes, and then you can be off on your own in areas they will point out to you as the best for underwater life. Otherwise dive schools will often take out snorkelers for a reduced fee, which gives you a much better chance of ending up with a leak-free mask. Most of the colors, in any case, are brightest near the surface.

In Lovina in north Bali it is possible to go out with local fishermen to snorkel among dolphins. It's the simplest thing in the world to arrange — you will be asked all the evening by half the locals you meet whether you'd like to go out to see dolphins or whether you'd like to go snorkeling. Mask and goggles are usually provided (check they fit and don't leak) and it costs a fraction of the fee charged by tour companies.

GOLF
Bali has four golf courses. Europeans will be alarmed, however, by how much they charge: usually more than US$120 for an 18-hole round, and with caddies expecting a commensurate tip. The huge green fees charged in Japan influence Asian golf courses, and it is much more expensive, in Bali, to play golf than to dive. The **Bali Golf and Country Club** ((0361) 771791 FAX (0361) 771797 E-MAIL baligolf@denpasar.wasantara.net.id, Kawasan Wisata, Nusa Dua, is generally assumed to be the best. This 18-hole, par-72 course is of championship standard and has already hosted several major competitions. Designed by Robin Nelson and Rodney Wright, it offers a special golfing experience with multiple tees to ensure playability for both professionals and novices.

The course has two parts. The first features waterfalls, creeks and canyons with small stone walls lining the sides of fairways and tees in the style of Balinese rice paddies. The second half runs through a mature coconut grove, with palms of up to 30 m (100 ft) tall. Fairways dominate here. Then for the last two holes you are by the sea. The seventeenth hole is played into the wind (usually), out toward the sea over sand dunes; the final hole sees you coming back from the sea's edge to a green beside a six-and-a-half-hectare (16-acre) lake.

You can rent clubs and shoes at the clubhouse, and electric golf carts stocked with cold drinks help you endure the rigors of the climate. Even so, it's best to book a time as early in the day as possible, or failing that in the latter part of the afternoon, any time after 4 PM, when it becomes much less expensive. Multilingual caddies, often with zero handicaps, will watch on as you fumble drives and miss puts. Green fees include cart and caddy and are US$142 for 18 holes, but if you start after 4 PM you can play as many holes as you can belt around for US$55.

In the Balinese-style clubhouse afterwards, you can eat an Indonesian meal, take a dip in the swimming pool, take a US$30 massage, or knock back a few well-deserved drinks at the bar.

At a somewhat cooler elevation stands the **Bali Handara Kosaido Country Club** ((0361) 22646 FAX (0361) 287358, Pancasari, Bedugul, on the main cross-island road from Denpasar to Singaraja and Lovina Beach, the first course to be set out in Bali. The 18-hole course was designed by Peter Thompson and Michael Wolferidge & Associates, and is also a championship-standard course. Apart from the altitude, a great advantage here is that you can also stay at the country club overlooking the lake. There's a karaoke bar, a traditional Japanese bath, and the place is also geared for business conferences, making it a great place to combine business with leisure. The complex has been voted one of the 50 best golf clubs in the world. Green fees are US$130, including caddy, but clubs and shoes — as well as the caddies' tip, of course — are extra.

Back at sea level, there's the congenial nine-hole golf club at the **Hotel Grand Bali Beach** ((0361) 288511 FAX (0361) 287917 at Sanur, referred to, rather dismissively, by the professionals as a "local course." It's okay for a hot Balinese day and guests at the Hotel Grand get to play for half price. The full fee is US$50 plus shoes, clubs, and the rest.

Finally, there's the new 18-hole championship course at Tanah Lot: the **Bali Nirvana Resort** ((0361) 815960, Jalan Raya Tanah Lot. Completed in late 1997, this is Bali's newest course and overlooks the famous island temple. It is similar in quality to Nusa Dua's market leader, but the views are more spectacular, making it well worth the drive from Kuta or Sanur.

The Open Road

For many visitors, a glance at Indonesia's roads, narrow strips of pavement crowded with overladen trucks and lumbering 4WDs and streaked by the buzzing blurs of scooters, undertaking and overtaking where there is space and where there isn't, is quite enough to put them off driving themselves. The road network seems to be in a constant state of repair, with deep holes and piles of road-building materials being constant obstacles. Traffic is often heavy and drivers, often inexperienced, seem to accelerate without the benefit of common sense or fear. Accidents are common. As a result, it is sensible to pass the responsibility for driving to a local chauffeur, but be sure your driver is experienced before heading off for a long journey.

One compensation is that generally transportation and car rental is relatively inexpensive. Gasoline is subsidized, and ludicrously inexpensive. Prices have recently increased — to about 15 US cents a liter. It is possible to hire a taxi for US$30 per day, though whether you're paying for fuel as well as meals for the driver is open to negotiation. To charter a vehicle with driver for an hour-long journey will cost less than US$5.

The route that visitors are most likely to experience is that running across the island from **Denpasar** to **Singaraja**. This is the most practical way of getting from the tourist centers in the southeast to the quieter north coast and the popular, small beachside places at Lovina. It's 88 km (55 miles) in all, but they're slow kilometers. Even if the traffic is sparse you still have to watch out for sudden hazards raining in from left and right.

Bali Handara Kosaido Country Club, voted among the 50 most beautiful golf courses worldwide.

The Open Road

The road rises soon after Denpasar and then enters a flat upland hollow. This is a quiet part of Bali, but the views are good, of paddies and small villages, cluttered with temples and markets. The road soon enough begins to descend, and often there are clouds and mist here, which doesn't usually spread down to the north coast, half an hour's drive further on. The north of Bali is one of the driest parts on the island, and the sun will in all likelihood have been blazing down all day while you were glowering at the raindrops splashing on your car's windshield.

Once in Singaraja, turn left and it's only another 10 minutes to **Lovina**, now the second-largest resort area in the island and certainly a good place to start looking for a restaurant.

The road that heads east, back through Singaraja and along the coast of north Bali makes fine driving. You can stop, if you like, to see the various sights along the way — the intricately carved temple at Sangsit, the slightly desolate beach location and natural pool at Air Sanih, both to the east of Singaraja, or the monkeys at Pulaki and the hot spring pools (these are wonderful) at Banjar.

Continue southeast and you will pass the fabulous diving location of **Tulamben** with its famous wreck, nowadays home to innumerable marine species. A mere 10 minutes farther on there is the road that leads off on your left for Amed, Bali's newest and still little-known beachside development.

If you want, you can take this left and attempt the drive all the way round Gunung Bisbis volcano, staying on the coast from **Amed** to the ruined floating temple at **Ujung**. There are rough parts where potholes will all but bar your way and you're in for an adventurous few hours. The state of the road changes from season to season and according to whether or not it has been repaired recently. Usually it is passable and the views of the coastline below are beautiful.

One of the most popular routes for visitors who have rented cars is up to **Kintamani** via **Bangli** on the other major road that crosses the island from south to north. This takes you to the volcanic area centered on **Lake Batur**, and you then have the choice of following the crater road west toward **Penulisan** or east to Besakih. Both ways are attractive. If you take the eastern option, you can descend the long country road that eventually leads to **Besakih**, Bali's preeminent temple.

This is a fine route with memorable views of **Mount Agung** on your left as you descend.

From Besakih there is another scenic road — this one running from the Mother Temple down to **Klungkung**. It's the road taken by almost all Balinese when approaching their temple for grand celebrations, and it goes nowhere else after **Besakih**. How could it? Besakih is the center of the Balinese spiritual world.

Another attractive country road — which is surprisingly quiet considering how close it is to the heavily populated and tourist-frequented part of southeastern Bali — is the road that runs from the great temple of Taman Ayun at **Mengwi** to the Monkey Forest at **Sangeh**. It's a cross-country route and not at all popular — perfect, in other words, for the motorcyclist, as in fact are all these country roads of the island.

But what many motorcyclists like to do is explore the *really* quiet roads of **upland Bali**. You can do this only by following your nose. One way of getting started would be to take the road that runs upwards into the mountains from the northern Bali coast road between **Sangsit** and **Kubutambahan**. You pass through the villages of Jagaraga and Sawan (where the gongs are made for the Balinese *gamelan* orchestras), and from Sawan onwards it's remote country where you're on your own.

There's no absolute need to arrange stopovers on these inland trips in Bali. The island is a mere 150 km by 80 km

---

TOP: The immensely fertile volcanic soils and abundant water supply near Ubud in Bali's mountainous center are the key to the area's voluminous rice production, which continues year-round. BOTTOM: Farmers with their fighting roosters.

(90 miles by 50 miles), but if the traffic is heavy and you stop to take photos and see temples, you'll find these click slowly on your odometer. Nor do the roads go in straight lines. The distance you'd drive to get from Gilimanuk, for example, to Amlapura (Karangasem) would cover 219 km (136 miles). You can, in fact, go to and from anywhere in Bali in a long day's journey, but with plenty of reasonably priced hotels around, often in beautiful settings, it's hard to see why you'd want to rush. This is also no place to drive when tired, as the chances of misjudging a situation rise dramatically, nor to drive at night, when road works, unlit vehicles and cattle all present unfamiliar hazards.

Backpacking

Bali has long been among the premier backpacker's destinations, particularly since the rupiah went into freefall on the international markets. This makes traveling independently in Bali very affordable. However, in recent years upmarket operators have noticed that backpackers are the first to find the best places, and more and more of the favorite backpacker haunts are being "developed" and turned into high-price destinations for affluent visitors.

Ubud is a prime example of this trend. Ten years ago humble *losmens* were everywhere. How different things are today. Now there are coffee-shops galore offering cappuccinos at Rp5,000 (a day's pay for the staff who serve you) and hotels where rates of US$200 are not at all uncommon (one charges in excess of US$450 for its cheapest bungalow).

There are still backpackers' places in Ubud, but they don't rule the roost and set the tone in the way they used to, and in the way they still do in other less frequented islands of the archipelago.

The same is true of Kuta, that former backpacker's resort par excellence. A huge new luxury hotel has been built in the very heartland of former backpacker territory. Kuta Square is already a glossy, high-priced reality, as is the Matahari department store.

The result has been that the backpackers have retreated to other necks of the wood. North Bali is still a good deal for anyone on a tight, or tightish, budget. Many such travelers spend months in the laid-back resort of Lovina. Air Panas, beside the crater lake under the shadow of mounts Batur and Abang, offers similar potential, despite the opening of a smart new hotel.

You can still stay in one of the nicest, quietest and most private places in all Bali, the Homestay Balakiran, right in the heart of the former royal palace at Amlapura (Karang Asem), for just Rp30,000 or so, the current floor price for budget accommodation on the island.

There are still places to be found, either with the help of this book or under your own steam, but this is no longer the 1970s and early 1980s. Bali tourism has become very big business, and as usual it's at the expense of the budget traveler and backpacker — and, of course, of the locals, who are as often as not deprived of their own entrepreneurial opportunities when the international companies arrive.

Fortunately, budget transportation is still available all over Bali. The celebrated (though frequently maligned) *bemo* minibus is still going strong. For instance, a *bemo* will take you from Denpasar to Singaraja and Lovina Beach for a mere Rp3,000 (about US$2) — a trip of two hours. Not bad value even if, like this writer, you have to sit on a pile of telephone directories in lieu of a seat.

On short trips along the beach road, such as those between Jalan Pantai and Legian, you'll find Rp500 (30 cents) will suffice. Usually the *kernet* (the boy who touts for passengers and takes your fare) will take more if you offer a larger amount or if you make it obvious you don't know the right fare. But if you get into the habit of offering Rp500, and looking confident, even nonchalant, it's probable he'll only ask for more if the fare truly is more — such as on the route from Kuta to Denpasar where it's Rp1,000 (about 30 cents).

Splashing around at the Nusa Dua Hilton Beach Hotel.

Backpacker citadels include Kalibukbuk village in Lovina, Padangbai and Nusa Lembongan. And while the travel industry seems to have taken a stranglehold on Nusa Dua and Sanur, there are still plenty of backpacker outposts hovelling in Kuta and Legian as well as, more rewardingly, in Ubud. They'll generally be listed in the inexpensive category of the relevant sections of the destination chapters.

Most backpackers get far closer to the Balinese than more moneyed travelers. This does, however, give even more opportunity to offend. Remember that even if temple festivals are free the unguided backpacker is also expected to wear a sarong and sash, and men should wear a little white headband. These are available for only a few thousand rupiah at any sarong stall that's catering to the Balinese rather than to the tourists. While tour-group travelers will have a guide to let them know the etiquette, backpackers have to behave with care.

Living It Up

Bali is, today, an enormously powerful magnet for the affluent vacationer. There's everything here anyone could possibly want, barring ski slopes and nightly performances of Italian opera. It has become a wonderful playground for those with the means to enjoy it to the full, and every year hundreds of thousands of such visitors fly in, from other parts of Indonesia and all points of the globe, expecting nothing less.

That said, all such temples to tourism are in the southeast of the island. Sanur, Nusa Dua, Ubud and Seminyak are the fashionable places in Bali.

Sanur is where many expatriates live, and has numerous fine hotels and restaurants. The beach is tame compared to Kuta's, and safe. Several hotels have nightclubs, all of them have restaurants that are delighted to welcome the well-heeled diner.

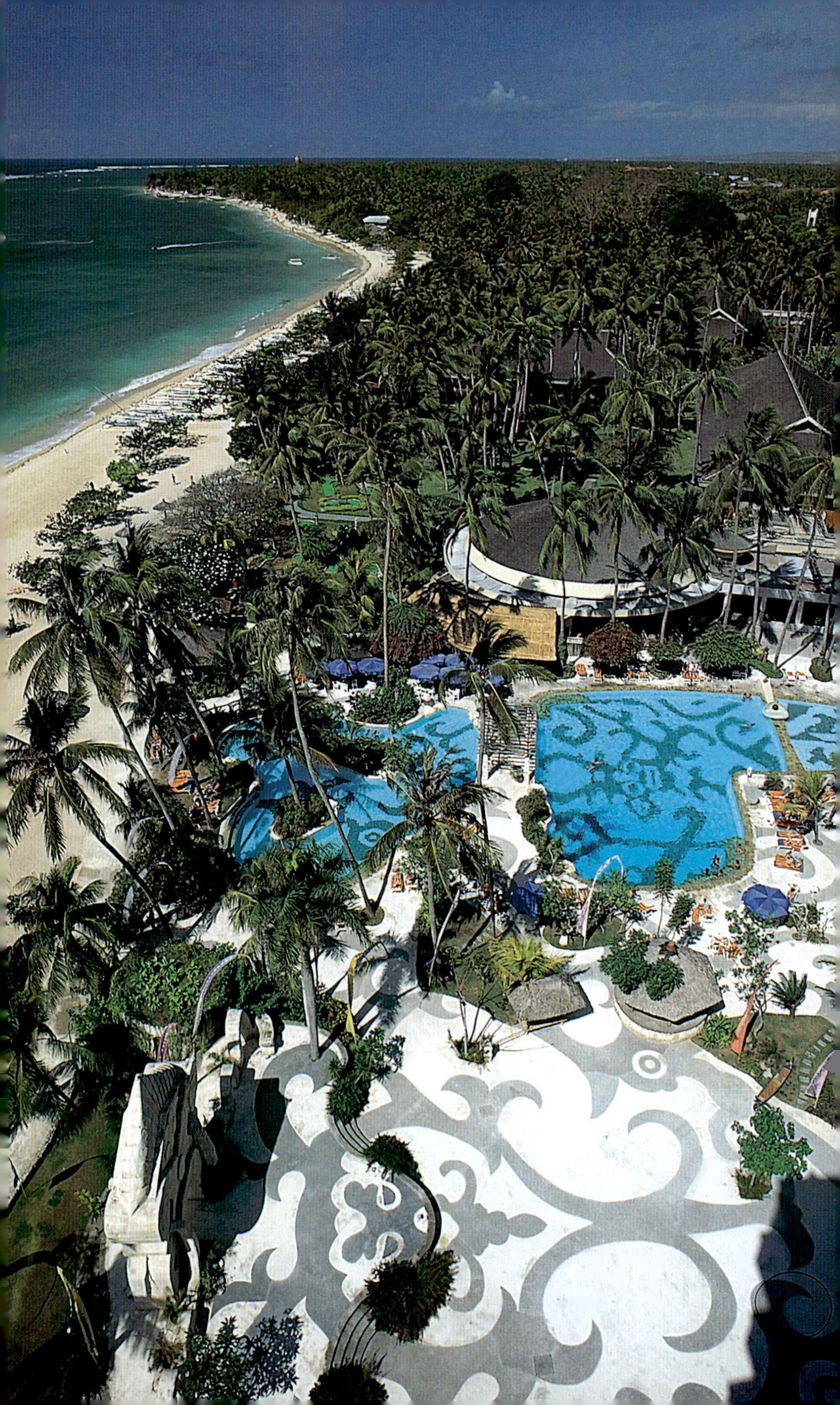

Nusa Dua is a purpose-built tourist enclave containing only five-star hotels. These too have their restaurants and nightlife, but the distance to Kuta or Legian is shorter — a mere 15-minute drive — and so the glittering lights of this brasher resort area are that much more attractive.

The long beach favored by surfers that extends from the airport (misleadingly called Denpasar Airport) through Tuban, Kuta, Legian, Seminyak and beyond is the center of both brashness and high society. You couldn't get much more brash than some of the nightlife places closest to Bemo Corner, but you can't get much more exclusive, either, than restaurants such as Seminyak's beautifully situated **La Lucciola** or hotels with Old World elegance such as the nearby **Oberoi** or the new all-suite hotel further along the beach from the Oberoi, called simply, the **Legian**. It's because of the youthful, sometimes rowdy crowd that gathers along Kuta's streets that the area's nightlife has a vibrancy that draws people to it from Sanur and Nusa Dua alike. Legian's **Double Six** is the finest discotheque on the island, and **Goa 2002** one of the nicest places to unwind and get into the mood before going there.

There are problems. There have been muggings in the narrow *gangs* (lanes) leading to houses where some expatriates live in the Seminyak area, and handbag snatching is becoming more common along the Kuta end of Jalan Legian, the main thoroughfare. If thieves see a camera bag, they might follow you all day until they get it.

Even so, the lure of the area is all but irresistible. The beach is wonderful, the nightlife is compelling, and the restaurants — **Café Luna**, **Poppies**, the **Swiss Restaurant**, and **Kafe Warisan** — are as often as not excellent. The little boutiques that are springing up all over Seminyak represent the most chic, up-to-date shopping in all Bali.

There are some particular gems. There are the famous Aman resorts, of which Bali now has three. They are the **Amanusa**, atop a hill overlooking the golf course at Nusa Dua; the **Amandari** just outside Ubud with its walled bungalows many of which hide private swimming pools, and **Amankila** with its stunning cliff-top location outside Candi Dasa. Nothing is overlooked here. They even have a helicopter to ferry you from one to the other without having to set foot in the ordinary world that separates them. You won't get in, or out, for less than US$460 a night, but you'll want for nothing. Then there are two Four Seasons Hotels, the **Four Seasons Sayan**, just outside Ubud, stunningly designed overlooking the paddies, and the **Four Seasons Jimbaran**, perhaps the finest hotel on the island, looking over at the bright lights of Kuta from its sheltered Jimbaran Bay setting. At either of these you'll get cuisine to die for, every comfort, and of course some of the best massage and spa facilities available.

These, then, are arguably the top hotels. The Legian and Oberoi are firm favorites on the Legian–Seminyak side of the island.

At Nusa Dua there is a choice of six hotels, but the original **Nusa Dua Hilton Beach Hotel**, with its gorgeous gardens, manages to be both smart and informal at the same time. On Sanur, head for one of the oldest hotels, still run by its family of owners. **Tandjung Sari** has hosted many a famous celebrity (though it would be indiscreet to mention more than Mick and Jerry, David…) and is renowned for its sophisticated seclusion. Then, you just have to see **Bali Hyatt**, another hotel where tropical gardens are given a special touch. The hotel is, as it always has been, one of the best on the island.

But the list grows by the hour. There are exclusive resorts and garden hotels in and around Ubud such as the small **Kupu Kupu Barong**, a wonderful, luxurious place. The Aman resorts have a sibling in the **Chedi**, a hotel that manages to offer much of the Aman class, at a slightly more affordable price. It's definitely the place for a weekend with a loved one.

The first stretch of Bali's coastline to be developed for tourism, Sanur is known for its tranquil luxury. Sanur is a lot quieter than Kuta, and is the favored place for expatriates to set up home.

Increasingly, and on all sides, there are secret little resorts, constructed and maintained with exceptional imagination and devotion, with perhaps only 10 or 12 private, flower-filled bungalows, tucked away in such a manner as, it seems, to give you all the more pleasure in seeking them out. They can all be booked via agents in Tokyo, London, Sydney and New York.

Whether you are looking for food, accommodation, or nightlife of the best possible kind, you're going to find it in Bali. Prices are rising steadily, but for now you can enjoy the high life in Bali for perhaps a third or less of the cost you'd pay a few thousand miles closer to home.

Family Fun

There are so many things for children to do in Bali, it's likely they'll never want to leave this kids' paradise. Best of all, perhaps, the risk of malaria is not great here.

The only real drawback for vacationing with children in Bali is the hot and often humid climate. They will need to dress appropriately for the heat, with hats, shorts and the flimsiest T-shirt or shirt you can find. Cotton is best — it's far cooler than anything else and doesn't irritate the skin the way synthetic fibers do. Loose-fitting shirts allow breezes in, cooling the skin and drying perspiration.

The **beach**, of course, is the prime spot for the family. Here again, you must be mindful of the sun, especially during the hours between 11 AM and 3 PM. Apply plenty of protective sunscreen, especially on shoulders, and top with a floppy hat that protects the neck as well as the head.

To all this, add frequent dips in the sea — children won't need much persuading on that count. On Kuta, Legian and Seminyak beaches, swimming and wading should *always* be in the company of an adult — the waves can be very big, and there are dangerous currents in some places. Adults and children alike should swim only between the red and yellow flags — this is the area designated as safe from dangerous currents, as well as the section watched over by the lifeguards.

At Sanur, Nusa Dua and Jimbaran Bay the beaches are safe. A coral reef protects the shoreline from waves, and the lagoon inside slopes gently toward the reef. Indeed, there may not be much water around at low tide, but then the kids can explore the rock pools, along with numerous locals who are there foraging for the booty of the sea. Jimbaran Bay, the ultra-luxurious Four Seasons Resort, is especially good with children, with their club for ages from five to twelve meeting storytellers, playing games, learning songs, dancing, painting and sculpture (no charge for children under 12 staying in the villa).

WILDLIFE

The celebrated Komodo dragon (actually a giant monitor lizard) can be seen at two places: the **Bali Reptile Park** ((0361) 299344 E-MAIL info@balireptilepark.com and the **Taman Burung Bali Bird Park** ((0361) 299352 FAX (0361) 299614 E-MAIL birdpark@indosat.net.id WEB SITE www.balibirdpark.com, both on Jalan Serma Cok Ngurah Gambir, Singapadu, Batubulan, Gianyar.

On the whole, the bird park is the best place to see the dragons, though there's no reason why you shouldn't visit both. The bird park, in addition to the fascinating lizards, has 250 exotic species of birds and a lovely garden to relax in. The reptile park, on the other hand, has

Family Fun

snakes and crocodiles which may make it popular with older kids.

Then there's dolphin watching. From Lovina, in north Bali, you can take the children out to see these beautiful creatures frolic at dawn (just about the time young children may be waking up and asking you to take them out anyway). It will cost you very little and it's an experience both you and they will not forget. For more details, see WATCH DOLPHINS AT PLAY, page 21 IN TOP SPOTS.

Children are fascinated by **monkeys**, and there are many places to see them in Bali. **Sangeh Monkey Forest** is the most famous, but it's overcrowded for most of the day. Better to go to one of the quieter locations. In northern Bali, don't miss taking the kids to the **Monkey Temple** at Pulaki. A tribe of the creatures virtually brings what little traffic there is to a halt as they scramble across the road competing for fruit thrown for them from passing vehicles. These monkeys are considered sacred, and the fruit given them is in the nature of a temple offering.

Then there are monkeys at **Ulu Watu temple** (refer to TAKE IN A TEMPLE, page 13 in TOP SPOTS), naughty ones these who will steal anything you happen to put down, even if you only leave it for a moment.

A special experience is to be had at the small monkey forest at **Kedaton**. Here there are only a relatively small number of monkeys, though their numbers are likely to grow if they see you have peanuts or bananas. Bear in mind that monkeys can bite hard and deep, and infection often sets in afterwards. Keep a good distance.

Also at Kedaton you can see the awesome giant fruit bats hanging in the treetops like torn strips of black plastic.

WATER FUN

Waterbom ((0361) 755676 FAX (0361) 753517 E-MAIL waterbom@denpasar .wasantara.net.id, Jalan Kartika Plaza, 8:30 AM to 6 PM, Kuta, is perfect for kids (Rp100,00 adults, Rp50,000 children, under fives free). The park features a set of pools, slowly moving artificial rivers and waterslides integrated in a beautiful garden setting. For the entrance fee you can stay all day and use all the facilities — except restaurants — free of charge (though there is a small charge for the use of lockers).

Some of the big slides are quite fast and on these children should be accompanied: in any case, children under 12 are only admitted to the park with their parents. The attendants know their jobs, however, and make sure that children comply with the park's rules and safety regulations. There's a particularly well-supervised and safe children's park where kids can play while you take a rest.

In fact, Waterbom is more suited to children than to adults. The biggest slides are tame for adults, and perhaps for this reason they have introduced spas to soothe grown-ups while children play around. Also ideal for children is the river, where you float slowly along with the water's movement in big rubber dinghies — one can meander along for

OPPOSITE: A monkey at Ulu Watu Temple takes a refreshment break. ABOVE: Learning to surf, Kuta.

Cultural Kicks

hours on end, shaded from the sun by overhanging bushes and trees, trailing hands in the warm tropical water.

You can be fairly certain that if you go once the kids won't let you leave Bali without taking them there again.

CLUB MÉDITERRANÉE

Anyone coming to Bali with children should consider booking into the **Club Méditerranée**. Much has been written about the advantages and disadvantages of Club Med vacations; but, if you have children to consider, the advantages decisively outweigh the disadvantages.

Club Med operates a Kid's Club in which all except the youngest children are taken off your hands for the daylight hours. They form a tribe with the other kids and, under the supervision of friendly and young group leaders, they dress up, have their faces painted, learn songs, swim and engage in all the games the imagination can devise. It's paradise for children and for their parents. Both have the vacation of their dreams.

No one else organizes this kind of holiday quite like Club Med. Children often spend their vacations longing to make friends and yet never quite getting it off the ground. Here the combination of kids from all over the world, new friendships, shared experiences, and activities geared especially for them is unbeatable, especially as parents are left free to relax.

Cultural Kicks

There are few cultures as fascinating as that of the Balinese. Even the colonizing Dutch appreciated what they discovered when they first visited Bali, and, unlike most colonizing forces, made a special effort to encourage the Balinese to maintain their traditional beliefs and ways of life.

At the heart of the Balinese culture is their religion, which is reinforced by a social system that groups local communities tightly together in *banjars*. It is this that informs the many rituals and festivals, the dance and the visual arts.

And the Balinese take religion very seriously — religious observance takes up 60% of the time and income of an average Balinese, and, luckily for us, results in an artistic outpouring that has mesmerized Western visitors from the moment the first Westerners set foot on the island.

In Bali, religion and culture are inseparable. Taken as a whole, this is what binds people together in a humane and life-enhancing way. Although observance may change with the times, the underlying premises remain fixed, expressing an attitude to the universe that is enacted in colorful rituals that ordinary people can both understand and participate in.

Bali is a living example of a world where the collective good still benefits the individual, a world that is coherent, hierarchic, ornate and sustaining.

The Balinese culture is, on many levels, visible and omnipresent. The small offerings, neatly presented on an intricately-folded leaf, placed outside your door keep evil spirits at bay. The flamboyant processions, where the Balinese dress in all their finery, proceed daily to the nearest temple with piled mounds of food, neatly arranged in bowls which the participants carry on their heads. The lavish ceremonial dances and shadow plays put on at the major hotels and cultural centers.

Other cultural manifestations are more subtle — but no less pervasive. Tradition and belief dictate the precise layout of the family homes, with different temples, niches and dwellings for the family members and visiting ancestors. In the symbolic design of villages in rural areas, ancient tradition separates the temples for the living and those for the dead. Tradition dictates the very identity of the recurring images that occur in sculpture, art and fabric.

There are museums in Bali, of course, but museums are a poor reflection of what Balinese culture is about. It's no wonder, nor does it perhaps matter much, that many of them appear neglected. When a

OPPOSITE, TOP: Musicians, *gamelan*-players at Besakih Temple and, BOTTOM, at Tanjung Benoa.

Cultural Kicks

people are living their culture in the way the Balinese are, they don't need museums. Perhaps it's only when cultures have died that museums spring up as a testimony to what has been lost.

Ideally, anyone hoping to come to grips with Balinese culture on a serious level ought to read something of the great Sanskrit poems, the *Ramayana* and the *Mahabharata*, which still have a pervasive influence on the Balinese. These convoluted tales of epic battles inform and give structure to many of Bali's shadow puppet shows and dance-dramas; their characters people the country's art and sculpture. In Bali today it is through the shadow puppet plays and the dance-dramas that the people make contact with these ancient symbolic stories. A knowledge of the tales being portrayed can add a welcome layer of interest to a live performance, just as it can add a new level of understanding to a canvas peopled with strangers or temple walls decorated in demons and ogres.

DANCE-DRAMAS

Dances of varying degrees of authenticity are put on to entertain, rather than inform, guests at some of the resort hotels. The best performances, however, take place in the town of Ubud, with four or five different performances taking place every day of the week. Others can be seen in temple festivals and genuine celebrations around the island.

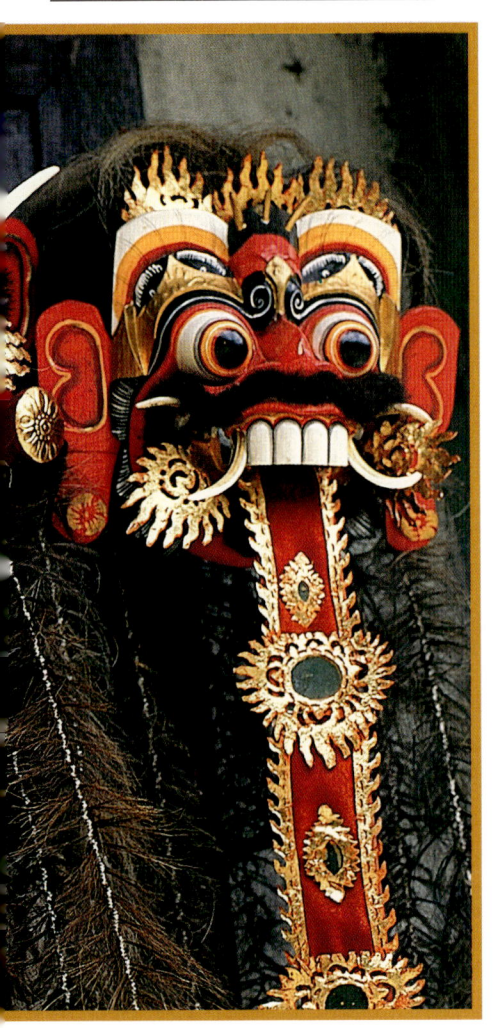

Some of the most famous dances visitors are likely to see include the *kecak*. There is no orchestra, but rather a continuous vocal background produced by a large group of men. This chorus dresses in black and white checked sarongs, with a red flower behind the right ear and a white one behind the left, and move around on their haunches, sometimes swaying from side to side, sometimes bouncing up and down, sometimes flinging themselves forward in a circle, with arms outstretched toward the center. All the time they chant, sometimes in unison, sometimes contrapuntally.

The central performance area is lit only by a flaming lamp. The gorgeously-clad characters in the drama usually arrive on the scene through a temple gateway, dramatically lit from behind.

The performance tells the story of Rama's trip to the forest with Sita to seek the golden deer. Rawana, king of the demons, kidnaps Sita, but Hanuman, the white monkey, comes to her aid by telling Rama what's happened. A son of the demon king fires an arrow (that turns into a snake) at Rama, but Rama calls on Garuda, the bird god, to save him. The king of the monkeys, Sugriwa, then arrives on the scene and the drama ends with a fight between the monkeys and the demons, with the *kecak* chorus dividing in support of the two sides. Rama is reunited with his beloved Sita.

The most classical of all Balinese dances is the **legong**, which is traditionally performed by girls who have not yet reached puberty. Two dancers enact the principal characters and a third plays the *condong*, or servant.

The dance is so formalized that it is difficult to follow what's going on. The plot involves a princess, Rangkesari, who has been forcibly abducted by a prince, Lasem. She refuses to have anything to do with him, and when she hears her brother, the crown prince of Kahuripan, is coming to save her, she appeals to her captor to release her and so avoid a battle. He refuses, and on his way out to fight sees a raven, an omen of his imminent defeat on the battlefield.

The dance tells only a fragment of this brief story. It begins with the *condong* dancing a prologue, then shows the two identically-dressed girls as the prince and princess. The prince is already about to leave for the battlefield when they first appear. He is sad that the princess has rejected him; she asks him not to fight her brother; he refuses and leaves. The *condong* then closes the performance by appearing with little gilt wings attached, representing the bird of ill omen.

Tourists like to buy colorful *rangda* masks like these as souvenirs.

Cultural Kicks

The **barong**, essentially an exorcism dance, features a benign monster — the *barong ket* — with long white hair and fitted with leather saddles. Its mouth opens and closes noisily. Its opponent is the *rangda*, a witch with long white hair, drooping breasts, bulging eyes and twisted fangs, flourishing powerful, magic white cloth.

The full version begins with introductory dances unconnected to the main action — a comic confrontation between the *barong* and three masked palm-wine tappers, and a short *legong* dance.

The play's essential feature is a battle between the good-natured *barong* and the *rangda*, with the *barong* assisted, not very effectively, by a group of men armed with *kris* (short swords). The plot involves a queen who has to sacrifice her son to the goddess of death. The son is saved, being given immortality by the god Siwa, but takes on a variety of heroic tasks, which quickly prove too much for him. He calls on the *barong* for help, and the *barong in* turn calls on the armed warriors. The *rangda* puts a spell on the men so that they try to kill themselves. The *barong*, however, renders their swords harmless; the impotent frenzy of the entranced warriors is a big feature of the show.

The *rangda* is finally defeated, but real magic is considered to have been brought forth by the performance — and indeed the warriors are often in a trance by this stage — and so a chicken is sacrificed and water sprinkled on the warriors by a resident *pemangku* as a conclusion to the dance.

A stalwart of the tourist circuit is the **sanghyang jaran** (also called the Fire Dance), which is more an event than a dance. A young man enters riding a hobbyhorse and proceeds to trample a pile of smoldering coconut husks with his bare feet. The performer is in a trance and sometimes kicks the glowing shells around violently. An assistant rakes them back into a heap. Afterwards, the entranced youth is brought back to normal consciousness with water. He then drinks holy water three times and offers blossoms three times in the direction of the temple.

A further variation on the physical dance-dramas is **wayang kulit**, or **shadow puppetry**, which tells similar stories with the silhouetted puppets throwing shadows on a sheet.

Enormously complex and highly stylized, puppeteer's skill is astonishing. Although tourists find shadow puppet performances just for them, the lucky can stumble upon performances in rural areas, simply by the side of the road, as itinerant storytellers bring ambitious plots to isolated communities who could never afford the lavish productions laid on for tourists.

SILVER RAIN

The music of Bali, the rhythmic *gamelan*, is an integral part of almost all-Balinese drama or dance. The *gamelan* derives from the indigenous orchestras of old Java, but what is played in Bali today is altogether more lively and progressive than anything you'll hear on the larger island. What characterizes the Balinese *gamelan* is its brilliance of sound, its sudden changes of volume and pace, and its virtuoso displays of precise, fast playing.

As with Balinese drama, the performers are not professional, and the music exists primarily as an accompaniment to rituals and dance performances (themselves also accompaniments to rituals) rather than as an entertainment in its own right. Of course, there are exceptions nowadays, such as the uprooted-looking performers seated in the lobbies of some big hotels playing with commendable spirit for a set portion of every hour. But the overwhelming majority of the musicians in Bali are farmers during the day, and *gamelan* artists after sundown.

A *gamelan* orchestra can, partly, be judged by the number of performers. A real *gamelan gong*, the commonest type of modern band, will have around 20 players and feature the several instruments. The xylophone-like *gangsa* consist of bronze keys over bamboo resonators. The player uses his right hand to beat the keys with a mallet, and then his left thumb and index finger to cut short the reverberation. Four players use sticks to strike the *riong*, a frame holding bronze "pots." A virtuoso solo player plays a *trompong*, an instrument similar to the riong. A *ceng ceng* is a frame with many suspended cymbals that are struck by another, handheld cymbal. And there are *kendang*, drums. Drums are the heart of the *gamelan*, the only instruments, the dancers need attend to, and they are played by the seasoned maestros of the orchestra. The first drummer is like the first violinist and conductor of a Western classical orchestra combined, the leader and controller of the *gamelan*. The musicians will all be male, seated on the ground and dressed in the colorful uniform of their particular orchestra.

The instruments are of invariable pitch, fixed forever at the time of manufacture. Where instruments are paired, there is often a slight and deliberate difference between their respective pitches designed to set up a thrilling dissonance that is an essential component in the brilliant, metallic cascade of sound that is Balinese music.

Here, then, is a music that, unless extra instruments are added, is entirely percussive. Nothing could be further removed from the Western classical tradition where the timpani have the lowest status of all the instruments in the orchestra. In Bali, they are everything, and the result injects energy into the sultry night air, music so vibrant and electrifying that the name *kebyar gamelan* says it all. *Kebyar* means bursting into flower, flaring up suddenly into jagged, passionate brilliance.

OPPOSITE: Masks make fun and inexpensive mementos of a Balinese visit. ABOVE: A vendor of non-traditional masks in Denpasar.

American Colin McPhee, author of *A House in Bali*, can be credited with first bringing this unique music to the notice of the West. He must have known his own attempts to transcribe the music for two pianos were doomed from the start, but the influence persisted nonetheless, in America especially, and found its first major flowering on the international scene in the 1960s with the music of such artists as Steve Reich, Terry Riley and, later, Philip Glass.

At the same time, don't feel you have to enjoy the music and drama of Bali. One person who thought a little of it went a long way was Noel Coward, who wrote:

> As I said this morning to Charlie,
> There is far too much music in Bali.
> And although as a place it's entrancing,
> There is also a thought too much dancing.
> It appears that each Balinese native
> From the womb to the tomb is creative,
> And although the results are quite clever,
> There is too much artistic endeavor.

Shop till You Drop

The creative and industrious Balinese supply the entire Indonesian crafts industry. In any Jakarta store you'll find an array of Balinese art and sculpture, and while the best quality might be exported, in its home island the prices are low and the craftsmanship confident and exuberant.

PAINTING

Art from Bali acquired some celebrity before the World War II due to the publicity given it by artists from the West coming to live on the island. They found a prolific but static local tradition and encouraged the practitioners to experiment along semi-Western lines. The results proved exotic yet familiar, just the thing the well-heeled tourists wanted to take home as mementos. It's a different story today.

It may well be true that you can resell Balinese pictures in the Gulf States and elsewhere for a handsome profit, if you know where to take them. But there is a vast amount of substandard work being produced these days in Bali merely to satisfy tourist market.

Much of the worst can be bypassed by going direct to the town of Ubud, the center for Balinese painting both good and mediocre. Here at least you will have a chance to inspect a wide range of work — particularly conveniently at the gallery across a rice field to the left of the Puri Lukisan Museum, where paintings by many artists hang with prices (not necessarily final) attached. A visit here will allow you to compare both artistic styles and going rates before you begin looking at the galleries showing a single artist's work.

Balinese painting before the 1930s was exclusively concerned with the production of hangings and calendars for temples. Production was centered on Kamasan, south of Klungkung, and work of this kind is now referred to as being in the Kamasan style. Subjects were scenes from the epic stories, painted in hand-ground paints, and the final result was not unlike a colored version of the *wayang kulit* shadow puppet plays. These types of paintings are still available and are still being produced in Kamasan.

For the rest, styles are nowadays divided into "traditional" and "young artists." By traditional is meant the style of painting encouraged in the 1930s by the Western artists Rudolf Bonnet and Walter Spies, painters who settled in Bali and lived in Campuhan, down by Ubud's suspension bridge. These paintings depict daily scenes as well as legendary ones, in restrained colors or even in monochrome. They are comparatively realistic, fill every corner of the canvas with detail, and lack any real attempt at light and shade effects.

The so-called young artists were set to work by the Dutch painter Arie Smit in the 1960s and are based in Penestanan, an extension of Ubud just over the bridge from Campuhan. Their pictures are vividly colored naive versions of daily life scenes.

Of course there are some fine pictures among all these, though originality is a rarer quality than technical skill. There is art across the whole range here. For major works prices are high, but for the visitor

Shop till You Drop

it is sometimes hard to distinguish the quality that underpins such high prices. It is perfectly possible to find smaller, less-regarded artists who sell their own works for less than the cost of framing back home. My favorite lives and works from a tiny shop in Ubud: try Agung, Jalan Monkey Forest, where I bought a number of works by Agung and his differently talented uncle for a very reasonable price. Framed, his smaller paintings go for as little as US$5, which I think means he is seriously undervaluing his talent. Beware, however, of the mounds of unframed works produced on an industrial scale and sold in the crowded area around the Tourist Office. Few of them are likely to travel well.

The booklet *Different Styles of Painting in Bali* by Drs. Sudarmaji, available at the Neka Gallery in Ubud (not to be confused with the Museum Neka) is helpful in getting an idea of what to expect.

WOODCARVING

Balinese woodcarving is renowned because a natural local aptitude has allowed itself to be influenced by Western styles, and the resulting hybrid artifacts consequently differ from anything found anywhere else in the world. The main place to see woodcarvings in Bali is the village of Mas, on the "Craft Corridor" south of Ubud.

A tradition of exquisite woodcarving, made famous by Bali's mastercarver Ida Bagus Tilem, is the best reason to stop at Mas, on the way to Ubud.

The craftsmen of earlier times were occupied with carving figures of gods and heroes for the adornment of the palaces of the local rajahs. The depiction of animals and trees, as well as nontraditional fantasy figures, came with the arrival of Western artists. A particular style involving smooth surfaces and elongated human bodies has become common, and is often looked on as quintessentially Balinese, but actually evolved in the 1930s under the influence of the European art nouveau style.

As with all art objects, the only advice that can be given is to buy what pleases you and what you consider to be of high quality. Despite the endless duplication, there are some wonderful craftsmen at work. Fashioning the wood with delicate steel tools and a lightweight hammer, and working with extraordinary speed, they have gained the reputation of being among of the finest woodcarvers anywhere in the world.

Painted carvings, made from local softwoods, are inexpensive and produced in huge numbers. Carved fruits — bananas in particular — almost all produced in the village of Pujung, can be found all over the world.

Hardwood carvings are produced using imported wood, as Bali's climate does not give rise to equatorial rainforests. Ebony, for example, is imported from Kalimantan and Sulawesi in eastern Indonesia. Beware of imitations of these woods. To be sure your ebony is ebony, there's a surefire test: ebony doesn't float. Whether your retailer will allow you to test it is another matter.

The famous shop for woodcarvings is Ida Bagus Tilem's in Ubud, where presidents and millionaires buy their Bali souvenirs. Quality is guaranteed, but prices are high; this is a place to see the best, then perhaps seek out comparable specimens in the numerous smaller establishments elsewhere in the village.

MASKS

Masks (*topeng*) are an important element in Balinese dance, and foreigners have been quick to see them as eminently desirable items.

Every actor knows the power of a mask. Hanging on a wall, it's merely decorative. Put it on and it comes alive, a part of the actor, but different — an altogether new being. Mask and actor combine to become something neither was before.

The Balinese interpret this psychological phenomenon as a sacred power that inhabits the mask. Many masks represent gods, and as the head is considered the most sacred part of the body, the special status of masks in Bali is assured.

Masks are made primarily at Mas and Singapadu out of the wood of the *pule*, the tree called the milky pine in Australia.

STONE CARVING

Carved stone is everywhere in Bali, but unlike the other arts, it never received the same attention from visiting Western "artists." Perhaps it was just too heavy. Bug-eyed monsters with lolling tongues and long fangs cohabit happily with figures on flowery motorbikes. In temples carvings are everywhere, and few are the public buildings and private houses that don't boast at least some examples of the art.

Stone carving is unlike woodcarving in that Western stylistic influence has been minimal, though figures from nature, as opposed to mythology, have long been incorporated into the designs. Balinese wit, with wry comments on modern fashions, is common.

Stone carvings also differ from woodcarvings in that the ordinary Balinese can afford to buy them. Prices are often low, as little as Rp20,000 for the smallest pieces. The only problem for the visitor is weight — even so, small items, a few centimeters in height, can be found depicting just about any animal, bird, mythological or fanciful character you could wish for.

Most Balinese stone carving goes on at Batubulan, home of the tourist version of the *barong* dance and on the road from Denpasar to Gianyar. Shops and workshops are one and the same, and all prices are negotiable.

The stone used in carving is a soft sandstone, extremely easy to work but friable. So pack your purchases carefully when taking them home, and remember they'll weather fast if kept outdoors. To some, though, the temptation to have a mock Balinese shrine in the garden may be irresistible.

TEXTILES

Weaving enthusiasts will be eager to seek out the local handmade cloth, **endek**, where a pattern has been dyed into the weft by tying it here and there with strips of plastic. The cloth is made on old European style hand looms in small factories, and is sold for local consumption in markets all over Bali.

Ikat, a cloth for which both warp and weft have been dyed before forming a pattern, is produced and sold in the Bali Aga village of Tenganan. The creation of *ikat* cloth is an astonishingly complex and time-consuming procedure, and you naturally pay for this when you buy the finished product.

Most visitors, however, will be content with the better-known batik from Java. **Batik** is not a Balinese product (though "Bali patterns" are always on offer), but both the brilliant "new" and the more delicately shaded "old" batik are on sale in all the main towns, and more or less everywhere that tourists frequent.

All three types of cloth — *endek, ikat* and batik — are sold either directly from the bolt or made up into attractive, if not always modern, articles of clothing.

Meanwhile Bali has an international reputation for its handmade **lace**. There are a number of smart, air-conditioned shops that specialize in the best quality, and perhaps the best is Uluwatu ((0361) 751933, with five branches in Kuta and outlets in Sanur, Ubud and Nusa Dua. Kuta, meanwhile, is at the heart of the textile and clothing industry, though for cutting-edge fashion it's best to look at the expensive boutiques in the major hotels. Buy from the streets here and you're likely to end up with a "Kuta look" which may not seem so appropriate back home.

GOLD AND SILVER

Despite the claims on the front of shops in Celuk, the center for gold in Bali is a small area of Denpasar, at the junction of Jalan Sulawesi and Jalan Hasanudin. Here, items of jewelry are sold by weight, prices follow the current price of gold, and the shops cater primarily to rich Balinese rather than to visitors and foreign tourists.

Celuk, just past Batubulan coming out from Denpasar on the way to Gianyar or Ubud, is the island's silverware center. Intricately-worked items — anything from rings to tableware — are a specialty, the smaller pieces virtually solid silver, the larger ones silver-plated. You can even watch the silversmiths at work. Prices, however, tend to be high; they are far more reasonable at the next village of Singapadu.

BARGAINING

Bargaining is a part of every transaction in Indonesia. The main tactic is to maintain a studied look of complete indifference as to whether or not a sale is made. This way the price plummets

---

Balinese silverware — the subjects are usually sacred and the technique invariably superb. The center for silverware is the village of Celuk.

satisfactorily until finally, you give in and buy. If, on the other hand, it isn't something you want, on no account give a figure as to how much you think it is worth. Once you've named a price, negotiations have started and it can be very hard to back out.

If the item is something you want, first get the price out of dollars and into rupiah. Even the most brazen vendor can feel shame when they transfer the price they're asking into what they see as a meaningful currency. The starting price can be anything from double to 40 times the actual value, and so don't be fazed by a high starting price, and bounced into making a high offer. Apart from really original creations (and there aren't too many of them in Bali) you're likely to be able to find the same thing a couple of stalls down the road and you can always buy later.

If you're getting confident about your bargaining skills, try looking around the giant shopping plazas that are now a feature of Indonesia and Bali. Bali Shopping World and Plaza Bali are both on Jalan Ngurah Rai (Bypass), near the airport, and are a good place to take a quick browse to get an idea of the top-end values. Visit early in your stay in Bali and you'll have a vague idea of the prices, which you should be able to halve buying on the streets.

Short Breaks

Bali might look small on the map, but if you have only a few days on the island you will quickly realize that travel eats away time without procuring, in the south at least, obvious pleasure. Pack too many destinations into a short break and you will see a lot but won't necessarily have much fun. Fortunately, it generally takes no more than four hours, and often much less, to drive from the airport to just about any place on the island.

When planning a short break, flight arrival time could influence where you stay. The least expensive flights arrive in the middle of the night, meaning that your first night is realistically going to be spent in the southern resort areas, near the airport. On a short break, the first night is often too near the last to relocate, which would limit your choice to the main resorts. Another factor specific to short breaks relates to budget: as time is important, it's not worth hunting around too long in search of bargains.

If you're trip coincides with high season, from June to September or over the Christmas period, book accommodation ahead of time, so as not to waste time hunting down a place to stay because the best places are filled up. It can also be wise to get your own transport immediately. There's a car rental stand at the airport, and although the rates aren't the best, venturing into the crowded world of independent rental agencies is very time-consuming.

For those whose with a cultural interest in Bali — or those who are just too pale to make the most of the beach — head for **Ubud**. A taxi from the airport will take about an hour and a quarter to reach this cultural center of the island. There's no better place to pack cultural dances and performances into a short stay, and there are endless opportunities to shop, see and buy art, or simply settle into the Balinese way of life. Its central location makes this a sensible place to stay for strategic reasons, and there are plenty of excursions here that are quicker and easier to accomplish than from other destinations. Within an hour you can make it to the beach at Candi Dasa or reach the towering volcanoes that are perhaps Bali's most spectacular feature, taking in beautiful views of lush rice terraces along the way.

For night-arriving flights, the major southern resorts are all near Ngurah Rai International Airport. Nearest of all is **Kuta**: drive a little further to the northern villages of Legian or, better, Seminyak. Bear in mind that from April to October this beach has plenty of heavy surf, so unless you're happy swimming in the break-line, this might not be the best place. As most of the island's very-late nightlife is based around Kuta and Legian this is a good

A trip on the crater lake, near Mount Batur.

place for those whose idea of a short break includes plenty of partying. **Sanur** is further from the airport in miles, but nearer in time, as access is by the fast-moving Jalan Ngurah Rai (Bypass). Protected by its offshore reef, bathing here is only good at high tide, but the resort is laid-back and has accommodation to suit every budget.

Nusa Dua is rather further away, south down a fast road across the Bukit. This is a good place to go for those who want international standards and a sanitized, luxurious atmosphere. There's less to appeal to budget travelers here, and the beach is rather frenetic at high tide, and a bit of a coral wasteland at low. At the same time, the Galleria is a pleasant place to stroll the restaurants of the world, and the standards of accommodation are high. It is a little cut off, however, and as the Bukit itself has no long tradition of habitation there's little of cultural interest to see nearby, save the fishing village of Tanjung Benoa to the north. In the main, southern part of Nusa Dua you could be at any beach in the world — and it's not a good enough one to merit a flight halfway across the world.

Bali isn't huge, though, and nohere on the island is out of range. The laid-back resort of **Lovina** is only about four hours from the airport, and there's a lot to be said for heading straight there to take advantage of calmer swimming conditions and a quieter atmosphere. The drive itself will also give visitors an idea of the layout of the island, something those who stay only in the southern resorts never see. Those who are interested in getting well away from the crowds can drive an hour further along the coast to the small settlement of **Pemuteran**, where a scatter of hotels are isolated near some of the island's best diving and hiking country.

The countryside of eastern Bali is within three hours of the airport and combines some of the most spectacular landscapes and scenes with a desirable distance from the crowds of the southern resorts. **Candi Dasa** has a range of small, character hotels, and is good for divers even though the beach is disappointing. Those really in search of the frontiers of tourism can drive further, skirting Mount Agung, and stop at **Amed**, where fishing and salt-making are still the main local activities and swimming is in the company of small, outrigger boats, brightly painted and made from local wood.

Festive Flings

There is perhaps no better place in the world to find a festival in progress. Bali celebrates festivals throughout the year. There are temple festivals, the *odalan* when temples are rededicated, always lavish and sometimes absolutely huge. There are village cremations, weddings and birth ceremonies. On almost any drive out through the countryside you'll see crowds outside temples, the women dressed in lacy tops and the men attired in neatly-tied headscarves. Roads are closed for major processions and chains of cars, buses and trucks ship celebrants to their pre-appointed destinations. Only on a few days deemed especially inauspicious is there nothing on.

The biggest festival of all precedes **Nyepi**, the Balinese New Year, and even visitors who stay snug in their resorts can't help but notice this event. On Nyepi, the Balinese deceive the evil spirits into believing the island is uninhabited. No one goes out, no lights are shown, and no fires lit. The island closes, as barren and bare as if swept by body snatchers. Many visitors are caught unawares by this holiday, when they find they are not allowed out of their hotels. No one is allowed on the beach, and anyone caught out can get into serious trouble. A light shown on the night of Nyepi (though not the eve) can result in stones being thrown through offending windows. The hotels apologize, caught half way between customer-satisfaction concerns and reverence for Balinese tradition. Fires are forbidden, power supplies are switched off in town (though the bigger hotels have their own generators, and shaded lights within their

Festive Flings

compounds are tolerated). Though flights continue to operate, and cars, with special permits, are allowed on the streets to take tourists to and from the airport, all other forms of transport are forbidden. Even on the day after Nyepi many shops remain closed, though beach life more or less gets back into full swing.

On the other hand, the night before Nyepi is a great and wonderful festival, the culmination of days of preparation and sacrifice. Giant images, known as *oggi-oggi*, are paraded through the streets, each section (or *banjar*) of a town competing in size and imaginativeness. Twenty or so young men carry the *oggi-oggi* down the streets on bamboo platforms, and in Denpasar the display is particularly marvelous.

If you don't want to experience Nyepi on your vacation, ascertain the exact date from your travel agent and plan accordingly. It can be a major cause of annoyance, especially if you only have a few days in Bali. Nyepi generally takes place sometime in late March or April, but the exact date, which depends on the lunar calendar similar to the one used in parts of India, varies from year to year.

The 210-day Balinese calendar alone dictates the date of the major national celebration — **Galungan** — which takes place every 210-days. This celebration has, inaccurately, been described as the Balinese Christmas. In the run-up to Galungan, specific days are set aside for ripening fruits, slaughtering animals and honoring ancestral spirits. On Galungan eve, *penjor* poles, high dangling bamboos draped in woven palm-leave patterns, are set up. On the day itself giant *barong* masked figures are paraded through the streets, long and elaborate dance-dramas are acted out, and the Balinese enter into a frenzy of visits to family and friends, feasting together and visiting recently cleaned and lavishly decorated temples. Ten days later there is a quieter day of purification, **Kuningan**.

Calculating the dates of **temple festivals** requires more than a knowledge of the lunar calendar, with its missing days ever nine weeks and intercalary, month inserted every thirtieth month to avoid losing contact with the solar year. It also takes a deep understanding of the Balinese calendar, which is either based on the growing cycle of rice, or an ancient Oedipal myth, depending on your source. The 210 days are divided into three-, five- and seven-day weeks, with different deities celebrated on different days. There are also days of fasting and cleansing, demon-appeasing sacrifices and all-night vigils of poetry and dance. Finally, the exact date of the building of the temple can add a further complicating factor.

For specific dates, either watch the moon for the latest information, contact the tourist office in your home country (see TOURIST INFORMATION, page 241 in TRAVELERS' TIPS) or, for the fullest information, contact the **Government Tourist Information Center** ((0361) 753540, Jalan Legian, Gang Benasari, Kuta, or the **Badung Government Tourist Office** ((0361) 234569 or (0361) 223602, Merdeka Building, Jalan Surapati 7,

---

The most classical of all Balinese dances is the *legong*, performed by girls who have not yet reached puberty.

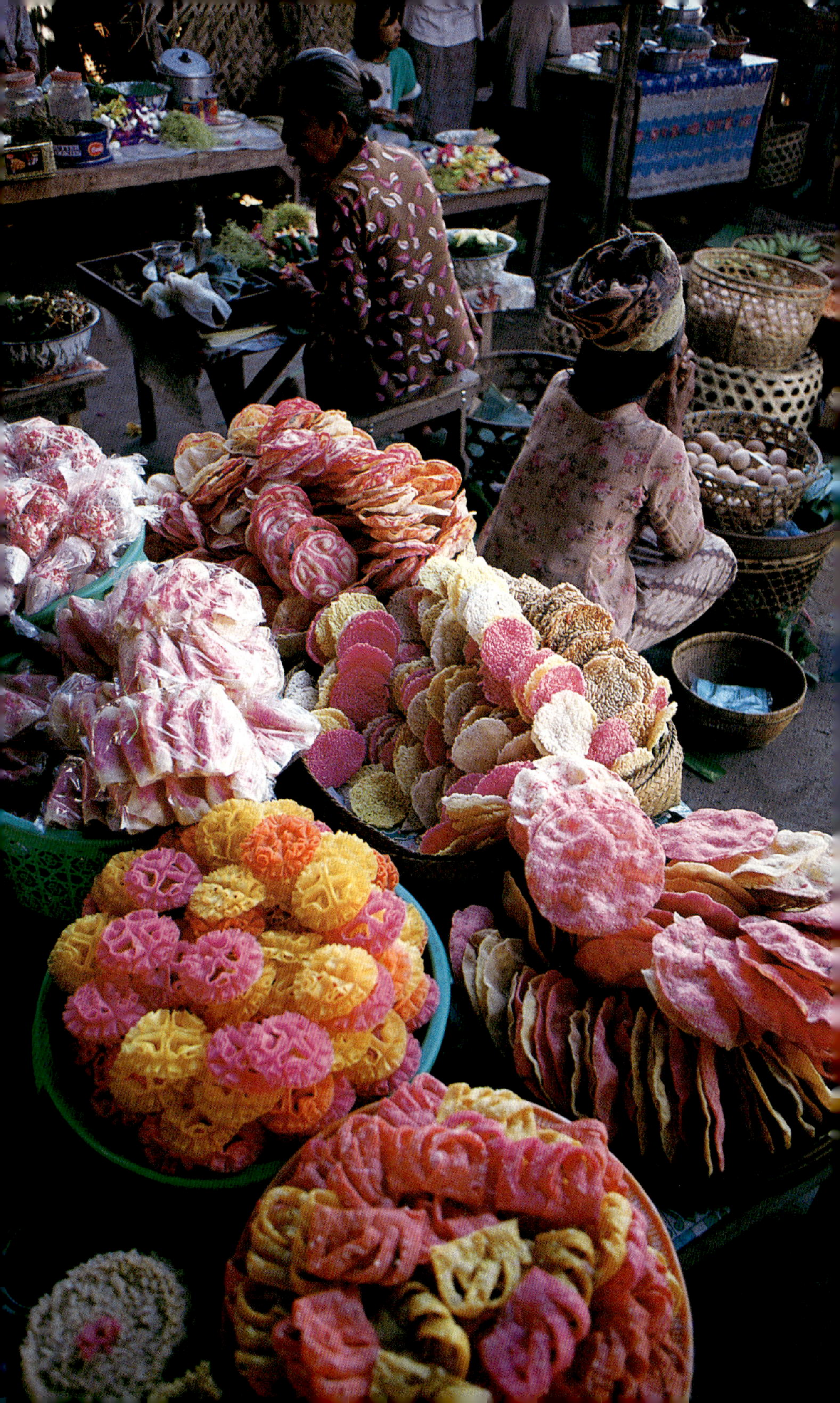

Denpasar, and ask them to fax you a calendar for the months ahead. This information is also available at WEB SITE http://bali-paradise.com/bali-events/index.html. Alternatively, most Balinese will know exactly what is happening, when, in their immediate area.

Galloping Gourmet

For the Balinese, to eat is to eat rice. As elsewhere in Indonesia — which indicates the cult is pre-Hindu — the rice plant is treated as a woman, and the stages of her birth, growth, pregnancy and final fruition are all celebrated. She is Dewi Sri, the rice goddess.

First comes the laying out of the seed to germinate, accompanied by a small offering, on a propitious date by the Balinese calendars. Some 45 days later the shoots are planted out in the waterlogged paddies, first in a ritual pattern — nine seedlings in the shape of a star — then in rows one hand-span apart. Nowadays such ceremonies are usually preceded by an application of trisodium phosphate, a government-recommended fertilizer.

Forty-two days later the Dewi Sri's "birthday" is celebrated with altars in the fields. When the grain first appears, she is said to be with child. Altars are again erected in the fields, and foods that pregnant women have a taste for are presented as offerings. Rites are performed to ward off the vermin (or evil spirits) that might attack the grain.

Four months after the planting (five months for traditional strains), comes the harvest. Effigies are made of Dewi Sri and her husband Wisnu from the first sheaves and taken to the cultivator's household temple. A Rice Mother is declared and placed to oversee the harvest to the end.

The ingenuous look on the face of the Dewi Sri figures called *cili* can often be seen in Balinese art, and in unexpected places. With their primordial simplicity, *cili* represent the impish soul of the island.

Only men plant and tend the rice, but everyone takes part in the harvest. It's a collective activity, too, and the harvesters go from one irrigation cooperative to another until the work is finished.

The rice cultivated in Bali is these days almost exclusively the new "miracle" rice, a shorter, less elegant plant than the old rice depicted in paintings from before the 1970s, but yielding at least a 50% larger crop, and over a shorter growing period. The older kind, however, is said to taste better and fetches a higher price in the markets than the new variety.

Local Balinese fare on ordinary days is very basic and consists of cold boiled or steamed rice *(nasi)* with a side dish of chopped and highly spiced vegetables, rather spicier than the food found in tourist-class restaurants. The dish is prepared early in the day and left out, covered with squares of banana leaf, for members of the household to help themselves to whenever they feel hungry. It's eaten, with the right hand and preferably alone, on a banana leaf plate that is then thrown to the pigs.

At festivals, however, far more complex dishes are prepared, and these, together with the tasty bits and pieces the Balinese love to eat at street stalls, are what the visitor is most likely to come across in the hotels and local restaurants. Only in the villages, or in the smaller eating places and small *warungs*, will you encounter daily Balinese fare.

Among the festive dishes, the best known is *be guling*, roast pork. It'll be labeled as *babi guling*, and you'll be told this means Balinese roast suckling pig, though it rarely will be. Usually the animal will have been three to six months old, hardly a suckling, and anyway *babi* is Indonesian, not Balinese. *Be* means meat and *guling* turned.

Bebek betutu, roast duck, is the easiest of the Balinese festival foods for the visitor to come to terms with. *Lawar*, or *ebat*, is a mixture of raw, finely chopped meat (usually turtle or pig) and fruits and spices, endlessly ground. Of the humbler local dishes, *nasi goreng* (fried rice) is the

---

Vividly colored rice cakes, *jaja*, the most popular breakfast with the Balinese.

commonest, and what most visitors, uncertain of what other options might imply, tend to fall back on. It can be anything from a sumptuous spread to little more than greasy rice with the odd shrimp, egg and spring onion mixed in. *Nasi campur* is another cheap filler, consisting of steamed rice with bits and pieces of everything on top. *Gado gado* is steamed bean sprouts and vegetables, all under a sticky peanut sauce.

Rijsttafel was the Dutch colonial standby — a wide variety of different side dishes served separately with steamed rice. It's usually ordered by a group, everyone taking what appeals to him or her. *Nasi padang* is also a set of side dishes with rice, but it's truly Indonesian (from the region of Padang in Sumatra). You order the things you fancy from a wide choice on the counter, and although they all come highly spiced, they are served cold. *Satay* is a popular Indonesian specialty of tiny kebabs — usually ordered by the half a dozen or more — served with peanut or hot pepper sauce.

With a few basic terms it is easy to recognize combinations on menus. Chicken is *ayam*, coconut sauce is *opor*, noodles are *mee* and bananas are *pisang*. *Goreng* means fried. Therefore *ayam goreng* is fried chicken, *opor ayam* chicken cooked in coconut sauce, *mee goreng* fried noodles and *pisang goreng* banana fritters. Rice cakes, the usual Balinese breakfast, are *jaja*.

On offer with virtually everything is *kecap*, this is not ketchup (although the pronunciation is identical) but soy sauce; *manis* is sweet, *asin* is salty.

In the resort areas of Bali, Western food is as common as or more common than Indonesian. Menus are self-explanatory — though perhaps non-Australians will need to be told that *jaffles* are toasted sandwiches sealed at the edges so that the contents become molten and gently bubbling. The new affluence brought by tourism has, however, led to an increased focus on taking the best of traditional Balinese cooking and developing these tastes further for an international market. There are courses in traditional Balinese cuisine, often conducted by leading chefs of international repute. Notable culinary schools include both Four Seasons Hotels (in Jimbaran Bay and Sayan, near Ubud) and Bumbu Bali in Nusa Dua. Full contact details are given in the touring chapters.

TROPICAL FRUITS

The range of fruit available in Bali is almost a reason for going there in itself. Pineapples, papayas, coconuts, bananas, avocados — all are common and cheap. In addition there are a number of fruits you might encounter here for the first time — and you should definitely give them a try. You don't want to find yourself tasting them for the first time on your last day and discovering, too late, that you and the fruit were made for each other.

Salak has a texture not unlike a Brazil nut but tastes like a lichee. **Rambutan** is also similar to the lichee but with a hairy red skin. **Mangosteen** is a fruit that travels poorly and so is little known outside the tropics. The outside is black, brown or purple and the inside stunning. When cut cross-section, **blimbing** forms a five pointed star, hence its Anglo-Saxon name star fruit. You can eat all of this refreshing pale green or yellow fruit. **Jambu-sotong** are guavas. **Markisah** are passionfruit. You'll see them on sale in the mountains. Break them open and eat everything you find inside, seeds and all. Exquisite is the only word for them. **Nangka** is jack fruit. They're so big you'll only want to buy a segment. You eat the yellow inner part and discard the white outer layer. **Jeruk** refers to all citrus fruits, but the pomelo, or *jeruk bali*, is the most common. It's like a grapefruit but bigger, and tastes much sweeter. Lemons are *jeruk nipis*, ordinary oranges *jeruk manis*. **Durian** — love it or loathe it — is the infamous fruit that stinks, but tastes to some people like heaven. You can even get durian-flavored ice cream — a good means of judging whether or not you want to brave the real thing.

The **coconut** palm provides oil for cooking and lamps, sweet water to drink, flesh to eat or to make "milk" from for use in cooking, wood for house building and furniture, leaves for offerings, the "palm cabbage" (just below the head) for food, and gum from its flower buds for palm beer *(tuak)*. Copra, the dried meat of the nut from which oil can easily be extracted, has been one of the main exports from the tropical belt for over a century.

Betel is often chewed in Bali. It's actually a combination of three basic ingredients folded together inside a betel leaf. Together they form a mild stimulant, aid to digestion and antiseptic all in one. But what is extraordinary, though hardly surprising, is that the Balinese have made it into a symbol of the three persons of God — Brahma, Wisnu and Siwa — and no temple offering is made without a sample.

BEVERAGES
Cold drinks assume a new and vital significance in the Balinese climate. Supreme among these are the exquisite mixtures — made everywhere but especially delicious on beaches — of fresh fruit, ice, syrup and a dash of canned milk whisked together in a blender. They're called simply *es jus*, iced juice, and the going rate on Kuta Beach is Rp10,000 (a little more if they're brought over to where you lie on the beach). Flavored yogurt drinks, *lassis*, are very popular with Balinese and visitors; *air jeruk* is lemon (or orange) juice made with fresh fruit, while *stroop* is fruit cordial.

Ordinary tap water is *not* drinkable. The better-off Balinese drink a commercial brand of bottled water called Aqua, and you should do the same.

This should make ice a problem. But for some years now the ice in Bali has been produced in approved factories and is, if not 100% safe, widely accepted.

Commercially produced ice cream is completely safe, but avoid the homemade variety peddled from street carts. Anything containing milk products needs careful handling and constant refrigeration in the tropics.

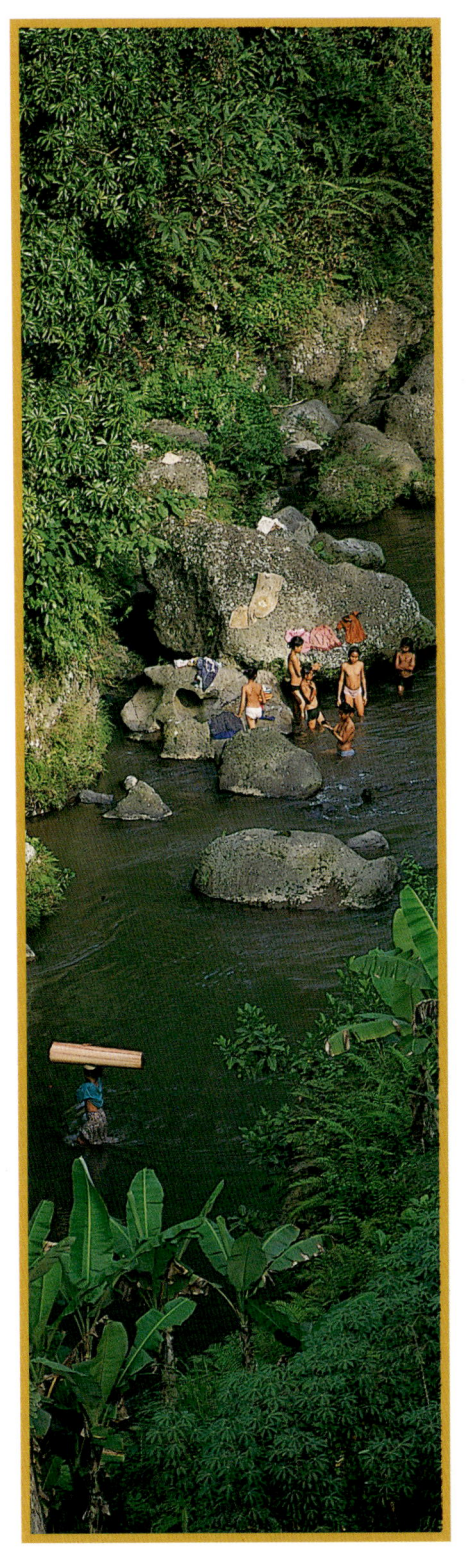

Bathing in a mountain stream near Ubud.

When it comes to alcohol, you are faced with the choice of expensive bottled products, similar to things you'll already know, and the inexpensive local brews.

The latter are essentially three — *brem*, a sweet wine made from black rice; *tuak*, a semisweet beer made from the sugar of the coconut palm; and *arak*, a deceptively tasteless brandy distilled from either *tuak* or *brem*. A beverage made of *arak* and *brem* mixed is excellent, while expats tend to favor *arak* served with lime and honey — *arak madu*.

There is now a Balinese wine, Hatten, made from imported syrups and darkened into a rose with local grapes. It's quite drinkable chilled. And there's a red wine made from grapes grown in the north called Indigo. It's a heavy, sweetish wine rather like Madeira — but it's there and the advertising image is nice: a Balinese worker pulling bottles from a paddy. Non-Balinese alcoholic beverages are invariably expensive. Beer comes in four brands, Bintang, Anker, San Miguel and Bali Hai. Foreign residents usually consider Bintang the beer of choice.

For the rest, tea is *teh* and coffee *kopi*. Each can be taken with milk (*susu*) and will come sweetened unless you specifically request it without sugar, in which case add the word *tawar*. Thus, coffee with milk but no sugar is *kopi susu tawar*.

Special Interests

There's plenty to appeal to special interests in Bali, whether natural or cultural. Most are best sought outside the major beach resorts, which have become so used to steering visitors straight down to the beach they've rather lost sight of Bali's other assets. If you're especially interested in any of the following topics you'll find a day-trip in a minibus with other people who are merely along for the ride a major disappointment. Take the trouble to travel inland, though, seek out the specialists, and enjoy the rewards.

FLORA AND FAUNA

Birdwatchers think they've landed in heaven here. Bali not only gets birds from both hemispheres, but also straddles the "Wallace Line" that divides Australian and Oriental bird regions. There are something like 300 different bird species on the island, and a keen birdwatcher won't take long to spot something unusual. The authority on the birds of Bali is Victor Mason, and his book on Balinese birds should be available at any good bookshop on the island. He also operates bird-watching walks, which he takes himself if he's in the country, from his base in Ubud: **Beggar's Bush (** (0361) 975009 or (0812) 391-3801 (cell), by the bridge, Tjampuhan. A trip to the **Taman Burung Bali Bird Park (** (0361) 299352, Jalan Serma Cok, Singapadu is a must.

The highlight of any birder's visit to Bali has to be a close sight of the ludicrously rare Bali starling, also known as Rothschild's myna. This is the only species endemic to the island, and there are thought to be only about 200 left in the wild, although there are more kept as pets. To try to increase the gene pool, a breeding and release program, using captive birds, has been established in the far west of the island, and you can certainly see captive birds awaiting for release, and with patience, the wild birds themselves. This should be arranged with the **West Bali National Park** (Bali Barat National Park), which has its headquarters at Cekik near Gilimanuk, about 40 minutes from the breeding program location.

Flowers proliferate on Bali, both native ones and species introduced by the island's many appreciative visitors. Margaret and Fred Eiseman's *Flowers of Bali* is a good reference for beginners, and a wide range of flowers can be seen at the often-overlooked Bali **Botanical Gardens**, Kebun Raya Eka Karya Bali (8 AM to 4:30 PM, Rp10,000), which contain 650 species of trees and 400 types of orchids. The crowds come up from Denpasar on weekends but through the week it's a delightful place to be, and the staff can be helpful.

There are also wonderful **butterflies**, some small, others flapping around heavily, resplendent with color. One place to study butterflies at close quarters is the Bali **Butterfly Park** ((0361) 814282 FAX (0361) 814281. It's on Jalan Batukaru, Sandan Wanasari, Tabanan.

CULTURAL EXPLORATIONS

A prerequisite for a deeper understanding of Balinese culture is to learn the **language**. To confuse matters slightly, there are three languages in use, depending on caste and status. Most visitors will be addressed in *bahasa*, the national language of Indonesia, which seems to come naturally to speakers of European languages. The big problem, in Bali, is finding those who will stop speaking English to you. To take a formal two-week immersion course as part of the LOTE (Languages other than English) organization, contact I Made Rajeg ((0361) 224121 FAX (0361) 223220 E-MAIL mrajeg@idola.net.id, Jalan Pulau Nias 13, Denpasar 80114.

The temple of Ulu Danu on Lake Bratan at Candikuning features a three- and an eleven-tiered *meru* on tiny islets in the crater lake.

Unquestionably, the village of **Ubud** is at the heart of the most well-developed cultural tourism network on Bali. Here you can take courses in a whole range of Balinese arts. There are day courses in carving and painting *wayang* puppets, singing and dancing, cookery and playing *gamelan* music. Other special interests include Balinese cooking courses and programs designed to turn visitors into Batik artists. Full details of these programs can be found in the Ubud section of the touring chapters (see page 148). More comprehensive tours can be tailor-made by **Dhyana Putri Adventures** ((0361) 975180 FAX (0361) 975162 E-MAIL rucina@denpasar .wasantara.net.id, Puri Kapal, Banjar Kalah, Peliatan, Ubud. Specialties include religion and the arts, development, food and textiles.

Massage and aromatherapy can also be considered cultural in this context, as they have long been important elements in the lives up upper-echelon Balinese royalty. Often this is now the preserve of top-class hotels, but there are both commercial health spas in the newer resorts and traditional healers and masseurs in traditional towns. For those with a serious interest it would be possible, with tact and time, to expand the passive massage experience at any of the smaller, more flexible establishments to learning more about the art. Be slightly careful of massage "courses" advertised on the Internet and elsewhere, as these can be an entry into one of several rather cultish, quasi-religious movements which aren't listed here. Where appropriate conventional establishments specializing in medicinal and purely pleasurable massages are listed in the text according to geographical areas.

Perhaps the most valid of all types of cultural tourism, however, is just to settle down in a small **home-stay**, and learn to share in the Balinese way of life. This is where the *losmens* have their origins, though many have now grown rather too large to maintain their intimate familiarity. However, there are still villages and settlements that don't get swamped by tourists, where the Balinese won't confuse you with your compatriots that speed by in an air-conditioned minibus: just look out for painted "home-stay" signs, or wait until someone approaches you.

Taking a Tour

If you intend to spend all your vacation in one of the Bali's more expensive hotels, it is well worth booking a package to the island, as international consolidators and discount agents are often able to arrange significant discounts, both on the airfare and the hotel nightly rates. Shop around is the watchword here. More varied tours of the island will usually cost more, and can leave you traveling in a large group. In Bali, small is beautiful and neither the roads, better hotels nor restaurants are really geared up for huge buses.

NORTH AMERICAN TOUR OPERATORS

There are a number of discount agents in the United States who specialize in arranging cheap airfares to Bali, including **STA Travel** ((212) 627-3111 TOLL-FREE (800) 777-0112, 10 Downing Street, New York, New York 10014, with branches nationwide; and **Travel Avenue** TOLL-FREE (800) 333-3355, 10 Riverside, Suite 1404, Chicago, Illinois 60606. For package holidays **Garuda Indonesia Vacations** TOLL-FREE (800) 342-7832, 9841 Airport Boulevard, Suite 300, Los Angeles, California 90045, is a subsidiary of Garuda, the Indonesian state airline, and **Himalayan Travel** TOLL-FREE (800) 225-2380, WEB SITE www.gorp.com/himtravel.htm, 110 Prospect Street, Stamford, Connecticut 06901, does tours and packages as well as customized tours.

BRITISH TOUR OPERATORS

For a smooth stay in Bali the luxury hotels tend to favor the upmarket tour operators. These include **Abercrombie & Kent** ((020) 7730 9600 FAX (020) 7730 9376 WEB SITE www.abercrombiekent.co.uk, Sloane Square House, Holbein Place, London SW1 8NS. For more imaginative options, including the chance to tour Bali

by bicycle, try the **Imaginative Traveller**
((020) 8742 8612 FAX (020) 8742 3045 WEB
SITE www.imaginative-traveller.com,
14 Barley Mow Passage, London W4 4PH.

The intensely competitive British travel industry means that some of the best bargains for travel to Bali can be found here. For flight only, try **Flightbookers** ((020) 7757 2444, 177-178 Tottenham Court Road, London W1P 0LX, or **Bridge the World** ((020) 7911 0900, 47 Chalk Farm Road, London NW1 8AN. Often, tour operators can undercut flight-only tickets and offer accommodation as well. Stranger still, they sometimes have access to more seats and can offer availability when consolidators can't. Two of the best are **Tropical Places** ((01342) 330740 FAX (01342) 330771 WEB SITE www .tropical.co.uk, Sussex House, London Road, East Grinstead, West Sussex RH19 1HJ, and **Travellers' Choice** ((0870) 905 6000 FAX (0161) 278 7755 WEB SITE www .tcdirect.net, Albert House, 17 Bloom Street, Manchester M1 3HZ. The latter once offered me two weeks in the

Grand Bali (room only), Sanur, for £495, including flights and transfers, when the cheapest flight only I could get through Flightbookers was £695.

AUSTRALIA AND NEW ZEALAND TOUR OPERATORS

Specialist operators to Bali from Australia and New Zealand include the **Bali Travel Service** ((02) 9264 5895, 302 Pitt Street, Sydney, who have a range of accommodation package deals, and **San Michele Travel** ((02) 9299 1111, 81 York Street, Sydney, with adventure tours and packages on offer. Discount flight agents in Australia and New Zealand include **Budget Travel** ((09) 366 0061, 16 Fort Street, Auckland; **Tymtro Travel** ((02) 9223 2211, Level 8, Pitt Street, Sydney, **Trailfinders** ((07) 3229 0887, 91 Elizabeth Street, Brisbane.

Everywhere you travel in Bali, you'll hear the sound of water. Each village has a water engineer who ensures the smooth flow of water from one rice terrace to another. In managing the water so efficiently, the villagers are able to cultivate three crops a year using simple, traditional methods.

ON THE GROUND

Once on the island, there's an intensely competitive world of tours in, around and beyond Bali. Everyone seems to be in on the game of taking you somewhere and showing you what to do.

It can often be worth taking advantage of local tour operators, especially when booking more expensive hotels. Quite simply, their rates for these are cheaper than you'll be able to get by yourself. One such is **KCB Tours and Travel** ((0361) 751517 FAX (0361) 752777 E-MAIL kcbtours@dps.mega.net.id, Jalan Raya Kuta 127, Kuta, Denpasar. It's worth giving them a call before you check in. With less expensive hotels you'll be able to arrange a better discount on your own.

Other tour operators offer added services to help explain what you're seeing in this sometimes inscrutable island. The services of a skilled and professional guide, not to mention an equally skilled driver, can transform your understanding of a place. The best, perhaps, is **Pacto** ((0361) 288247 FAX (0361) 288240, The Grand Bali Beach Hotel, Jalan Ngurah Rai (Bypass), Sanur. This is a large, professional Indonesian ground handler, but the local staff is given a great deal of freedom in what they do and say to tourists. Another big operator is **Bali Indonesia Ltd** (BIL) ((0361) 288271, Bali Hyatt Hotel, Sanur. The tours usually follow a similar pattern: one will be to Bedugul, for the lakes and mountain scenery, which will probably also include Sangeh Monkey Forest and Mengwi temple, perhaps taking in the sunset at Tanah Lot. Denpasar tours will take in the city highlights and the Bali Museum. Karangasem tours will explore the east of the Island, driving through some spectacular terraced landscapes and visiting the water palace at Ujung and the Bali Aga village of Tenganan. The Kintamani tour will head up to Lake Batur and might give you the chance to get across to Trunyan or a short stop in Ubud. The Monkey Forest tour will head out into the highlands west of Ubud, Tanah Lot will be a quick one, heading to the temple and running you past the vendors, and their Ubud/Handicraft tour will sweep you past this cultural center's many attractions.

If you've got more money than time then these can represent an easy way to skim the surface of the country. But bear in mind you'll have to tip your guide, who is also likely to get a percentage of anything you buy along the way. A full day is likely to cost about US$25 per person, and a fair bit of this might be spent picking up other clients from other hotels and even other resorts. If, on the other hand, you hire a vehicle for yourself, with driver, you should expect to pay about US$50, if the air-conditioning works, and for many visitors the experience is better this way. Other reputable tour operators include **Jans Tours** ((0361) 232660 FAX (0361) 231009, Jalan Nusa Indah 62, Denpasar, and **Satriavi** ((0361) 287074 FAX (0361) 287019, Jalan Danau Tamblingan 27, Sanur, and **KCB Tours and Travel** ((0361) 751517 FAX (0361) 752777), Jalan Imam Bonjol 599, Kuta. One company running special tours is **Waka Louka** ((0361) 426792 FAX (0361) 426283 E-MAIL wakalandcruise@wakaexperience.com WEB SITE www.wakaexperience.com, Jalan Padang Karika 5X, Kuta, with itineraries including day-trips by Landrover into the rainforest (US$83 with lunch) and trekking in the rice paddies (US$40).

If you would like to get closer to the intricacies of Balinese culture, it can be worth tailor-making a tour with a Balinese tour operator. One of the best is **Bali Origin** (/FAX (0361) 238504 E-MAIL baliorg@indo.net.id, Jalan Pulau Saelus 2, Denpasar, who do the standard range of tours to volcanoes and lakes, but will also plan more ambitious itineraries if requested. This small operator is run by a sensitive, intelligent Balinese man called Dedy who speaks English well. None of these qualities are hard to find in Bali (although the name Dedy is a bit unusual), but Bali Origin is a good recommendation for those who have to arrange their tours remotely.

A procession to the temple. Bali is extraordinary in the continuance of Hinduism thousands of miles away from its Indian home.

Many of the active options are listed under SPORTING SPREE (see page 29), but it's worth noting that when adventure is mentioned, prices go up sharply and group sizes increase.

Some of the least expensive tours on the island, however, are organized by the tourist offices, and leave every day from outside the regional tourist office nearest to you. This is, perhaps, why all the tour operators try to look official and plaster "information" all over their shops. The various tourist offices' contact details are listed in the appropriate section of the touring chapters in this book and, 99% of the time, it's the official one you want.

No matter where in the island you start, tourist office tours generally follow well-established itineraries, displayed on boards outside. You'll find most, if not all, the places these tours visit in the following pages, and costs usually run no more than Rp60,000 for a full day, starting between 8 AM and 9 AM.

Finally, a last option for those with money to spare is to explore Bali from the air. A six-seater Cessna can be hired for a mere US$1,400 (+15% tax) to take a close look at the volcanoes and terraces, with a four-seater available for rather less. Book through **Golden Wings Bali Avia (** (0361) 751257 FAX (0361) 752282 E-MAIL baliviatr @denpasar.wasantara.net.id.

ALL AT SEA

Because so many of the key Bali attractions are to do with the sea, there are plenty of tours on the water as well.

You can, for example, go on one of the various interesting tours organized by **Bali Hai (** (0361) 720331 FAX (0361) 720334 E-MAIL balihai@indosat.net.id WEB SITE www.baliparadise.com/balihai, which leave from Benoa Harbor. Two tours take visitors out to Lembongan Island for the day. The Beach Club Cruise Family Package includes snorkeling, buffet lunch on the beach, a special children's program, optional scuba diving (recommended) or glass-bottom boat trips (not recommended on account of the poor condition of the coral reef in the area) and fun rides on banana boats — long inflated sausages you sit astride in a line and hope for the best. Or you can opt for all of these activities in a single package, called the Lembongan Island Reef Cruise.

Bali Hai also offers the Sunset Dinner Cruise (two and a half hours) where the entertainment is one of the most amusing around — an all-Indonesian drag show.

Quicksilver Tours ((0361) 771997 FAX (0361) 771967 will take you over to Nusa Penida, the large, mostly barren limestone island east of Benoa and Sanur. Departures for this are from Tanjung Benoa (not to be confused with Benoa Harbor, where most of the other tours leave from, a 20-minute drive away on the other side of the bay).

Quicksilver's deal is similar to Bali Hai's, with a semi-submersible coral-viewing submarine, optional snorkeling or scuba diving, and trips onto the island.

To visit the island of Nusa Lembongan, **Lembongan Express** ((0361) 724545 or (0811) 393387 (cell) is a locally-run operation that gives you the offshore experience at about half the price of the others. Using a traditional 20-m (65-ft) outrigger, they also offer an overnight option on the island. "Secure jobs for locals and protect our environment!" they say. You could certainly give them a try, though the smaller size of their vessel may upset some people in the often heavy swell of the Badung Strait that separates Nusa Lembongan from Bali.

The organization known as **Waka Louka** ((0361) 426792 FAX (0361) 426283, Jalan Padang Karika 5X, Kuta, runs several tours. One of them is again to Lembongan Island, but in this case it's by sailing ship. The 23-m (75-ft) catamaran sails from Benoa Harbor, and, in addition to all the facilities offered by the other Lembongan cruises, you have the option of staying at the small but upmarket Waka Nusa Resort on the island.

Small catamarans such as these can be rented on most of the more popular beaches in Bali.

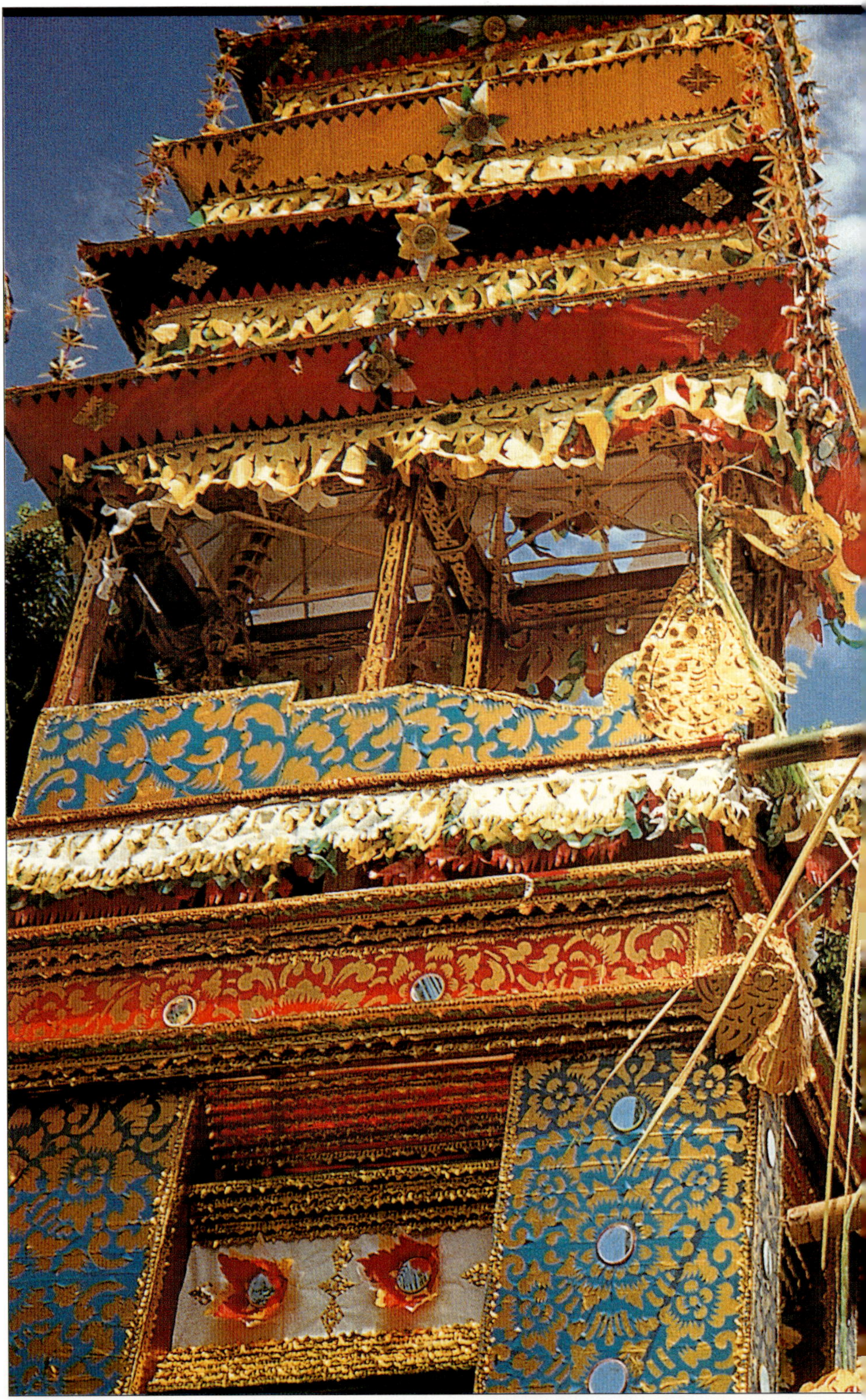

Welcome to Bali

THE TINY ISLAND OF BALI is known throughout the world for rose-tinted images of palm-fringed beaches, smiling locals, neatly tended rice paddies and spiritual calm. Travel agents everywhere think Bali, and think honeymoons.

There are elements of truth in the image. It is a beautiful island, with even the most developed resorts low-rise. Over the years hotel height has been restricted to not exceed the height of indigenous palm trees. Rice terraces still lattice the interior, stepping up lush valleys into a landscape dotted with the perfect cones of still-active volcanoes. Look closer and the spiritual element is very obvious. In the home, women are constantly occupied, readying delicate sacrifices to grace thousands of temples and shrines. Endless processions and dramatic, colorful festivals glorify the deities of an ancient religion, and it is religion, not politics, that fills the minds of this devout and spiritual people. Mysticism rules in this island that has somehow bypassed many of the changes wrought in a material age.

The reality, of course, is rather more complicated. Seventy years of tourism flooding in from the West has transformed the roads into dangerous alleyways of speeding trucks and motorcycles, made even worse by huge Javanese buses that tear through towns and villages, waving vehicles into the verge and brushing cyclists aside. Hotels have been built on every flat patch of land, and even hung onto the sheerest cliffs. Insiders of the now-disgraced Suharto regime secured huge sums of money to gobble up tracts of prime beachfront real estate and develop vast, international-quality resort hotels, displacing local Balinese, who were relegated to waiter status, or reduced to setting up small shacks in the few slivers and pockets of remaining land, where they desperately tried to attract the attention of free-spending tourists who rarely risk stepping out of the air-conditioned, international hotels.

Deforestation inland has upset the water supply, and now one of the world's most lush landscapes periodically runs out of water. Tourist development is damaging some of the surrounding coral reefs, while more remote marine beauty-spots have fallen to fishermen hunting with dynamite or cyanide. As the young people gravitate to the easy tourist dollars in the major resorts or the capital city, Denpasar, only the old are left to continue maintaining the rice terraces that are such a key part of Bali's scenic beauty.

The tourist brochures also omit to mention that Bali is in Indonesia, and that it shares the turbulence that has affected one of the world's most populous nations and bought the economy to its knees. Alone of all the Indonesian islands, Bali has weathered the economic storms that have battered the Indonesian economy, thanks to its buoyant tourism industry, and its progress is jealously eyed by 120 million people just across the water on the island of Java. And though the Balinese economy has come through these crises well, the gap between rich and poor gapes as widely as ever. For every Balinese who rides past on a Harley-Davidson — there is a dealership in Denpasar — there are countless more laboring in

ABOVE: Weeding between the growing rice plants; note the low banks between fields and the subtly varied water levels. Such terraces are maintained, and the water flow controlled, by close cooperation among and within villages. OPPOSITE: Part of the palace of the Rajah of Kerangasem (modern Amlapura), with Mount Agung behind.

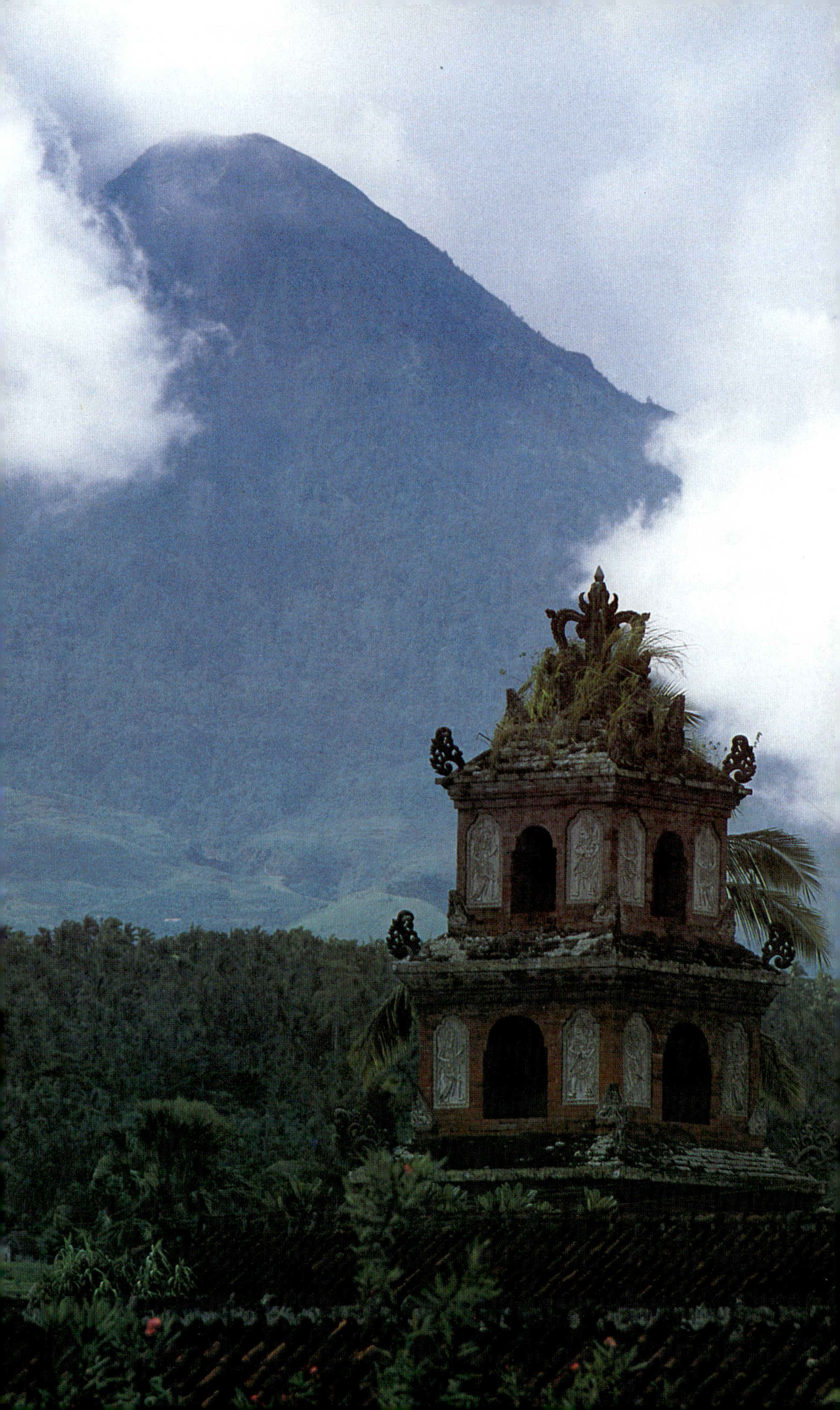

construction, often young women carrying huge loads of concrete and mortar on their heads, and thousands carving wooden handicrafts to tempt foreign visitors, earning each day the amount of money a tourist will spend on a beer.

To date, however, the Balinese culture has held together with an impressive strength and social unity. This is partly through the *banjar* network, social groupings of up to 300 families that act as community council, social services and youth groups for all ages. These organizations have their own meeting halls and are in constant contact as they work toward the next festival or ceremony. It is, more than anything, the *banjar* that holds communities into tight conformity and ensures that the musical and artistic skills that have made the island famous are passed through to new generations. These social groupings of families bind together communities on a local level, providing support for their members and helping to maintain one of the world's most complex and least-understood religions. Up the social ladder, a four-cast hierarchy also plays its part in a tightly-knit society that tolerates and caters to tourists, allowing them to watch, photograph, document and observe. Only rarely, however, does it allow foreigners true in-depth contact with the dense and all-encompassing island culture.

Although much of the culture remains shrouded, some aspects of Balinese society are open to view, such as the devout temple festivals, the art, and the dance. Even the constant cockfights — the essential, bloody prelude to any temple festival, giving a disquieting hint of a society that can reconcile a belief in reincarnation with this vividly bloody sport — are open to view. Any tourist who dresses correctly is freely allowed to watch any of the spectacular spiritual ceremonies that, in other countries, would be far more hidden. It was this apparent openness that charmed the early Dutch colonialists, and persuaded them to actively try to preserve the Balinese culture while shipping out spices as fast as they could.

Gamelan music and street processions often combine to add delight to the most oppressively humid day.

Welcome to Bali

But such openness to outsiders masks a society that is far more restrictive to its own members. The caste system exists more than ever, being continually adapted to maintain a strict hierarchy, despite the blurring of distinctions by education or employment. The financial and social burden of constant religious observance ties every member of the community into constant interaction with their *banjar* members, as the money and time required in preparing for, and celebrating, the many religious ceremonies is just too much for any individual to cope with alone.

Those who don't have time to help with the *banjar* quickly find themselves politely outcast, with far less chance of getting help should they need it.

In many ways, this social interaction is what has kept Balinese society cohesive and tightly-knit, and has contributed to the fact that crime, on the island, is rare. It is also one reason why few visitors manage to penetrate far through a wall of smiles and welcomes, the endless processions and the constant offerings. Bali's perfectly preserved façade of a gentle, Asiatic culture, first recognized and protected by the colonial forces and now being entrenched and reinforced by the tourist industry, seems set to define Bali's "difference" for many years to come.

Administratively, Bali is divided into nine Regencies, but for most visitors a simpler way to get the island into perspective is to separate it into the following regions. Southern Bali and the Bukit includes most of the main tourist resorts. Surrounded by the white-sand beaches and rolling surf, this area was seized upon by developers seeking the "Fly and Flop" market, and this is where you'll find most of the large mid-range (which in Bali means fairly luxurious) hotels in the resorts of Sanur, Nusa Dua and Kuta. The largest development is around Kuta and the surrounding villages of Legian and Seminyak, where the tourist industry to Bali started, and where you'll still find the greatest range of accommodation and facilities. This section includes the capital, Denpasar, which is rarely visited by tourists as most of the relevant offices and facilities are more conveniently available in Kuta.

An hour and a half's drive to the north, Ubud and Bali's heartland appeals to a slightly different, more reflective type of visitor. Many choose to make it their base for a stay on the island, from where they can drive to the coast for a day on the beach while spending most of their time following more cultural pursuits. East Bali and the mountains, although visited mainly in day-trips from the coastal resorts, offer incomparable landscapes, hiking opportunities, and spectacular village cultures that have come unscathed through the eras of colonization and westernization. The north coast and the eastern parklands include the area that saw the first invasions of the Colonial Dutch, the popular beach destination of Lovina and also the little-visited east of the island, with its spectacular parklands, not just on land but also stretching out to include some of the area's finest marine reefs.

ABOVE: A *meru* at Ulu Danu temple in Candikuning. RIGHT: All the sultry, languid beauty of the tropics is suggested by this young performer in the *barong* dance. Children are trained in the art of dance from an early age, and often continue to perform throughout their adult lives.

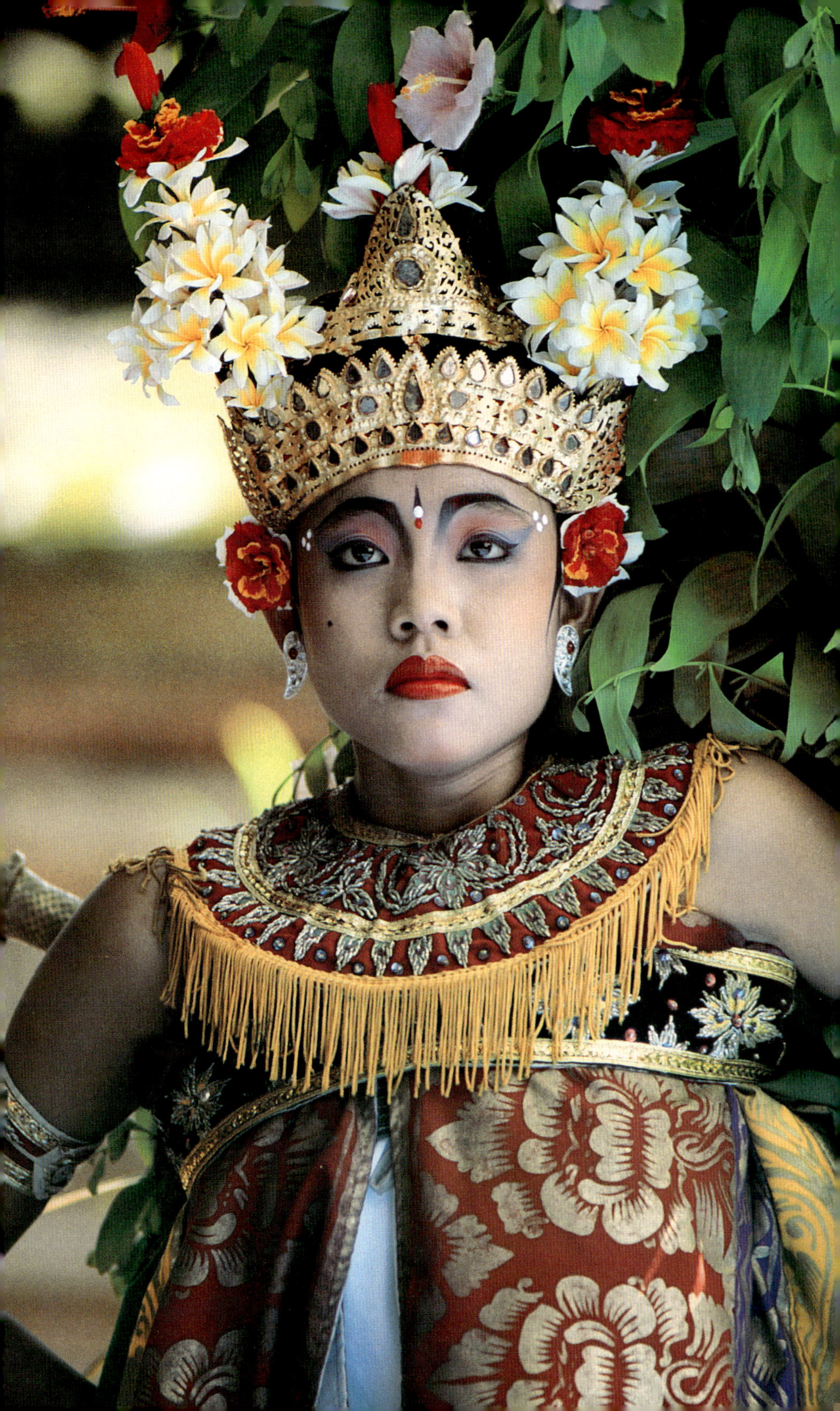

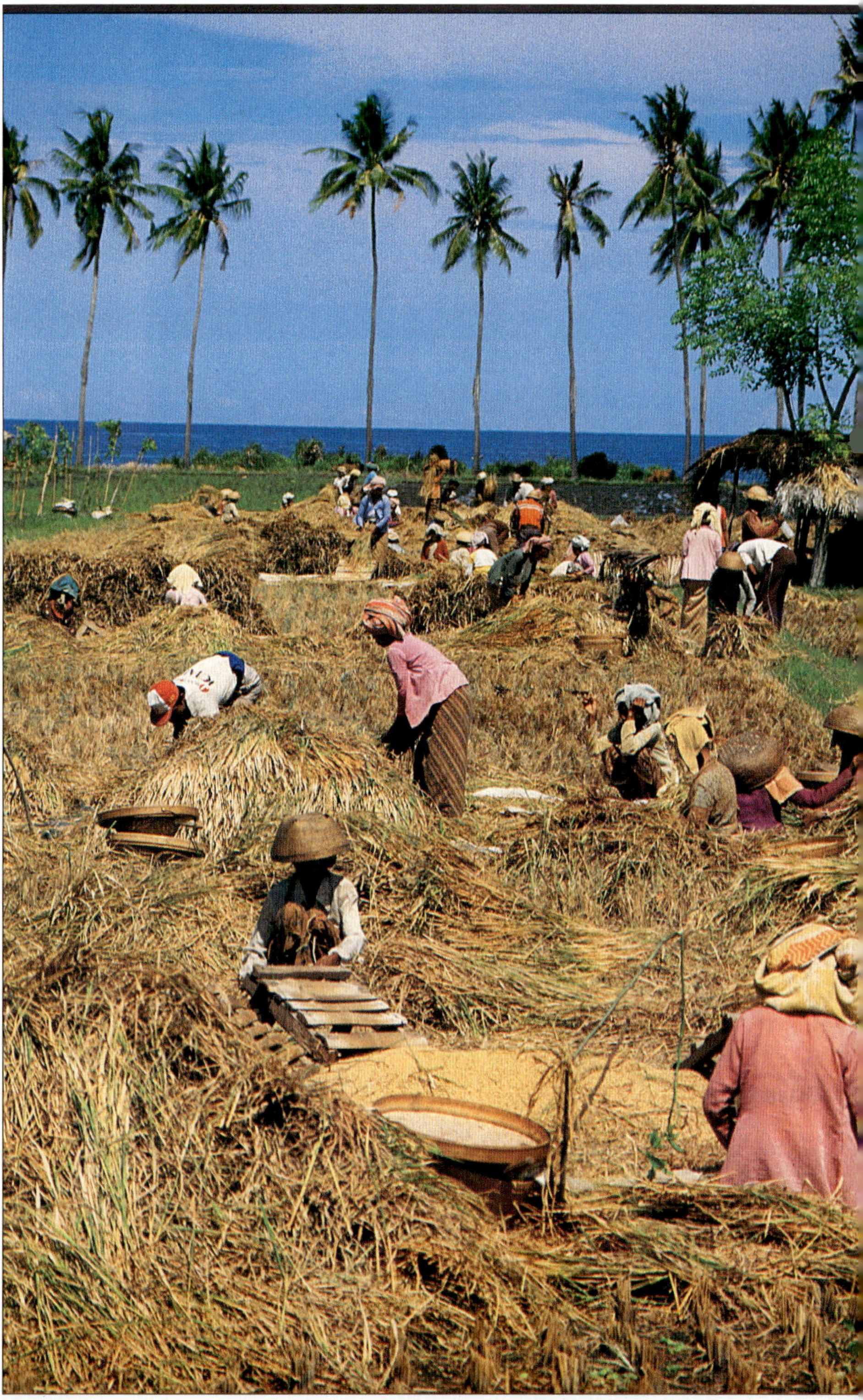

The Country and Its People

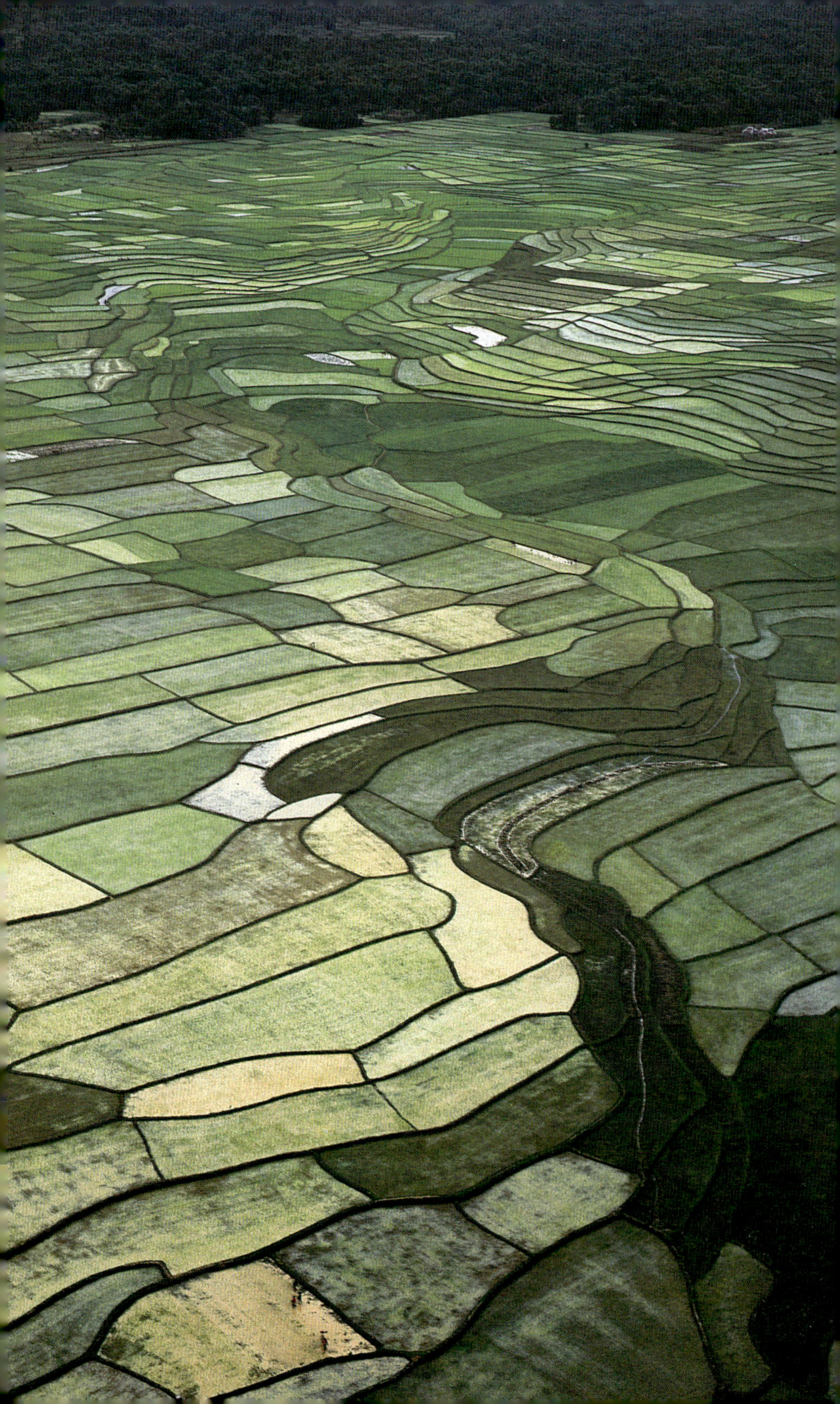

PHYSICALLY, BALI WAS BLOWN OUT OF THE DEPTHS OF THE INDIAN OCEAN by the string of volcanoes that form its central spine. They fall steeply to the sea in the north, where there are only a few valleys and a narrow coastal strip where agriculture is possible. To the south and east of the mountains, however, because the land has been lifted by the deeply burrowing edge of the Australian Coastal Plate, the slopes are gentler and alluvial plains have been deposited. This area of rich volcanic soils, cut into by fast flowing streams, is the Balinese heartland, and the home of its greatest kingdoms and their highly developed cultures. Western Bali is also volcanic, as it tapers away toward Java, but these are older and decrease in size. The larger and more distinctive volcanoes in the west are still, technically, active, though major eruptions are rare.

The same lifting that produced lush southern Bali also raised from the sea bed the large limestone island of Nusa Penida, and the peninsula south of the airport, probably also once an island, known as the Bukit.

FROM JAVA MAN TO AN ISLAND EMPIRE

Some of the earliest remains of the prehuman *Homo erectus* have been found in Java, at a time when the landmasses of Indonesia's archipelago were almost certainly joined into a single, long ribbon, and it would have been possible to walk through Malaysia to the Asian mainland. *Homo sapiens* came later, around 40,000 years ago, developing through the Neolithic and the Bronze Age, thanks to contact with China. The basic Malay-type population of modern Indonesia appears to have been there for several thousand years at least, and the evidence of the wide extent of peoples speaking Malayo-Polynesian languages points to a large ethnic group extending from peninsular Malaysia in the west eastwards to the Philippines.

To this population, with its belief in spirits that inhabit all places and all things, came Indian Hinduism, in about the second century AD. The reasons for this are easy to see: To travel from India to China without crossing the highest mountain ranges on the planet, you must sail south down the coast of Myanmar (Burma) and through the narrow Straits of Malacca that lie between peninsular Malaysia and Sumatra.

Once trade became established along this route, it cannot have been long before the desire of the Indian merchants to trade with the islands, and especially with rich Java to the south, combined with the ambitions of the Sumatrans to exert some measure of control over the trade sailing past their shores — all factors which contributed to extensive cultural interaction. Then the natural tendency of the more complex and highly organized culture to dominate the simpler and less sophisticated one meant that both Indian and Chinese influences on the tropical islands south of the Asian mainland began early.

Along with Hinduism, the Indian merchants and priests brought with them their complexly interrelated culture — Sanskrit, the caste system and Hindu mythology. Remnants of all these aspects are still found even in Moslem Java, where the shadow puppet plays and the dance-dramas continue to portray the characters of the great Indian epics.

Under these influences, and with a naturally rich soil, Java eventually produced a series of powerful Hindu, and later Buddhist, civilizations, from the Majapahit to the Mataran. Sumatra, less easy to cultivate, concentrated on the control of trade, and its Srivijaya empire too flourished. At their most extensive, the maritime trade routes stretched from China to Arabia and East Africa, and all through the Straits of Malacca. Bali, rather on the edge of things, and lacking both the natural resources and harbors of Java, joined and left empires as they waxed and waned.

These old Hindu empires, with connections as far west as Madagascar, must have been quite exotic. How far their imported culture penetrated into the lives of the ordinary people is another matter. The immense Buddhist temple at Borobudur in central Java and the nearby Hindu one at Prambanan are, however, evidence both of extraordinary dedication and exceptional powers of organization.

Rice is central to the island's life. Some of these beautifully terraced fields have been flooded for the planting of the young shoots.

Just as trade with India and China had brought Hindu and later Buddhist priests to Indonesia, as well as Chinese scholars, so trade with Arabia eventually led to the arrival of Islam in the archipelago.

Everywhere along the coast of Java in the fifteenth century, rajahs were becoming sultans, and the final outcome of this expansion of Islam was the fall of the great Majapahit empire and the flight of its aristocracy, priesthood and community of artists and scholars across the narrow strait from east Java onto the neighboring island of Bali. This did much to graft Hinduism onto ancient animist beliefs.

The emperor became the king of Bali and rajah of Klungkung, and the rest of the island was divided up into seven diminutive kingdoms—Bandung, Tabanan, Bangli, Gianyar, Karangasem (Amlapura), Jembrana (west Bali) and Buleleng (Singaraja)—and given to members of the ex-Majapahit royal family to rule. Men used to ruling an empire now began to focus their attention on a medium-size island.

These Balinese kingdoms vied with one another over the centuries, first one becoming dominant, then another. But culturally, and, more important, religiously, the island was a whole. On great festival days Balinese traveled to the Mother Temple at Besakih irrespective of the kingdom they resided in. Though there were wars between them from time to time, it seems these kingdoms were largely the playthings of the rajahs who ruled them. Their boundaries form the basis for the island's modern administrative districts.

Why Islam never moved into Bali remains something of a mystery. Islam certainly extended further east into Sulawesi and the Moluccas. Nevertheless, prolonged interaction with Islamic and other cultures did leave its mark on the island. There are Moslems in the east-facing ports of Padangbai and Kusamba, and Buddhist priests work alongside the Hindu ones. Up in the mountains, the Bali Aga, who never accepted the caste system or other Hindu imports, continue their intransigent existence.

Thus Bali (with a section of western Lombok) became what it remains today, the only predominantly non-Islamic territory in the archipelago, and an isolated outpost of Indian Hindu culture gorgeously stranded in the tropical seas south of the equator.

Rather than fade away, cut off from its source, Balinese culture has flourished, apparently intact, and continues to do so today.

It could be argued that the Balinese had their first experience of keeping foreign influences at bay by three hundred years of contact with the Dutch. Improved ship production brought the various European powers to the East in the sixteenth century. Acquiring spices quickly became the prime object of their expeditions; these were used not only to flavor meat but, far more importantly, to preserve it. Soon cloves, cinnamon, nutmeg and the rest were fetching staggering prices in Lisbon and Amsterdam. It was the Dutch who eventually came to dominate this immensely lucrative business and, as the British were later to do in India, soon began administering the territories they were exploiting. The former trade of what became known in Europe as the East Indies was suppressed, surplus clove trees (which threatened to lower prices in Europe) were burned down, and the islands were made to grow an ever-increasing proportion of crops marketable back in Amsterdam. Cloves were sold there for approximately 15 times the price paid for them. The old Arab–Chinese–Malay monopoly of the trade was at an end. The Dutch, charmed by the flowery Balinese culture they encountered, resolved not to destroy it in the way of most colonists.

The Dutch first set foot in Bali in 1597, taking home glowing reports. Despite this aesthetic appreciation, the search for profits led them to Java and the eastern spice islands of the archipelago. Again, Bali was ignored. The Dutch had enough on their hands in the more profitable corners of the region. The trade in spices, it is true, ceased to be the license to print money that it had been, and control of the islands was even temporarily lost to the British during the Napoleonic wars, when the French occupation of Holland was taken as an excuse for seizing all Dutch possessions in Asia as war booty. Nevertheless, the peace treaty saw the Dutch colonies

---

Turn-of-the-century Balinese. Western influence on the East Indies began early, but Bali was largely left alone because of its lack of ports and its mountainous interior.

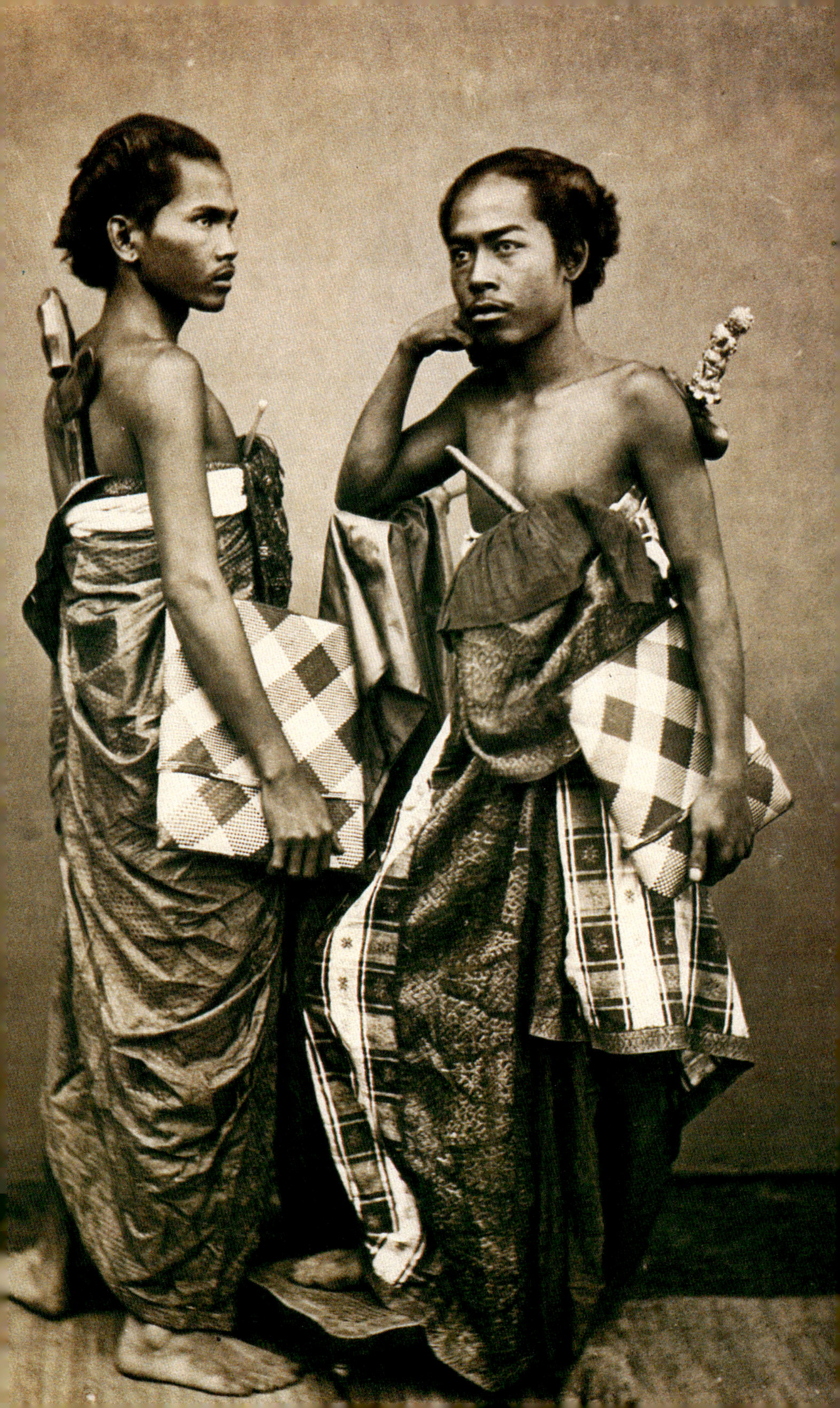

FROM JAVA MAN TO AN ISLAND EMPIRE

return, with minor adjustments which basically led to more oppressive control. Interest in the region was revived by the introduction of American cash crops such as cotton and tobacco into the islands.

One export Bali had traditionally been valued for was slaves. By the end of the eighteenth century up to 2,000 Balinese were being shipped abroad into slavery annually, ending up in South Africa, Madagascar, and Mauritius among many other places. Balinese women were especially prized as concubines by Chinese men, as they were obedient, quiet, and, unlike slaves from India, didn't mind preparing beef and pork. The slave trade was finally abolished in 1830.

The nineteenth century, like the centuries before it, saw several revolts against Dutch rule. The most notable was the so-called Java War of 1825–30, when the resistance was led by Prince Diponegoro. Major streets in Klungkung and Denpasar are named after him.

The first Dutch attempt to occupy, as opposed to keep an eye on, Bali came in 1846 when the Balinese plundering of a wreck was used as a pretext for moving in and eventually controlling the northern and western districts of the island from the Dutch capital at Singaraja. From then on a policy of divide and rule set the remaining Balinese kingdoms against one another, until one side made the tactical error of appealing to the Dutch for assistance against its neighbors. This was what the Dutch had been waiting for and they promptly annexed the kingdom they were helping, Gianyar, in 1900.

Another looting of a wreck, this time off Sanur, led to the completion of Dutch control. This, however, did not become final until after the massacre of 4,000 Balinese in Denpasar when the aristocracy presented itself in full ceremonial dress for ritual *puputan*, or resistance to the last man, against what were clearly superior forces. This was on September 20, 1906. A similar heroic but suicidal last stand took place in Klungkung, and then it was all over and the Dutch were masters of the island.

Even at home in Europe, accounts of their ceremonial massacres shocked a population

---

Arms and eyes are far more important in Balinese dance than the legs, which makes it far removed from every kind of Western dance.

already throwing off monarchist rule. On Bali their rule was even less popular. A rigid policy of white supremacy was enforced and little was done to benefit the Balinese.

In the 1920s the Royal Dutch Steam Packet Company introduced Singaraja on their sailing schedule, and placed Bali, for the first time, on the tourist map. The early 1930s was the time when the first Western artists began arriving in Bali, men like Walter Spies, who lived in Ubud, and Miguel Covarrubias and Le Mayeur, who settled near Denpasar and in Sanur respectively. They lived with, or at least alongside, the local people, and made a point of being independent of the Dutch administrators. They were in Bali because of the idyllic existence to be had there, in which culture and an easy life seemed to go hand in hand, and they had no use for the distinctions deemed necessary by the colonial masters for the perpetuation of their system.

Wealthy tourists, too, began arriving at this time. Rarely were the visitors interested in the politics of colonialism, but usually were more drawn by the prospect of a subservient, cultured nation. Despite the recent colonial outrages it's estimated that about a 100 tourists a month were visiting Bali by 1935.

A good account of the period is K'tut Tantri's *Revolt in Paradise*. This American citizen settled in Bali in 1933, adopted local dress and a Balinese name, and stayed in Bali and Java until the late 1940s. Her book is also a good guide to the events that followed the outbreak of the World War II.

The Japanese entered the war in 1941 and proceeded quickly to overrun Singapore, Malaya, Burma, the Philippines and the Dutch East Indies. The Dutch colonial army finally surrendered to them on March 7, 1942. Japanese anticolonial propaganda did not win the support of the Indonesians for long, but the opportunity was taken by some of the emerging nationalist leaders to advance their cause, and on the defeat of Japan the independent Republic of Indonesia was proclaimed on August 17, 1945.

The Dutch, however, had other ideas. In association with British forces they landed in Indonesia with the ostensible purpose of disarming and interning the Japanese there. Before long, however, troops of both nations were fighting armed Indonesian volunteers, and in November 1945, Surabaya was shelled from the sea and bombed by British forces.

Eventually the British, already troubled in their colonies in India, fell back into the role of go-betweens, but the Dutch continued, spending all the money granted to them under the Marshall Plan, designed to help them rebuild their home country and recover from World War II, on trying to preserve their East Indian Empire. The Americans were not amused, and on December 27, 1949, the Hague bowed to international pressure and agreed to recognize the sovereignty of the Republic of Indonesia.

The country's first president was the long-established leader of the independence movement, Sukarno (who had a Balinese mother). He held power through a period marked by a declining economy, militant anti-Americanism, growing corruption and little western investment. The increasing influence of the Indonesian communist party (PKI) alarmed the army. On the night of September 30, 1965 there was an attempted coup, allegedly by the PKI, though most onlookers suspect a military involvement. This was swiftly put down by the army, and Major General (later President) Suharto seized control. He embarked on a terrible purge of communists, suspected communists, and, most notably, Chinese in the last months of 1965. The total number of victims has never been agreed on — indeed the account of this period is only now becoming a permitted subject of debate in Indonesia. In Bali alone the number of dead almost certainly exceeded 100,000; the killing there was more extensive and brutal than anywhere else in the country. According to one observer, "Whole villages, including children, took part in an island wide witch hunt for communists, who were slashed and clubbed and chopped to death by communal consent." It's a sobering thought when considering a culture dubbed by so many as one of beauty, harmony, and a serene adherence to the will of the gods. The Balinese won't often speak of this period, and, especially among those too young to remember it themselves, often claim not to know anything about such a slaughter.

Suharto was to rule, as a dictator, for the next 31 years. His policies were pragmatic and pro-Western, and the PKI was declared illegal, but the rush of foreign investment seemed mysteriously to disappear into Suharto's own family group. Democracy was never fully restored and the nearest the government got to dealing with the corruption of the governing elite was to bear down increasingly on democracy, dissidence and the freedom of speech.

OPPOSITE: Traditional farming methods are still employed on Bali's rice terraces. ABOVE: Episodes from the Sanskrit epic poem, *Ramayama* are frequently represented in Balinese art, dance and theater.

The Country and Its People

A VILLAGE UPBRINGING

The Balinese have never been very political, probably because so much of their time is tied up with religion, but could hardly fail to notice the floods of Jakarta money that steamrollered huge hotels into stretches of prime beachfront with little account taken of local people, many of whom had ancestral claims to the land. The Balinese undoubtedly shared the resentment felt by most Javanese that led to increasing civil unrest in the regions and spectacular riots of students in Jakarta. In 1998, Suharto finally resigned, placing his friend and chosen successor, B.J. Habibi, into the position of president, but the people were not satisfied. In 1999 elections removed him from power, but although the popular vote went to charismatic woman politician Megawati Sukarnoputri, at the head of the Indonesian Democratic Party of Struggle (PDIP) power transferred to the acerbic, blind and elderly Abdurrahman Wahid. Corruption seems to continue as the Indonesian economy continues its long slide into crisis and the military seem constantly prepared to enter actively into politics — though not, so far, in Bali. In an atmosphere of panic conservative forces insist on stability and moderation, whereas in fact democratic change might be the only hope for the world's third-most populous nation.

Even though it is clearly and inescapably a part of Indonesia, Bali is in many ways distinct. In most of Indonesia, Islam is the predominant religion, and a government decree states that all religion should, at least, be monotheistic. Balinese Hinduism, with its belief in spirits and demons as well as the countless figures of mythology, clearly isn't. While Indonesia's economy freefalls, today Bali, alone, basks in the relative prosperity brought to it by tourism. Eighty percent of all Indonesia's tourists visit Bali and nowhere else. Although some of the largest payments go to expensive hotels built and still owned by consortia headed by Suharto connections and the Javanese business elite, the influx of foreign tourists bring enough money to transform the island's economy and encourage ancillary employment in sculpture, art and handicrafts. For the rest, the economy remains agricultural, dominated by rice production, of which the island produces a surplus for export, as well as copra and coffee.

A VILLAGE UPBRINGING

With the exception of the Bali Aga settlements, Balinese villages all follow a similar pattern. The village is invariably on either

A VILLAGE UPBRINGING

side of a road. Along this road run thatched walls with somewhat higher roofed gateways, also thatched, leading into the family compounds. Side roads at right angles to the main road lead to the rice terraces, while immediately behind the family compounds are kitchen gardens where crops such as green vegetables and corn are grown.

Somewhere in the center of the village stands the communal buildings: the village temple *(pura desa)*, the assembly pavilion *(bale agung)*, the *kul-kul* tower and, more often than not, a sacred banyan tree.

Balinese villages are shady, well tended places where gardens and the communal manipulation of running water give a strong sense of security and order.

Villages are run by a council *(krama desa)* of which every married householder is a member. This council elects one of its members as leader *(klian desa)* and meets in the *bale agung*. It orders the life of the village and makes arrangements for festivals. The council can also administer punishment, essentially expulsion. This is a serious punishment in Bali as, once expelled from his village, a

Some distance away is the cemetery, a rough grassy field surrounded by trees where cremations take place and bodies are buried temporarily prior to cremation. A small temple of the dead *(pura dalem)* also stands there.

Low bellied pigs forage freely around the village and mangy dogs hang out, despised but tolerated. Fighting cocks in round bamboo cages are often placed on the ground where they may be seen and admired, and where they can peck at the earth before being moved on to a new patch.

Chickens, too, wander at will, but ducks are herded daily into the rice paddies where they are kept together by means of a tall pole topped with a white cloth. The ducks never stray far from this marker.

man will find little refuge anywhere else on the island, and in times gone by would have to settle in the unhealthy swamps of pre-tourism Kuta or the arid limestone island of Nusa Penida. Historically, it wasn't necessary to do anything wrong to get expelled: until 30 years ago or so the parents of different-sex twins would be evicted and their house burned down, as this was regarded as a very sinister omen.

It isn't long before the visitor realizes that every hotel worker he comes into contact with identifies strongly with his village and hur-

Purification ceremony on Kuta Beach —
OPPOSITE: A *pemangku* distributes holy water.
RIGHT: Facing the ocean, the devotees venerate a temporary bamboo shrine. Such ceremonies take place after, for example, a cremation.

The Country and Its People

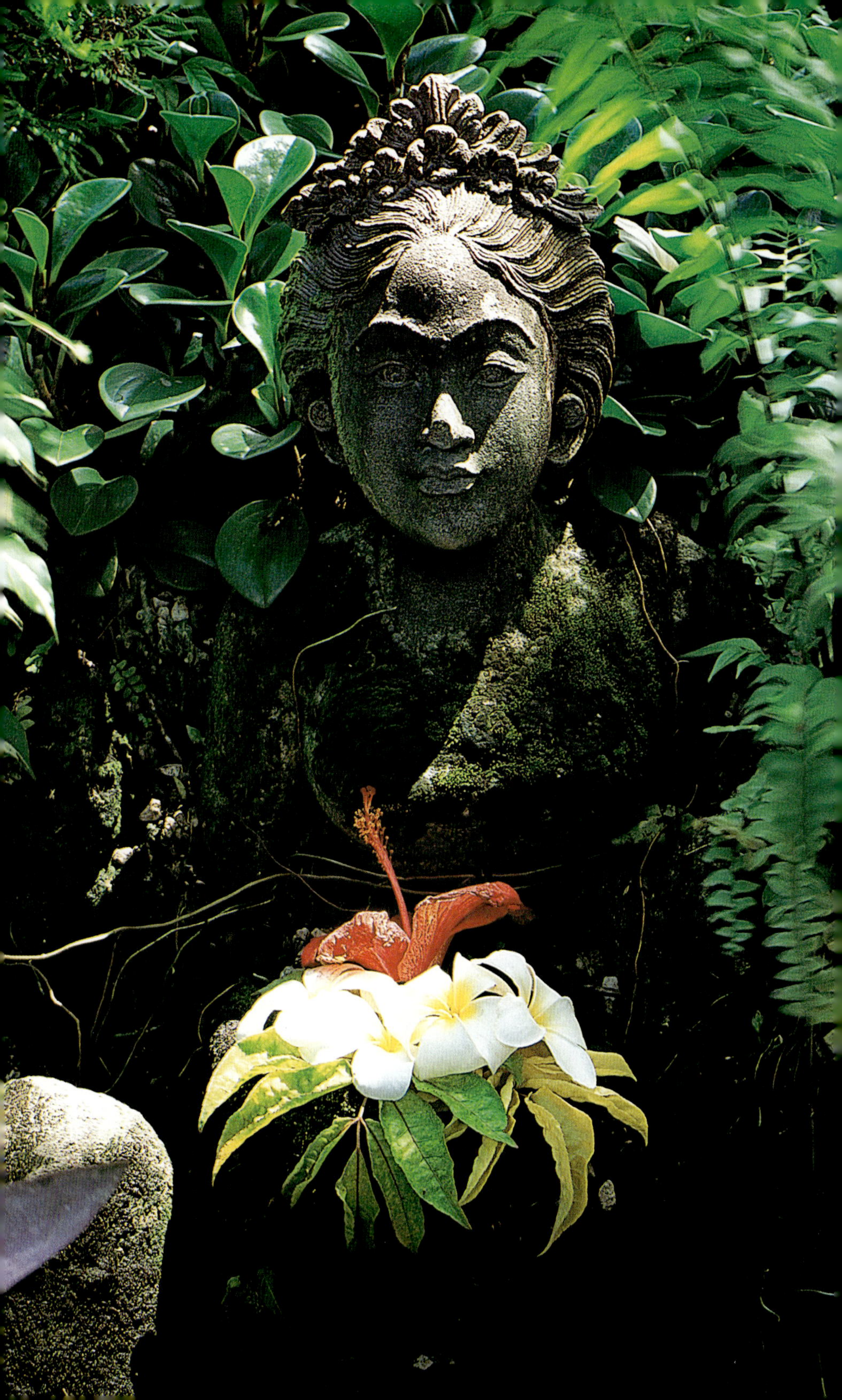

ries back there whenever he has a couple of days off, even if it's on the opposite side of the island. This is because large villages and towns are subdivided into *banjars*. These operate as youth groups that span the generations, each with its own temple, council, *bale agung* and the rest. In this way, village organization continues, even in the capital of Denpasar. Each *banjar* has its own festival on its temple *odalan*, or anniversary, and on the night before Nyepi — a great island-wide festival — each *banjar* in Denpasar parades its own lovingly-made monster through the central streets without any hint of rivalry. When *banjars* become too large — more than 300 families or so — they split and form two, but membership of a *banjar* is the central lodestone of Balinese life — almost always more important than work and second in importance only to the family.

In many cases Balinese aristocrats still live in their palaces (*puri*), and these are situated within villages rather than outside. These large walled compounds are like miniature villages in themselves, containing houses for different family members, each with its own garden and subdividing wall. There is no real middle class in rural Bali. The Chinese businessmen and the shopkeepers of Kuta, together with the other self-made people, tend to live in or just outside of Denpasar.

Although rice fields are nowadays owned by individual villagers, the old cooperative system of agriculture continues to exist. One of the reasons for this is that irrigation is necessarily communal, and the flow of the water, the careful provision of exactly the right amount of water for all the fields before it is allowed to flow away downstream to the next village, requires careful cooperation and management.

The organizations that oversee this operation are known as *subak*; everyone who owns a rice field is a member. The *subak* meets monthly, sometimes more often, at the shrine in the rice field dedicated to the deities of agriculture, where they makes decisions about what repairs or improvements are needed, and who will be responsible for carrying them out.

Partly for the gods, partly for the aesthetic, stone statues such as this one at Poppies, Kuta, are decorated daily with fresh flowers.

WHERE DO YOU SIT?

Caste is more deeply embedded in the Balinese psyche than it may first appear.

In the same way that the Hindu religion was brought, in the Majapahit invasion, to a people previously content with worshipping spirits of place and of their ancestors, so too the age-old Hindu distinction between people born to different roles in life was superimposed on a culture that was essentially collective and probably relatively classless. Just as the Balinese took to the one, so they accepted the other. Despite the fact that 93% of the population has to be content with membership of the lowest of the four castes, the Sudra, they appear to accept uncritically the claims of the other three castes, and at times, even when away from their home villages, seek to adopt their status for themselves. Some commentators have judged that caste in modern Bali represents little more than a pleasant diversion. Perhaps this is the impression the Sudras would like to give, and that the top-dog Brahmanas can afford to give (seeing as they are often also the wealthiest people around). Nevertheless, the complexities of an inter-caste marriage have not lessened with the arrival of a few hundred thousand tourists on the beaches of Kuta and Sanur.

Essentially, the Brahmanas were the priestly caste; the Satrias, the warriors; the Wesias, the merchants; and the Sudras, the ordinary people. A long-standing struggle between the Brahmanas and the Satrias over which of them was the senior group seems to have been resolved in a de facto victory for the Brahmanas.

The four groups prefix distinguishing titles to their names. Brahmana men us Ida Bagus, the women Ida Ayu (Dayu for short). Both these mean "highborn and beautiful." Satrias men use Cokorde, Anak Agung, Ratu and Prebagus, while the women use Anak Agung Isti, Dewa Ayu. Wesia men affix I Gusti or Pregusti, and the women I Gusti Ayu. Sudra men use I and the women Ni.

Legally, feudal discrimination according to caste is forbidden. It is true that Brahmanas can be found waiting tables in restaurants and Sudras occupying reasonably important government positions. Nevertheless, socially the habits of deference persist, and "Where do you sit?" (referring to the custom of always sitting lower than someone of a higher caste) remains a question strangers will often ask each other on first acquaintance.

NAMING OF NAMES

Balinese personal names usually refer to the position of the child in the family order. The firstborn is Wayan — or, in the higher castes, Putu or Gede. The second is Made — or Nengah or Kadek. The usual name for the third born is Nyoman, with Komang as an alternative. The fourth child is Ketut. These names are used for boys and girls indiscriminately. After four, the cycle is repeated, with the fifth child Wayan again and so on.

SEX ROLES

Distinction according to sex is more rigorous than that according to class.

Only men work as craftsmen (weaving excepted), climb coconut trees, tend cattle or cultivate the fields (though women invariably help with the rice harvest). Only women do the housework, look after the chickens and pigs and prepare offerings for temples.

It often surprises Westerners is to see women doing all the heavy labor on construction sites and road works. The principle here is that, whereas it's the men who build the traditional Balinese wooden houses, the women do the dirty work in Western-style building.

Also, it is the custom for women to carry goods on their heads, men to carry them slung at either end of a pole they carry on their shoulders. It's normally women who carry offerings to the temple, but when a man does this, he too must carry them on his head.

Nevertheless, Balinese women do enjoy a measure of independence by Asian standards, keeping the profits from economic activities for themselves, and they can easily obtain a divorce from an unsatisfactory husband without incurring any serious social disapproval.

BIRTH, CHILDHOOD, LOVE AND MARRIAGE

Family life is particularly important to the Balinese. The existence of offspring to ensure an adequate cremation is essential, and the more children there are to bear the cost of this expensive ceremony the better. In earlier times, and possibly still, Western contraception devices were considered akin to black magic. Failure to bear children is an acceptable ground for divorce (as is male impotence) in Balinese society.

Three months into pregnancy, the mother-to-be is subject to a ceremony, and during the gestation period she will probably wear one or more amulets to protect her from the attention of *leyak* (witches) anxious to feed on the entrails of the unborn child. After the birth itself, the mother is considered unclean (*sebel*) for 42 days (and the father for three days).

The newborn child is considered to be accompanied by four "brothers" in the case of a boy, or four "sisters" in the case of a girl: the *kanda empat*. These have their physical manifestation in the placenta, blood, skin-coating and amniotic fluid, all of which are saved and buried with great solemnity, the place being marked with a shrine.

Not so long ago, the birth of twins was considered a disaster by ordinary people, and a sign of serious spiritual evil. If the babies were of different sexes this would be such an evil event it would necessitate the removal and eventual destruction of the family's house and the impoverishment of the father of the ill-begotten unfortunates. Among the upper castes, however, twins were considered the reincarnations of two souls previously happily married, and their birth the occasion for great rejoicing. Some experts have suggested that these different reactions to a similar situation illustrate the continuance of ancient Balinese beliefs among the ordinary people, in their fearful reaction, and the Hindu approach of the upper classes, many of whom descended en masse on Bali from Java in the sixteenth century. Perhaps.

After 14 days, the newborn is named, but it's only after 105 days (three months of 35 days each) that the child is allowed to touch the ground for the first time, the occasion being marked, not unexpectedly, with a ceremony. Another similar ceremony takes place after one Balinese 210-day year, although in practice the two ceremonies are frequently combined on the later date to reduce the expense of the necessary feasting of guests and hiring of priests.

The Balinese allow their children to live an unusually natural life. They are suckled for as long as they want, often over three years, and allowed to eat — as their parents do — whenever they're hungry. They are held in permanent bodily contact with either the mother or another woman of the family for every moment of the first three months of life, and throughout early childhood fathers cuddle or carry their children almost as often as their mothers. Not surprisingly, Balinese children rarely cry.

Once they're able to walk, the children live a free and easy life in the village in the company of other children of their own age. They are never beaten, and little in adult life is hidden from them, so that they appear to enter the world of sex at adolescence without surprise, guilt or neurosis.

Sexual relations between Balinese teenagers are left to proceed in a natural way without interference from the parents, at least in the Sudra class that makes up the vast majority of the population, and there's no expectation that early affairs will necessarily lead to marriage. Love charms and magically potent amulets are often used when the girl seems reluctant. Homosexuality is frowned on and seems rare.

The charm of the Balinese is the charm of a people whose natural grace has been sustained and augmented by a religion that is based on respect and reverence for the life of all things.

A VILLAGE UPBRINGING — BIRTH, CHILDHOOD, LOVE AND MARRIAGE

The relaxed attitude to sex continues on into marriage. Parents have a minimal part to play in the arrangements, and in the commonest form of marriage the ceremony doesn't take place until several days after the announcement of consummation. Even in upper caste arranged marriages, the couple may sleep together for an agreed period before the wedding.

The commonest form of marriage ceremony in Bali is a theatrical kidnapping (*ngrorod*). The boy seizes the girl in some public place and, after token resistance, the couple speed off to a prearranged hideaway where offerings are set out for the gods and the union consummated. It's considered vital this happens before the offerings wilt in order for the union to be valid. This is the real marriage, performed in the sight of the gods, and the subsequent public celebration is merely a recognition of the couple's new status.

Arranged marriages (*mapadik*) are commonest among the aristocracy, but only with the full agreement of both parties.

The wedding ceremonies take place at the home of the boy's father. A tooth-filing ritual (see below) will be incorporated if this operation hasn't been performed already. There's much feasting and music, but the actual ceremony is a simple one with the priest blessing the union amid much throwing of flowers, ringing of bells and dashing with holy water.

In the past, a Balinese woman could not marry a man of lower caste than herself, thus keeping daughters from descending the social scale when marrying. If this is changing nowadays, it is changing slowly. Marriage with divorcees and widows, however, is freely allowed.

Balinese women can divorce their husbands — for cruelty, impotence or failure to support them — by simply walking out of the house. The divorce is then confirmed by the village council; this is generally a formality as there are no set criteria by which "support" or "cruelty" can be judged.

The phenomenon of "possession" — entering a trance during a temple festival. While these men are possessed, they can endure extremes of pain without any apparent ill effects.

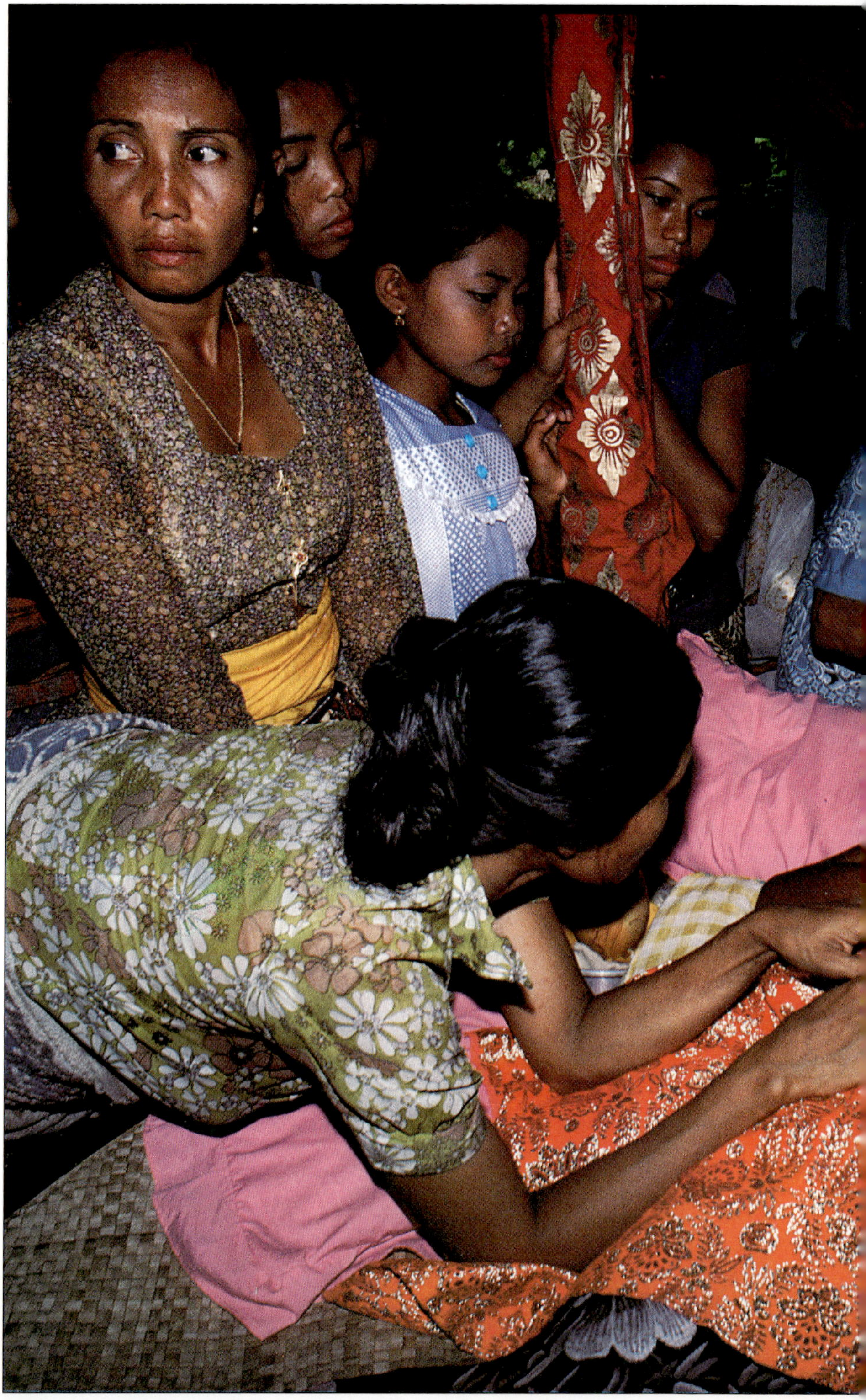

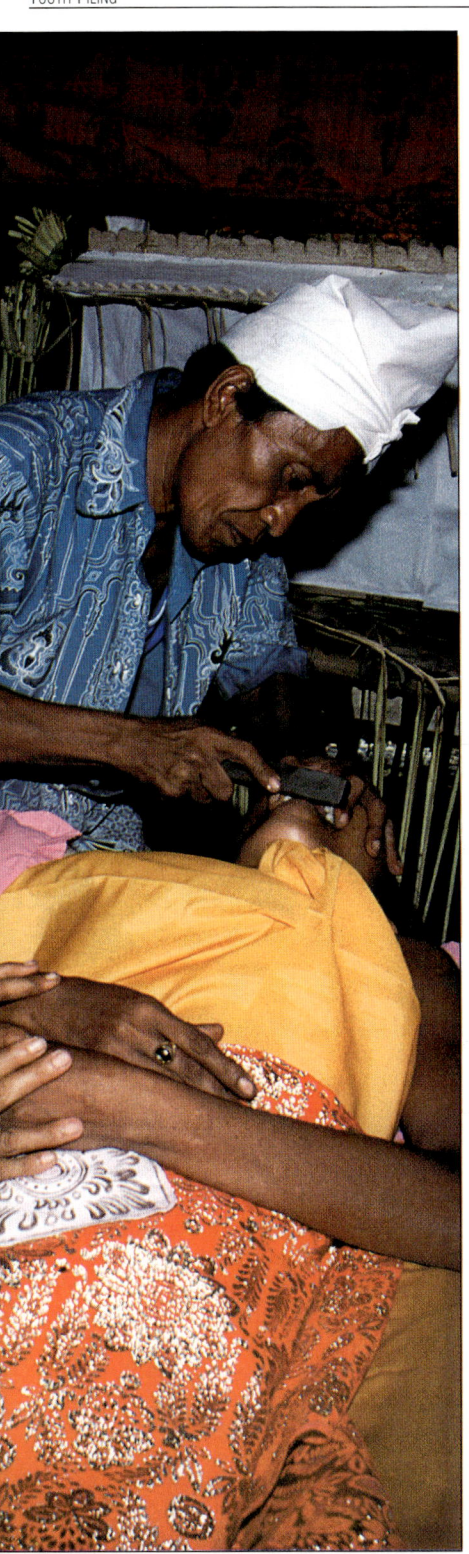

Tooth Filing

It is considered essential for every Balinese adult sooner or later to have his or her teeth filed — so much so that in the event of accidental death in youth the teeth of the body will be filed before cremation.

The purpose of the ceremony is to reduce the power of the vices of greed, jealousy, anger, drunkenness, lust and "confusion" that are considered more appropriate to animals than to humans. Consequently, the two upper canine teeth, and the four incisors between them, are filed down amid feasting and general celebration. Because of the cost of the hospitality involved, tooth-filing ceremonies are often held in conjunction with other rituals. Because it's thought desirable to have had your teeth filed before you get married, the ceremony is frequently held in conjunction with a wedding.

Ideally, the six teeth are filed down by someone of the Brahmana caste, perhaps the upper-caste patron of the family concerned. The patients, dressed in their finest, lie down in a pavilion, usually two at a time, surrounded by offerings. They are then wrapped in a white cloth while family and friends gather round.

The extent to which the teeth are filed down depends largely on the wishes of the subject, but as filed teeth are considered beautiful as well as an aid to virtue, it's not uncommon for a thorough job to be requested. The filing usually takes between 15 and 30 minutes. The mouth is held open by a short piece of sugarcane and from time to time the patient spits out the filings into a yellow coconut which is later buried in the family temple. A small mirror allows the victim to inspect the work and request improvements. Often, to save on expense, hundreds of young men and women have their teeth filed together in one ceremony.

Tooth filing — a custom that is still rigorously observed by all Balinese, and no young man or woman can be married before the ceremony has been completed. Groups of adolescents often have their teeth filed together, and marriage and tooth filing rituals frequently take place together.

RELIGION

Every Balinese will describe himself to you as a Hindu, but in reality the elements of Hinduism found in Bali include a far older belief system of gods and demons, spirits of protection and of danger.

The central tenets of Hinduism fit in well with the belief that the world is everywhere populated by spirits. A people who believed from the start that in every tree, animal, bush, volcano — and in every fortunate or disastrous event — there is an invisible intelligence at work cannot have found it difficult to take to a philosophy that taught of a World Soul of which we, and all other living things, are temporary embodiments.

To the educated Hindu, the universe is ordered by a controlling spirit, Brahman. Your inner essence, the silent core of your being that remains when all the lusts for money, sex and power are stilled, is your Atman. The innermost secret, the core of the mystery, is that the two — your "soul" and the vast spirit of the universe — are one and the same thing. You are a part of it, manifested for a brief time in matter. So is a mouse, a tree, a grain of corn.

The cycle of birth and death, creation and destruction, goes on forever, the essence of all things constantly embodying itself in matter. In just the same way that all things are part of the great World Spirit, so their death is no tragedy, merely the returning of the part to the whole, a whole from which innumerable new iterations will be born.

This constant rebirth of the spirit, at a higher or lower level of creation according to the place your actions have brought you in your last incarnation, is natural and inevitable. But it's wearisome to the high-aspiring soul who longs for permanent rest, for final union with the creating spirit itself. Because the spirits of all things and the great universal spirit are essentially one and the same, this ultimate union, or reunification, is possible. Reject all desire, which holds you down among the world of material things, and you might attain that final fusion with the ineffable and unimaginable, known as *moksa*. You at last realize the potential that was in you all along and become one with Brahman.

This is the philosophic heart of Hinduism. Over the millennia, innumerable manifestations of it have grown up in India and elsewhere. In Bali, orientation of temples toward the volcanoes and the use of cock's blood (obtained at cockfights) in temple rituals seem remote from the pure spirituality of the Chandogya Upanishad, but reflect the ancient, ancestral practices.

Despite differences from Hinduism in India, the influence of the Hindu vision in Bali is remarkably pervasive. Balinese cremations are genuinely cheerful affairs, and the numerous rituals preceding them, symbolizing the cutting off of attachment to the soul of the dead, are living parts of ordinary village life. The soul must be allowed to go free, and not be held back by grief — so teaches the religion; and the result is that, remarkable as it may seem to Westerners, the ordinary Balinese at a cremation do not mourn.

The variety of religious practice, the number of places and things that can be venerated, is astonishing. There's hardly a field, a large tree or even a disco on the island that doesn't have its incense-burning shrine. The same is true, it might be argued, of Hong Kong or Bangkok, but the constant attention to these household shrines in Bali and the frequency and elaborateness of temple festivals have no match in any other culture.

Every village *(desa)* has its temple of origin *(pura puseh)*, its temple of the dead *(pura dalem)*, its temple for the irrigation system *(pura subak)*, and any number of temples and shrines dedicated to local streams, lakes, springs, hills and waterfalls. All must have their offerings on their holy days. In addition, evil spirits, thought to occupy their own special sites, but proliferating at crossroads, must be placated with offerings too, thrown down casually and quickly crushed by the first passing car (but not before the greedy spirits have wolfed up their meager essence).

Thus the spirits of goodness are constantly being invited down into the world of everyday life and feted at festivals, and the evil spirits kept at bay by regular, bribes.

A young girl takes an offering to the temple. Under a very liberal system of child rearing, the Balinese mature early and retain a natural dignity throughout adult life.

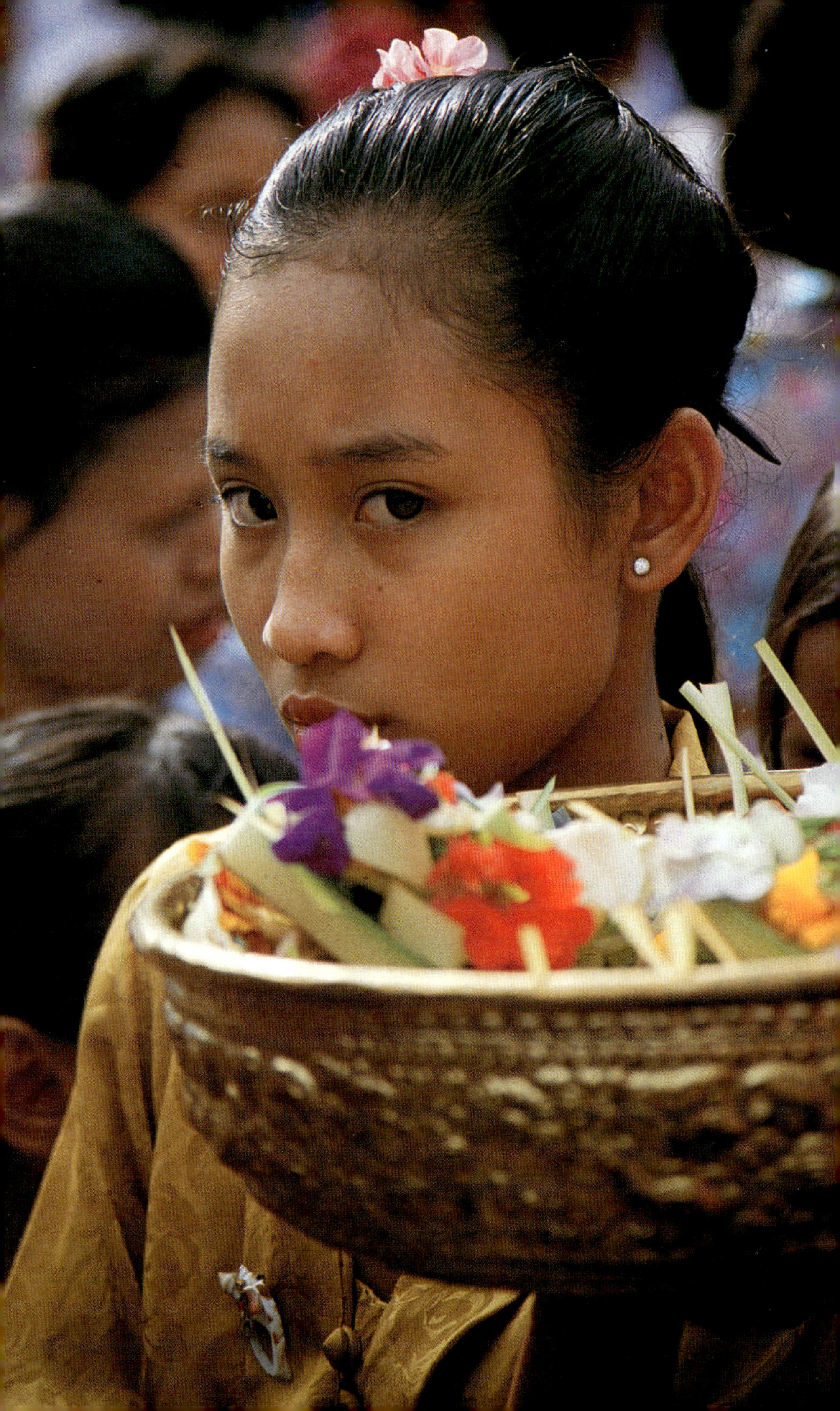

RELIGION

For the Balinese, volcanoes are the seat of the gods. Every structure in Bali is to some extent influenced by this sense of "to the mountains" *(kaja)* being pure and the opposite direction *(kelod)* being impure. Thus, a house will have its shrine in its most *kaja* corner, and its pigpen and garbage area in its most *kelod*.

This doesn't mean that to the Balinese the sea is impure, though some Western writers have inferred this. It is true the Balinese historically have not been seafarers, but the sea itself is seen as a purifying element, used for cleansing symbolic items from the temple *(arca)* and one source of holy water.

The mountain-oriented temples of Bali often have a deserted, even shabby look. They contain no idols, and no priests are in attendance. Only the temple keeper *(pemangku)*, dressed in white, is usually somewhere around to keep the place tidy and accept the donations of visitors. On festival days, though, things are very different.

The principal festival of any temple is its anniversary *(odalan)*, occurring every 210 days from the date of its founding. Then bamboo altars and tables are put up, and offerings of fruit, cakes and flowers, piled high on the heads of the women, are brought from nearby houses. The *pemangku* receives them, pours holy water onto the hands of the villagers and places grains of rice on their temples and brow. The villagers take flower blossoms and, holding them between the tips of their fingers, raise them to their foreheads three times before throwing them toward the shrines.

The high caste priests *(pedanda)* are said to be the direct descendants of the Indian Brahmins who officiated in the old courts of Java. They only attend temple ceremonies on the most important occasions, such as aristocratic weddings, at which they sit on a high platform ringing their bells and reciting their mantras. They can be either Buddhist or Hindu *(pedanda bodda* or *pedanda siwa)*, the former going bareheaded with long hair, the latter wearing a gold and red miter crowned with a crystal ball. The chief use of

---

The village cremation. These days the fire is largely kerosene sprayed onto the bier from a portable tank. The actual cremation takes place at a burning ground just outside the village.

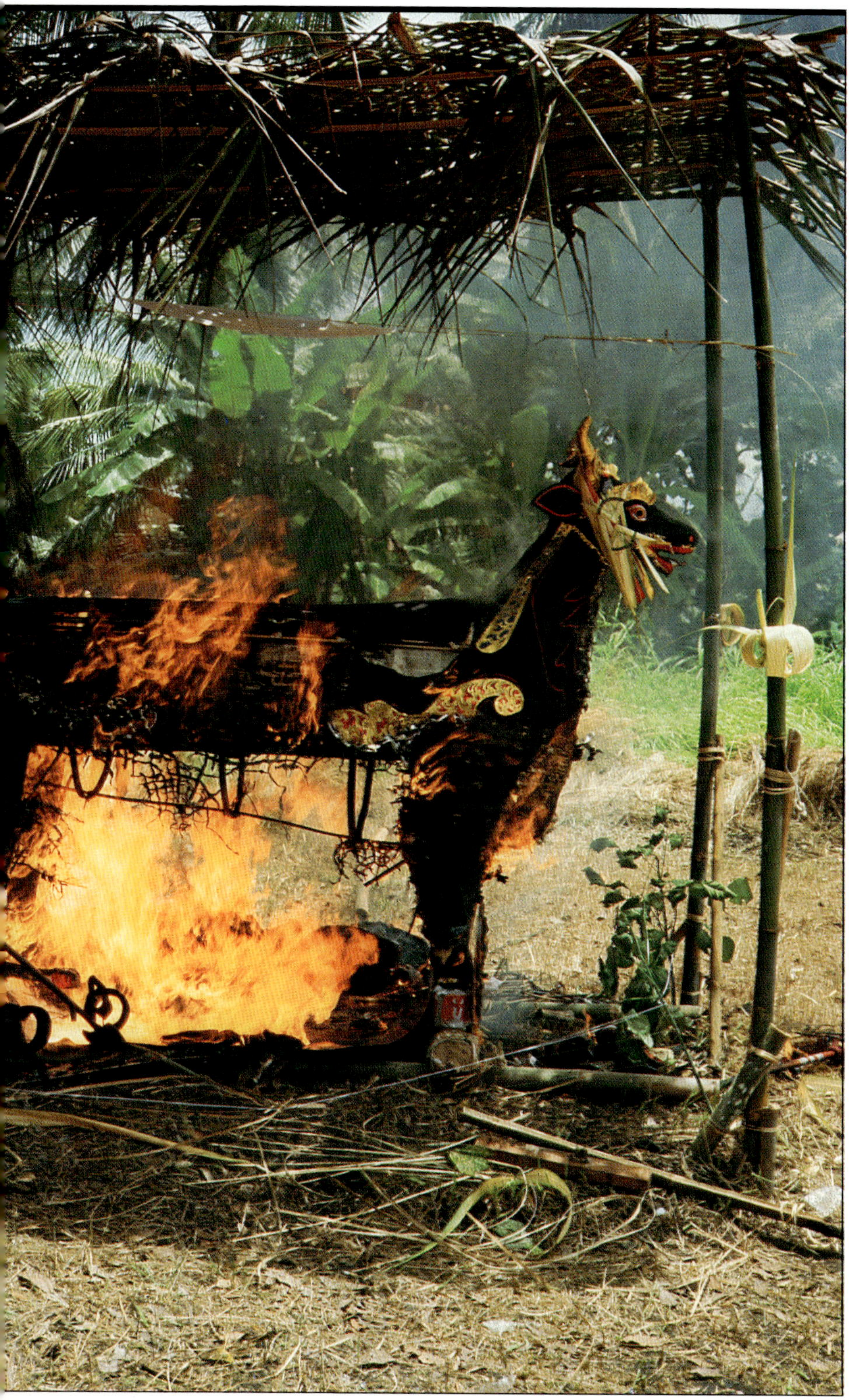

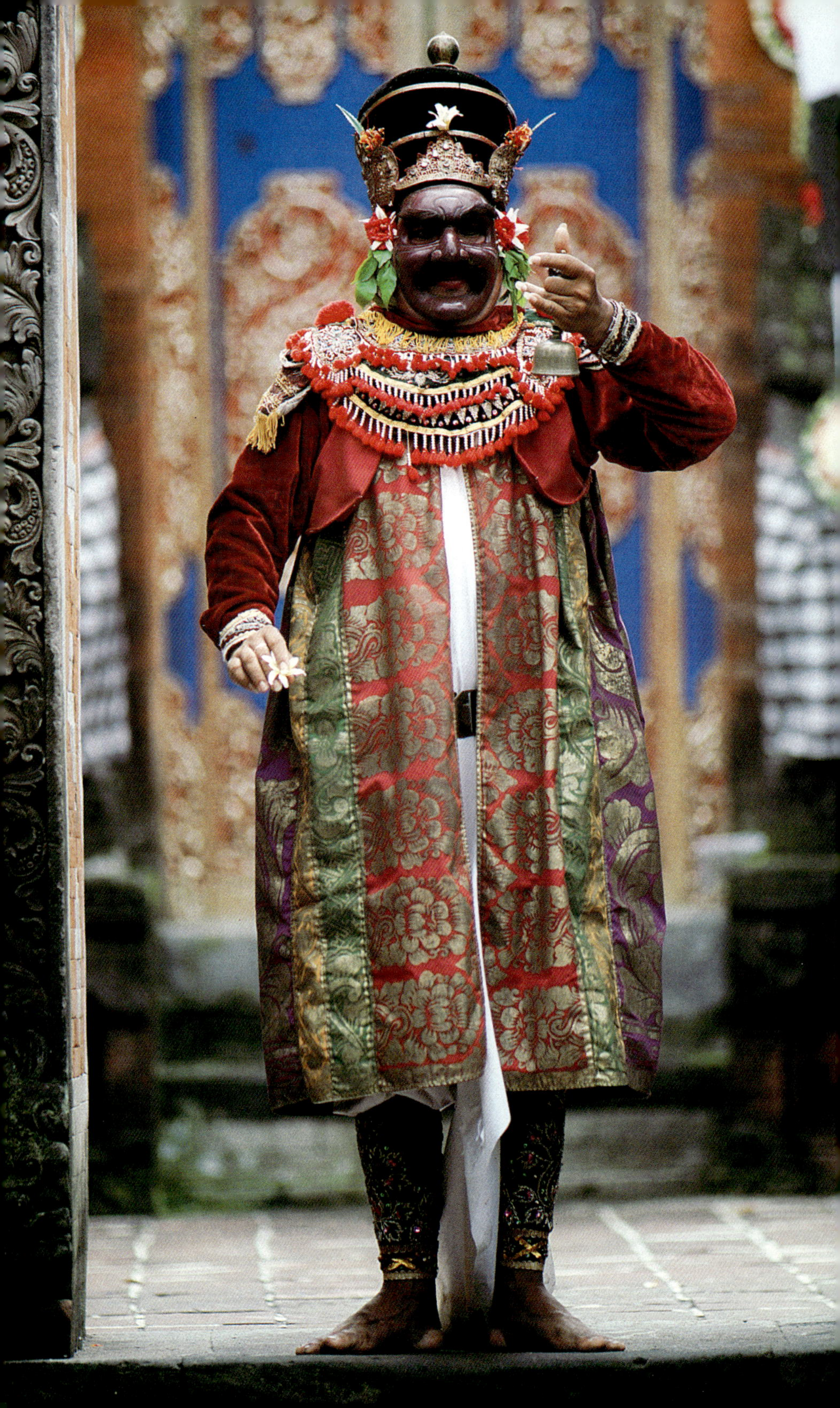

these learned *pedanda* as far as the ordinary people are concerned is to bless the holy water used in all temple ceremonies.

At these temple anniversary festivals, male and female figures, the *arca*, made of sandalwood, or of old Chinese coins (*kepeng*), symbolize the gods and are taken during the day to a river or the sea and symbolically washed. In addition, cockfights are sometimes staged in the afternoon. *Gamelan* orchestras play, and dance-dramas may be performed. As the evening wears on, coffee and cake are offered to everyone present, and certain villagers will go into a trance (during which they may also perform a sword dance) when a spirit, it is believed, will speak through them and report on how the offerings have been received by the gods.

At dawn, the women dance in honor of the rising sun, and the elaborate offerings, their essence judged to have been devoured by the gods, are taken back home and eventually eaten by the weary devotees.

Hotels for the Gods

Balinese temples have the same mixture of diversity and similarity as a similar selection of Christian churches. A typical Balinese temple, however, might present itself as follows:

From the street the first, or outer, compound is approached through two carved stone structures, the inside (facing) walls of which have been left smooth. The general effect is of a structure, tapering upwards, that has been split down the middle. This split gateway is known as a *candi bentar*.

The first compound is spacious and almost empty. It does, however, contain a *pemangku* clad in white who asks visitors to sign a visitors' book and pay a donation of a couple of hundred rupiah. The compound also contains some ordinary-looking pavilions (roofs resting on four posts, with a waist-level floor) and a brick tower. Climb the tower and you'll find hanging at the top some hollowed out tree trunks with slits cut into them: these are *kul-kul*, and they are hammered in times of emergency to call the villagers to the temple compound. The pavilions are used by the *gamelan* orchestras, and for preparing offerings and cooking food, on festival days.

If the temple has a second, outer compound it will simply contain further pavilions.

At the top end of the outer court, oriented directly toward the mountains, there is a wall with a door in it. Around this door are ornate decorations, and the door itself is intricately carved. It's called the *padu raksa*. The door stands half open, and there are a few steps to a short wall, an *aling-aling*, which bars direct access. This is actually meant to bar the way of evil spirits which are thought to travel in straight lines, as well as to be rather stupid—seeing their way barred, it's hoped, they'll reverse direction and fly back out again. Turning left or right and going down the steps into the inner courtyard brings you to the holiest part of the temple.

There are a considerable number of shrines along two walls, either the eastern and northern walls in south Bali or the eastern and southern walls in north Bali, as the shrines must face the mountains. Some of these shrines are small structures a couple of meters high, little more than high tables with roofs of black thatch (*ijuk*). Others are high towers with multiple roofs. These are

OPPOSITE: An official in the *barong* dance. The courts of the old Hindu rajahs of Java and Bali have left their mark on a number of Balinese dramas. ABOVE: Dancers' costumes are made and maintained with extraordinary care and attention to detail.

known as *meru*, and the roofs are always of an odd number. The number signifies which deity they are dedicated to, as follows: three roofs means it is dedicated to Dewi Sri (the rice goddess), five to Isawa (an incarnation of Siwa), seven to Brahma, nine to Wisnu, and eleven to Siwa. The finest *meru in Bali* can be seen at Besakih and Mengwi.

Close to the eastern wall there is a sounder structure with locked doors. This is the *gedong pesimpanan* and contains various dusty items — masks for *barong* dances, for instance — communally owned by the villagers and occasionally used in festivals.

Situated in the corner between north and east in southern Bali or south and east in northern Bali is a stone throne placed at the summit of an elaborately carved structure also of stone. This is the *padmasana*, the chair for Ida Sanghyang Widhi Wasa, the supreme deity in the Balinese pantheon. The support for the chair is carved to represent the world as imagined in Balinese mythology: mountains supported by a turtle entwined with snakes. When there are three chairs instead of one, they are for the godhead in the form of the trinity Siwa, Wisnu and Brahma.

THE AFFRIGHTED SUN

The gamecock clipped and armed for fight
Does the rising sun affright.
—William Blake, *Auguries of Innocence* (1805)

The tending and care of fighting cocks is one of the most visible parts of Balinese life. Men sitting in circles preening their birds is one of the most common sights on the island, and the early-morning alarm cackles a daily feature in the cheaper *losmens*, where the owner's fighting cocks are likely to have their beds near yours.

Gambling has been illegal throughout Indonesia since 1981. In Bali, however, where the letting of blood is deemed a necessary part of temple festivals, permits are issued by the police allowing three cockfights on the days of temple anniversary celebrations. Both the restriction on the number of fights and the general prohibition on gambling are regularly ignored on these occasions.

Bets are placed nominally in the ancient currency of the *ringgit* though in reality in the rupiah equivalent. A lay priest (*pemangku*) gives offerings to both the good and evil spirits before the fight begins.

The Balinese word for cockfights is *tajen* (blades), after the razor-sharp knives that are attached to the cocks' left legs.

Cocks naturally fight each other over the female birds. But it's only with the lethal blades attached that they slash their opponent almost to death, often in a matter of seconds. They are not armed with blades in the trial bouts, of course, but in the fight itself nature becomes hideously armed, a flurry in the air becomes a flashing of steel, with the defeated bird lying bleeding in the dust.

The blade becomes the property of the specialist (*pekembar*) the owner has employed to fix it in place. As soon as the winner has been declared, the legs, blade attached, are chopped off the losing cock, almost invariably while it is still alive. Photography is not welcome at cockfights.

The Balinese also bet on crickets; it's a sort of poor man's cockfighting. The creatures are caught in the cracks of the dried-out rice fields after harvest and fed on grains of rice and flower petals. They are exercised and bathed, and kept in tubular cages made of sections of bamboo. The fights take place inside a pair of cages placed together end to end. The winner is the cricket that forces the other to retreat to its furthest corner. Bets are in the region of a few thousand rupiah — on cocks they can be millions.

In another practice, bells and small flutes are attached round the necks of doves so that when they wheel overhead they produce a delicious tinkling and humming. Covarrubias says in *The Island of Bali* that these aerial musical instruments are a protection against birds of prey. If this is not the case, then bird orchestras are the only form of Balinese music created purely for pleasure.

Even so, it would be very Balinese to make them for fun, and then say they were to accompany the gods on their way down to the temples. Whatever their original purpose, the unexpected sound of these tiny instruments borne on the breeze is one of the real delights of the island.

Men preening and matching their fighting cocks — a common sight all over Bali. Cock fights are nowadays only permitted before temple anniversary ceremonies.

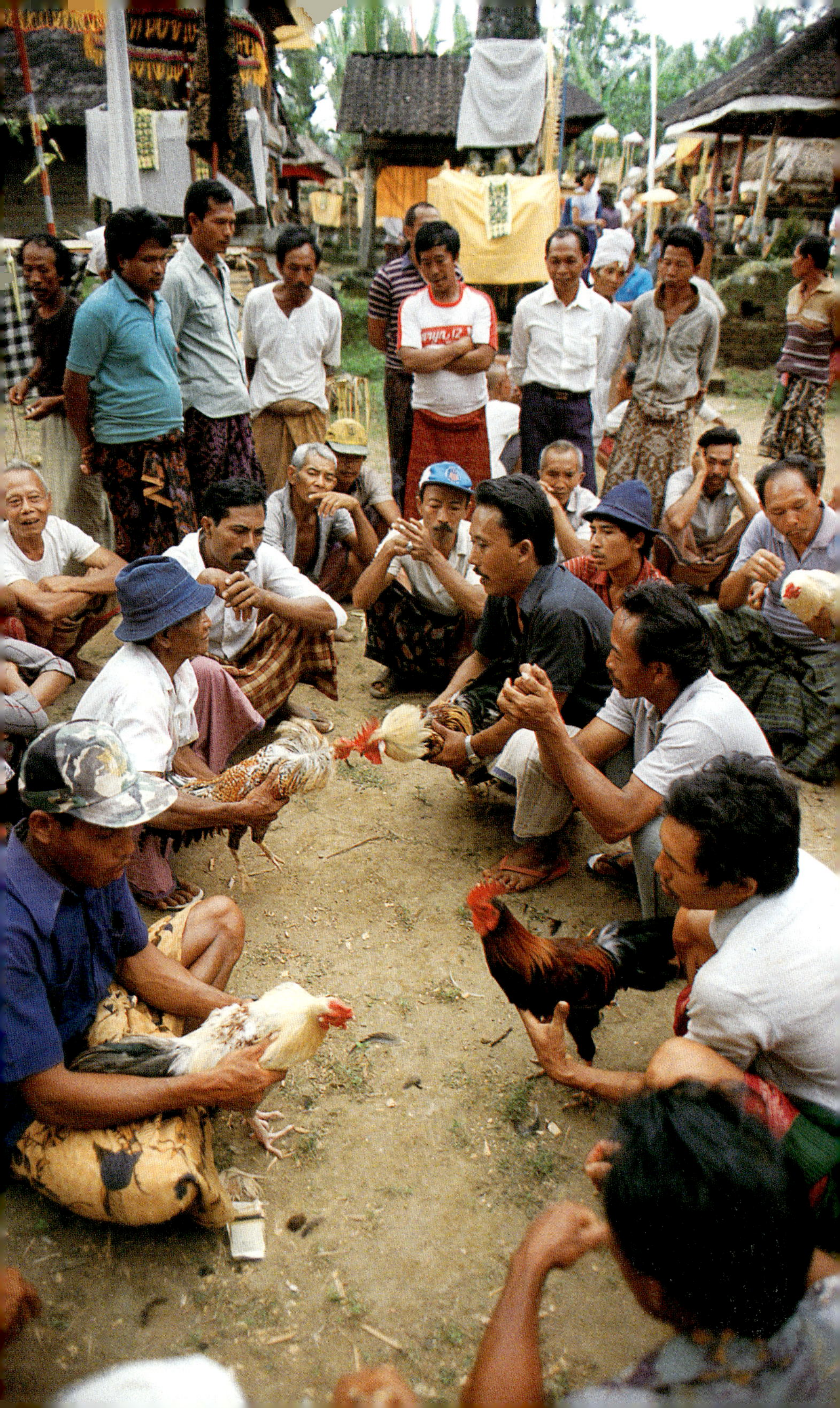

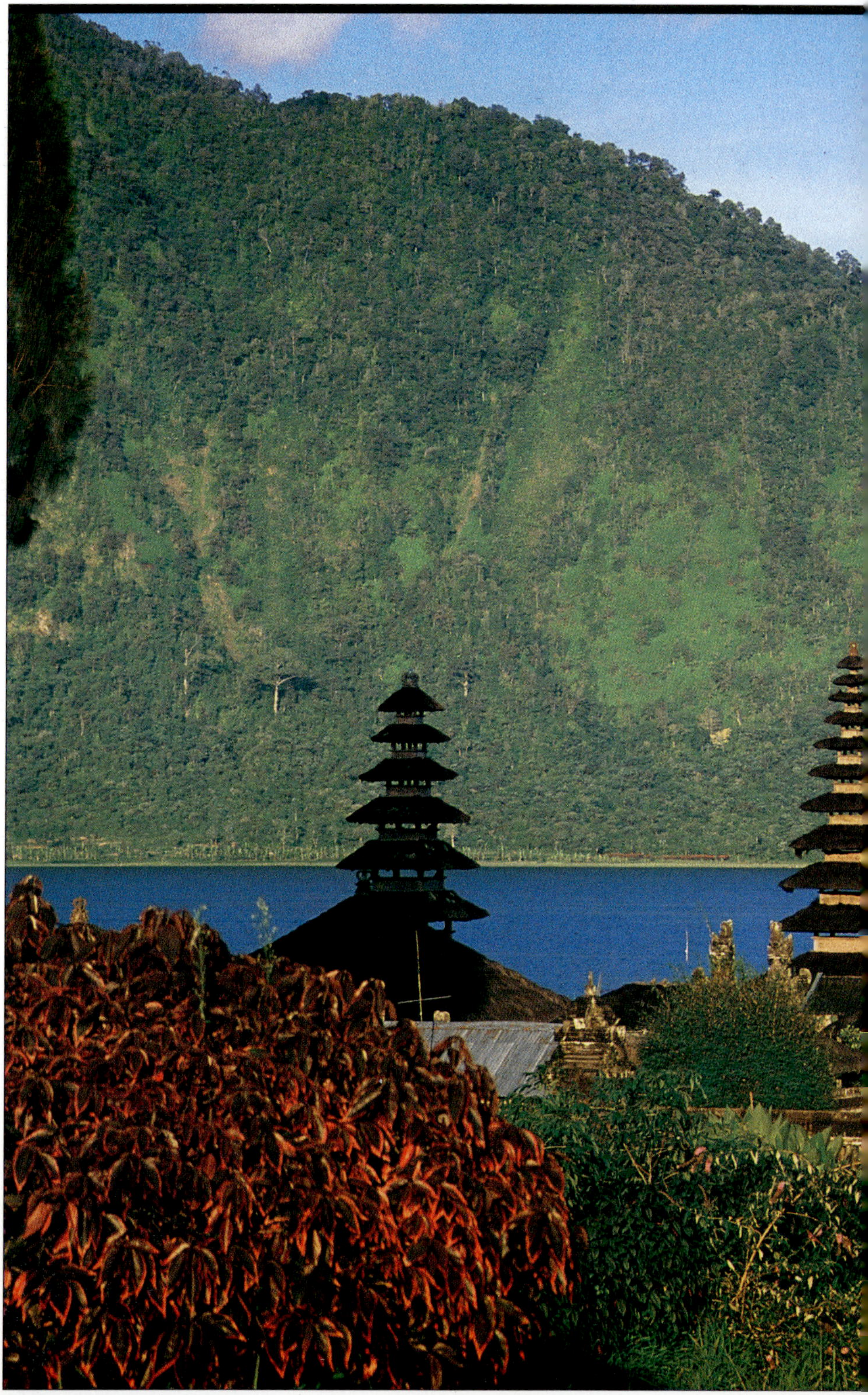

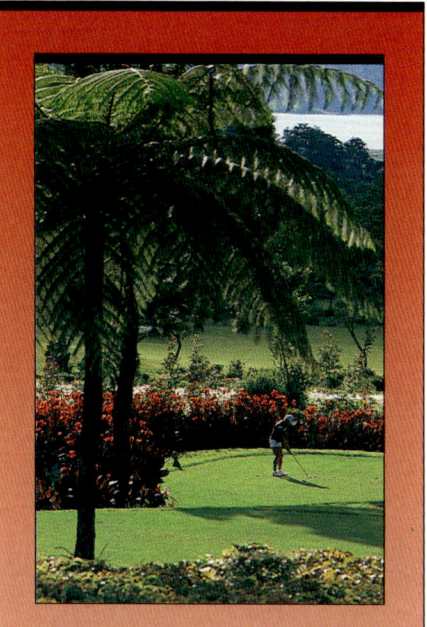

Southern Bali and the Bukit

BALI'S CAPITAL: DENPASAR

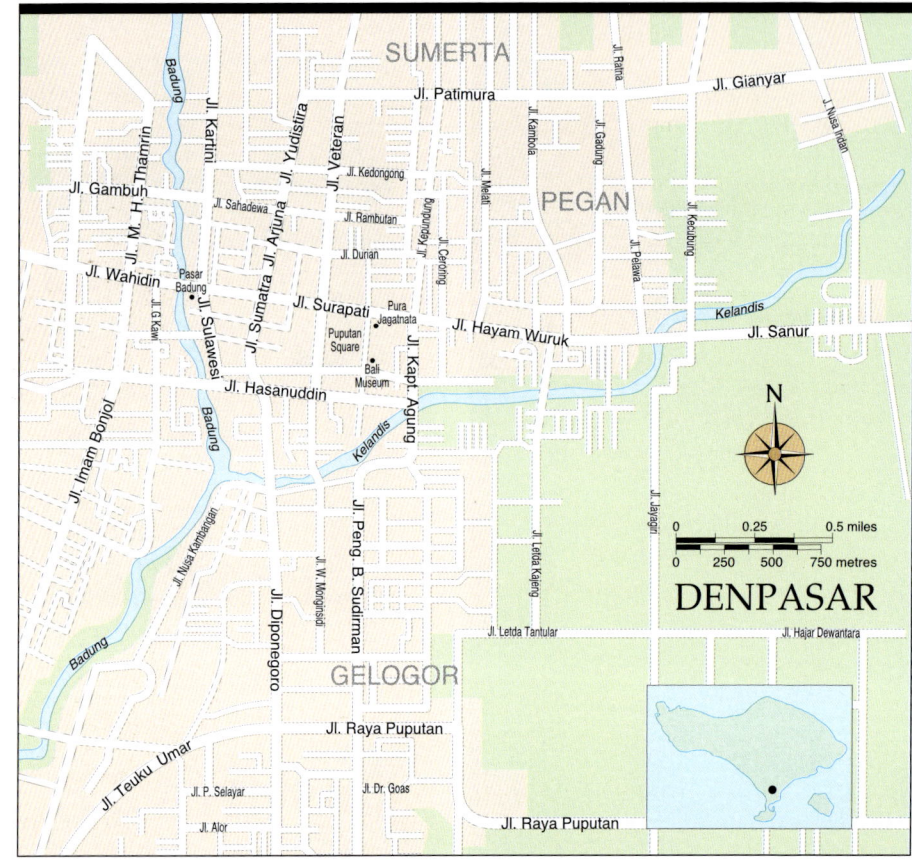

THE FERTILE FLATLANDS OF BALI'S SOUTH have long been the most populous of the island. At the heart of it all, Denpasar is the island's capital city, buzzing with scooters and growing fat on tourist revenue. Most visitors avoid it — most goods and services relevant to the tourist industry have shifted, in any case, to Kuta — and few long to return.

Where overseas visitors do go, and stay, is to the resort areas around the south. It's here you'll find the resort of Kuta, long since grown into one with the neighboring villages of Legian and Seminyak, where tourism started in the 1960s with a few wide-eyed souls following the southern end of the hippy trail. South of here, the teardrop that is the Bukit is a peninsula pushing out into the Indian Ocean: once a barren patch of land thought all but useless by the Balinese, this was given a whole new value first by surfers and then the "fly and flop" travel market. The neck of the peninsula has become the super-exclusive resort of Jimbaran Bay, while out on the Bukit itself, the western tip, previously cut off by swamps and mangroves, has been transformed into the sleek resort of Nusa Dua. Back up on the mainland, its fishermen growing rich on the constant demand for lobster and prawn, the busy port of Benoa still retains the painted fishing boats and small-scale beauty that first attracted visitors to the island. As the coast curves north and east it is taken over by the mass-market resort of Sanur, where large hotels, but still infused with the special qualities of Balinese spirituality and grace, line the beach.

BALI'S CAPITAL: DENPASAR

Denpasar makes few concessions to tourism. It is Bali's capital, but tourists rarely any need to go there, and there are few good reports of it from people who have been and escaped back to Kuta or Sanur to tell the tale. There are, for instance, numerous small hotels and *losmens* there, but it's rare that anyone other than Indonesians on business in Denpasar stays in them.

It's a crowded, noisy, polluted town, the very antithesis of everything people come to Bali to find. Like many other cities, Denpasar is caught between two moments in history: It was built for an age of horse-drawn and pedestrian traffic and now endures the full force of modern mechanized transportation.

So great is the tourist concentration in Kuta and Sanur that even shopping and such services as banks, telex offices and travel agents are as good there as in Denpasar, or better. A visit to the Immigration Office, or the Denpasar Police Office to get a license to drive a motorbike on Bali (if you don't have an international driver's license), is the most likely reason for paying a visit to the town.

Nevertheless, Denpasar does have one or two places of interest, and these will be dealt with briefly below.

GENERAL INFORMATION

The **Badung Government Tourist Office** ((0361) 234569 or (0361) 223602, Merdeka Building, Jalan Surapati 7, Denpasar, is open 8 AM to 1 PM Monday to Thursday and 8 AM to 11 AM on Fridays and Saturdays. It provide's maps, lists of festivals (valuable, as these go by the Balinese calendar and so vary from year to year), and details of dance and other performances. It's not the full service provided by some of the regional tourist offices, but the attendants are helpful and do respond to personal inquiries.

The **Bali Government Tourist Office** ((0361) 222387 FAX (0361) 226313, by contrast, is difficult to find, as it is located in a complex of government buildings and not oriented to the needs of the individual traveler.

The easiest way to get around town is by taxi. These can be flagged down (Rp2,500 flag fee), and some can be called by phone, in which case there will be a minimum fee. The major (metered) taxi companies are **Bali Taxi** ((0361) 701111, which has blue vehicles; **Pan Wirthi** ((0361) 723366, in green; and **Praja** ((0361) 289090, in orange. There are also taxi motorcycles (*ojèks*), which can be useful in heavy traffic. Driving yourself is difficult due to one-way systems and poor signposting,

but is possible. Denpasar is home to the island's major hospital and only decompression machine. **Sanglah General Hospital** ((0361) 227911 (switchboard) or (0361) 227915 (emergency), Jalan Kesehatan Selatan 1, Jalan Diponegoro, Sanglah. Denpasar is probably the best place in Bali to sort out any major medical emergencies.

Should you happen to hold a visa of the kind that can be, or needs to be, renewed (see ARRIVING page 237 and LEAVING, page 238 in TRAVELERS' TIPS), then you will need to go to the **Immigration Office** (Kantor Imigrasi) ((0361) 227828, between Jalan Panjaitan and Jalan Raya Puputan, Renon, open Monday to Thursday 8 AM to 3 PM, Friday 8 AM to 11 AM, Saturday 8 AM to 2 PM.

WHAT TO SEE AND DO

The center of Denpasar is a large grassy square known as the **Tanah Lapang Puputan Badung**. Its notable feature is a heroic, three-figure statue standing in pools amid fountains, a memorial to the 4,000 Balinese who died defending the city against the Dutch on September 20, 1906.

If you face the monument from the center of the square, the building on your right is the **Bali Museum** ((0361) 222680, Puputan Square (admission Rp1,500; open 7:30 AM to 3:30 PM Sunday to Thursday, 7:30 AM to 11:30 AM Friday, closed Saturday and holidays. They are not above shutting early or changing these hours to suit themselves.

Renting a motorbike is easy in Bali — but you do need a license.

Although the museum does contain a lot of important ethnographic material, there is not much labeling and no English-language catalogue, so the average visitor will blunder around in a bit of a haze unless he or she hires one of the "guides" who hang around the door. The basic concept is attractive: that its very buildings should in themselves be exhibits of Balinese temple and palace architectural styles. Unfortunately, the contents have neither the range nor the organization to make them the major resource that such an institution ought to house. The exhibits include a model of a tooth-filing ceremony, some interesting masks, some paintings and woodcarvings, a display of agricultural tools and implements, and a good collection of terracotta.

Next door, the **Pura Jagatnatha** is a modern temple dedicated to the whole of Bali. Unlike most Balinese temples, it is closed to the public except at festival times.

Art Centers

Two art centers provide useful indications of what artistic riches the island has in store.

The **National Art Center**, between Jalan Abiankapas and Jalan Palawa Pagan in the east of the town, contains exhibits of shadow puppets and giant barong landong puppets, as well as silverware, carvings, basketry, paintings and weaving. Further east—you'll need to take a taxi—is the government-run, fixed-price art shop; ask the driver for **Sanggraha Kriya Asta**. It not only has a wide range of items, but also provides a convenient indication of the kind of prices to be paid for similar objects elsewhere, useful knowledge when you bargain for them later.

You can attend lessons in Balinese dance at two places in Denpasar: the **Academy of Dance Indonesia** (ASTI) on Jalan Nusa Indah and the **Conservatory of Performing Arts** (KOKAR) on Jalan Ratna. Lessons take place in the mornings.

There is an annual six-week-long Bali Arts Festival between mid-June and the end of July at the **Werdi Budaya Arts Center**, Jalan Nusa Indah, off Hayam Wuruk, where you'll also find nightly *kecak* dances at 6:30 PM. The city center also explodes with papier-mâché monsters (*oggi-oggi*) on the eve of Nyepi, the Balinese New Year, usually in March or April.

Finally, Denpasar has the island's only proper **Cinema** ℂ (0361) 423023, Cineplex, Jalan Thanrin 69, Denpasar. It shows a range of movies, and usually these have subtitles with the soundtrack in the original language.

SHOPPING

Denpasar has plenty of fixed-price shopping malls and supermarkets. The biggest market on the island is **Pasar Badung**, on the eastern side of the Badung River, which used to have three floors of produce and traditional handicrafts. Sadly it burned down in 2000, but it is hoped that it will be rebuilt.

The best place to buy sarongs and Indonesian fabrics in Denpasar is the local **cloth market**, Jalan Sulawesi, where prices are far lower than in tourist outlets. Note that taxi drivers are more likely to know the street by its old name of Jalan Kampong Arab.

Almost opposite the Natour Bali Hotel (see below) on Jalan Veteran there is an outdoor **bird market** and a covered **jewelry market** (at No. 66). For gold or silver try Jalan Hasanuddin and Jalan Sulawesi.

If orchids are your interest, you will be in paradise at the **Flora Bali Orchid Farm** ℂ (0361) 225847 FAX (0361) 232877, Jalan Noja 102. You can inspect acres of infant plants at your leisure. It's not the place for spectacular floral shows, but specialists will not be able to drag themselves away. Note that only vacuum-packed specimens can be taken out of the country legally.

WHERE TO STAY

The first hotel to be built in Bali is still the best in Denpasar: the **Natour Bali** ℂ (0361) 225681 FAX (0361) 235347, Jalan Veteran 3 (moderate). It's the old Dutch colonial hotel (Charlie Chaplin and Noel Coward, among many other celebrities, stayed here) and, though now over 60 years old, it has been tastefully modernized. It has a swimming pool and an ambiance that manages to be both efficient and relaxed. There's no real need to spend even this modest amount of money, however, as there other options. The budget-priced **Pemecutan Palace** ℂ (0361) 423491, Jalan Thanrin 2, occupies a wall of the Badung palace grounds, and has a rural feel to it. On a really tight budget, **Darmawisata** ℂ (0361) 484186, Jalan Imam Bonjol 83, Denpasar, is very reasonably priced for basic Indonesian-style accommodation, and also has a swimming pool, which helps after a day of Denpasar's traffic.

WHERE TO EAT

There is fantastic food in Denpasar. However, as foreign tourists are not common, it tends to be Indonesian or Chinese. The Natour Bali provides a varied cuisine, and is famed for its *rijsttafel*. But why not eat with the locals. The **Ayam Bakar Tallwang** ℂ (0361) 241537, Jalan Teuku Umar, serves spicy Lombok cuisine. For Padang Food, try **Bundo Kanduang** ℂ (0361) 228551, Jalan Diponegoro 112A. In general, good areas to look for restaurants are along Jalan Teuku Umar, Jalan Sumatra and near the Satria bird market.

HOW TO GET THERE

There are three main *bemo* stations in Denpasar: Tegal, Ubung and Batubulan. Each serves a different area of the island, and small light-blue vans shuttle back and forth between them for Rp1,000 (but don't expect to have room to breathe). The shuttles also run to Kereneng, the home station for *bemos* plying routes within Denpasar.

Tegal serves Kuta, the airport, Ulu Watu and Nusa Dua. Ubung serves the west and north; full-sized buses, both ordinary and air-conditioned, leave from here to Gilimanuk and across to cities in Java, plus minibuses to Singaraja/Lovina. Batubulan is the station for services to Ubud, Kintamani and eastern Bali. For a *bemo* to Sanur, go to Kereneng. A further small station, Sanglah, serves Benoa Harbor.

Although a major link for public transportation, with your own transport it's best to bypass Denpasar using dual carriageway Jalan Ngurah Rai (Bypass), as traffic can be heavy and it's easy to get lost. Denpasar is seven kilometers (four and a half miles) from Sanur, ten kilometers (eight miles) from Kuta, and 89 kilometers (55 miles) from Lovina.

One final point — all over Bali you will hear *bemo* drivers touting for passengers calling out "Badung!" In fact, "Badung, Badung!" rings through the dusty evening air from Klungkung to Kuta and from Ubud to Tabanan. You won't find it on any map, but just as Karangasem is the old Balinese name for Amlapura and Buleleng the old name for Singaraja, Badung is the name by which all Balinese know the Denpasar area, and these tired and hungry drivers are looking for their last fares of the day before finally heading home.

KUTA AND AROUND

If, as countless visitors before you, you fly into Bali with no fixed plans, perhaps even arriving late at night, you're most likely to end up in Kuta. Five hundred years ago you'd have been cast into a wasteland of lepers and misfits. It was probably here that Gajah Mada invaded from Java in the fourteenth century with his Majapahit forces. In 1580 the Englishman Sir Francis Drake may have called in for provisions. In 1597 a small Dutch expedition of three ships under Cornelius de Houtman dropped anchor off Kuta, and a party was landed. Later, the ships sailed round to the better anchorage off Padangbai, with the added purpose of being near the Dewa Agung, the most powerful of Bali's chiefs, and his court at Gelgel, near Klungkung.

In the succeeding centuries Bali became a source of slaves, sold to Java but also as far afield as Mauritius. Kuta (encompassing also the anchorages nearby on the east coast) was the center for that trade.

The tone of Kuta only changed in 1839 when Danish adventurer Mads Lange landed. He set up a trading empire here, even as the Dutch colonizing forces made incursions from the north. In the 1930s Kuta saw one of the first Western-run hotels in the island, established by Bob and Louise Koke. After the hiatus of World War II, Kuta was ready to greet the hippy flood of the 1960s. What is now the splendid Oberoi Hotel was then a semi-derelict drug city of international standing, where life was free and magic mushrooms were consumed under the palm trees and among the grazing cattle.

Kuta is in every possible way the diametric opposite of the other main resort areas of Nusa Dua and Sanur. Its development was unplanned; it is in many places ramshackle; very cheap food and accommodation are available everywhere. There are touts at every turn, and at the south end of the beach barely five minutes pass without someone approaching you to sell you a T-shirt or give you a massage. To some people this is an intolerable intrusion, but the level of harassment fades as you head north. At its worst in Kuta, there is little harassment in Legian, and almost none by the time you reach the smarter, less frantic village of Seminyak.

The fact remains that, in addition to its supremely magnificent beach, Kuta teems with irrepressible liveliness. The beach scene at the southern airport end resembles nothing so much as a circus, but it's the circus of democratic life in the early twenty-first century, and is something not to be missed. It's doubtful that there's anywhere else in the world quite like it.

Australian grannies, who no doubt live modestly back home in Adelaide, can be seen surrounded by a veritable court of hair braiders, hair beaders, massage artists, runners bearing iced beer from the beach restaurants, sellers of Dyak elixirs fresh from the jungles of Borneo. Add an Italian tenor and it would be the opening scene from the German opera *Der Rosenkavalier*.

Yet a few hundred meters away, a hundred or more Balinese may be performing a post-cremation ceremony involving a procession in full traditional dress and the scattering of ashes on the waves, accompanied by the release onto the waters of ducks, chickens and doves.

The key to it all is that, while Kuta remains an extraordinarily cheap and "exotic" destination for the huge numbers of French, Australians, Japanese, Germans, British and others who flock there, this same conglomeration is an unparalleled magnet to the Balinese, for whom tourism represents an opportunity to make profits unheard of in, for example, agriculture. Locals and Westerners alike think they have a bargain at Kuta, and the result is a fairground of happy buyers and enthusiastic sellers, all under the glorious sun on one of Asia's most fabulous beaches.

Because Kuta grew without official planning, many of the businesses in the area remain in local hands. Thus the profusion of

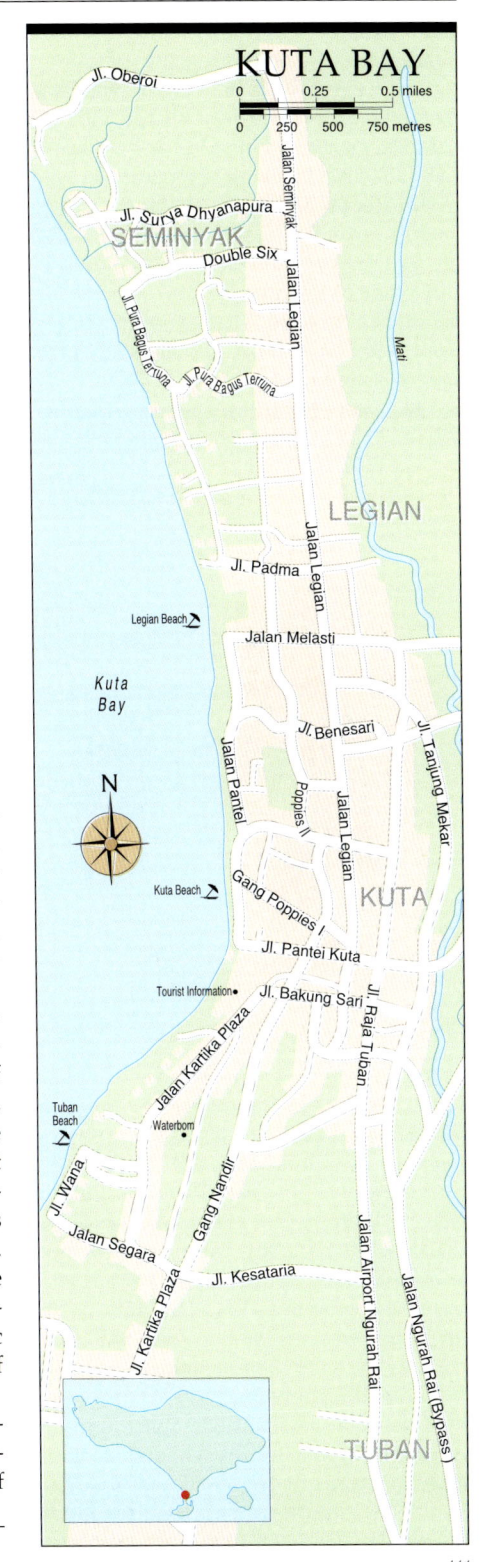

The clothes market on Jalan Bakungsari.
Southern Bali and the Bukit

small, budget-priced *losmens* is no coincidence: They exist because Kuta grew from travelers in the 1960s arriving at what was then only a medium-sized village and asking to be provided with food and a place to stay. First-class hotels have, of course, moved in since that time, and today there is a huge amount of top-price accommodation in Kuta, too. But this only contributes to the democracy of the place: All tastes and all bank balances are catered to. All the world comes to Kuta Beach, and almost all Bali, it sometimes seems, is waiting there to greet them.

The first thing the early hoteliers saw was the beach. While the land wasn't very good for farming, and fishermen used the port of Lemboa, the white sands of Kuta, washed by rolling warm waves from the Indian Ocean, offered palm-fringed paradise by the sand-bucket-load. Although now not as clean as it once was, Kuta Beach is still the best on the island, spreading sand in an unbroken scimitar up along the coast fronting the once-separate villages of Kuta, Legian and Seminyak.

Kuta has always been to some extent disreputable, an area where vagabonds congregated and foreigners were allowed to settle. Parallels with its modern character need not be emphasized. So now if you fly into Ngurah Rai Airport in the middle of the night and travel north through the always-crowded roads to the frantic resort town of Kuta and the animated villages of Legian and Seminyak, you're following a noble tradition. Leaflike, you've blown into what is at once the best, and the worst, place to stay in the island.

GENERAL INFORMATION

Kuta's **Tourist Information** ((0361) 751419, Jalan Bakung Sari, open 7 AM to 5 PM Monday to Saturday, is at the airport end of the development. The **Bali Clinic** ((0361) 733301 FAX (0361) 733302, Jalan (Oberoi) Laksmana 54XX, Br Taman Kerobokan, offers 24-hour medical service. If you're seriously injured it's probably best to go to the major health facilities in Denpasar. Taxis, which are metered, are rarely hard to find. When getting in a taxi, make sure the meter is turned on, and be sure to have plenty of Rp1,000 and Rp500 notes with you, as drivers invariably have no change. Car rental agencies are everywhere: one is **Bali Bahagia Rent Car** ((0361) 751954, Jalan Raya Kuta 72X, or at the airport **Toyota Rent Car** ((0361) 751356, Jalan Raya Airport 99X, Tuban. This being Kuta, many scooters have been adapted with large hooks on the side for carrying surfboards. Avoid these, unless you're a keen surfer, as they make the machines too wide for the traffic and complicate any accident. For the best deals on motorcycle rentals, try any of the dealers at Jalan Legian near Bemo Corner. One is **Wayan Kantra** ((0361) 487889 or (0812) 834-6952 (cell), Jalan Legian Kelod, in front of San Club Bar, which has particularly keen prices. This is the man I rent my scooters from.

If you need to send or receive a fax, a useful place is the **Krakatoa** cybercafé/accommodation bureau/veggie whole-food shop ((0361) 730849 FAX 730824 E-MAIL krakbc@indo.net.id, Jalan Raya Seminyak 56, open 8 AM to 10 PM Monday to Friday, and 8 AM to 8 PM Saturday and Sunday. They have typewriters for your use, too, as well as a bank of computer terminals with Internet access. More important, though, is that the place is a major center for Westerners living in this part of Bali, and its large noticeboard is one of the best ways of finding such things as houses for rent.

For e-mail messages and access to the Internet, there are countless new bureaus, though, as always, rates can vary, as well as minimum connection charge. Rp500 per minute, with no minimum connection charge, is standard, though some go as low as Rp300 per minute. One is **Impian Nusa** (/FAX (0361) 761326 E-MAIL hchua@singnet.com.sg or hchua@idola.net.id, a cybercafé on Jalan Pura Bagus Terruna, and another is the **Wartel Kambodiana** ((0361) 753330 FAX (0361) 753331 E-MAIL kambodiana@denpasar.wasantara.net.id, on Kuta Square.

The **GPO**, like most in Bali, is open in the mornings. It is at the junction with Jalan Bakung Sari and Jalan Raya Tuban.

THREE VILLAGE CENTERS

Known, collectively and from a distance, as Kuta, the eight kilometers (five miles) of development that follows the broad sweep of sandy beach heading north from Ngurah Rai Airport consists of three main villages, now all-but merged into a single urban conglomerate. The resort is bounded on the west by the sea and to the east by a main road, always crowded with cars and scooters, variously known as Jalan Raya Tuban, Jalan Legian and Jalan Seminyak. Most of the hotels, shops and restaurants are on roads and alleyways between this main road and the beach.

Although the visitor will not immediately be able to spot the ancient village boundaries, the three settlements of Kuta, Legian and Seminyak have individual characters of their own. Kuta covers the region nearest the airport until Jalan Melasti, Legian runs from there up to Jalan Double Six (also known as Arjuna), with Seminyak carrying on north to the Oberoi Hotel.

Although the distance between these villages isn't huge, getting from one to the other usually involves taking a long sandy walk on the beach or getting into a car or onto a motorbike and heading back to the main road, several hundred meters inland from the beach. And while in the north Jalan Seminyak allows travel in both directions, at the southern end inland from Kuta one-way systems make joining the queues of jostling drivers time-consuming and to be avoided. Perhaps for this reason the traditional cultural distinctions remain, and it is worth putting some thought into which village will suit your own purposes best and choosing your accommodation appropriately. It's not a matter of cost: each village has a full range, from the smartest hotel to dingy beachfront chalet. Nor is it a matter of the beach, which is brilliant all along. You'll find good — and bad — restaurants in each village. The distinctions are social.

Kuta is the rowdiest. This is where the Australian surfies land when they're starting off, or ending, long holidays around the islands. True, it does have many of the best shops and largest banks, and it also has the most hustlers, masseurs and bars. The beach is crowded, but that's how Kuta guests — and residents — seem to like it.

Legian is a step removed from all this seething activity. The alleys seem that bit wider, broken by fewer awnings and temporary stalls, a bit more mature. People who stay here are a bit more mature too, although there are plenty of bars and discotheques, including some of the island's best and that stay open the latest.

Kuta — "The circus of democratic life in the early twenty-first century." OPPOSITE LEFT: Surf, sun and sand. RIGHT: Hair beaders at work.

Seminyak is a huge stride nearer to the untouched topical paradise, partly, it seems, because of the calming influence of the Oberoi Hotel. You can't imagine Julia Roberts, say, or David Bowie, being woken up every 10 minutes by a strolling beach hustler offering a massage, very cheap. The restaurants round here tend to be better, and the shops more exclusive. They also tend to be more spread out: in the Balinese heat you'll want a scooter, or perhaps a car, to get around; or rely on local taxis, which should be metered. When swimming, bear in mind that, apart from the Oberoi, which employs its own lifeguard, there are no official surf rescue stations in Seminyak.

In view of the strong differences in character, it seems sensible to list the main accommodation facilities separately, yet to treat the resort's facilities, restaurants and attractions, which are often worth making an effort to reach, as being open to all three of Kuta's village centers.

ORIENTATION

Driving north from the airport, you're in Kuta when the road dives off to the left on Jalan Bakung Sari, the first of a clogged, interlocking one-way system that makes orientation in Kuta just that little bit tricky. It's here you'll find the first of two Government Tourist Offices. After completing a reverse "S" bend of tarmac, through heavy traffic, you'll arrive at the area's only traffic circle, known as Bemo Corner. The *bemos* stop just to the east of here, at the junction of Jalan Raya Tuban and Jalan Pantai Kuta for the run into Denpasar, but Bemo Corner traffic circle is a useful landmark. It is also where you'll find the second official tourist information office, which is not as good as the first.

From Bemo Corner, heading north, you loop around by the sea through Kuta, to later swing left onto Jalan Melasti heading inland. From here you can go left onto Jalan Legian, uncomplicated by any one-way regulations, to Legian and Seminyak, or you can turn right and head back down through Kuta's "High Street," Jalan Legian, returning to Bemo Corner. This stretch is where you'll find most of the scooter-rental stands, cheap car rental companies, and plenty of bars, cybercafés, travel agents and handicraft shops.

WHAT TO SEE AND DO

Most people in Kuta base their simple daily cycle on that of the sun. The Surf Rescue guards take up their positions at 6 AM, and even then early morning joggers and swimmers are out before breakfast. By 9 AM the beach is filling up and many of the suntan zealots are already in place. Soon the colorful scene is at the first of its two daily heights. The beach traders are all at work: boys with a single woodcarving wrapped in its cloth and constantly being polished, children offering to bring you cold drinks for a Rp200 commission, an elderly lady bearing ancient *lontar* (strips of palm leaf inscribed with sacred texts), and the inevitable sellers of hats and beach mats.

There is only one setback to Kuta Beach, but it's one that could prove serious. Hundreds of thousands of people swim safely at Kuta every year, but the fact remains that at certain points along the beach currents pull out seawards from the shore, and, on average, six people a year drown, especially inexperienced surfers. The strength of Kuta's rips varies according to the size of the surf and the phases of the moon. These danger areas are well known to the Kuta Surf Rescue teams, and safe bathing areas are marked and watched all along the beach every day.

The problem is that the best surfing areas are exactly those areas where the currents are dangerous.

The **Kuta Surf Rescue** service is run by the Badung Government Tourist Office in Denpasar. It maintains four stations along the beach, at Kuta, Half Legian, Legian and at the Kuta Palace Hotel. In addition, the Bali Oberoi pays for a private service at the northern end of Seminyak. The staff are on duty every day of the year, with the one exception of the Balinese New Year, Nyepi, when no one is allowed on the beach anyway. Their hours are 6 AM to 6 PM. The service operates with additional help from their counterparts at Cottesloe Beach, Perth, in Western Australia, from whom advice and materials have come over the years.

Remember, if you are in danger, try not to panic. Raise one hand high above your head. This is the international distress signal and is what the Surf Rescue are looking for. If you do feel strong enough to swim, paddle sideways and parallel to the beach, across the current, not against it.

Whether or not any bathers have been lost at sea, midday sees a dramatic diminution, most of the Balinese retreating from the sun's ferocious glare and only small clutches of sun-drunk tourists remaining to play Frisbee relentlessly before collapsing in one of the beach bars for protracted lunches of local seafood, beer and grainy Indonesian coffee, to the sound of dated Australian and American pop hits.

If the afternoon seems slow to take off, it's no doubt because the morning went on so long, and sunset here in the tropics is very early anyway. This, you quickly realize, is why the Indonesians get up at 5 AM — in this land of eternal summer, light is gone by 6:45 PM. But before it goes, the sun puts on a display. Kuta's sunsets were renowned even in K'tut Tantri's day (see RECOMMENDED READING, page 258) and nowadays, as the buses pull up from Nusa Dua's five-star hotels, which, facing east, offer a similar, but often unappreciated display at dawn, all of Kuta, from its tattooed Japanese surfers to its Jakarta businessmen down for a week by the sea, set up their cameras and tripods where they will best catch the reflection on the wet sand, and wait.

Every Balinese is an artist, or so the early visitors to the island claimed. OPPOSITE: A handpainted T-shirt. ABOVE: Work is displayed and admired in a fashionable boutique in Kuta.

The event itself is very much like a prima donna's operatic performance — maybe the miracle will happen, maybe it won't. Sometimes Great Nature has a cough and, despite cloudless skies, the sun sinks with no more attendant glory than a fifty-cent piece dropped into a puddle. But sometimes, ah, sometimes… then the beams shoot up like chiseled shafts, the colors deepen through apricot to salmon to a final consummating crimson, the great Indian Ocean surf laps as if entranced, as aeroplanes drift in to land stage right like windblown stars. All at once it's night. The moon has established her quiet sovereignty above the palms, the motorbikes — mere spots of light — putter across the sand, plying their night trade, and the audience disperses to supper and other pleasures and diversions.

Beyond the Beach

There is life, of course, beyond Kuta's beach. The surf, which is such a draw for many, makes swimming a rather frantic affair and rules out most other water sports. For these you'll probably want to head east to the major resort areas of Nusa Dua and Sanur.

Much of what is best about this buzzing resort is the sheer vitality of it all. Inland, Kuta resembles a cut-price Hollywood set. A couple of paces behind the single-story façade of boutiques and restaurants is another world, one of pastoral *losmens*, coconut groves, tethered cattle and free-ranging poultry. Take your choice of which is stranger — the magical world of the immemorial pastoral round or the tacked-together world of Kuta's main streets, part fashion shops, part potholes.

Stand at night at **Bemo Corner**, with your back to the beach, and the two faces of urban Kuta lie at either hand. To the right is the **Night Market**, pure Indonesia. It is a world of interiors illuminated by kerosene lamps, hemmed in by the black and humid night. The small restaurants have adapted themselves to tourists needs, but otherwise you could be anywhere in the archipelago.

But you're not. You're in Kuta, and if you're looking for things to do, bear in mind it's a young resort and the things to do tend to be active. One way of getting in some exercise without giving yourself heatstroke is at **Waterbom** ((0361) 755676 FAX (0361) 753517 E-MAIL waterbom@denpasar.wasantara.net.id, Jalan Kartika Plaza, open 8:30 AM to 6 PM (Rp12,000), with waterslides, water volleyball and helter-skelters. Families lose whole days here.

Bungee jumping has become, unsurprisingly but rather depressingly, one of the most popular ways for Kuta's visitors to put a buzz in their day. Several operators offer jumps from specially constructed towers, usually with a swimming pool underneath you. The harness is tied around your ankles, and the pool exists not in case of mishaps but to give you the added pleasure of a quick dip in the water at the end of your initial descent. There are three thicknesses of cord, depending on your weight. You will be offered a video at the end with a history of bungee jumping, ending with recorded interviews with you, before and after your leap. One of the originals is **A.J. Hacket Bungee** ((0361) 730666 FAX (0361) 730466, Jalan Double Six, right next to the shore at Legian's Blue Ocean Beach. On Saturday nights you can disco, then jump, then disco again. This particular bungee-jumping site shares a compound with Bali's nicest dancing space. Only the swimming pool separates the dance floor from the bungee tower, and rows of nightlife aficionados sit along the pool wall, beers in hand, and cheer the jumpers as they come hurtling down through the warm Balinese night air.

Every day at sunset there is a lucky draw at the bar. The prize? What else but a free bungee jump?

For those whose idea of fun is an adrenaline-kick from fear, bungee jumping OPPOSITE and the catapult slingshot ABOVE provide the means.

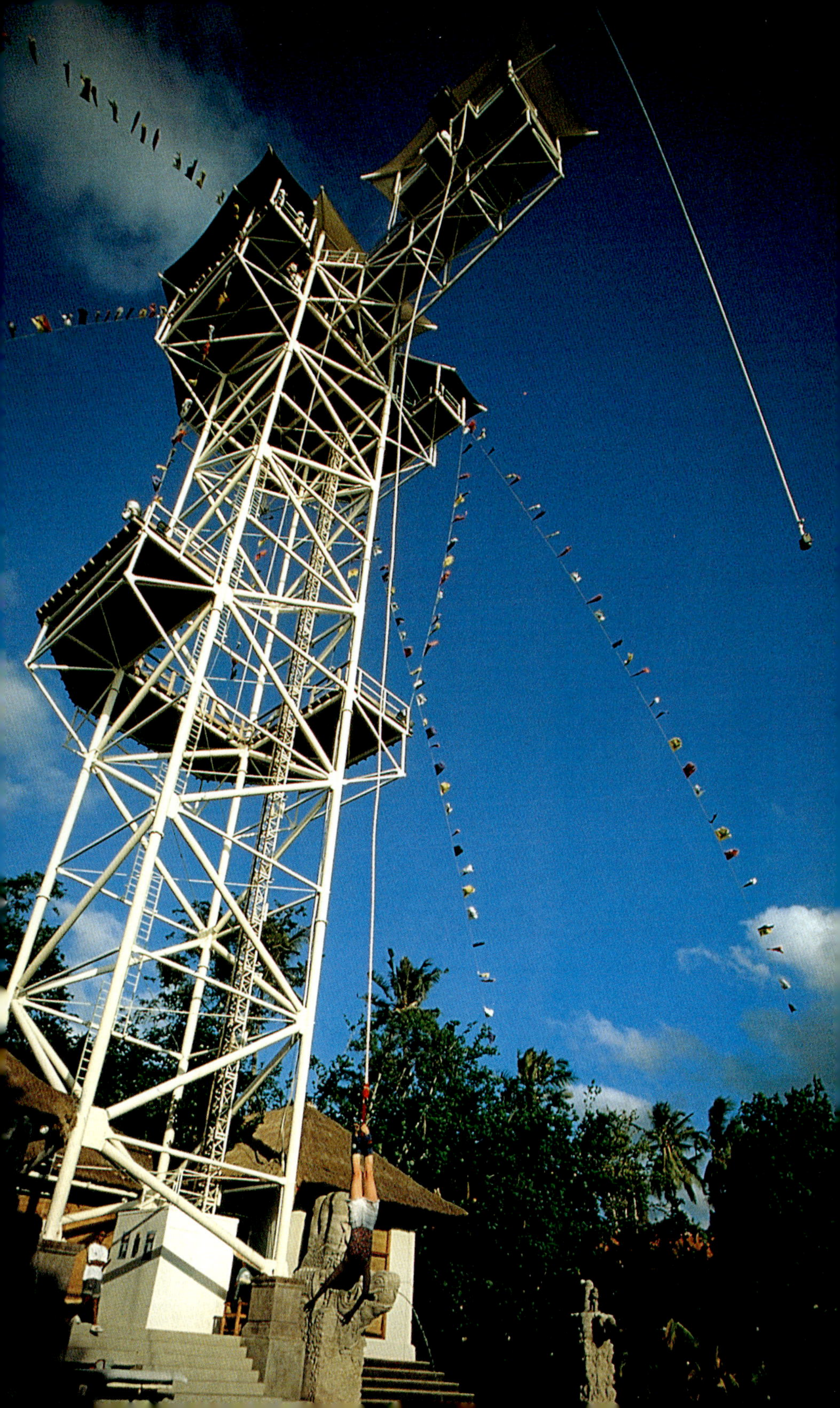

The other bungee jumping centers in Bali are Bali **Bungee Co**. ℂ/FAX (0361) 752658, Jalan Pura Puseh, slightly inland at Kuta, and the nearby **Adrenalin Park** ℂ (0361) 757841, Jalan Benesari Kuta. Adrenalin Park has additional attractions. As well as a climbing wall, there is the terror-inspiring Bali Slingshot. Here you are harnessed, alone or in twos, inside a padded open-air capsule which is then catapulted into the air. A video camera records your facial distortions as the thing swivels round and is propelled up and down several times by the diminishing thrusts of its elastic cords. Since this feature recently killed three members of a visiting rugby team, however, you're not going to get me onboard. Costs for a bungee jump generally stay fairly well in line: Adrenaline Park, for example, charges Rp350,000, for which you get a video and a T-shirt thrown in.

Horseback riding along the beach is a great way to appreciate the cool of sunset. There are **stables** near the Mesari Hotel ℂ (0361) 730401, Jalan Abimanyu in Seminyak; expect to pay around US$10 per hour.

For those who want to try surfing without ending up a statistic swept out to sea, try Kuta's surf school **Surf@Soda Club** ℂ (0361) 756735, Jalan Double Six (Arjuna), 7A Legiankaja, which has a shed behind the Soda Club. It's expensive, though, at US$55 for one day and US$135 for three days, and you can do cheaper courses, surprisingly, from Ubud.

If, however, you're not tempted by the varied restaurants, shops, and bars of Kuta, get out and give yourself some air. The Bukit Peninsula is a short drive away, or head inland: Ubud can be reached in little over an hour and there's not much of the island that can't be reached in a day.

Massage is a big thing in Kuta, most especially with licensed massage girls who hang around the beach touting for business. These can be quite good, and the girls certainly seem to enjoy giving them, but it's a little bit public to really relax. The going rate has gone up a lot over recent years, though even now it stands at only about US$3. There are more exclusive — and more expensive — massages available, of which the best is perhaps at the Hotel Sahid Bali ℂ (0361) 753855, Jalan Pantai, Kuta.

Shopping

Kuta is an excellent place for shopping, combining quality and value for money. There is a huge choice in Kuta in general, and in particular for clothes and leather goods.

Visitors staying in upmarket hotels in Nusa Dua and Sanur invariably come to Kuta on shopping sprees, and shops selling good quality goods are plentiful, mixed in with those offering tourist souvenirs.

The trade in cheap cassettes and CDs is not what it was before Indonesia agreed to comply with international copyright. Even so, at Rp20,000 a foreign tape (those by Indonesian artists are cheaper) and Rp60,000 per CD, there is still a savings over prices elsewhere, and there are a dozen shops in Kuta selling nothing else.

There are several bookshops specializing in vacation reading. Particularly recommended, both for the range and quality of its stock, is the **Kertai Bookshop** on Jalan Pantai, on the left as you walk toward the beach. New and secondhand books are available and can be traded in at half the price paid for them.

The further you go up Jalan Legian toward Seminyak the classier things become, and eventually it's all boutiques where a tiny number of exquisite objects are sold in grand and resplendent surroundings.

Good buys can be found everywhere. You'll find designer sunglasses at **Sol** ((0361) 755072 on Kuta Square, Australian sportswear at less-than-Australian prices at **Dreamland** ((0361) 755159, also on Kuta Square, and surfing gear at **Aloha Surf Station** ((0361) 758286 at the Kuta end of Jalan Legian.

Fabrics with crazy designs, fabulous for wall-hangings, can be seen at **Irie Collection** (/FAX (0361) 754732, and bizarre candlesticks are a specialty at **Titien Collection** (/FAX (0361) 730448 in Seminyak. Custom-made picture frames are the specialty of **Toko Kaca Taman Sari** ((0361) 730424, while **Ulu Watu** ((0361) 753428 Jalan Bakung Sari branch specializes in Balinese lace. They have locations in most popular tourist areas in Bali.

A road to visit if you're looking for sarongs is Jalan Double Six where there are many shops specializing in fabrics.

Back on the main road, **Nona** ((0361) 755919 sells a little bit of everything — furniture, ceramics, wood carvings and mirrors — while **Tidore** ((0361) 730934 sells antiques and collectibles. Gems and jewelry can be seen in many places along the main road too, including at **Miko Opals** ((0361) 761231 on Jalan Pura Bagus Terruna. Fine silver is sold at the shops of **Suarti Designer Collection** ((0361) 754252.

Sunsets at Kuta Beach on the Indian Ocean the draw huge crowds for a show renowned since travelers have come to Bali.

Furniture can be found in many places, too; try **Setya Budi Art** ((0361) 730560 on Jalan Tunjung Mekar. More furniture and *objets d'art* are on sale in Seminyak at **Warisan** ((0361) 730710, and both clothes and furniture are sold by **E. Ekstra** ((0811) 398685 (cell) in the same area.

Back in Kuta, the island's biggest department store is **Matahari** on Kuta Square (not to be confused with the smaller Matahari building containing Kuta's cinemas on Jalan Legian). A new Kuta shopping complex focusing on the arts is Bali **Plaza**, close to Waterbom. Meanwhile, every evening Kuta's **Night Market** takes place by the light of dangling bulbs at the inland end of Jalan Bakung Sari.

WHERE TO STAY

There is so much accommodation in Kuta and Legian that it would be impossible to give a full listing here. They basically divide into two types. The large resort-type hotels where you'll find plentiful water sports and other amenities, often including live performances of Balinese music and dance, are usually less expensive when booked as a package, including a flight. Once you're in, they rely on marking up drinks and meals (on Bali the more expensive hotels are generally priced at room-only rates) and so are not of great interest to cost-conscious travelers. They are only mentioned here if they offer something slightly out of the ordinary or are of especially high standards. The hotels that are more in keeping with the Balinese tradition are small, cottage-like establishments, such as *losmens*. At these, you'll always have self-contained accommodation surrounded by temples and offerings, and breakfast is almost always included. The many small and inexpensive *losmens*, which can still be found in Kuta, unlike some of the other resort areas, take some ferreting out and are best selected by personal inspection. Only a few favorites are listed here, and are divided into their locations in the three villages of Kuta, Legian, and Seminyak.

Kuta

In the south, the area nearest to the airport known as Tuban, the **Holiday Inn Bali Hai** ((0361) 753035 FAX (0361) 754548, Jalan Wanasegara, offers comfortable accommodation at moderate rates, yet with a Balinese ambiance. Although the hotel is on the sea, it is a 10-minute walk from the best part of the beach.

Slightly further north, you are in the heart of Kuta, the center of the beast. The giant new department store, Matahari, dominates a most un-Balinese shopping mall called Kuta Square, which pavement cafés and struggling palm trees do little to domesticate. Once you arrive at Jalan Bakung Sari, you are in the thick of things. Of all the expensive hotels to settle here, one of the most popular is the **Hard Rock Hotel** ((0361) 761869 FAX (0361) 761868 E-MAIL hardrock@bali-paradise.com, Jalan Pantai Kuta, Banjar Pande Mas, whose Hard Rock Café showcases the island's best bands. Good value here is the **Naga Sari Beach Club** ((0361) 751960, Jalan Bakung Sari, with peaceful and pleasant chalets, bathroom downstairs, room above (moderate).

The **Natour Kuta Beach** ((0361) 751361 FAX (0361) 751362, Jalan Pantai Kuta, has a superb location, actually fronting on the beach, but the rooms disappoint (expensive). There's a Garuda office in the lobby and Japanese food in the restaurant.

Tucked away inland along Poppies Lane and just past the restaurant of the same name prices drop. **Poppies Cottages** ((0361) 751059 FAX (0361) 752364 E-MAIL info@bali.poppies .net WEB SITE www.poppies.net, Gang Poppies I, are built to the same design as the pioneering "Old Poppies," but with new facilities and a swimming pool. It's very popular though, and reservations are essential. Self-catering facilities and babysitters are available. If close access to the beach isn't important, then double back on Jalan Legian and check into the inexpensively-priced **Agung Cottages** ((0361) 757427 FAX (0363) 751147, Legian Street, which has friendly staff, comfortable facilities and a superb, central location.

Backpackers, here, are spoiled for choice, with a number of budget *losmens* crowded into a warren of alleys and tracks. Old favorites include **Komala Indah 1**, Gang Poppies 1, which has terraced accommodation around a central courtyard, and the **Losmen Arthawan** ((0361) 752913, Gang Poppies II.

But if you're walking here with a backpack someone, somewhere, will probably tempt you to a *losmen* of his or her own.

Legian

Legian tends to be best at the middle range of hotel accommodation, with few really outstanding international-standard resorts, but plenty in the inexpensive and moderate price ranges. The **Legian Garden Cottage** ((0361) 751876 FAX (0361) 753405, Jalan Double Six, has a swimming pool and is also a minute's walk from the beach (moderate).

The **Sri Ratu Cottages** ((0361) 751566, Jalan Three Brothers, provides good value, with bungalows sleeping up to six (inexpensive). A newcomer in the heart of Legian is the moderately priced **Suri Wathi Beach House** ((0361) 753162 FAX (0361) 758393 E-MAIL suriwathi@yahoo.com, Jalan Sahadewa 12, which is a largish, newish chalet-hotel desperately growing lush gardens, dropping down a price level for rooms without air-conditioning.

Backpackers, for once, stay right on the waterfront here, and in rooms large enough to swing a couple of cats. The **Blue Ocean** ((0361) 730289 FAX (0361) 730590, Jalan Double Six, provides fairly clean bungalows with gas burners blackened by people who surf better than they can cook (budget). It's between two bars but most people sit on their verandas and drink their own. Don't rely on the hotel management for too much help: the last time I visited, admittedly late at night, they couldn't stand up.

Seminyak and Beyond

Far and away the best place to stay here is the **Oberoi Bali** ((0361) 730361 FAX (0361) 730791 E-MAIL obrblsls@indosat.net.id WEB SITE www.oberoihotels.com, Box 3351, Denpasar 80033, Jalan Laksmana (expensive). This exclusive establishment is a member of the Leading Hotels of the World and the Small Luxury Hotels of the World, and is sited on a holy beach with several especially important shrines. Double rooms cost from US$200 to US$750, and the 74 rooms are all set in private villas among the gardens, which front directly onto a beach. Although not a private beach, it certainly is not prey to hordes of hustlers. The only people you see on this stretch of sand are the occasional cremation party, respectful at that.

Struggling rather to catch up is the **Legian** ((0361) 730622 FAX (0361) 731291 E-MAIL legian@idola.net.id WEB SITE www.ghmhotels.com,

The beach at Legian offers a relaxed alternative to the hectic pace of Kuta Beach.

Jalan Laksmana, Seminyak (moderate). With a large and beautiful garden, a swimming pool and access directly onto the sand, this three-star hotel offers four-star value. Hawkers are prohibited from the areas around the sun chairs immediately in front of the hotel, and it is generally a friendly, welcoming place. The hotel has some rooms that have been specially adapted for the disabled.

For the less financially advantaged, there are still plenty of opportunities to breathe the same air as the rich and famous. Along Jalan Abimanyu there are several overgrown *losmens* that offer plenty of character and charge from US$30 per day. One is the **Puri Bunga Cottages** ((0361) 730939 FAX 730334 E-MAIL puribungacottages@yahoo.co.uk WEB SITE www.baliweb.net/balipuribunga, Jalan Abimanyu (Gado Gado), Seminyak (inexpensive). Try to get room 1104: its bathroom wall is made up of the dramatic lower part of a huge Banyan tree, surreally decorated with plastic leaves.

Further north still, beyond Seminyak in Canggu, stand the **Legong Keraton Beach Cottages** ((0361) 730280 FAX (0361) 730285, Jalan Pantai Berawa (moderate). This is well away from the action at Kuta, and you have to drive well inland to get there, so it suits those who want a quiet time. Be careful, however, of strong currents here.

WHERE TO EAT

The restaurants in Kuta and its neighboring villages are as varied as the accommodation. Prices, however, don't reflect this range. The variety in Kuta's eateries lies not in their prices but in their cuisines. You can eat Japanese, Mexican, German, Chinese — the only problem posed might be finding Balinese food, but even that is possible.

Made's Warung on Jalan Pantai is a historic site, the first place, 25 years ago, to offer high-quality Western dishes in Kuta. At the time of writing it was closed for renovation. Traditionally lunch here extends into dinnertime, with a couple of glasses of *arak madu* (palm spirit with lemon juice and honey) leaving some patrons barely able to stumble the short distance along the road and collapse on the beach just in time for sunset.

Made's Warung II ((0361) 732130, Jalan Raya Seminyak, at the center of a fashionable shopping square in Seminyak, gets more attention and a more chic set of diners than its parent in nowadays-raucous Kuta.

A few yards down the narrow lane immediately to the left of the Jalan Pantai Made's lies another fine establishment, **Un's** ((0361) 752607, Jalan Pantai, named after the Swiss owner's wife. Set in a beautiful courtyard with flowering trees, it is deservedly popular at dinnertime.

Poppies ((0361) 751059, Gang Poppies I, is an old favorite now become trendy; the food remains excellent, and the restaurant is so popular that tourists come from Sanur and Nusa Dua; it is advisable to book in advance. For a touch of the Americas, **TJ's** ((0361) 751093, Gang Poppies I, is close by and serves excellent Mexican food.

Northerners who long for potatoes and homemade sausages will find their heart's desire at the **Swiss Restaurant** ((0361) 751735, Jalan Pura Bagus Teruna. Bratwurst, wiener *kartoffelsalat* and *apfelstrudel* rub shoulders with *fondue bourguignonne*. The owner is the Swiss Consul.

For French food at a very reasonable price try The French Restaurant **Topi Kopi** ((0361) 754243, Jalan Pura Bagus Teruna, a few yards along from the Swiss Restaurant. By far the classiest place for dining French-style is the **Kafe Warisan** ((0361) 731175, Jalan Raya Kerobokan, overlooking rice paddies not far from the Oberoi Hotel. This place reopened recently to much acclaim. Food and wine are of a very high standard.

Italian food is big business in Legian and Seminyak. Top prices can be paid at the ultra-fashionable **La Lucciola** ((0361) 730838, Oberoi Road, Kaya Ayu Beach, right on the Beach in Seminyak, and booking is essential for tables from sundown onwards. Many enthusiasts believe the food is even better at the **Café Luna** ((0361) 730805, Jalan Raya Seminyak, opposite Goa 2002, where they make fresh pasta every day on the premises. It's an elegant establishment that mounts fashion shows in a large and beautiful hall behind the main restaurant space at 11 PM every Friday. It's as much a cult place as La Lucciola and particularly popular with the nightlife set. New kid on the block is **Fabios** ((0361) 730562, on Jalan Raya Seminyak.

A good, attractively-housed coffee shop is **Warung Kopi** ((0361) 753602, in Legian on Jalan Legian. It serves homemade ice cream containing only natural ingredients, and meals including an Indian buffet on Wednesday. There's another branch on Jalan Padma Utara.

Good Thai food is served at the **Kin Khao Thai Restaurant** ((0361) 732153, which has a second location in the heart of Kuta on Jalan Kartika Plaza. Should you hanker for Jakarta-style food there's **Warung Batavia** ((0361) 243769, on Jalan Raya Kerobokan in Seminyak.

The increasing wave of Japanese visitors to Bali means that there are plenty of good and improving Japanese restaurants. Those who think that Japanese meals have to be delicate and small can think again after they've eaten at the **Hana Restaurant** (no phone), Jalan Raya Seminyak, where helpings are huge. The most significant Japanese restaurants remain, however, the **Yashi** ((0361) 751161, Jalan Patra Jasa Bali, or the **Ryoshi** ((0361) 731377, Jalan Raya Seminyak 17. And for Indian curries the best, though far from the smartest restaurant is the **Gateway of India** ((0361) 732940, Jalan Abimanyu 10, Legian Kaja, Seminyak.

If you want to eat overlooking the surf, then head for the **Surya Café** ((0361) 757381 at the end of Jalan Padma. The food is average but the location excellent. Further north in Seminyak the **Soda Club** ((0812) 380-8846 (cell), Jalan Double Six (Arjuna) 7A, has grown from a beachfront shack to a friendly bar/restaurant, especially busy as the sun drops into the sea. Immediately next door, the **Zanzibar** ((0361) 733527, Jalan Double Six (Arjuna), serves Mediterranean and Indonesian food all day long. In addition, many of the tiny outlets with pointed roofs on the beach serve simple meals; the one known as **Tivoli**, close to the part of the beach just before the Oberoi known as Blue Ocean, is good and fastidiously clean.

Lastly, for cheap but often excellent food, try **Depot Kuta** ((0361) 51155, in Kuta's Night Market. There are several very inexpensive restaurants and food stalls in this area, but this one, specializing in Chinese food, is among the best.

NIGHTLIFE

Kuta's nightlife is both raucous and extensive. The pace is set by Australian surfers: they land here, flooded with money, to arrange their onward travel to distant islands in the archipelago, and later return to sell off their boards and spend what cash they have left. It's not always a pretty sight, but it does keep the place moving.

In Kuta itself there are a string of places catering for the young surfing crowd. Among them is **Peanuts** (entrances on Jalan Legian and another from Jalan Melasti), which has live music every day and is the start of the twice-weekly pub crawls (Tuesday and Saturday) that have, apparently, spawned

OPPOSITE: A cremation ceremony at Seminyak Beach, just past Legian. ABOVE: The best eating in Kuta combines quality with informality, amiability with economy, and all under a traditional Balinese roof.

200 "Peanut Clubs" worldwide. Another is the **Hard Rock Café**, Jalan Melasti, that despite being a recent import has settled well into the Kuta "scene" and has many of the best bands in the island performing live, every night. Until about 11 PM the action is at the Hard Rock Café, then it shifts a few meters to the **Hard Rock Hotel**. There are more — the **Sari Bar**, **Bounty Ship 1**, **Tubes**, the **Apache Reggae Bar** and the **All Stars Surf Café**. All are open nightly and cater to a partying, rock'n'roll clientele. Enough said.

Head east along the coast and things calm somewhat. Legian and neighboring Seminyak are rather less determinedly youthful, while still containing a number of friendly, lively bars. The main Jalan Legian has, by here, changed its name to Jalan Seminyak, and if you start here the first bar you'll get to is the **Jaya Pub**, which has live rock most nights, and **Goa 2002**, whose name changes to keep a year ahead of the dateline. Cross the road and you'll find **Café Luna**, which was always lively but recently revamped its image to head upmarket. Even the barstaff question the wisdom of this. Take a left down Jalan Double Six and there are some great bars: the **Buddha Bar**, grooving with a Latin accent and the **"A" Bar**, where you don't have to drink Absolute Vodka to be given a seat. Most of these bars are rather sad places until about midnight, when suddenly they fill. After about 2 AM they close and folks left standing make their way to the **Double Six**, which has the area's best dance floor and a pool. When, at 4 AM or so, this place closes, your last chance is the **Villas Club**, Jalan Kunti 118, which keeps going for two more blurred hours. A few hundred meters in the other direction is the flashing world of bars and discos, each attempting to outdo the other with amplified noise. Entrance is usually free at Kuta's nightclubs for tourists, but for Indonesians only if they can be seen to be bringing in a tourist. A tourist, it is assumed, can be guaranteed to cover the assumed value of entrance with drinks bought at the bar.

How to Get There

For international arrivals, getting to Kuta couldn't be simpler: prepaid taxis line up at the Ngurah Rai Airport on fixed fares. If you're on a tight budget, you'll save money by taking a dark blue *bemo* which can be found if you walk the 750 featureless and poorly-lit meters (820 yards) to the airport front gate. Go left and you'll tour Kuta, before traveling on to Denpasar, where you'll need to transit for *bemo* connections to other parts of the island. Kuta is three kilometers (two miles) from the airport, 10 (long) kilometers (six miles) from Denpasar.

Excursions from Kuta

The southern resorts, as they are broadly equidistant, have operators providing most of the same excursions. These excursions are listed in this book based on their proximity to each resort. Near Kuta is **Tanah Lot**.

The spectacular offshore temple of Tanah Lot, perched on a rocky islet 100 m (330 ft) out from the coast, has had its charm buried by the tourist industry. Today it hosts the unwelcome addition of kiosks selling T-shirts and sarongs, two small hotels, a shop selling Polo Ralph Lauren fashions, and the vast Le Meridien Hotel with its 18-hole golf course.

Except at high tide, you can walk over the rocks to the site of the temple, but you will not be allowed into the temple itself — it's locked except at festival times. Most people have little desire to go there; what they want to do is photograph it from the shore, preferably against the backdrop of a sunset.

There are essentially three places from which this picturesque if slightly twee ensemble can be captured on film: from down in the cove itself, from along the low cliff, and from the headland on the right. From this last position a natural arch in the rocks to the north can also be taken in, with Mount Batur in the background.

Tanah Lot has little to keep you for more than a brief visit. You can, however, while down in the cove, see the "holy snake" or guardian of the temple, which lies conveniently coiled on a ledge in a small cave. Boys will illuminate it for you with a small flashlight and collect a donation for the service.

The temple itself has five small thatched shrines and is thought to date from the six-

---

Tanah Lot — The bus-loads of tourists arriving to photograph the temple outlined against the sunset have rendered this particular image one of modern Asia's archetypes.

teenth century, when the priest Danghyang Nirartha is believed by the devout to have crossed over to Bali from Java floating on a leaf. He instructed several temples to be built, Tanah Lot among them, as was the far more spectacular temple at Ulu Watu.

Entrance to the beach area adjacent to the temple is Rp10,000, half-price for children. You will be asked to pay an additional donation, but there's no need to do so.

If for some reason you should desire to stay the night at Tanah Lot, the two small hotels are the **Dewi Sinta** ((0361) 812933 FAX (0361) 813956 (inexpensive) and the **Mutiara Tanah Lot Bungalows** ((0361) 225457 FAX (0361) 222672 (moderate). Amid considerable controversy the Bali Nirwana Golf Course has now spread along this stretch of coast.

Tanah Lot is 12 km (seven and a half miles) south of Kediri, a town on the busy main road heading west from Denpasar to Tabanan. If traveling by *bemo*, Kediri is where you need to turn left, and find someone to take you down the road to Tanah Lot by motorbike. Most people, however, arrive on organized tours.

SANUR

Sanur is altogether a comfortable place — not cheap, but long-established, leafy and reassuring. The beach, placid and sheltered behind a reef, is not the broad sweeping expanse of sand that is found in Kuta, but then no other beach in Bali can match up to this standard. In compensation, it is much more relaxing for swimming. An offshore reef breaks the surf, and even children can safely bathe. There is a catch: at low tide the sea retreats to the horizon and there just isn't enough water inside the reef to swim. Venturing outside the reef for a dip is only a good idea for experienced swimmers with flippers; otherwise the currents are too strong.

Sanur was the first stretch of coast to be developed for tourism, with expatriates setting up their homes here well before Kuta became infested with hippies. The Belgian artist Le Mayeur was perhaps the best known, while other illuminati have included Vicki Baum (who wrote *A Tale from Bali*) and, later, the Australian artist Donald Friend. To this day it remains the favored area for expatriates to build their homes.

The refined and quiet atmosphere of Sanur took a step toward that of a modern beach resort when, under Sukarno, the huge Bali Beach Hotel was built. In 1993 this eyesore suffered serious fire damage, but not enough. It has now been rebuilt and is called the Grand Bali Beach, and remains the largest hotel in the area.

All of the tourist facilities available in such profusion in Kuta are here too, but presented in a more genteel, affluent way. Sanur is a lush garden where visitors lie on beach beds under palm trees sipping their Camparis, or flop splendidly into a pool. (Hotels without pools can't compete in Sanur.) Leather traveling bags replace canvas ones. It's as discreet, worldly and wise as Kuta is fresh, brash and youthful. You pay your money — more than in Kuta, but less than in Nusa Dua — and you take your choice.

With a few exceptions, most of the other places to stay are medium-sized hotels of self-contained rooms and cottages, usually, these days, with air-conditioning and swimming pools. You won't find Kuta's low-priced flophouses here and the nightlife tends to be quiet and low-key, but then you don't have the seething traffic nor the glittering rows of high-rent shops selling counterfeit goods to naïve shoppers. Instead you've got small, mid-range hotels and a range of foreign embassies that find Sanur far more accessible to most of their expatriate citizens, and a nice place to stay as well. And that is just the way the residents of Sanur like it.

GENERAL INFORMATION

The easiest way to get to Sanur from the airport is by prepaid taxi, which shouldn't cost more than Rp30,000; it's not straightforward by *bemo*. From elsewhere in the island, shuttle buses are the most convenient way to get here. There is no official tourist information office here, though there are several travel agents and the larger hotels have travel desks. For medical attention the second branch of the 24-hour **Legian Clinic** ((0361) 758503, Jalan Danau Tamblingan 154, is probably the best place to start. Taxis generally cruise around Sanur, but it is also the home of the **Praja Taxi Company** ((0361) 289191. Car rental is easy to arrange, with Bali **Car Rental** ((0361) 288550, Jalan Ngurah Rai (Bypass), and many other smaller operators practicing from roadside stalls or through travel agents.

There are a number of cybercafés of which one, with particularly helpful staff who can cope with Internet virgins, is the **Ocha Internet Café** ((0361) 264186 E-MAIL ocha@dps.centrin.net.id, Jalan Danau Tamblingan 84.

ORIENTATION

In common with many of Bali's resorts, Sanur consists of three separate villages, with the Grand Bali Beach Hotel counting as a fourth all of its own. Each village retains its own character in many ways, but they all share a leafy, relaxed atmosphere as they spread along the coast to the east of Denpasar's new dual-carriage ring road, known, universally, as Jalan Bypass.

Most northerly is the antiseptic "village" of the Grand Bali Beach Hotel. If you're after a beach vacation, this isn't a bad place to stay, as the sand is kept very clean and the rooms are of an international standard. It's especially good value if you've flown to Bali on a package, when your hotel accommodation is, effectively, free. It's not the hotel that takes up the space but its golf course, which is the cheapest — especially for guests at the hotel — but not the best on the island.

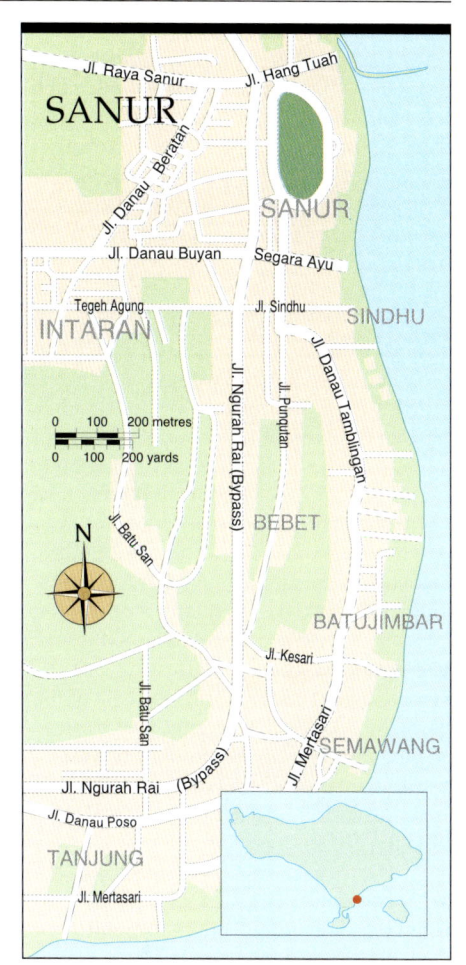

What is, effectively, Sanur's main street loops in a crescent east of the main Jalan Ngurah Rai (Bypass), reaching, at its nearest, about 100 m (330 ft) from the beach. In the north this street is known as Jalan Danau Tamblingan, changing its name in the south to Jalan Mertasari. As it progresses south it links the villages of Sindhu, Batujimbar and Semawang.

Sindhu is the most upmarket, with night markets and art shops as well as some better restaurants. **Batujimbar** is where the expatriates live, and several foreign embassies

---

The sight of Tanah Lot at sunset epitomizes the beauty and force of Bali, an arresting image that remains in the minds of travelers long after they have returned home.

shelter in shady lanes that lead down to the beach. This is where you'll find most of the busiest bars. Then, after a small blank patch caused by the looming bulk of the Hyatt Hotel, the southern village of **Semawang** is perhaps the most varied, with a smattering of very expensive hotels rubbing shoulders with a number of Sanur's least expensive home-stays.

WHAT TO SEE AND DO

Sanur, with its sheltered waters, has the best facilities for water sports on the island in terms of cost and of sheer variety. Many of the major hotels offer facilities of their own, and plenty of beach vendors and touts take care of any visitors who feel left out, usually undercutting hotel rates. There are canoes, windsurfers, and jet-skis available. It is possible to explore the underwater world using a glass-bottomed boat, snorkeling on the reef, or, if qualified, diving in the area, but the diving is easier in the north and east of the island; most operators arrange day-trips. In the wet season, from September to March, the monsoon winds bring **surfing** to the coast off Sanur, which is useful as this is just when the waters of Kuta go flat.

There are more attractions further out to sea. A row of outrigger canoes are pulled up on the beach in Semawang, to the south of the resort, and can be chartered for visits to Serangan Island, better known locally as Turtle Island. There are a couple of temples on the island and a rather depressing pond full of turtles: this project is supposed to help breed the massively endangered species but doesn't fill the visitor with confidence. Turtle Island can be visited from Nusa Dua, or even Kuta, but the southern end of Sanur is the closest. At low tide you might have to wade some of the way, so take appropriate footwear. There are a number of diving companies based, or with offices, here, of which one is **Bali Safari Dive** ((0361) 282656 E-MAIL bsdive@indosat.net.id, on Jalan Mertasari 15. Another good one is **Aquapro** ((0361) 270791 FAX (0361) 287065 E-MAIL aquapro@balidiving .com, Jalan Ngurah Rai (Bypass) 46E, Blanjong, Sanur. Although the north coast dives are quite far away, Sanur is well-placed to explore the very good diving around the small islands of Nusa Lembongan and Nusa Penida. For **big-game fishing** contact **Atlantis** ((0361) 283676 E-MAIL kertimas@denpasar .wasantara.net.id, Jalan Danau Tamblingan 188, which charges US$180 for four hours open-water trolling, with coral fishing somewhat cheaper. Sanur is home to Bali's only diving and sailing charters to the island of Komodo: contact **Grand Komodo Tours** ((0361) 287166 FAX (0361) 287165, Jalan Hang Tuah 26. For fishing, **charter boats** can be found just down the coast at Tanjung Benoa (see under NUSA DUA, page 134).

On land, Grand Bali Beach provides the least expensive place on Bali to play **golf**: the green fees are US$50, with golf club and shoe rental and caddy fees on top. Guests at the hotel get a 50% discount. The same hotel also has a **bowling** center, charging US$2.50 per game.

For a touch of culture, one of the few historical sites in Sanur here is the house, now known as the **Museum Le Mayeur** (Tuesday to Thursday and Saturday 8 AM to 4 PM, Friday 8 AM to 1:30 PM), where the Belgian painter Le Mayeur lived from 1932 to 1958. The place has been left more or less as it was, with his books still on his desk and so on. What is so striking about the house is that his painting explodes from the framed pictures onto the walls and eventually all over the window frames. Fantastic scenes from the *Ramayana* epic in augmented Balinese style feature prominently.

Hydrotherapy and Massage

In keeping with Sanur's ambiance of genteel comfort there is a sauna, spa and massage club known as **Sehatku** ((0361) 287880, Jalan Danau Tamblingan 23, where you can relax and have all those worries kneaded. It also offers *lulur* baths, whirlpool, sauna and steam treatments. It isn't as inexpensive as massages on Kuta Beach, but it's undoubtedly more congenial to its clients and truly in the gracious Sanur style. Pedicures, manicures, facial and body massages are the specialty at **Peruna Beauty Line Salon** ((0361) 289536, Jalan Danau Tamblingan, further down the same street.

Meanwhile makeshift bamboo stands do busy business in cut-price beach massages on the southern stretches of beach.

Shopping

Sanur is a good place to shop if you are looking for quality. You won't find many bargains in Sanur's smart boutiques and art shops, but if shopping at the countless stalls that line Jalan Danau Tamblingan bargaining skills can get prices down to much the same level as Kuta. Almost all the following shops are on Jalan Danau Tamblingan.

For ceramics, there's the **Miralin Collection** (/FAX (0361) 286061 and **Earth and Fire**. Puppets (some originals, some reproductions) and Javanese terracotta figurines are on offer at the **Lama Gallery** ((0361) 286809 FAX (0361) 751468. For leather try **Rafflesia** ((0361) 288528, Jalan Danau Toba 10. For *ikat* and handwoven fabrics there is the **Nogo Ikat Center** ((0361) 288765, with two outlets in Sanur, at Jalan Danau Tamblingan 98 and 208, selling the best in handwoven knit designs. For clothes in general and hand-embroidered Balinese lace there is the **Mama & Leon Boutique** ((0361) 288044 FAX (0361) 288150, Jalan Danau Tamblingan 99A. It's a beautiful showroom and shop, and the factory is just behind. The even smarter **Uluwatu** ((0361) 288977, on Jalan Danau Tamblingan, also has fine lace and linen. For international fashions, however, you're likely to be best off in the major hotel's own boutiques. Export quality silver jewelry is at **Suarti Designer Collection** ((0361) 298914, at Jalan Danau Tamblingan 69, while for

The sheltered waters off Sanur's beaches are perfect for sailing and swimming.

inexpensive souvenirs and gifts the Sanur Beach Market will have the best choice and, for those who convincingly feign complete indifference throughout the bargaining process, the best prices too.

WHERE TO STAY

Most of the hotels, except the Grand Bali Beach and the Bali Hyatt, are of the bungalow type and are often set in shady tropical gardens, most of them facing the (generally safe) beach. Almost all of the more exclusive hotels in Sanur are right on the beach. In each category here listings start from the north and work south.

Expensive

The irritating thing about the more expensive hotels here that if you walk in off the streets you are charged US$200 or more for a room while if you book it as a package you get accommodation, effectively, for less than nothing (see TAKING A TOUR, page 62 in YOUR CHOICE). This is true of most of this area's expensive hotels.

The **Hotel Grand Bali Beach** ((0361) 288511 FAX (0361) 287917, Jalan Hang Tuah 58, has every facility anyone is likely to require. It's the only hotel in the region built upwards, eschewing the more conventionally Balinese bungalow/garden style, but it also has its low-rise wing and cottages. You approach the hotel down a long drive with a nine-hole championship golf course on the right, where figures in white tropical suits swing their clubs with Balinese caddies in attendance. A *gamelan* orchestra celebrates your arrival for lunch, and many of the airlines have offices in the hotel to facilitate your smooth departure. However, although there is a shuttle bus to Kuta and Nusa Dua, to get to any local shops or restaurants it is a very long and hot walk. The sheer expanse of their golf course imprisons most guests, so that packaged tourists shall pay for their stay in overpriced beers and facilities.

Just behind the Grand Bali Beach is the new **Radisson Bali** ((0361) 281781 FAX (0361) 281782 E-MAIL radbali@indosat.com WEB SITE www.bali-paradise.com/radissonbali, Jalan Hang Tuah 46 (expensive, although special deals can bring rates down to average and above), which is a good, international-standard hotel in the heart of Sanur that, when offering special promotional rates, represents good value.

Continuing south, the attractive **Hotel Tandjung Sari** ((0361) 288441 FAX (0361) 287930 E-MAIL tansri@dps.mega.net.id, Jalan Danau Tamblingan, Batujimbar, with only 26 rooms, is the preferred hideaway for celebrities and jetsetters in Sanur. The food is good and the atmosphere that of a raja's garden. The hotel actually dates back to 1962, but it still has a regular returning clientele, as for many, it is the only place to stay in Bali.

The **Bali Hyatt** ((0361) 288271 FAX (0361) 287693 E-MAIL bhyatt@dps.mega.net.id, Jalan Danau Tamblingan, set in an astonishing 15 hectares (36 acres) of land, combines very Balinese public areas with four-story accommodation. High thatched roofs rise over restaurants serving food from Indonesia and Italy, and a sauna and discotheque complete the international part of the ambiance. This used to be the place to stay in Bali, though now it has been rather eclipsed by other luxury hotels on Jimbaran and Nusa Dua. Once more, its grounds are so large they might as well be specifically designed to prevent escape.

At the far south of the beach is the **Sanur Beach Hotel** ((0361) 288011 FAX (0361) 287566 E-MAIL sanur-bch@dps.mega.net.id, Jalan Mertasari, Semawang, which claims to be the friendliest of the big Sanur hotels. It's usually booked solid by tour groups. For a much better atmosphere go to the most southerly of all the expensive hotels and the **Raddin** ((0361) 288833 FAX (0361) 287303 E-MAIL radsanur@indosat.net.id WEB SITE www.raddin.com, Jalan Mertasari.

Moderate

Sanur has a good range of accommodation options in the moderate category. These rarely form part of the package-tourism industry and while their facilities might not be as grand as their more expensive neighbors, the welcome is often more sincere. To the north the **Diwangkara** ((0361) 288577, Jalan Hang Tuah, has classic Balinese bungalows set out in gardens on the beachfront. The **Segara Village Hotel** ((0361) 288407 FAX (0361) 287242 E-MAIL segara@denpasar

.wasantara.net.id, Jalan Segara Ayu, with two-story cottages in garden surroundings, is unpretentious, quiet and relaxing and faces the beach, though only its less expensive rooms fall into this price category. It has a good reputation for its children's programs. Off the beach and the ethical place to stay is the **Hotel Santai** (/FAX (0361) 281684 E-MAIL sontai@indosat.net.id, Jalan Tamblingan 148, which combines an environmental resource center, a very complete library on ecological issues, and a cybercafé. Although the public areas are expansive, the rooms themselves are slightly cramped around a swimming pool there isn't really space for. Better perhaps to head for the less doctrinaire **Hotel Bali Warma** ((0361) 285618 FAX (0361) 285154, Jalan Wira HBB 2, centrally but quietly positioned, which may care less about the environment but don't charge guests for it.

South a bit and the **Baruna Beach** ((0361) 288546 FAX (0361) 289629, Jalan Sindhu, is well-located on the beach and popular with travelers and surfers. Just across the road is the **Natour Sindhu Beach** ((0361) 288351 FAX (0361) 289268 E-MAIL nsindhu@denpasar .wasantara.net.id, Jalan Pantai Sindhu 14, is part of an Indonesian chain that provides good value here. Meanwhile the **Santrian Beach Resort** ((0361) 288009 FAX (0361) 287101, Jalan Cemara, offers the usual one- and two-story bungalows in the usual verdant tropical gardens.

Budget

Sanur isn't known for its bottom-end accommodation, but there are some places worth checking out, especially in hotels that don't actually front the beach. Those who don't mind walking a hundred meters to the beach will find they get much more for their money. It would be hard, in Sanur, to get more than a 10 minute-walk from the sea in any case.

In the far north of the resort, squeezed above the Grand Bali Beach, there's the **Ananda Hotel** ((0361) 288327, Jalan Hang Tuah 43, which provides clean rooms with fans and cold water, right next to the sea though at the very end of the beach. In the central village of Sindhu, **Yulia Homestay** ((0361) 288089, Jalan Danau Tamblingan 38, provides classic home-stay accommodation in basic rooms. More comfortable is **Ida's Homestay** ((0811) 387211 (cell) FAX (0361) 288598, Jalan Danau Toba, Gang 1. The owner describes it as "central" but perhaps he just means it isn't on the beach. Air-conditioned rooms here slip up to the next price bracket.

Images of turtles and fish illustrate the importance of the ocean in Sanur.

Southern Bali and the Bukit

Centrally located on the main strip and within staggering distance of Sanur's two sleaziest bars is the surprisingly salubrious **Puri Suar** ((0361) 285572, Jalan Danau Toba 9, which has air-conditioned rooms and handcrafted, hand-painted furnishings blasted by quiet, glacial air-conditioning (no breakfast or restaurant). This is something of a bargain for this part of town.

Further south, **Bali Senia Hotel** ((0361) 289358 FAX (0361) 288951 E-MAIL bsenia@ indosat.net.id, Jalan Danau Poso 23, Blanjong, provides good value for Balinese-style rooms with air-conditioning, although the dining area is a little depressing.

WHERE TO EAT

Sanur teems with fine restaurants, although they tend to be reasonably expensive by Balinese standards. They also generally shut early: leave your dinner until later than nine at night and you might be looking at a taxi-ride to Kuta to dine at all. One advantage is that almost all the restaurants tend to be set along the main, looping street that brings Sanur together: stroll along Jalan Danau Tamblingan and you'll be spoiled for gastronomic choice.

The best restaurants tend to be sited in the better hotels. Thus the restaurant of the **Tandjung Sari** ((0361) 288441, Jalan Danau Tamblingan, is famous for its *rijsttafel* in a classically Balinese garden, and the Chinese restaurant, run by the Bali Hyatt, known as **Telaga Naga** ((0361) 281234 extension 8080, Jalan Danau Tamblingan, is set a short distance from the main hotel in an enchanting — if rather over-the-top — Chinese style garden. Both Sichuan and Cantonese dishes are served.

On the same street is the **Kul Kul Restaurant** ((0361) 288038, Jalan Danau Tamblingan, offering Western and Indonesian food, with traditional Balinese dishes available if ordered in advance. Similar in style is the Gazebo's **Krui Puti** ((0361) 288212, Danau Tamblingan 35. South a bit and the **Trattoria Da Marco's** ((0361) 288996, Semawang, is well-known for it's Italian cuisine. Japanese cuisine is fast becoming a Balinese specialty, and **Kita** ((0361) 288453, Jalan Danau Tamblingan, and **Ryoshi** ((0361) 288473, Jalan Danau Tamblingan, are two exponents here.

The further south you go along Jalan Danau Tamblingan the cheaper the restaurants get. Once past the Hyatt there are a number of very reasonable *warung* bars and small restaurants to be found. For even fresher local food try the **Night Market**, which sets up by the Art Market by Jalan Mertasari in Semawang.

There are also some fine eating places on the main road known as Jalan Bypass. One of the most unusual is Bali's only Korean restaurant, the **Chong Gi-Wa** (/FAX (0361) 287084, Jalan Ngurah Rai (Bypass). Hearty servings of magnificent northern food, cooked up on your table, are accompanied by the unique Korean pickled cabbage known as *kimchi*.

NIGHTLIFE

Nightlife isn't a prominent feature of Sanur as young people make for charismatic venues at Kuta and Legian, only a 15-minute drive away. There are, however, a number of pubs and relaxed drinking places as well as some traditional dancing shows in Sanur. At major hotels dances are usually only shown as part of an expensive buffet dinner, but various restaurants have, often quite lavish, dances at minimal cost. For example, free *legong* shows are the backdrop to seafood and lobster at the **Legong** ((0361) 288066, Jalan Danau Tamblingan, which picks guests up from their hotels free, and Happy Hours can stretch all night as venues compete to snare strollers who've escaped from their large hotels and a hard core of expat drinkers. Among these are **Lazer & Sport Bar** ((0361) 288807, Jalan Danau Tamblingan 82, where big screens show live world sport, and live music is the draw at **Planet Sanur Café** ((0361) 287597, Jalan Tamblingan 202; the **Mango Café** ((0361) 288411, Jalan Danau Toba 15; and the **Jazz Warung** ((0361) 287761, also on Jalan Danau Tamblingan.

If you're up to paying international drink prices the Hyatt's **Grantang Bar** has live jazz every evening from 8 PM until 1 AM, except Wednesday. If you don't mind a short taxi ride try the **Jazz Bar and Grill** ((0361) 285892, Jalan Ngurah Rai (Bypass), Komplek Sanur 15, seven nights a week, or on Friday and Saturday the **Kafe Wayang** ((0361) 287591, Jalan Ngurah Rai (Bypass), Komplek Sanur 12.

HOW TO GET THERE

The easiest way to get to Sanur is by shuttle bus from one of Bali's other resorts, or by taxi. Driving, it is conveniently signposted of the Jalan Ngurah Rai (Bypass), with three exits leading into the resort. Sanur is 15 kilometers (nine miles) from Kuta, seven kilometers (four miles) from Denpasar and 14 km (nine miles) from the airport.

EXCURSIONS FROM SANUR

As the most northerly of the mainstream coastal resorts, Sanur is well-served by tour operators offering day-trips into the heart of the island. One such is the **Waka Land Cruise** ((0361) 426972 FAX (0361) 426971 E-MAIL wakalandcruise@wakaexperience.com WEB SITE www.wakaexperience.com, Jalan Padang Kartika 5X, Padang Sambian Klod, Denpasar, whose Landrover tours of rice paddies, farmhouses, quarries and mineral springs provide lunch with ingredients straight from the rainforest. Day trips run from US$83 per person. For a fuller list of tours — and operators — see TAKING A TOUR, page 62 in YOUR CHOICE.

Taman Burung Bali Bird Park

The Taman Burung Bali Bird Park contains 250 kinds of Indonesian birds spread over two hectares (nearly five acres), and there is a walk-in rainforest aviary. Several of the park's species are endangered; a permit is required for the park to hold these and an extensive breeding program is being undertaken.

Most popular of the park's inhabitants is the king bird of paradise, little bigger than a canary but with a long and spectacular tail. This tail was nearly the cause of the bird's extinction as it was much prized in ladies' hats in the nineteenth century — at the height of their popularity some 50,000 bird of paradise pelts were exported annually to Europe and the United States. The bird can be difficult to spot as it tends to sit high up in trees.

Taman Burung Bali Bird Park ((0361) 299352 FAX (0361) 299614 is worth a visit from any of the southern resorts, but as it is only 30 minutes by road north of Sanur it is listed here. It is situated on Jalan Serma Cok Ngurah Gambir in Singapadu, the village just after Celuk on the road from Denpasar to Gianyar. The park is open from 9 AM to 6 PM. Entry, if traveling independently, is Rp57,000 but most visitors arrive as part of package tours which are priced somewhere around US$35 and include transport and

OPPOSITE: Enjoying a ride on a *prahu* off Sanur. ABOVE: Grilled corn cobs are a welcome hot snack after an active day on the beach at Sanur.

Turtle Island

Pulau Serangan, also known as Turtle Island, is a low, sandy spit cut off from the mainland to the north at high tide. Variations in tidal levels, however, make it inadvisable to cross other than by boat, even from Sanur, its closest resort. It can also be reached from Nusa Dua. The island is covered by palm trees and at its one village, turtles are kept in a small arena ready for inspection by visitors — a holdover from the days when they arrived spontaneously on the beach in huge numbers. Formerly they were kept on a much larger scale for eventual sale for as food or sacrificial offerings.

It has been 50 years since these mass arrivals ceased, but the island remains a popular destination for half-day tours. Travelers visiting individually will have a nicer time if they visit early in the morning or at the end of the afternoon to avoid coinciding with the tour groups.

For the Balinese the main significance of the island lies in the important temple **Pura Sakenan** which attracts thousands of worshippers during the festival of Kuningan.

NUSA DUA

The region south of the airport is generally referred to as the Bukit. This is the Balinese word for hill and strictly refers only to the high ground southwest of Nusa Dua. Nevertheless, the peninsula is of one piece; whereas the rest of mainland Bali is made up of volcanic rock and soils, the Bukit, like the nearby offshore island of Nusa Penida, is entirely limestone. Indeed, it is probable that at one time the Bukit was once an island too. Even today it is only connected to Bali proper by a low-lying and narrow isthmus.

Rainwater runs straight into the ground in limestone country, and the consequent lack of surface streams means there is no water available for irrigation during the dry season. As a result, life in the Bukit has traditionally been hard. The selection of Nusa Dua (literally "Two Islands") for development as a major tourist complex has done little to alter the traditional life of the region. The area includes the five-star complex of Nusa Dua itself, the fishing village of Tanjung Benoa situated at the end of a five-kilometer (three-

some other destinations in the island. These can be a good way to get there — at least there's less chance of getting lost — but if too much time is spent picking up guests at other hotels — and other resorts — the whole day quickly becomes quite a trial.

mile) sand strip directly to the north of Nusa Dua, the village and bay of Jimbaran (located on the neck of the isthmus immediately south of the airport), and the upland area itself which culminates in the magnificently situated temple of Ulu Watu, washed by some of the island's greatest surfing waves.

The development of Nusa Dua only truly got under way in the early 1980s. Prior to that time, the area was an infertile coastal patch featuring the two small "islands," connected to the mainland by sandy strips, which give the place its name. Mangrove swamps made the area all-but inaccessible, and only the arrival of big Indonesian money established access to what is now one of the island's most luxurious, if not exclusive, hotel developments.

Nusa Dua's hotels tend toward the five-star rating and each is, in its own style, the last word in luxury; all meet the highest international standards. They stand in their own ample grounds complete with several restaurants, swimming pools and more. Indeed, each of them is a self-sufficient vacation environment and anything that might be thought to be missing — Balinese local culture, for instance — is brought in and presented for the hotel guests' exclusive delectation.

Nusa Dua's beaches may not be the finest on the island, but they are safe and adequate for many people's needs. They are sheltered behind reefs and thus are shallow and placid, and they have white sand. Once again, at low tide swimming in the sea becomes impossible, so most guests here spend these times clustered around the hotel pool. Rocks and seaweed become more common as you move south, so that Club Méditerranée enjoys the best beach and the Grand Hyatt the least pleasant. On none of them are you likely to meet people other than fellow guests at the Nusa Dua hotels. To some people, however, this is an advantage, and certainly anyone concerned about security can be confident that here they are staying in a place specially designed with their safety in mind. Along the long avenues of palms that link the access roads to the hotels, security men are stationed on their motorbikes, lolling in boredom across the handlebars of their machines. Their main function in normal times seems to be to keep hawkers away from these wide acres in which are concentrated many of the richest people staying on Bali.

The atmosphere created by well-trimmed verges and impeccable tarred driveways is more that of a presidential golf course than somewhere given over to free-and-easy relaxation. In the southern area of Nusa Dua the only Balinese you're likely to encounter will be wearing hotel uniform, but as you head north things get less sanitized. The beach gets better and inland from huge hotel blocks stalls and houses jostle for space, and those who stray out of their air-conditioned palaces will still find restaurants, cybercafés and shops where the Balinese live on the scraps from the rich table of tourism. The northern village of Tanjung Benoa, largely untouched by tourism in its minor alleys and streets, still retains the feel of a traditional Balinese fishing village.

GENERAL INFORMATION

The resort of Nusa Dua spreads in a line of hotels from the northerly Balinese village of Tanjung Benoa down to the southern, central area where you'll find the Galleria Shopping Complex, which houses some of the best, though not the cheapest, restaurants and shops on the island. The **Bali Tourism Development Corporation (BTDC)** ℂ (0361) 771010 FAX (0361) 771014, Box 3, Nusa Dua, lost in the manicured grounds of Nusa Dua's most expensive real estate, claims to be open five days a week from 8 AM to 5 PM, but is often unexpectedly closed and is, in any case, not worth the trek to reach. The Galleria Shopping Complex, whose information desks are open seven days a week, is a much better place to present any questions about the wider environment, the area's best shops and the logical place to use ATMs or money changers.

For medical attention your hotel will probably be your first recourse — most have nurses, at least, on duty 24 hours — but the best of the clinics is the **NDC** ℂ/FAX (0361) 771324, Jalan Pratama 81, which also has a dentist on hand. Their treatment is likely to much less expensive than the hotel facilities, though this is rarely top of most agendas when sickness or injury strikes. They cater mainly to Balinese here, and the arrival of a Western patient causes no little hilarity and excitement, though most hotels will use their ambulance facilities if needed.

The resort area stretches six kilometers (nearly four miles) along the coast, but most of hotels run complimentary shuttle buses to and from the Galleria from 8 AM to 11 PM. For taxis, call **Bali Taxi** ((0361) 701111 FAX (0361) 701628, Jalan Ngurah Rai (Bypass) Nusa Dua 4. If you need a taxi and driver you won't be short of offers, but one option is **Made Latra** ((0361) 773763, Jalan Pratama 67A, who is a nice man and will you anywhere on the island for US$30 a day including gas, which is enough to get you to the volcanic heart of Bali and back. He prefers clients who want to go to Mengwi because it gives him a chance to visit his family.

The area is too moneyed to encourage many cybercafés, but if you find you need to log on the **CV Nusa Dua Internet** ((0361) 775496 E-MAIL bagir@astaga.com.id, Jalan Pratama 93, is well-priced although their connection isn't fast.

WHAT TO SEE AND DO

Of all Bali's southern resorts, Nusa Dua has, perhaps, the least to offer in terms of local culture. Newly built, its strong suit is international luxury, with the Balinese culture sneaking in only in decor and design, corporatized by world-renowned architects for an international clientele. Most guests here are after sun and sand, rather than exploring the spiritual dimensions of Bali's Hindu culture. The nearest most visitors will get to experience Balinese dance is in their hotel's own performances or in the daily dances put on at 7:30 PM at the Galleria Shopping Center (admission free).

However, if the Balinese culture was this easy to swamp, Bali wouldn't still be one of the world's most rewarding destinations. The local culture lives on most strongly in the northern extent of Nusa Dua and the fishing village of Tanjung Benoa. It has a raffish, freewheeling air, like a place long forgotten but determined to survive. And while the development of Nusa Dua to the south has seen a string of new hotels along the road joining the two places, there is a steady growth, also, of smaller and more individual places on the less expensive real estate to the western, inland side of the main road.

The most obvious entry point for new arrivals to the vacation scene is in undercutting the, generally fairly expensive, water sports available from the resort hotels. So Tanjung Benoa is now becoming an important center for diving, parasailing and windsurfing. Be aware that prices won't necessarily be lower if they think they can get away with fleecing a naïve Westerner.

Dominating the place is the new, bizarre but wonderful **Beluga Marina** ((0361) 771997 FAX (0361) 771967, Jalan Pratama. It's of most interest as a water sports center, with a submarine so you can see the local fish even if you can't swim, a dive school, and two silver catamarans that run over to Nusa Penida. With prices considerably lower than what hotels charge for the same services it tows parascenders up and down the coast and runs banana boats and jetskis. Beluga Marina also makes a serious attempt to entertain through the day, with white-uniformed waitresses shouting out enthusiastically to stop slow-moving vehicles to recruit a new audience for Italian food, live jazz in the afternoons and Western pop from the same Javanese musicians in the evenings. *Kecak* dances are also staged every night right in the middle of one of its two extraordinary restaurants. They offer free pickup from the major hotels but charge US$15 for the show. On the other side of the peninsula **Lingga Sempurna** ((0361) 774761, Perh Puri Mumbul, Jalan Sandat 1/15, is another water sports specialist; and another is **Waterworld** ((0361) 772781 FAX (0361) 774350 E-MAIL wwBali@indo .net.id, Jalan Ngurah Rai (Bypass) Km 25.

The view north from Tanjung Benoa is of Bali's major fishing port, **Benoa**. It's a longish way round from one to the other by road or a short trip by boat, but Benoa Port itself is not a favored excursion. There is little charm in watching mid-sized fishing boats shoveling aboard ice and the constant smell of rotting fish detracts further from its charm. Between the two, however, sheltering the entrance to the bay, lies Pulau Serangan, commonly known to tour operators as Turtle Island. Transport can be arranged from the beach over to Turtle Island for around

Rp15,000 per person, each way (see EXCURSIONS FROM SANUR, above). In addition, the village of Tanjung Benoa has an important **Chinese temple**, open from 6 AM to 9 PM daily. There is a wonderful view across the strait to the sun-and-shadow-etched cliffs of Nusa Penida in the late afternoon.

As the resort heads southwards it becomes ever more refined, spreading out into large and generous manicured greens dotted with palm trees and traversed by smooth tarmac roads. The principal attraction in the south is the Galleria Shopping Center, which has a collection of restaurants and fixed-price shops that offers quality, but at prices that would be more expected in Europe. This is also where you'll find the **Bali Golf and Country Club** ((0361) 771791 FAX (0361) 771797, an 18-hole golf course of championship standard. It stands on a lush swathe of land overlooked by the Amanusa. It's expensive though, but some Nusa Dua hotels include use of its facilities as part of a package or negotiate some reductions (see SPORTING SPREE, page 29 in YOUR CHOICE).

A very Nusa Dua thing to do is to take a **massage**. Most of the hotels offer massage facilities, though the rates are usually high. The leading Mandara Spa chain is represented at the Bali Golf and Country Club — which you'll need after 18 holes here — Club Med and the Nikko, but most of the smarter hotels provide spa services of their own. Of the top-class massage centers, the largest thalassotherapy center in southeast Asia is run by the Grand Mirage group: the **Thalasso Bali** ((0361) 771888 FAX (0361) 772148 E-MAIL gmirage@denpasar.wasantara.net.id, Jalan Pratama 72-74, Tanjung Benoa. Prices here are fairly international, with a day — including a light meal — costing US$95, though a popular option is to take a spell in their Aquamedic Pool, where seawater is jetted and poured and flowed into massaging currents, guaranteed to give your skin a boost: this costs just US$25.

Meanwhile across the main road there are other centers offering more conventional Balinese massage services. For example, the **Sri Agung Spa** ((0361) 772828 FAX (0361) 773703 E-MAIL sriagung@indo.net.id, Jalan Pratama 79X, Nusa Dua, offers a full range of treatments including aromatherapy, Shiatsu and reflexology and traditional massage with prices starting at US$30 per hour — and not getting too much higher. Another is **Aroma Talk** (/FAX (0361) 771458, Jalan Pratama 87C,

The Nusa Dua Hotel, one of the many five-star hostelries in this ultra-exclusive enclave: all have international-standard facilities.

Tanjung Benoa, with rates from US$25 per hour and around US$70 for three hours.

Finally, one of the best places to learn about Indonesian cooking is available here. Established by noted food writer Heinz von Holzen and his Balinese wife Puji, this one-day course starts at 6 AM (buying fish) and lasts all day; the cost is US$85 (US$55 for a half-day). The courses are run in the very professional kitchen of the **Bumbu Bali Restaurant and Cooking School** ((0361) 774502 FAX (0361) 771728 E-MAIL hvhfood@indosat.net.id WEB SITE www.balifood.com, Jalan Pratama, Matahari Terbit Bali, Tanjung Benoa, Nusa Dua. Courses are run from Monday to Friday.

Shopping

Those staying at Nusa Dua start their shopping with a serious disadvantage. Everyone in the area knows how much they are paying for their rooms and so the traders' expectations are correspondingly high. This needn't be an insuperable problem, however, if you practice your bargaining skills: outside the main gates of Nusa Dua there is a huge market where all the handicrafts of Bali are on display, and although the expectations of traders might, here, be higher, the price they have paid for the goods is just the same as they would if they were operating in Kuta. Those with a clear idea of the local value of what they are buying can achieve much comparable prices if they combine seeming indifference with persistence.

Most of Nusa Dua's shoppers are fed toward the Galleria center, where set prices are the norm. Unfortunately, these set prices are relentlessly high. There are the ubiquitous Uluwatu and Mama and Leon for upmarket lace, Nogo for *ikat*, Ralph Lauren, Versace and Benetton. More usefully though, there is a **Tragia Supermarket**, which provides some unexpected bargains, including great deals on software and perhaps the cheapest Dutch hand-rolling tobacco in the world. Perhaps the only really useful shop in the entire place is **Yakkum Craft** ((0274) 895386 E-MAIL yakkum@idola.net.id, WEB SITE www.yakkumcraft.org, which only sells handcrafted goods made by disabled people. Their rocking-horses are superb, and they have a number of excellent wooden jigsaws, all sold by gracefully disabled staff. Shops like this, give Nusa Dua prices a very welcome ethical dimension. Most of the other shops just make you feel like a complete sucker.

Strangely, the Galleria is not a good place to find ATMs. There is one, and although the Galleria management would never lose face by putting up an "out of order" sign, it often fails in its basic function of handing over cash. If you need to draw money on a credit card it's best to head out from the Galleria for two kilometers (a mile and a half) on the road to Denpasar, where you'll find, on the left, another Tragia Supermarket aimed at the local market: in the shade of the supermarket there are four ATMs and one or more of these can be guaranteed to work correctly.

Where to Stay

Most of the accommodation in Nusa Dua falls firmly into the luxury bracket. When it was first established, this was the sort of place heads of state would be lured — the Reagans, among others, stayed here — though now the guests here tend to be Europeans and Japanese attracted by package deals made available to tour operators in their home countries. Almost all of these international-standard hotels are much less expensive booked as part of a package from abroad (see TAKING A TOUR, page 62 in YOUR CHOICE), and booked in this way it has to be admitted they provide excellent value. For those who either book directly or just drift in and try to check in at reception they will prove hugely expensive. Not least because most published rates don't include the 21% "tax" that will be added when you check out, raising the tariff still further.

For this reason we don't, here, aim to be comprehensive on the international hotels that line the beach in the southern, snooty area of Nusa Dua, as information about them is widely available through tour operator brochures that are freely available abroad. Mid-range accommodation — which does exist here — is more useful and more difficult to discover. Inexpensive home-stays are, as yet, barely present, though it has to be said that Nusa Dua is not the most rewarding place for backpackers to spend their time.

Those on a budget will want to focus on the northern area of the resort toward Tanjung Benoa where there are more Balinese shops and homes, the only option for those who wish to live and eat inexpensively.

Expensive

There is a plethora of places offering high-standard resort facilities here. The **Nusa Dua Beach Hotel** ((0361) 771210 FAX (0361) 772617, Lot N4, Nusa Dua, is where heads of state stay when they visit Indonesia; government officials fly down from Jakarta to meet them here rather than having to face the security nightmare presented by the nation's capital. The architectural style of the Nusa Dua Beach Hotel is solidly generous, while its rooms are in four-story blocks.

The **Melia Bali Sol Hotel** ((0361) 771510 FAX (0361) 771360 E-MAIL melia-bali@denpasar.wasantara.net.id, Lot N1, Nusa Dua, by contrast, mixes Balinese style and Spanish ownership, with daily cabarets and flamenco played by Balinese musicians. It too has rooms in four-story blocks.

The **Putri Bali** ((0361) 771020 or (0361) 771420, Lot N3, Nusa Dua, is the other big, traditional hotel and, managed by the government, offers relatively good value. The name means "Balinese Princess."

The **Bali Club Méditerranée** ((0361) 771520 FAX (0361) 771835, Lot N6, Nusa Dua, offers a unique vacation experience. Three extensive buffet meals a day, all sports equipment and instruction and supervised activities for children (see FAMILY FUN, page 40 in YOUR CHOICE) plus a lively cabaret show every night, are provided for in the all-inclusive price. This is about the best of Club Med's Asian properties. Note that non-guests interested in savoring the distinctive Club Med style can come in for lunch or dinner and use all the facilities on a day-long or evening pass.

The **Grand Hyatt Bali** ((0361) 771234 FAX (0361) 772038, Box 53, Nusa Dua, opts for the grand hotel style, and has developed a swimming maze, including slides and chutes, to make up for a less than ideal beach that, nonetheless, takes up 650 m (710 yards) of coast. It is allied to its nearby conference center though, and so can be a bit institutional.

At the northern end of the resort, toward Tanjung Benoa, is the **Grand Mirage** ((0361) 771888 FAX (0361) 772148 E-MAIL gmirage@denpasar.wasantara.net.id, Jalan Pratama 74,

---

Painting from life is not typical of Balinese practice, though the island's painters have been influenced by western trends since the 1930s.

Tanjung Benoa. Next door to this is the **Grand Mirage Club** ((0361) 772147 FAX (0361) 772156 E-MAIL kbmbali@denpasar.wasantara.net.id WEB SITE grandmirage.com, Jalan Pratama 72, Tanjung Benoa, which offers full food and drink for an all-inclusive price. People who just want to take in the cabaret and drinks can buy four-hour passes here for US$12 and serious drinkers can make a good deal out of this. Such all-inclusive vacations can represent terrific value if bought overseas, but always run the danger that you'll never stray from the hotel to experience Bali in any more meaningful way.

On the southern edge of Nusa Dua is the Japanese-owned **Nikko Bali** ((0361) 773377 FAX (0361) 773388, Jalan Raya Nusa Dua Selatan, which has dramatic sea views.

Finally, overlooking Nusa Dua from a nearby hilltop is the only really desirable luxury hotel in Nusa Dua. This is the ultra-luxurious and exclusive **Amanusa** ((0361) 772333 FAX (0361) 72335 (rates for its 35 suites start at US$460), the sister resort of the Amandari at Ubud and the Amankila near Candi Dasa. The Amanusa is classically beautiful and you are treated like the royalty who may well prove to be your fellow guests.

Moderate

One of Nusa Dua's smallest beachfront hotels is the **Hotel Bualu** ((0361) 771310 FAX (0361) 771313, Box 6, Denpasar. It is well suited for children, and, like most of its more expensive neighbor hotels, has a PADI-certified diving instructor and free sporting facilities. Another is the **Tamen Sari Suite Hotel** ((0361) 773953 FAX (0361) 773954 E-MAIL tarisuit@indosat.net.id, Jalan Pratama 61B, Nusa Dua. Otherwise, in this price range, you'll have to look nearer to Tanjung Benoa where the best value is the **Rasa Sayang** ((0361) 771643, Jalan Pratama 88X, which offers straightforward accommodation with some rooms including air-conditioning.

Budget

There are not many inexpensive places to stay, but one stands out as offering a good atmosphere and value. That is the **Pondok Agung** ((0361) 771143, Jalan Pratama 99, Tanjung Benoa, a traditional *losmen* with *mandi* bathrooms but comfortable furnishings. Handily, should they be full (not in itself very likely) there is another, even less expensive, *losmen* right next door. That is the **Rasa Dua Homestay** ((0361) 772726, Jalan Pratama 98. The telephone number above is actually that of Baruna Water Sports, where the *losmen* owner works.

WHERE TO EAT

All of the Nusa Dua hotels have extensive restaurant facilities and are probably likely to beat any of the independent restaurants in the area. The biggest selection of restaurants are collected together in the Galleria Shopping Center to the south of the resort. Most aim to please everybody but end up rather bland. Of the better options **Sendok** ((0361) 772850 offers Swiss and German specialties, **Galih** ((0361) 775740 is a quasi-European pasta bar, and — perhaps the best of them all — the **Matsuri Japanese Restaurant** ((0361) 772267. All these are expensive — think European prices — but if you wander past early they offer discounts of 30% to 50% on the rates, perhaps out of embarrassment. As such they eventually offer reasonable value.

Apart from the Galleria — and the hotels' own very professional restaurants — there are a few restaurants scattered along Jalan Pratama that are worth a visit, including the **Taman Sari Thai Restaurant** ((0361) 773953 at No. 61B, Nusa Dua.

Those on a budget will find the southern region of Nusa Dua a taunting desert of irrigated lawns and long hot pavements, broken only by major hotels. But there are also a few restaurants that offer more conventionally-priced Balinese and European fare in the northern area of Tanjung Benoa. For those on a budget one option is the **Bola Bali** ((0361) 775490, Jalan Pratama Nusa Dua, which makes a sterling attempt at about four different culinary traditions without coming halfway to the prices charged on the other, beachfront, side of the road, or the rather cleaner and smarter **Warung Bali** ((0361) 775523, Jalan Pratama, Nusa Dua, right opposite the Grand Mirage Hotel.

How to Get There

Bemos travel to Nusa Dua from Denpasar's Tegal terminal, but it is unusual for Westerners to use them and, traveling through Kuta and the airport, they take time. They're not allowed into Nusa Dua itself, either, and will drop passengers at the main gates, still a long hot walk from any hotels or facilities. Taxi is easiest. It's not a pleasant drive as the dual carriageway road is busy and fast. Nusa Dua is clearly signposted from Denpasar and Jalan Ngurah Rai (Bypass). It is 11 km (seven miles) from the airport and 25 km (16 miles) from Sanur.

Excursions from Nusa Dua

The classic excursion from Nusa Dua is across the Bukit to **Ulu Watu Temple** (see TAKE IN A TEMPLE, page 13 in TOP SPOTS). About 30 minutes by car from Nusa Dua, this clifftop temple is among the most important in Bali, and the setting is spectacular — especially at sunset, when the cliffs are gently lit with the low evening light. Admission is Rp1,000, including sash and, for those wearing shorts, a sari. There is a nightly *kecak* fire-dance performance at 6 PM, at a cost of Rp15,000.

The area is not just important for its religious significance, however. It is also a Mecca for surfers all over the world. **Ulu Watu Surfing Beach** is six kilometers (four miles) to the north of the temple, along a quiet road that drops down between kapok trees and prickly pear hedges. At the end of the road pushy women will demand money for parking on what is merely the verge of a dead-end road but it is, perhaps, easiest to comply. Then some concrete steps drop into a dry valley. From here you can climb down a short bamboo ladder into the so-called cave (actually its roof has collapsed) that leads to the cove, or follow the path up to the line of *warung* and souvenir stalls that enterprising Balinese have established on the steep sides of the slope overlooking the ocean.

There's not much to be seen from the little cove itself, just to the left of where the cave meets the sea. The sand is gritty and the sea bed rocky, but at least it's a place to get wet and cool off, and someone may try to sell you a silver amulet.

The wonderful place is the highest of the *warung*. This is perched on the edge of a ridge running up the cliff and commands a stupendous view out over the incoming surf. The spectacle is extraordinary. The sea is spread out before you in all its majestic fury. Away to the right Mount Agung is outlined — on a good day — against the blue. You can sit there under the thatched roof of the *warung* and sip your iced fruit juice and watch the figures far below skimming along the great glassy slopes as if they were on skis, playing with the ocean like children in the vast lap of the gods. As the sun goes down, straight ahead of you, it shines through the waves like light coming through the green stained-glass windows of a cathedral.

JIMBARAN BAY

The village of Jimbaran straddles the road running south from close by the airport to Ulu Watu, and sprawls out toward the five-kilometer (three-and-a-half-mile) crescent of sand which is Jimbaran Bay. Just over 10 years ago this was a fishing beach virtually unknown to tourists, with a small flotilla of fish-

Poised above the surf, Ulu Watu Temple is especially beautiful at sunset.

ing boats providing an income through its important daily fish market. The beach, while beautiful, free of coral, and relatively safe from currents, never seemed to catch the imagination of the crowds who thronged to the other side of the airport. Somehow the village seemed immune to the rampant development rapidly sweeping across Bali.

Then two things happened. Firstly, some major hotels, on the run from the bustle — and soaring property prices — of Kuta, leap-frogged south of the runway, putting the village on the tourist map. This in itself wouldn't have made much of a difference, as most of the hotels, manicured in huge grounds, exist on a rather different plane to village life of fishing and religious observance. But then a handful of enterprising *warungs* built thatched shelters on the edge of the beach, and started to sell seafood fresh from the market, priced by the kilo and cooked over coconut husks. Gradually, plastic tables and chairs appeared on the sand, set out each evening to catch the sun as it set over the sea. The idea proved phenomenally popular. Indonesian and Western visitors liked the experience of eating simply-cooked fresh seafood against the sunset while they watched the planes land at Ngurah Rai's airstrip, built out to sea like some huge breakwater against the distant lights of Kuta and Denpasar. The simple economics of selling seafood priced by weight appealed first to Jimbaran fishermen surviving on reducing fish supplies and then, rather quickly, to many other Balinese from other parts of the island. Now there are probably a hundred *warungs* lining the beach in two main groupings, interspersed with beached boats and boat-builders. Through most of the day Jimbaran remains a sleepy place with few facilities for visitors, but as the sun drops the waterfront comes to rather hysterical life.

General Information

Jimbaran is too small to have any separate Tourist Information office, and in any case, Kuta is only a five-minute drive past the airport. There is a 24-hour medical clinic in Jimbaran, however: the **Jimbaran Clinic** ((0361) 701467, Jalan Ngurah Rai (Bypass) 95SS, Jimbaran. The conventional way for tourists to this part of Bali to get about is by *ocek*, small motorcycle taxis that, although they only take one Western passenger at a time, can often be seen transporting whole Balinese families. Foreign passengers are required to wear a crash helmet. Jimbaran is near enough to use the airport taxi service if required.

What to See and Do

There are no sights as such at Jimbaran, though the fish market, especially early in the morning, is always a colorful experience, and hours can be happily spent watching the comings and goings of *jukung* on the water's edge. This is a good place to watch the local boats being built, with the body of a *jukung* being carved out of a solid tree-trunk, with prow and gunwales added separately. In the central area of the beach, squeezed rather between the two main stretches of beach *warungs*, you'll see boats in every stage of their development. For guests of the major hotels in the area, entertainments are likely to be far more limited, confined to the immediate vicinity of their luxury villa, spa or pool. At every level the village is refreshingly free from vendors and is noticeably less stressed than either Kuta or Sanur.

Where to Stay

Most of the accommodation at Jimbaran Bay is aimed comfortably at the top of the market. The most important of all the hotels in the area is the **Jimbaran Bay**, run by the Four Seasons group, set well above the bay itself and to the south of the beach, but with fantastic views to compensate. This is a great place for honeymoons and for those interested in enjoying the spa facilities, with hot and cold soaking pools and full massage services. There are 147 villas, divided into seven village squares, and are all self-contained and large enough to live in. The food, particularly the seafood, is among the best on the island. This all comes at a cost, however, with villas US$525 upwards per night, and it is hard to suppress a rush of irritation to learn that Four Seasons have trademarked the phrase "Alternative Cuisine" which seems a tad presumptuous. Perhaps, as they own the copyright on any new culinary forms, their extra service of supplying airline food for their guests to carry home instead of risking eating on-flight meals is only their duty. For further details contact Jimbaran Bay ((0361) 701010 FAX (0361) 701020 WEB SITE www.fourseasons.com, Jimbaran 80361 (expensive).

Three kilometers (two miles) south of here is the second major hotel, the four-year-old **Ritz-Carlton** ((0361) 702222 FAX (0361) 701555 WEB SITE www.ritzcarlton.com, Jalan Mas Sejahtera, Jimbaran (expensive). This is so far out of the village that guests here only make the trip down to the waterfront if they're taking part in one of the expensive cooking courses. They have their own beach, a short drive south from the hotel, but mainly relax in the succession of pools that flow, with infinite horizons and a steady stream of waterfalls, down from the hotel's lobby. Comfort and privacy are what you get here, although with 340 rooms and suites it is privacy from the outside world of Bali, rather than privacy from other guests.

There are only three hotels that directly front Jimbaran Beach. They start, heading south, with the **Keraton Bali Cottages** ((0361) 701961 FAX (0361) 701991 E-MAIL german@denpasar.wasantara.net.id, Jalan Majapati, which caters mainly to German tour groups (expensive). Less ethnically-focused are the **Pansea Puri Bali** (701605 FAX (0361) 701320, Jalan Uluwatu, with just 41 rooms in cottage compounds (expensive), and the Bali **InterContinental** ((0361) 701888 FAX (0361)

High up on Bukit Badung, the Hotel Bali Cliff has a spectacular outlook over the Indian Ocean.

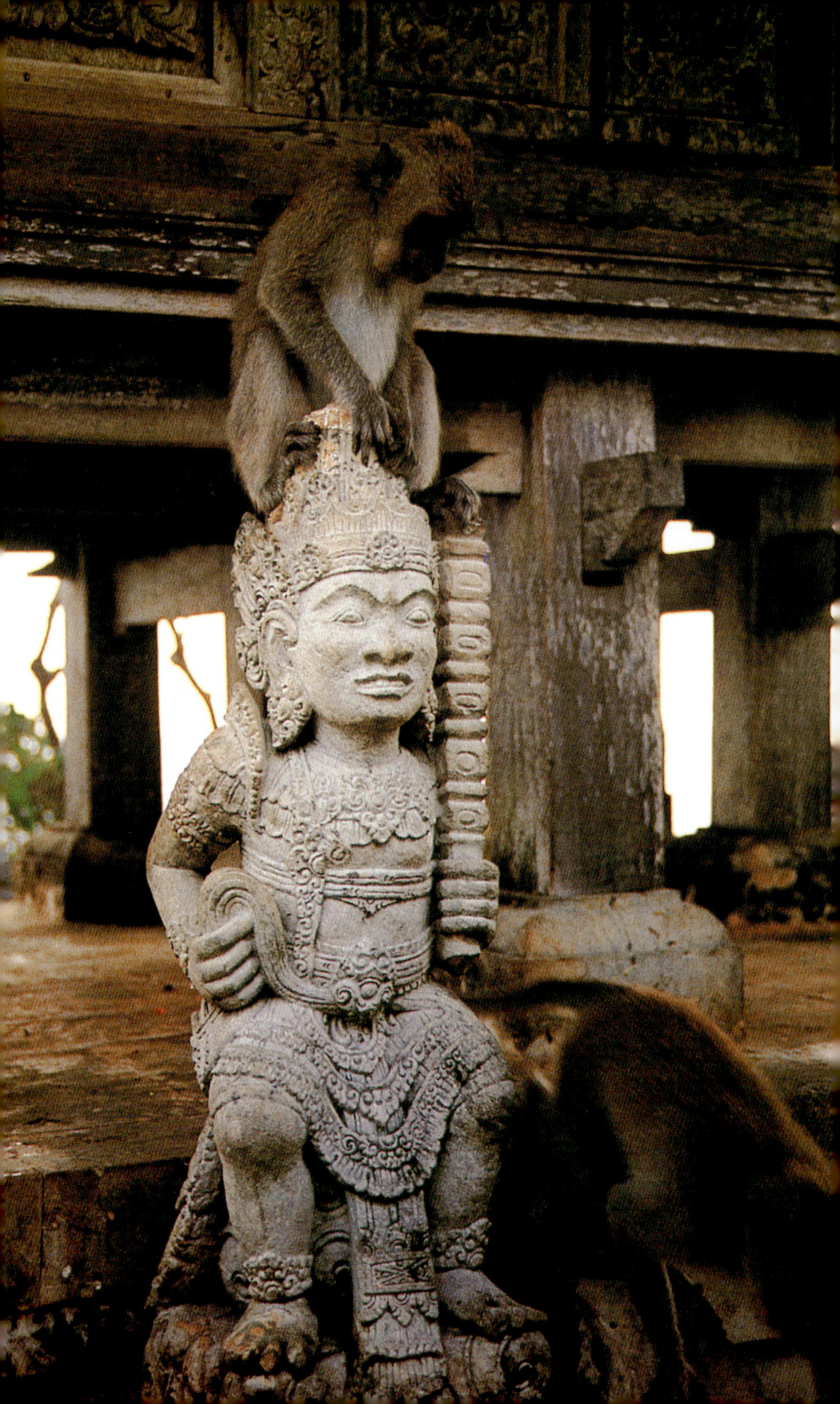

701777 E-MAIL bali@interconti.com, with views of the Bay from every room (expensive).

With their value inflated by their illustrious neighbors, even the humbler places here seem to charge beyond their facilities. The **Puri Bamboo** ((0361) 701377 FAX (0361) 701440 E-MAIL balipbh@indosat.net.id, Jalan Pengeracikan, Kedonganan, is 200 m (about 220 yards) from the beach but still charges more than you'd pay for similar properties in Kuta, Seminyak or Sanur (moderate).

On a budget, good luck. Perhaps one of the fishermen will open some new place. Well-positioned (on the waterfront), the far from exceptional, inexpensive **Netayan Jimbaran Restaurant and Accommodation** (/FAX (0361) 702253, Jalan Pantai Jimbaran 3, whose restaurant boasts of its "special European taste." It's clean enough though, and the roof terrace provides great views of the bay, for the price. Surfers favor the **Puri Indraprasta** ((0361) 701552, Jalan Uluwatu 28A, but it's hard to see why as it is basic, on the main road, and some way from the beach (inexpensive).

WHERE TO EAT

The Ritz-Carlton is rather far out of town to consider as a venue to dine out; the best place to eat is undoubtedly at one of the restaurants in the Jimbaran Bay Hotel. There are several well-respected restaurants sited, rather unromantically, on Jalan Ngurah Rai (Bypass). These include the **Café Latino** ((0361) 701880, which serves Italian food, with a disco on Fridays, and **Bali Edelweis** (772094, which for reasons best known to itself brings Austrian cuisine to the heart of Bali.

The obvious place to eat here, however, is the beachfront, with crowding *warungs* competing to entice with the freshest (often live) seafood. It's worth being cautious here: all the *warungs* have printed sheets with the price per kilo of their various dishes, but their costs differ wildly. On the same day I have seen lobster priced at Rp180,000 per kilo and Rp100,000 further down, with other *warungs*, even less helpfully, claiming to sell at "market rates." Check they're talking fish market rates, not gullible tourist rates.

Meanwhile, owners, managers, staff and even names of the *warungs* can change quickly. Currently good is **Antar Café** ((0361) 703382, Jalan Pantai Kedongan, who offer good-looking fish and lobster and reasonable prices, and the **Ramayana** ((0361) 702859, Jalan Pantai Kedongan, one of the longest established and popular establishments. But of course there are a hundred others, with names such as "Wendy's" and "Uganda," and choosing is half the fun. The *warungs* are open through the day but you'll be eating alone: they're far livelier at night.

Later on, most guests return home to Kuta or beyond, and the nightlife dies. The village pretty much goes to sleep, ready for the next day's fishing.

HOW TO GET THERE

Jimbaran is immediately to the south of Ngurah Rai International Airport, on the eastern neck of the Bukit Peninsula. Taxis from the airport or even Kuta are the best way to get here, and it is a logical place to stop on the way back to Kuta or Sanur after watching the sun set over Ulu Watu Temple.

OPPOSITE and ABOVE: Pura Luhur, Ulu Watu and its sacred monkeys.

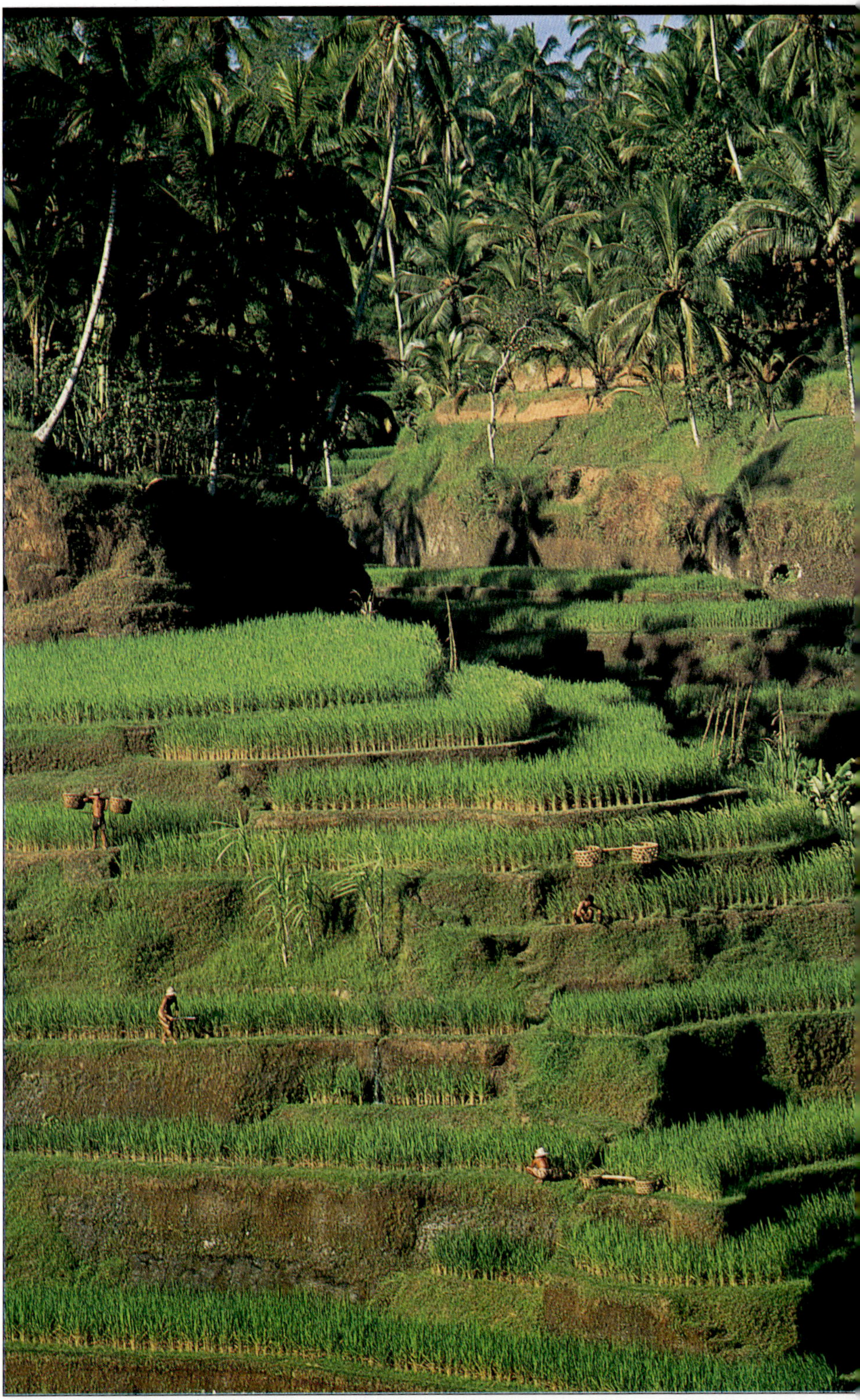

Ubud and the Bali Heartlands

UBUD

THE AREA NORTH OF THE MAIN COASTAL TOURIST RESORTS — and the capital — in many ways embodies the island's essence. Here is the intense rice cultivation on the banks of the fast-flowing rivers that rush down mountains, cutting earthy gorges as they do and providing for the irrigation that has always been the basis of the island's prosperity. This abundant water supply and the immensely fertile volcanic soils that it feeds are the key to Bali's ceaseless rice production, which continues regardless of season, so that the rainy season is as much an inconvenience as a blessing. The great lakes in the volcanic calderas ensure an endless water supply, and this in turn guarantee food production.

Famine, so common elsewhere in Asia, is in Bali only the product of political upheaval or volcanic eruption. The relatively new "miracle" rice produces three crops a year, and all stages of growth can be seen in the fields, providing varying tones of yellow and green that have so delighted painters.

This agricultural abundance has allowed Bali to develop its arts. Leisure time has never been in short supply, and with carving, painting and metalwork all originally dedicated to a religion that looked to the hills from which came the abundance, it can seem as if the whole formed a self-contained, beautiful and life-enhancing system. It was thus that many of the first visitors to the island regarded Bali.

Ubud is at the heart of it all. East Bali is lush too, but the plains are less extensive, there are many subsidiary ridges of hills, and the region is subject to earthquakes, albeit rare ones. North Bali is a mere coastal strip. The area of Bali south of Denpasar, now so prosperous on account of tourism, was not so long ago seen more or less as an arid waste. West Bali has always been considered a rocky, waterless and infertile wilderness. It is the area of central Bali to the south of the main volcanic range, the area around Ubud, that has always been the productive and most populated center of the island culture.

UBUD

Now very much at the heart of Bali's cultural life, Ubud has not always been so eminent. Historically it was ruled by the Sukawati family, who reigned over the area from a royal court 10 km (seven miles) to the south of the city. For 200 years these rulers patronized the arts, supporting dancers, artists, sculptors and puppeteers. When, in 1908, the Dutch took over the island, the Sukawati Kingdom was one of only two regional powers to be left untouched, and it became a focus for the national culture. The area became known to the West largely thanks to German artist Walter Spies, who settled here in 1928 and helped draw in a range of artists, anthropologists, and musicians. This influx of Western artists continued through the 1930s and gave a new impetus to the development of arts in the region, formalized by the foundation of the Pita Maha Arts Movement in 1936, which attracted adherents from all over the island to meetings and exhibitions. Although this movement died with Walter Spies in 1942, Ubud is still very much at the forefront of Balinese culture.

This long tradition of entertaining cultured Western visitors has set Ubud apart from the surf 'n' sand resorts in the south. It has range of accommodation to suit all budgets and many of the best restaurants in Bali, all within easy strolling distance of timeless rice paddies and idyllic rural scenes. It can satisfy most tastes: to some it is an upmarket resort where you'll find spiritual healers, aromatherapists and reflexologists; to others it is a place to enjoy the arts, while still more

ABOVE: Deer-like Balinese cattle being taken for a walk. RIGHT: At the house of Catalan artist Antonio Blanco, Ubud, one of several Western artists who made their homes in Bali.

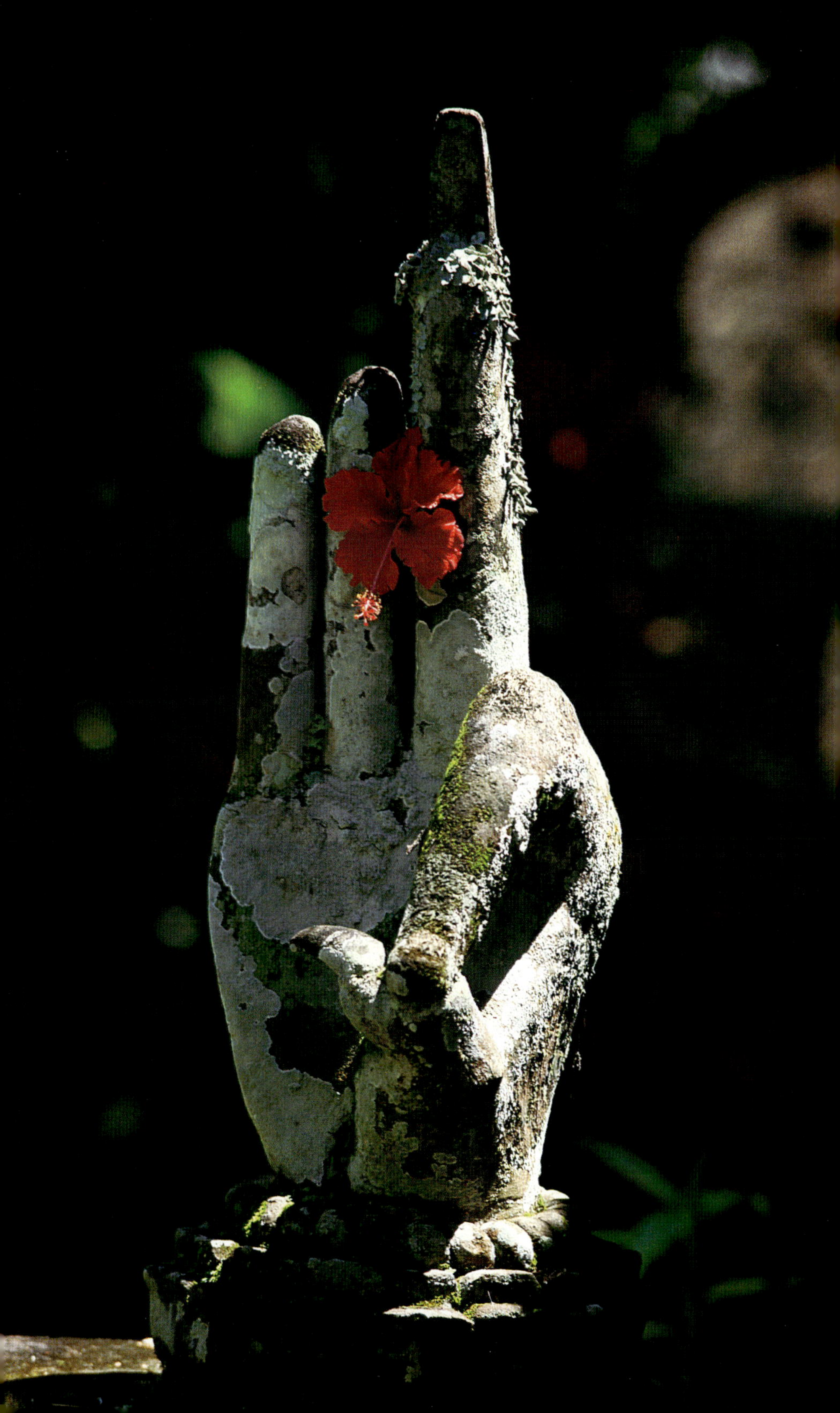

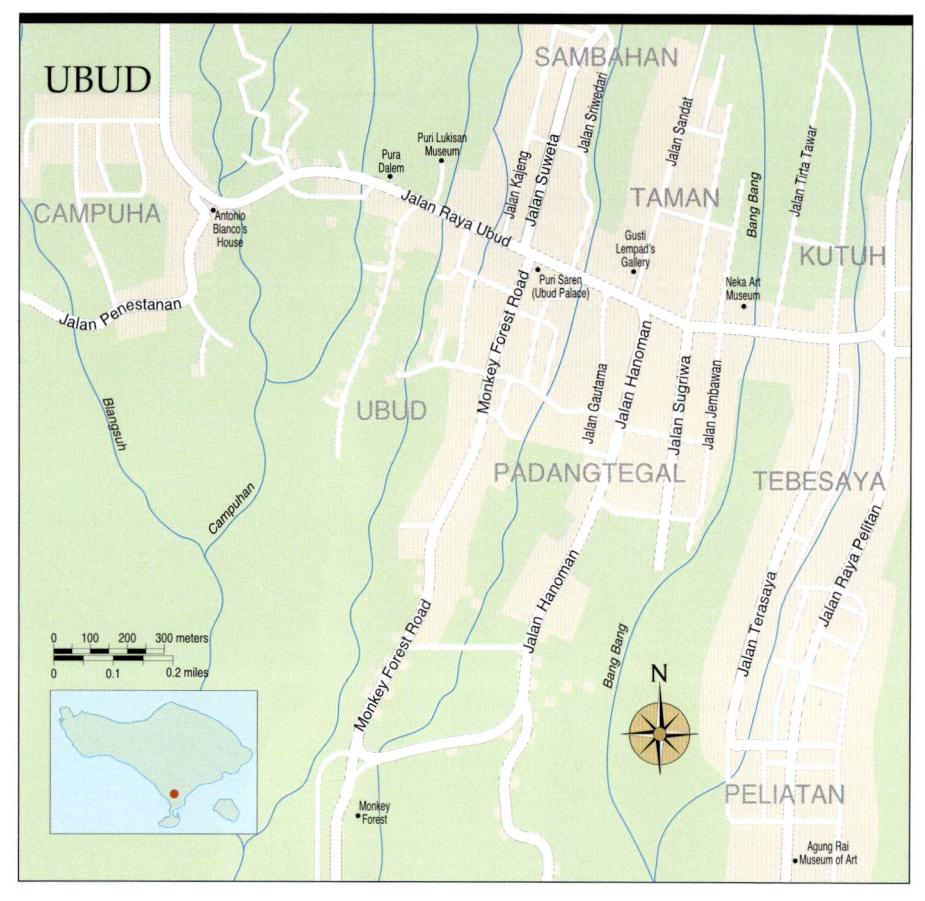

just find its gentle, relaxed pace of life a sympathetic environment to settle in to Bali. It's also well served with tourist-class shuttle buses that link Ubud with the rest of the island: there aren't many parts of Bali you can't reach from here in a day.

Ubud itself doesn't have the feeling of a town — more an extended village. Its long main street, running east to west, is on the main road to nowhere, and a relaxed, well-heeled ambiance pervades the place. You can begin the day with an expensive cappuccino, have your hair cut, or simply wander out along unmade paths to watch the rice farmers as they till the soil into terraced paddies of vermilion rice.

People read books in Ubud, unlock rental mountain bikes in the morning air, still remembering the *kecak* or *legong* dances they saw the previous evening, and positively wince at the thought of Kuta and the Hard Rock Café.

Ubud is the best place in Bali to see dance-dramas, to buy art or sculpture, and to simply absorb the local culture. These days, it is true, the Balinese seem, in the central streets at least, to be almost outnumbered by the Western visitors, but they retain their culture and dignity; and the tourist dollar, here, is more likely to go into the performing arts than into new shiny cars.

General Information

Bemos and shuttle buses stop in the center of Ubud, at the junction of Monkey Forest Road and Jalan Raya. This is where you'll find the **Ubud Tourist Office (** (0361) 973285, Jalan Raya; open 8 AM to 9 PM. Under the glass counter of the enquiry desk here you'll find a complete schedule of dance events. They also arrange tours around the island and sell tickets for the shuttle bus. There are plenty of other signs around town advertising "Tourist Information," but these are mere travel agents. Facing the tourist information office you'll find the market and the first people to rent you a mountain bike (costing around Rp10,000 per day). Whichever way you go down Jalan Raya you'll find ATM machines (the nearest is if you turn left) if you need to draw cash. There are also a number of cybercafés and fax bureaus, but the speed of connection, standard of computer and charges vary. One of the better ones is the **Darma Tourist Service** ((0361) 978410, at the junction with Monkey Forest Road and De Wisita Road.

Several hopeful taxi-drivers/guides will be quick to offer you their services, as will plenty of people wanting to rent you cars or motorcycles: there's not much to choose between them, but one possible operator near the tourist office is **Bakor Motor** ((0361) 973405, Jalan Suweta 34. Stroll far down Monkey Forest Road and you'll be offered solutions to any of your travel needs. This is at the heart of a looping one-way system which makes navigating around the city easy but, if you're driving, lengthy. It can be hard to find smaller houses and homestays, as the growth of the city has not been matched by the addition of any new street-numbers: refer to the map to locate your precise destination, as the addresses are rarely conclusive.

The 24-hour **Ubud Clinic** ((0361) 974911 FAX (0361) E-MAIL ubudclinic@ubudclinic.com WEB SITE www.ubudclinic.com, Jalan Raya Tjampuhan 36, is one of the best in the Bali. Their main business is stitching up people who've stepped into one of Ubud's many holes, where pavement slabs have been removed for some inexplicable reason. These holes drop about a meter (three feet) into drains, so watch your step: Lorne Blair, who produced and directed *The Ring of Fire* and coauthored the book of the same name, recounting his experiences over 10 years adventuring in Indonesia, died from complications after falling down one of Ubud's famous missing paving slabs. Although the Ubud Clinic has oxygen and IV drips, for major problems, of course, they'll rush you to the main hospital in Denpasar, half an hour down the road.

WHAT TO SEE AND DO

Ubud is a major center for traditional dance, art and culture in general. Some of the country's most respected galleries and most of its dance troupes are found here and in the surrounding area.

Dance and Drama

You can see the authentic dance-dramas of Bali in context at a temple festival, where the dances are performed, as they were intended, for the benefit of the gods. As these depend on the fiendishly complicated 210-day calendar and other local factors, you'll need the informed advice of a Balinese guide to track them down. But in Ubud, though the dances are being put on for your benefit, at least they are being done well, for connoisseurs and not for a mass audience.

The following schedule for dance performances in and around Ubud may have changed by the time you arrive in Bali, but it's unlikely. In its essential form it hasn't changed in many years. Most performances start at 7:30 PM and tickets are generally priced around Rp20-25,000.

Monday, there is a performance of the *legong*, preceded by other dances, at the Ubud Palace. At the same time, in nearby Bona Village, there is a *kecak* and Trance Dance, while at Ubud's Jaba Pura Padang Kerta, Padang Tegal Kelod, there are *barong* and *kris* dances.

Tuesday, see the Mahabharata Dance at Teges Village, three kilometers (two miles) from Ubud, the Ramayana Ballet in Ubud Palace, and several other dances elsewhere.

Wednesday, see the *wayang kulit* (shadow puppet plays) at Oka Kartini, the *legong* and *barong* dances at Ubud Palace, and a repeat of Monday's *kecak* dance in the same location as on Monday.

Thursday, it's the turn of the *gabor* dance at Ubud Palace and the *calonarang* dance at the village of Mewang, nine kilometers (six miles) away (transport from Ubud is provided for these out-of-town shows).

Friday, see another *barong* dance performed by a different troupe at the Ubud Palace, a *legong* dance at Peliatan Village (two kilometers or just over a mile from Ubud) and a *kecak* and Trance Dance at the Pura Dalem.

Saturday, there is another *legong* program at Ubud Palace from a different troupe plus a *calonarang* dance (as on Thursday).

Sunday, see the *kecak* dance repeated as for Monday, and another *kecak* in Ubud itself.

The full list can be obtained from the Ubud tourist information office on Jalan Raya. This list is useful, indeed vital. They also sell tickets.

In the daytime, all these accomplished performers work in restaurants, shops or in the fields. These Ubud performances are genuine folk dramas, like the European medieval morality plays. You see the Monkey King or Shiva, but he's really the local butcher or candlestick-maker.

Try It Yourself

Having seen so much of Balinese culture, don't miss the chance of trying out some of the skills involved yourself. The **Dwi Bhumi** ((0818) 351393 (cell) offers day and half-day courses in various aspects of the culture, including carving and painting *wayang* puppets, singing and dancing, cookery and playing *gamelan* music. A half-day course costs from Rp45,000. They will pick participants up from the Bali 3000 Internet Café, Jalan Raya, or you can make your own way to their base at Melati Cottages (/FAX (0361) 975088, Penestanan. Other music courses are arranged by **Ganesha Bookshop** ((0361) 976339, Jalan Raya. If you'd like to try your hand at Balinese cuisine the **Casa Luna** (see WHERE TO EAT, page 159) runs courses. To learn how to make batik **Nirwana Batik**, Jalan Gautama, near the tourist board, will be happy to help: in a two-day course costing Rp60,000 you'll get to make your own three-color batik, but longer courses are available.

Art Museums and Galleries

There are four important museums exhibiting Balinese paintings in Ubud. The **Neka Art Museum** ((0361) 975074 FAX (0361) 975639, Jalan Raya Ubud (9 AM to 5 PM Rp10,000), has 13 rooms spread around airy pavilions overlooking a river valley. It orders its material into styles and so is the place to start if Balinese art still seems either uniform or a confusion of contrasting tendencies. The museum is about one kilometer (just over a half mile) beyond the bridge by Murni's Warung; carry straight on up the road on the other side of the river, and it's on your right.

Puri Lukisan Museum ((0361) 975136, Jalan Raya Ubud (9 AM to 5 PM; Rp10,000), the oldest (founded in 1954), is in the center of the village and contains 10 rooms — seven in the main building and three in a separate gallery on the left as you arrive. All styles of Balinese art are on show, though less neatly categorized than at the Neka. Nevertheless, here you can see many paintings crucial to the history of Balinese art and the changes brought about by the arrival of artists from Europe between the wars.

More useful still is the display in a separate building, a short walk across a paddy field (follow a sign labeled "exhibition" pointing right as you come out of the main museum). There are a large number of pictures for sale here. As they are by a wide variety of artists, and have fixed prices marked on the back of their labels, a wander around can give you a fair idea of the going rate for Balinese art and the prices you might consider reasonable should you want to negotiate with the local painters themselves in their private galleries elsewhere in the district.

Newly opened, the sprawling **Agung Rai Museum of Art** (ARMA) ((0361) 976659 WEB SITE www.chica.com/arma, Jalan Peliatan, Peliatan (9 AM to 6 PM, Rp10,000), is a good place to see art at the permanent exhibition and learn more about Balinese culture in general. There are *gamelan* and dance shows at all times, including every Sunday at 7:30 PM. The museum has a magnificent collection of work by artists who have lived and painted in Ubud. The exhibit here formed part of the private collection of the art dealer Agung Rai, until he mounted this museum complex as a cultural counter-blast to "young men calling out on the streets after Western women and drinking beer." There is a fine restaurant and a hotel under the same management as well as a center for education in dance and drama. If, after seeing this interesting collection, you want to buy something of quality, there are also paintings for sale.

A final gallery is dedicated to art by women — generally underrepresented in Balinese painting. The **Seniwati Gallery** ((0361) 975485 WEBSITE www.seniwatigallery .com, Jalan Sriwedari 2B, Banjar Gaman, has a permanent collection, changing exhibits and a number of works for sale. Most interesting perhaps is the work of Ni Made Suciarmi, who specializes in the ancient *Kamasan* style of painting, where the canvas is primed with rice starch, polished with a seashell and then painted with pigments ground from stone.

An Artist's House

If museums tend to make you cross-eyed with their bewildering variety, the houses of several of the early influential Western artists who made their homes in Bali are open to the public. Most impressive is the most recent: Catalan artist **Antonio Blanco's House**, four kilometers (two miles) out of town toward Payangan, is still the artist's home. Erotic illuminated poems hang beside fantasy portraits of the painter's Balinese wife, but the house itself, with a huge dome, gilded sculptures and over-the-top decor, is the main attraction. This gives an idea of what Ubud and Bali once were, both for him and for the other expatriate artists who made it their home. A photograph of Blanco talking to Michael Jackson hangs in the reception area, where you will pay the Rp10,000 entrance fee if you feel his ego (he calls himself "The Dali of Bali") needs any further support. Bear in mind he is still resident and you might have to talk to him. The house is open daily from 9 AM to 5 PM. The former home of the far more influential Walter Spies is now the **Hotel Tjampuhan** on Jalan Raya.

While almost swamped by this influx of Westerners, one Balinese artist did manage to squeeze in an open house of his own. I Gusti Nyoman Lempad, a versatile artist who

---

Music and dance are an essential part of life in Ubud. OPPOSITE: *Gamelan* musicians accompanying *legong* dancers. ABOVE: The popular *kris* or sword dance.

died here in 1978 at an age of approximately 116, has **Gusti Lempad's Gallery** on Jalan Sandat (open 9 AM to 5 PM, free admission), but most of the pictures are by more recent artists and for sale.

Ubud Palace

Just across from the tourist information office, Ubud Palace (9 AM to 5 PM daily, Rp10,000), also known as the Puri Saren Palace, is well worth a stroll. Parts of it are used as a hotel, and others are given over to dance performances, but the courtyards and temples still retain much of the grace you'd expect from the heart of a major Balinese Kingdom, even if it ceased to operate as the administrative heart in 1940. Next door is the Pura Pamerajaan Sari Cokorda Agung, which is where the royal family stored their regalia, and it's an atmospheric place, especially early, before the crowds arrive, or lit by the reflected glories of light shining on a troupe of traditional dancers as they go through their graceful movements. Outside, an impressively grotesque set of statues portray the many gods of the Hindu religion.

The Sacred Monkey Forest Sanctuary

A regular fixture on the tour-bus route is the Sacred Monkey Forest Sanctuary (open during daylight hours; Rp10,000) at the end of Monkey Forest Road, within walking distance of the tourist office and a surprising thing to find in the middle of town. The sanctuary itself is small, and although the entrance, where you buy a bunch of bananas, is impressively overgrown with huge fig trees, as you walk into the sanctuary the trees thin out and man-made terracing and landscaping reminds you that this is in the heart of a city. The effect is strengthened by the fact you're soon likely to be mugged by one or more of the 125 resident Balinese macaque monkeys. They are determined and observant and you don't get any peace until your food supply is exhausted. It's wise to treat the monkeys with respect, and not just because they're very important in the Balinese culture: they also have quick, sharp teeth.

Once relieved of your bananas, there are three holy temples that can be visited, and there are a number of sculptures (and graves) scattered around the cobbled pathways.

Lay Out, Relax

If all these galleries and museums start getting to you, lay out and relax for a traditional — or not-so-traditional — massage. Some of the most luxurious hotels have their own spa and massage, but for a cut-price version of even higher quality, visit **Nirvana** ((0812) 394-6702 (cell), Monkey Forest Road. Their massages start at a very reasonable US$5, for which you get an excellent half-hour massage, a shower and a cup of tea. They also do the full range of beauty and health treatments offered by the international spas but at a fraction of the price. Another specialist place for massage as well as haircuts, pedicures, etc., is quietly set among the rice fields: the **Tri Nadi Health Center** ((0361) 977934, Jalan Bisma 69, with *mandi lulur*, for instance, taking an hour and a half and costing Rp65,000. Their prices are low perhaps because they're well off the beaten track. The oldest herbal treatment center in Ubud is **Nur Salon** ((0361) 975352, Jalan Hanoman, which specializes in *mandi lalur*. Reservations essential. Taking it rather more seriously the **Mentari Massage Centre** ((0361) 974001, Anoman 1, Jalan Raya, is run by a well-respected Balinese healer.

More medicinal massages can be found up the road at the **Ubud Sari Health Resort** ((0361) 974393, Jalan Kajeng 35, who offer Reike, Shiatsu and reflexology along with the full range of mud and mineral baths; prices start at about US$10 and they also have lectures in their amphitheater. For personal yoga training contact **Sri Jane** ((0812) 398-5048 E-MAIL sriaurora@hotmail.com, a fully-qualified United Kingdom expatriate.

A big step further are the activities at the **Daya Putih School** ((0361) 975467 WEB SITE dayaputih@tripod.com, Jalan Andong 1, who, for around US$85 per day, teach breathing techniques and meditation as part of their own non-contact martial art. If the thought of that makes you weary, there's a public meditation room at the **Meditation Shop**, Monkey Forest Road.

Active Ubud

The River Agung, to the west of Ubud, is where Bali's whitewater rafters venture out into the rapids. Tickets can be bought at any of Ubud's travel agents. There are two companies here: one of the oldest is **Sobek** ((0361) 287059 E-MAIL sobek@denpasar.wasantara.net.id and the other is the **Spirit of Adventure** ((0361) 973405. Costs are about US$60 per day.

Several operators offer specialized walking tours. The first to do so was Birdwatching Walks, started by expatriate Englishman and leading ornithologist Victor Mason and conducted, if not by the man himself, by his longtime secretary. They can be contacted through the **Beggar's Bush** ((0361) 975009 or (0812) 391-3801 (cell), by the bridge, Tjampuhan. You can also do a three- to four-hour **Herb Walk** ((0361) 975051, with a cup of herb tea thrown in. There are **Downhill Mountain Bike Tours** ((0361) 975557 organized by Bali Cultural Tours, which take riders through paddies to temples and promise not to make you pedal uphill. A full day including fees, breakfast and lunch costs Rp360,000. Another operator is Bali **Bintang Tour** ((0361) 975992, Jalan Raya Ubud, opposite the market, who drive cyclists to Mount Batur and let them ride back to Ubud through the dropping terraces at a cost of US$40 per person, including bike rental.

You can even, surprisingly, go surfing from Ubud — and it not only costs less than similar courses at Kuta, it offers a much better chance of getting you up and on your feet. Courses are booked at the **Café Bukit Bamboo** ((0818) 550725 (cell) FAX (0361) 974338, Jalan Rayan Sanggingan, and leave at 7:30 AM for a full day on the beach, including breakfast and lunch, for only US$45. Unlike the coastal operators, this surf school starts beginners on smooth waters so they can master the vital art of paddling the board correctly. Therefore, as the owner Patrick Flanagan asserts "everyone we teach gets to stand up on their first day, usually on their second or third wave."

Shopping

The streets of central Ubud are lined with shops, often of very high quality. There's even a small Ralph Lauren store catering mainly to Japanese office workers. There are, of course, innumerable shops offering sarongs, wooden fish mobiles and woven bits of luggage and furniture, but there are also some outstanding outlets where individual designs of jewelry and sculpture are imaginatively — and expensively — displayed.

The market is one of the best places to browse and compare the different standards of workmanship and design, and this is by the junction of Jalan Raya and Monkey Forest Road, a few paces from Tourist Information. Many of the endless woven place mats, brightly colored wooden mobiles and puzzles, and vivid sarongs start to look almost mundane when seen in such profusion. But don't worry: they travel well, are very inexpensive and improve hugely on your return home. The market improves out of all recognition when, once every three days, a traditional produce market swamps the tourist tat. Near here, on Jalan Raya, Ary's Bookshop has newspapers and books from around the world. For paintings and carvings, good places to look are the **Agung Rai Fine Art Gallery**, Jalan Peliatan, Peliatan, and **Munut's Gallery**, Jalan Raya, the **Neka Gallery** (not to be confused with the Neka Museum, although the same family is involved) is opposite the GPO on Jalan Raya.

For pure browsing, nothing beats a stroll past the many small, specialized shops that line Monkey Forest Road. Woven place mats, painted fish mobiles, sarongs and batiks paint vivid colors onto every verge. As an artist's colony since the 1930s, there are undeniable European influences, and you're as likely to find Chez Monique as Warung Wayan. When you do actually come across Café Wayan on Monkey Forest Road, check out **Archipelago**, just opposite, for clothes, jewelry and housewares. Whatever the cultural background, however, some of Bali's finest creations are to be found here. **Tugen** ((0361) 973161 WEB SITE www.balitrade.com, Jalan Hanoman 44, has a good collection of carvings and sculptures. The Ubud artists working in silver and precious stones produce many works which compare well with the finest international craftsmen and artists, and the upmarket jewelers and galleries in the center of town are kept on their toes by the knowledge that it's an easy stroll for their customers to reach the next competitor. This usually keeps prices attractive to hard-currency spenders. Follow Jalan Raya west to the Campuhan region and the art element gets stronger: check out **Seni Echo**, Jalan Campuan 18, for some revolutionary uses of papier-mâché in art and furniture. As with buying art or sculpture, the best advice is to see the major galleries listed above to give yourself a smattering of education and then let your taste do the judging.

Where to Stay

It may come as a surprise to those who only see Bali as a beach destination that some of the very finest hotels in Indonesia are found in Ubud and the surrounding area. Bali as a whole is a fashionable destination, and even those who don't know where it is — or that it's part of Indonesia — are happy to pay handsomely for a slice of the Balinese dream. The top end of the market, for better or worse, seeks to provide the quiet and the sense of exclusivity these travelers will be cocooned in. But, wonderfully, Bali has accommodation and facilities to appeal to travelers on any budget, and the choice extends to the least expensive levels. There are 250 guest houses in the Ubud area, with more coming on stream all the time: this is only a selection of the best.

Expensive

The most expensive hotels are situated just outside the main town, in the exclusive village of Sayan (pronounced, and very occasionally spelled, Sayang), six kilometers (four miles) west of Ubud. They line up along the Agung River, with views across to the terraced paddies, and each strives to outdo the other in sheer luxury. Queen of the bunch is without doubt the most southerly. The **Four Seasons Hotel** ((0361) 977577 FAX (0361) 977588 WEB SITE www.fourseasons.com, Sayan (starting at US$375), which is not only the newest but also the most beautifully designed and run. The hotel cascades down the slopes of the Agung River Valley in tiers of lotus pools, reflecting the rice paddies opposite. The spa here specializes in Ayurvedic therapies, but most of the guests are on honeymoon: the place is littered with chairs set neatly out in pairs, sometimes occupied by quiet couples from the 46 private villas terraced onto the hillside.

A few hundred meters to the north, but safely out of sight, the **Amandari** ((0361) 975333 FAX (0361) 975335 E-MAIL amanres@indosat.net.id, Box 33, Sayan (starting from US$600), has views of an upstream kink in the river valley. Each suite has a walled garden, and many have a private pool. The ambiance is relaxed and even informal, at least until you have to settle up at the end of your stay.

A kilometer (just over half a mile) north again, the Australian-owned **Kupu Kupu Barong** ((0361) 975476 FAX (0361) 975079, Sayan, has 19 villas (starting from US$450). This is another ultra-luxurious hideaway organized on the same principles and sharing a view of the same river. It has a particularly fine restaurant.

North again from Kupu Kupu Barong for almost another kilometer there's the larger **Chedi** ((0361) 975963 FAX (0361) 975968 E-MAIL chediubd@ghmhotels.com WEB SITE www.ghmhotels.com, Desa Melinggih Kelod, Payangan, with beautiful rooms in two-story blocks, plus top-ranking suites with baths surrounded by carp pools. As a larger establishment it manages to offer similar facilities as its more exclusive neighbors at a rather lower cost. If you want to stay in any of the above, consider buying a travel package including flights before you leave home, as this will almost certainly end up costing less.

Moderate

For moderately priced accommodation in Ubud itself, beginning from the Campuhan end, the area down by the two bridges and Murni's Warung, there is the **Hotel Tjamphuan** ((0361) 975368 FAX (0361) 975137, Jalan Raya, Campuhan. On the site of Walter Spies first-ever home-stay in Ubud this long-established bungalow hotel sits on the steep, sloping bank of the river. A path zigzags down and there are bungalows dotted around at various levels. It has a tennis court and swimming pool. It aims to be somewhat exclusive, but these days finds itself out-

Rice terraces near Ubud. Bali's intricate terracing system, is best seen in the center and east of the island.

classed in the frantic Ubud scramble toward super-exclusivity.

In the center of Ubud, close to the *puri* and the intersection with the Monkey Forest Road, are two mid-priced places offering good value for money. Sited at another former artist's home is **Han Snel's Siti Bungalows** ((0361) 975699 FAX (0361) 975643, Jalan Kajeng. A short way down a lane, this is a pleasant place with an adjacent restaurant and cocktail bar of the same name. Simply graceful rooms, scattered in traditional self-contained chalets, are available at the **Ubud Inn** ((0361) 975071 FAX (0361) 975188, E-MAIL ubudinn@indosat.net.id, Monkey Forest Road. Rooms with air-conditioning cost a little more.

Budget

There are literally hundreds of home-stays in Ubud. This doesn't actually mean you're sharing a bathroom or kitchen: these are homes where a walled courtyard contains several family bungalows — and a few temples in most cases. Unlike more expensive establishments, breakfast is invariably included, usually consisting of a banana pancake and a bowl of fresh fruit.

In the center there is a slew of budget home-stays for just over the floor price of US$5 per night. They are inexpensive and convenient and are often run by artists or sculptors — or, at least, picture-framers — and offer a far closer involvement with the people of Ubud than the faintly commercial smiles of more polished operators. Invariably they offer self-contained chalets within a family courtyard that includes family temples of their own, and you wake in the morning to find offerings placed, on your behalf, outside your door. Some are very central, of which one of the best is **Alit House** ((0361) 973284, 64 Monkey Forest Road. Although in the heart of the city, it is beautifully quiet with a gallery of art lining the footpath into the home. South down Monkey Forest Road past the town football pitch and the **Gherhana Sari Art Shop** ((0361) 975392 offers home-stays in another quiet quarter. There are plenty more to choose from outside the town center, especially south along Jalan Hanoman, where you'll find **Brata 1** ((0361) 975598, Padang Tegal, which even provides hot water, and **Wayan Family** (no telephone), Padang Tegal 52, Jalan Hanoman, which is even cheaper.

Some provide quiet oases in the heart of the town, but Ubud is surrounded by rice-paddies, and for a couple of dollars more you can stay out among the growing rice in a timeless atmosphere that can't be matched by the center. A good place to look is just west of the tourist office: cross the river on Jalan Raya and turn left up an unmade road called Jalan Bisma. There are several along here. One of the first you'll pass is the **Menara Café** ((0361) 975142, Jalan Bisma; it has a light and airy restaurant, strangely almost always empty. It's nearest to town though, so you won't feel fully rural. There are more: just watch their paths snake off on either side. Most edge up toward the "moderate" price category. A few hundred yards further my favorite is called, simply, **Vera** ((0361) 975960, Jalan Bisma, reached by a long snaking path between paddies. It has just three guest rooms, is sparkling clean, and very inexpensive. Further still along Jalan Bisma and a long side road leads down to **Bucu View** ((0361) 975976 FAX (0361) 975082, which is set in a private valley, all palmed and lush, over a waterfall. It has great views and a swimming pool, but after breakfast you've a longish walk for your next meal as, like many home-stays, it doesn't have a restaurant and the nearest café is fairly distant.

These home-stays won't be as convenient as those in the town center, and will usually cost a little more, but tend to have a village network that supplies most immediate needs. Jalan Bisma, for example, has a couple of local shops selling essentials and luxuries, a massage clinic, and a cybercafé, all in the middle of the countryside. It's hard, after a while, to force yourself back into the buses, minibuses and traffic chaos that is daytime Ubud. A stay among the rice paddies is as much a part of the Ubud experience as any number of museums.

Some people still come to Ubud for a short visit, get to know people, find places to stay far from the tourist trails, and live on for months virtually as part of local families.

Where to Eat

Many of the most expensive restaurants so characteristic of Ubud share the same features — homemade cakes, European-style bread, tiled floors, antique wooden doors, a view of a lotus pond or a river gorge, original paintings on the walls — and an assumption of superiority over all the others.

For the most luxurious meals, head out to Sayan to the **Four Seasons Hotel** (see above), where, if you have a reservation, you'll be able to treat yourself to a meal and complement the experience with a good, if expensive, European wine.

There are a number of established, if fairly expensive, restaurants along Jalan Raya. The first upmarket eatery in Ubud was the **Café Lotus** ℂ (0361) 975660, Jalan Raya. It is almost opposite the tourist office, and the ambiance makes up for the standard of the food and the price of the bill. Pink flowers stretch their necks like flamingos in the pond, and music chosen with discretion (no Vivaldi's "Four Seasons" here) plays unobtrusively. The menu still offers wheat bread, salads with olive oil dressing, freshly made pasta with mushrooms, and strawberry tart, but prices keep creeping upwards. The same group runs better restaurants elsewhere.

Other places in the center of Ubud include the **Casa Luna** ℂ (0361) 977409, Jalan Raya Ubud, who serve good Italian food in elegant surroundings. More importantly, they also offer a free shuttle bus out to their satellite restaurant, **Indus**, where you can enjoy pesto among the rice paddies — always a highlight for newcomers to the region, and faily reasonably priced. **Ary's Warung** ℂ (0361) 975063, Jalan Raya, serves what they describe as "Balinese Fusion" while also playing mellow jazz.

Too chic now for its former clientele, like so many places in Ubud, **Murni's Warung** ℂ (0361) 975233, west along Jalan Raya where the old suspension and modern road bridges cross the river in Campuhan, occupies four levels. It offers Indonesian and Western specialties — look for unexpected items such as vichyssoise and gazpacho, as well as "Upper Elk Valley authentic hamburgers." Murni's also stocks souvenirs and books on Bali, and a collection of art and sculpture from around the archipelago that, at times, approaches museum quality. It is owned by the publisher of an excellent map-guide, "Bali Pathfinder," and opens from 9 AM to 11 PM. Murni's lower levels drop down near the river, letting you eat in peaceful and beautiful surroundings. Prices here are reasonable.

The **Nomad Wine Bar and Restaurant** (moderate), Jalan Raya, further down the main street in the direction of Denpasar, is a pleasant place, open from 8 AM until the last diners have finished their beer, and sometimes has live music.

Many more rewarding — and less expensive — experiences can be found by a simple stroll down Monkey Forest Road. After 100 m (110 yards) you'll find the friendly **Gayatri**, which offers a limited range of rather ordinary European, Mexican and Balinese food in airy surroundings: if it's hot, head upstairs for air and views. The owner offers a guide service with car and simple accommodation. Left into Jalan Dewi Sita and there's good Western food (though the local dishes are a bit ordinary) and the best expresso in Ubud, at the inexpensive **Tutmak Warung Kopi** ℂ (0361) 975754, Jalan Dewi Sita.

Further down Monkey Forest Road, past the football pitch, and prices go up a little bit, but so does the quality. There's delicious Thai cuisine, at very reasonable cost, at the **Thai Restaurant and Bar** ℂ (0361) 977484, with lots of low, Thai-style tables — but a scatter of conventional Western seating as well. The green chicken curry, their most frequently ordered dish, is served in a coconut shell. Next door, the **Lotus Lane** ℂ (0361) 975357, serves fairly expensive but totally

---

The lotuses that give their name to one of Ubud's upmarket restaurants.

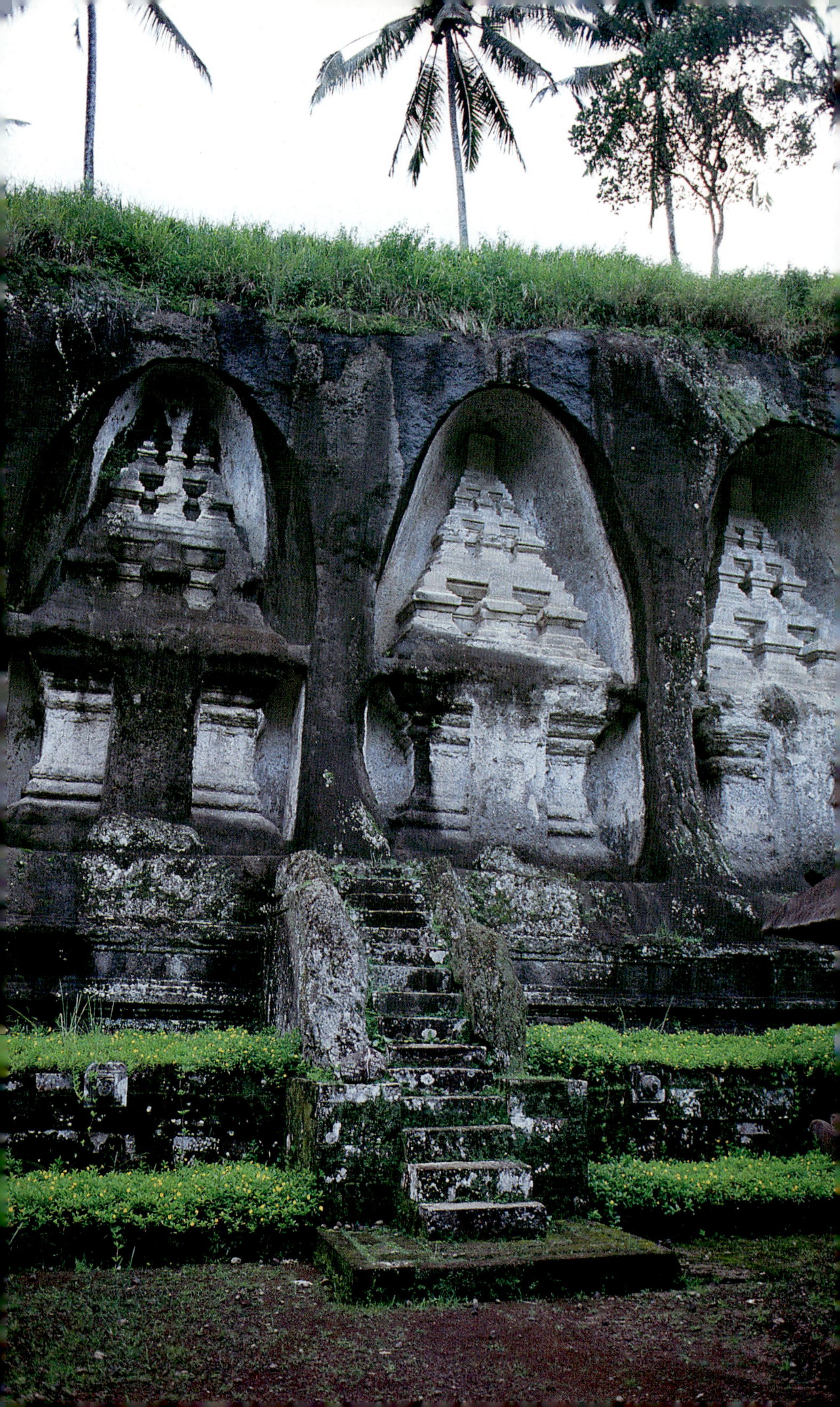

authentic Italian cuisine among water-features. Don't order their wine though: the markup is huge even on domestic brands. Nearby is the **Café Wayan** ((0361) 975447, Monkey Forest Road. The chef trained in Thailand and California and takes his food very seriously. So do his clients: in the evening reservations are needed, but try for a space at lunchtime.

Eating cheaply is no problem in Ubud. Many of the *losmens* down along the Monkey Forest Road have small restaurants attached to them where you can eat well for under US$3.

Nightlife

Ubud is not known for the rowdiness of its nightlife. After darkness falls, visitors tend to go to *gamelan* concerts, traditional dances or shadow-puppet displays, and these cultural pursuits often seem to rather knock the stuffing out of its audiences. Early evening places include the friendly **Café Bukit Bamboo** ((0818) 550725 (cell), Jalan Rayan Sanggingan, has one of the finest collection of early (1930s) American blues and jazz records you'll find in Asia, even after 1,700 LPs were lost some years ago in a fire. You'll find a sprinkling of approachable expat drinkers here, unless they're in **Nuri's Warung**, some 25 m (30 yards) up the road toward Ubud. A few bars, such as the very central **Putra Bar** ((0361) 975570, Monkey Forest Road, show videos, advertised nightly on a blackboard, starting at about 6:30 PM, but this bar is much better attended later on, when it goes on to have live music nightly, with the reggae nights being by far the most popular. The music itself leaves a lot to be desired but the atmosphere is good.

The other notable venue in the town center is the **Jazz Café** ((0361) 976594, Jalan Sukma 2, a magnet for Ubud's smarter expats and upwardly-mobile locals who gather for the live music and arty ambiance. It's likely to have the best live jazz you'll find away from the coast. Live cover bands also play at **Exiles** ((0361) 974842, Jalan Pengosekan Kaja, from about 9 PM, and although this is a fair way from the center it can be lively. Civic regulations insisting that every-

one closes by — or at least near — midnight cramp the nightlife scene still further, and the only place to get anywhere near pushing this boundary is the British-run **Funky Monkey**, Monkey Forest Road, usually gets well underway by 11 PM and, especially on Thursdays, can be heaving by midnight dancing to music from all over the world. Otherwise it is often empty, but hey, at least it's open and enthusiastic.

How to Get There

Bemos from Denpasar to Ubud leave from the Batubulan terminus, usually charging Rp2,000 for individual passengers (not charter). Shuttle buses link the Tourist Office directly to most other major towns in Bali: there are six a day to Kuta, for example, and five to Sanur. The two main companies are **Cahaya Sakti Utama Tour and Travel** ((0361) 975520, or **Perama** ((0361) 974772, though the latter is also handled by the Tourist Office. It's barely an hour's drive north from Sanur, and a little more from Kuta. It's easiest to use Jalan Ngurah Rai (Bypass). If driving yourself follow signposts for Gianyar and finally you'll see signs for Ubud, turning left at Sukawati.

EXCURSIONS EAST FROM UBUD

While travel to the area west of Ubud is complicated by the sheer gorge of the Arung River, which few bridges traverse, the area to the east is easily accessible and particularly rich in archaeological and historic sites. The following takes in the most interesting of these sites in a round-trip tour. Note that to do justice to all of these places in a single day would be, in the Balinese climate, a near impossibility, but these can be reached easily on a self-drive tour by car or motorbike. If you'd rather look around with a well-informed guide, various combinations are offered from the Tourist Office in the center of town, with full-day set-departure tours costing in the region of Rp60,000.

The great rock tombs at Gunung Kawi, situated on the valley floor of the Pakrisan River, are probably 1,000 years old and thus testify to a formal culture on the island long before the Majapahit invasion.

Tegalalang, Pujung and Sebatu

Leaving the center of Ubud on the road that leads eastwards (towards Denpasar), keep a lookout for a sign to Pujung (15 km or just over nine miles) away. This is an attractive road, scenic in a typically Balinese way and brimming with artists' workplaces and sales stalls.

On the way to Pujung, you pass through Tegalalang, a small center for the production of painted, softwood carved statues, usually depicting fruit or plants. As you drive up the road, you will pass small shops, each specializing in one particular form or style. At Pujung, the main occupation of the populace is the manufacture of the banana tree carvings to be seen at tourist centers all over the island, and increasingly in many places elsewhere in Asia as well.

Turn right at Pujung and descend to the bottom of the valley where, at Sebatu, there are some attractive public baths. From there the road climbs again — past many shops offering painted softwood carvings of various kinds — to the junction where you bear left, after one kilometer (just over half a mile), for Tampaksiring.

Tirta Empul

The **Sukarno Palace** at Tampaksiring is reached after climbing a good number of steps. The palace — a 1950s-era pile with Western-style carpets, Western-style windows, and international-level security — is built in two sections connected by a footbridge over a small valley.

At the foot of the steps is the Tirta Empul, the holiest place of pilgrimage in Bali for over 1,000 years. It consists of holy springs, public baths and a temple. Water emerges from the rock into a large basin and from there into the bathing pool. The water is considered sacred and magic, so bathing in it is a popular pursuit. The temple itself is one of the six most important in Bali, and the sight of it creates a particularly vivid impression. Entrance is Rp 10,000, which includes the sarong rental. An additional Rp1,000 is charged for any visible camera and Rp5,000 for a camcorder. The site is open from 8 AM to 5 PM.

Gunung Kawi

Take the road south from Tampaksiring in the direction of Gianyar and you will shortly arrive at the King's Tombs, or Gunung Kawi, on the left side of the road.

Near the parking lot, steps descend the side of the steep valley. If you arrive at the end of a long day or, worse still, in the heat of the early afternoon, you might be content to view the site from above — if so, there is a convenient viewing point a few dozen steps from the parking lot. If you opt to inspect the site at close quarters, descend until the path crosses the River Pakrisan by a bridge, where far below, young boys have set up a lucrative business diving for coins thrown from the parapet above.

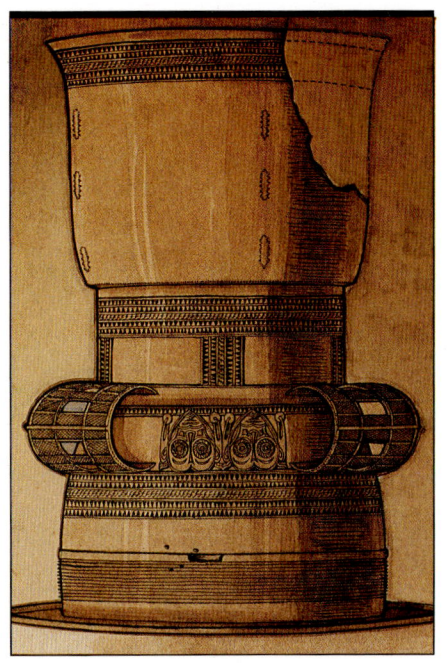

The ruins consist of large mausoleums, formal rectangular shapes cut into the rock and without ornament. There are four on your left before you cross the bridge, five ahead of you on the other side and a last one further down the valley. There are also passages cut into the rock, reminiscent of modern wartime pillboxes. Taken together, the site has a feeling that is almost Egyptian in its formality. The monuments are thought to date from the eleventh century and to be the resting place for the remains of King Anak Wungsu, who ruled Bali from 1049 to 1077, and the remains of his wives and sons.

The charge for entrance is Rp10,000, plus a bit more for your sash, and the site is open from 8 AM until 6 PM.

THE MOON OF PEJENG

Continuing further south, after another 11 km (around seven miles) you reach Pejeng and, on the left side of the road, **Pura Panataram Sasih**.

This temple, another of the Balinese top six, is above all famous for its gigantic bronze drum, known as the **Moon Face**. At more than two meters (six feet) high and with its striking end 160 cm (5 ft) in diameter this is the largest such drum in Southeast Asia. It is over 1,000 years old, dating from the ninth century, and vividly demonstrates the advanced level of the Bronze Age in the region. Unfortunately, it is kept high up under a roof, and is not clearly visible; it is beautifully decorated with frogs and geometrical patterns.

A kilometer (half a mile) further on, to your right, is **Pura Kebo Edan**, or Crazy Buffalo Temple, best known for its statue of the dancing Bhima, strongman from the epic poem *Mahabharata*, with its multiple penises.

Only a short distance further, on the other side of the road, is the **Archaeological Museum** (Museum Arkeologi), which contains a variety of historical objects and fossils.

YEH PULU

Shortly after the museum, the road divides, turning right for Ubud and left for Gianyar. There is, however, a third, unpaved road that leads off from this junction — follow it for two kilometers (one and a quarter miles) and, after passing through a village, you will arrive at Yeh Pulu.

A short walk between rice fields at the point where the road ends takes you to the site of a frieze, of about 40 m (120 ft) in length, carved in the rock beside the path. Depicting men on horses in a hunting scene, it is strangely dynamic and forceful; there is an energy and a simplicity here that vanishes from later Balinese work, where the emphasis is on poise and the sublime. These carvings at Yeh Pulu are more reminiscent of the rough but vigorous archaic Greek sculpture, heroic and independent of the requirements

---

OPPOSITE: An early twentieth-century drawing of the great drum of Pejeng. ABOVE: One of the stone fountains in the Goa Gajah, or Elephant Cave.

of a later orthodoxy. The frieze is thought to date from the fourteenth century.

GOA GAJAH: THE ELEPHANT CAVE

Back at the crossroads, take the road toward Ubud. After about a kilometer (just over half a mile) you will arrive at the popular Goa Gajah or Elephant Cave.

Visitors to the cave might be excused for thinking the place had received an excess of publicity. Bus-loads of sightseers unload every day to stumble through a small cave, knock their heads against the roof in the inadequate light and stare at a single small sculpture of Ganesa (elephant-headed son of Siwa) illuminated by an oil lamp. Yet the usual array of *warung* and souvenir stalls is assembled and a charge of Rp1,100 is made as if this were one of Bali's great splendors.

Even so, the manmade cave does date back to the eighth century, and the carving around the rectangular entrance of the cave is indeed marvelous, a typically bug-eyed monster appearing to prize open the rock with his fingertips. The statue to the left of the cave entrance is of Durga, destructive mother and consort of Siwa. In front of the cave are some large baths, with six standing figures holding bowls from which water pours. They are a testimony to past splendor and are basically in good condition; they could easily be restored.

Some 50 steps lead down from the temple compound that contains the cave and baths to a pleasant natural amphitheater where ponds and a small altar to Buddha enhance the natural serenity of the area. As neither Buddha nor elephants have ever been native to Bali, the site is something of an historical mystery.

From Goa Gajah, it is five kilometers (three miles) back to Ubud, turning right at Teges where you meet the road from Denpasar.

BANGLI

Bangli is a small town (though referred to in Penelokan as a "city") on the border of the central and eastern regions, 14 km (nine miles) from Gianyar.

Bangli's main temple is **Pura Kehen**. Carvings of trumpeting elephants welcome you to the flight of 38 steps leading up to a highly ornate gateway. The temple is built in tiers up a steep slope, and its obligatory banyan tree is vast. This was the state temple of the old kingdom of Bangli, its doors are vividly painted in gold, black and red. It is generally thought to date from about AD 1200, but the temple opposite, the restored **Pura Penyimpenan**, contains bronze relics even older than this. At the other end of the town is the **Pura Dalem Pengungekan**, the Temple of the Dead, with the outer walls painted with a bloodthirsty *Ramayana* scene of a voyage into the underworld.

The small, inexpensive hotel–restaurant, the **Artha Sastra Inn** ((0366) 91179, Jalan Merdeka 5, is actually the old palace of the former king of Bangli. A photograph of the young rajah, with two attendants, hangs on the walls of the verandah where lunch is served. It was apparently taken as recently as 1950. Together with the painted doorways and faded gilt mirrors, it provides a key to the atmosphere of a former world. Lewis Carroll's Alice could have slipped through a time warp and been there in a trice, you feel. One of the attendants told me a figure sweeping the steps was the former king's daughter. A glimpse into the once great rooms reveals camping furniture and a table with shampoo and a toothbrush.

Bangli is 29 km (18 miles) east of Ubud, and 47 (29 miles) northeast of Denpasar. The best way to get there is to drive yourself, though *bemos* head this way from Denpasar's Batubulan Terminal, and cost just Rp1,500.

EXCURSIONS WEST OF UBUD

The area to the west of Ubud is not an immediately straightforward drive, as the road networks must cross the lateral valleys that run down from the volcanic highlands toward the southern coast. It won't deter a taxi driver, nor anyone who can read a map with ease, but for this reason the following excursions are more commonly reached by tour buses from the southern resorts, often on their way up to the central highlands. Their location near Ubud, however, means that they are listed here.

Women returning from the fields near Ubud. The central area of Bali is the island's heartland, a rich alluvial rice-growing region where the many ancient monuments testify to a long history of human settlement and cultural sophistication.

Mengwi

Taman Ayun, the Water Temple at Mengwi, was once an attractive, peaceful place, but now, like so many other celebrated sites on the island, it has been all but taken over by vendors selling T-shirts and trinkets.

Built on rising grass slopes and partly surrounded by a wide moat, Taman Ayun is one of the great Balinese temples, spacious and almost trim in a way that is uncharacteristic of most of the others. As if to establish this garden-like quality, there is a pool with a fountain in it on the left as you enter the first compound.

In the second compound, in the bottom left-hand corner, is a small tower that can be climbed; the top provides a good viewpoint of the temple and its watery surrounds. Immediately below, gnarled frangipani trees exhibit their fabulous blossoms.

The last, or inner, court contains 10 fine *meru*, the tall, tiered towers thatched in black *ijuk*, a fiber derived from the sago palm. The number of tiers is always uneven, as with the tiers on cremation towers. Here the tallest have 11.

The inner court also contains a fine stone *padmasana*, in effect a giant and highly ornate chair on which it is hoped the unseen supreme god will deign to sit on days of high festival. The back of the chair is oriented toward Mount Agung. Also notable, on the left, is an ornate brick and stone shrine with a thatched roof. At the corner of each base is a carving of Garuda attacking Naga. The inner court is surrounded by a miniature walled moat that echoes the great moat that nearly encircles the temple.

To the left of the upper part of Taman Ayun is a lush, overgrown area, abandoned to nature and silent except for the chirping of insects.

Food and drink are available on the far side of the outer moat overlooking the temple. Mengwi is 18 km (11 miles) northwest from Denpasar, conveniently on the way from the south to Bedugul.

Taman Ayun is particularly spacious and, surrounded as it is by a wide moat, the peaceful ambiance is remarkable. Note one of the temple's multi-tiered black *meru* in the background.

Sangeh

An exceptionally pleasant winding country road links Mengwi and the Monkey Forest at Sangeh, nine kilometers (six miles) away. Take the road on which the Water Temple stands, turning left as you leave the precinct. Turn left after five kilometers (three miles), then left again after a further two kilometers (one and a quarter miles). The forest is then on your left, opposite a parking lot.

Sangeh consists of some 10 ha (24 acres) of pala trees in the middle of which is a temple. It is in fact a sacred wood. About 1,000 monkeys are said to inhabit the area, and they too are believed to be sacred.

There are stories of bus-loads of tourists overwhelming Sangeh from morning till night, a horror only exceeded by the bands of thieving monkeys that leap on you at the least rustle of a packet of peanuts. A visit at about 4 PM, however, makes it possible to appreciate the beauty of the place.

The trees are tall and symmetrical, some reaching a height of 50 m (164 ft) with no side branches. The place is scented by the five-petaled flowers of the trees which lie scattered underfoot. The shady cool and the silence induce an air of sanctity, and the temple is simple and potent. There, monkeys organize in two groups, east and west, each with its king. No monkey will cross into the other group's territory. At sunset, they retreat to the tree tops to sleep. Locals will tell you the biggest monkeys are the kings (thereby providing an insight into Indonesian attitudes to politics). They also insist that no dead body of an old monkey (as opposed to younger ones killed accidentally) has ever been found. Perhaps, though they won't countenance the prospect, their brothers eat corpses.

Entrance to Sangeh is by donation. Young men will attach themselves to you and chat as you walk along, but be warned they'll expect payment for the dubious privilege of their company.

The statue at the entrance is of Hanuman, the white monkey god of the *Ramayana* and the *kecak* dance. Sangeh is 21 km (13 miles) north of Denpasar, and 15 km (nine miles) from Mengwi; most operators combine the two attractions in a single tour.

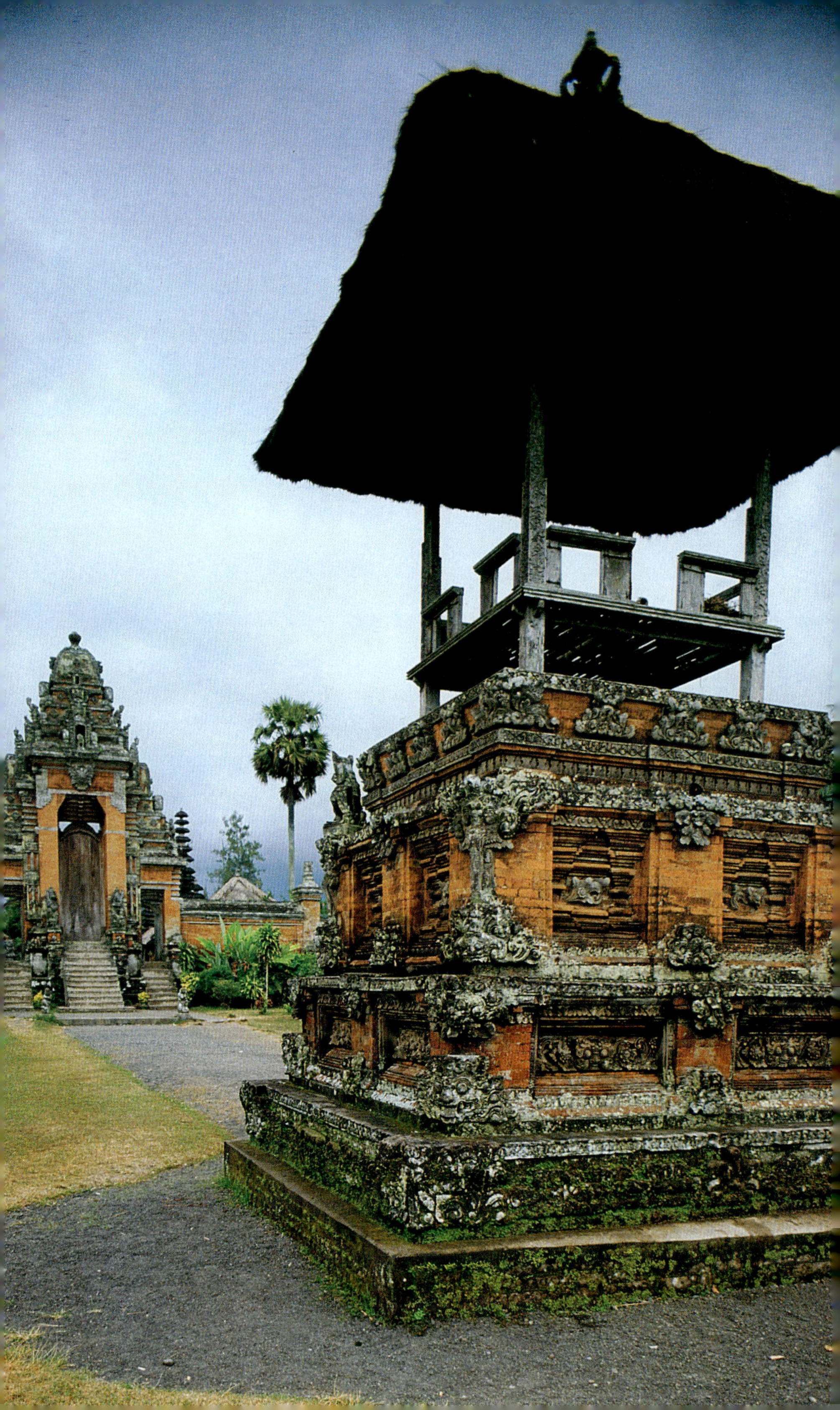

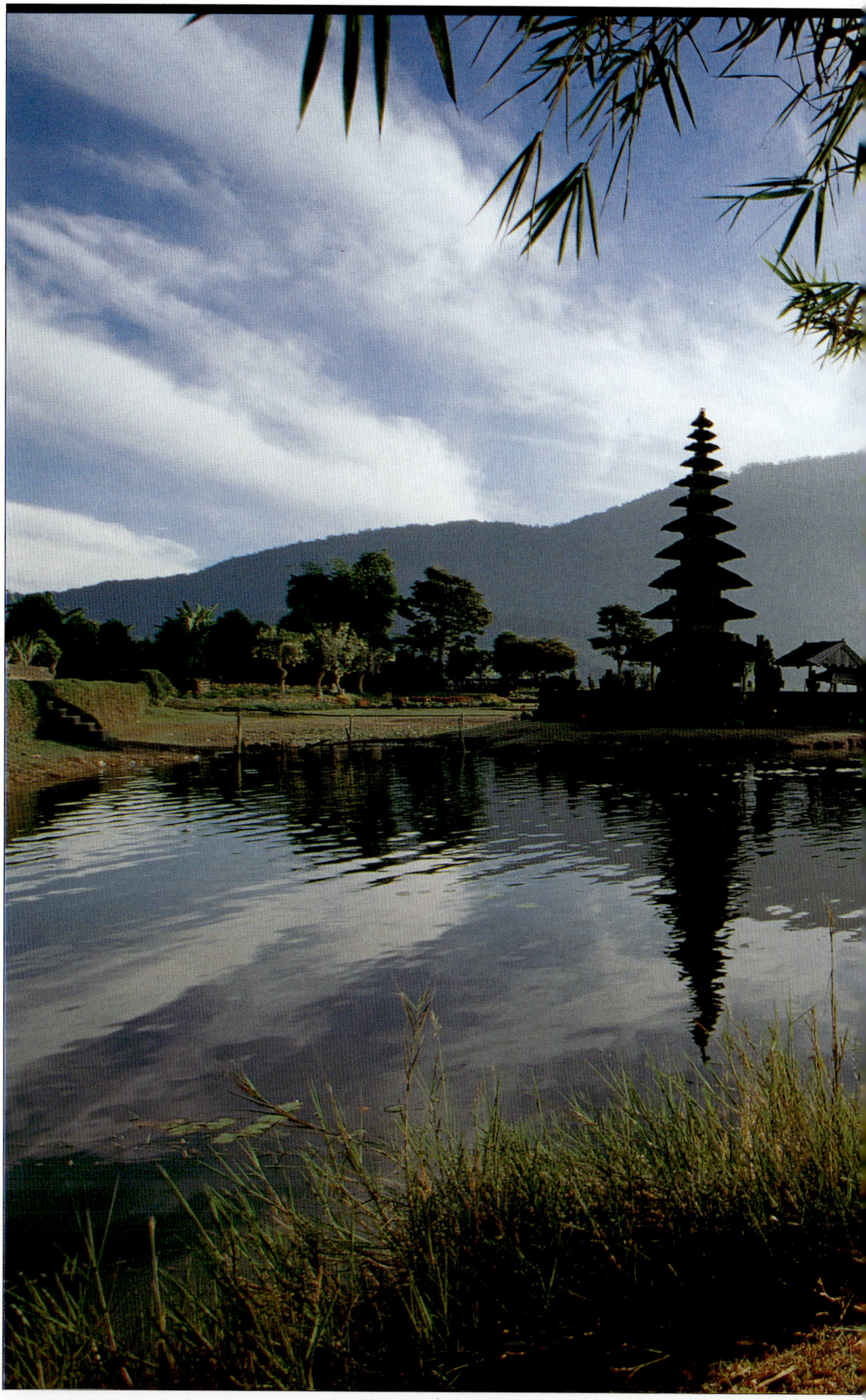

The Heights

FROM THE SOUTH, THE ISLAND OF BALI RISES STEADILY, culminating in its northern half with a dramatic range of volcanic landscapes, folded into mountains and valleys by unimaginable forces. This is where, according to geologists, the subcontinental Australian Plate nudges, at tectonic speeds, underneath the edge of the Asian Plate. As it pushes northward, it is forced deeper and deeper into the molten magma of the earth's inner mantle.

The phenomenal heat in the earth's depths has caused these slowly descending rocks to melt. Movement on such a scale has also caused unimaginable pressure to build up underground. Consequently this newly molten material has taken advantage of weaknesses in the earth's crust to burst through and surge upwards. The result is, strung out along a line marking the meeting point of two continents, a chain of volcanoes that have pushed through the ocean floor to create islands. Among them is Bali.

Not all the islands of Indonesia, this immense country that straddles the equator for 5,500 km (3,400 miles) and spreads itself over three time zones, are volcanic in origin. Bali is, though. Virtually the entire island is made up of what volcanoes past and present have pushed above the waters of the Indian Ocean. And at the heart of Bali's past, present and future is the revered chain of volcanoes that make up the Bali highlands. Two of them, Agung and Batur, have erupted in the past century, Batur twice. This has created chaos, immense loss of life, and set the Balinese people into turmoil as they attempt to explain the eruptions in the terms of their religion. But, with time, the molten flows of disruptive lava has proved to be a blessing, fertilizing the land and enabling the Balinese to live in a society where famine and hunger are not everyday threats.

Most visitors to the highlands do so as day-trips from the southern resorts. This is not the best way to do it, however, as the morning light is by far the best time to see the volcanoes and the views: everything tends to get hazy as the mornings wear on, and the afternoons are frequently cloudy. Tours that have to start by collecting their various clients from different hotels and even resorts are lucky to reach the volcanoes before lunchtime. It is better, and for two or more people, less expensive, to drive yourself or hire a taxi for the day.

There are three main routes from the south crossing the highlands heading north. The most easterly is the main road to Singaraja on the north coast, passing Bedugul and Lake Bratan. This is the least dramatic of all the high volcanic landscape but rewarding for its Botanical Gardens, one of the country's finest golf courses and wonderful, if not overly dramatic, general scenery. Most visited, with the best mountain views, peaks to climb, and cultural sights to see, is the central route to the volcanic peaks. This comes up through Bangli and reaches Penelokan, where the views are supplemented by the options of visiting the Bali Aga village of Trunyan and climbing Mount Batur before proceeding on through lush steep landscapes to the south-coast town of Kubutambahan.

While both these roads go do cross the island, as they get higher in the mountains interconnecting roads become rarer and less passable. The route you choose will dictate which highland scenes you see, though a circuit would make a demanding, but not impossible, day-trip itinerary. The third route dead-ends on the higher reaches of Gunung Abang at the temple of Besakih, Bali's "Mother Temple" and an important site of pilgrimage for the Balinese. This is also the road to take for those who wish to climb Gunung Agung.

Bear in mind that if you're staying overnight in any of these places, warm clothes — at least a sweater — will be essential.

THE ROLLING HIGHLANDS

The area known (here) as the Rolling Highlands is reached along the route that is most commonly used when traveling from the south to the north coast. Traffic is not intolerable and the road passes through several towns of interest, notably the lowland town of Mengwi (page 166 under UBUD AND THE BALI HEARTLANDS) and becomes ever more spectacular as it gains altitude.

The rice paddies that blanket the lower slopes of Mount Agung give way to temperate rainforest as you get higher up.

Bedugul

Fifteen kilometers (nearly 10 miles) west of Kintamani, but not linked to it by any road, Bedugul is a lakeside mountain resort 51 km (32 miles) north of Denpasar. It provides welcome relief from the heat, and especially the humidity, of the coast, and is especially popular with domestic tourists. As such it is perhaps best avoided on weekends, when it can become crowded.

Lakes Bratan, Buyan and **Tambingan** fill a huge caldera, comparable to Batur's. Here, however, the crater's northern walls have slipped seawards, and it is consequently neither as distinctive nor as impressive.

Ulu Danu

The temple of Ulu Danu is set in delightful gardens on the edge of Lake Bratan (35 m or 115 ft deep) at Candikuning. Temple buildings occupy two minute offshore islets, and these, with their three- and eleven-tier *meru*, are much photographed. The temple is dedicated to the spirits that control the irrigation systems drawn from the lake; there are also Buddhist and Islamic temples close by.

It is possible to be taken by rowboat on a 45-minute lake trip to see a cave and visit the **Bedugul Hotel and Restaurant** (moderate), where waterskiing and parasailing are on offer. Accommodation and meals can also be found at the **Bali Handara Kosaido Country Club (** (0361) 22646 FAX (0361) 287358, Pancasari (expensive), whose 18-hole golf course is one of the finest in the country, and, for that matter, the world. Green fees are US$130, including caddy, but renting clubs and shoes, plus the inevitable caddy tip, adds a bit extra. There is a trail encircling the lake; the walk takes about three hours.

Botanical Gardens

Half a kilometer (550 yards) from the lake (along the road back toward Denpasar) by a flower and vegetable market, a road runs off to the right to the Botanical Gardens.

The gardens consist of a large wooded parkland. Pathways have been established, and the clearly labeled trees on this south facing upland slope are fine. Flowers bloom in what look like natural conditions. It's a place for quiet, extensive walks among glades, with views up to the wooded hills, and, on a weekday at least, a place for almost total solitude. On an island where a huge variety of tropical and subtropical plants, both native and introduced, flourish with ease, the variety here is immense. The gardens are open daily 8 AM until 4:30 PM.

How to Get There

Most people drive themselves here, as the attractions are a bit spread out. Otherwise they pass through on shuttle buses destined for the north coast. There are shuttle buses to Bedugul from the southern resort areas, while *bemos* leave from Ubung terminal in Denpasar.

THE VOLCANIC PEAKS ROUTE

For sheer variety of sights and experiences, the most attractive parts of Bali's volcanic peaks are found on the central highlands routes, where the roads north from Payangan (near Ubud), Tampaksiring, and Bangli meet to funnel over the central range of volcanoes through the highland town of Kintamani. Each of these three routes has different qualities to recommend it, but the best tarmac is found on the road coming up from Bangli, while the Payangan road will involve a little backtracking to reach Penelokan, which is very much the epicenter of the views, if not the area's popular excursions.

Penelokan

The approach to the mountain area is most dramatic if you arrive there at Penelokan, whose name means "good view." Of the two roads up to this village, the main route is through Bangli, and nothing is seen of the country you are approaching as you ascend until you pass through a ceremonial gateway. The other route is from Ubud, where you drive through increasingly sheer and dramatic scenery of paddies and palm trees. Whichever way you come, eventually you pass through a set of ceremonial gates and suddenly a massive view lies out before you. The effect is only somewhat spoiled by the immediate approach of a policeman who asks you for a view donation (compulsory, apparently, and a minimum of Rp1,000) and then recommends his hotel down in the valley. There is no tourist information office here as such, and little beyond a chain of hotels and restaurants, cashing in on the view between plate-glass picture windows, in case the afternoon cloud comes down wetly.

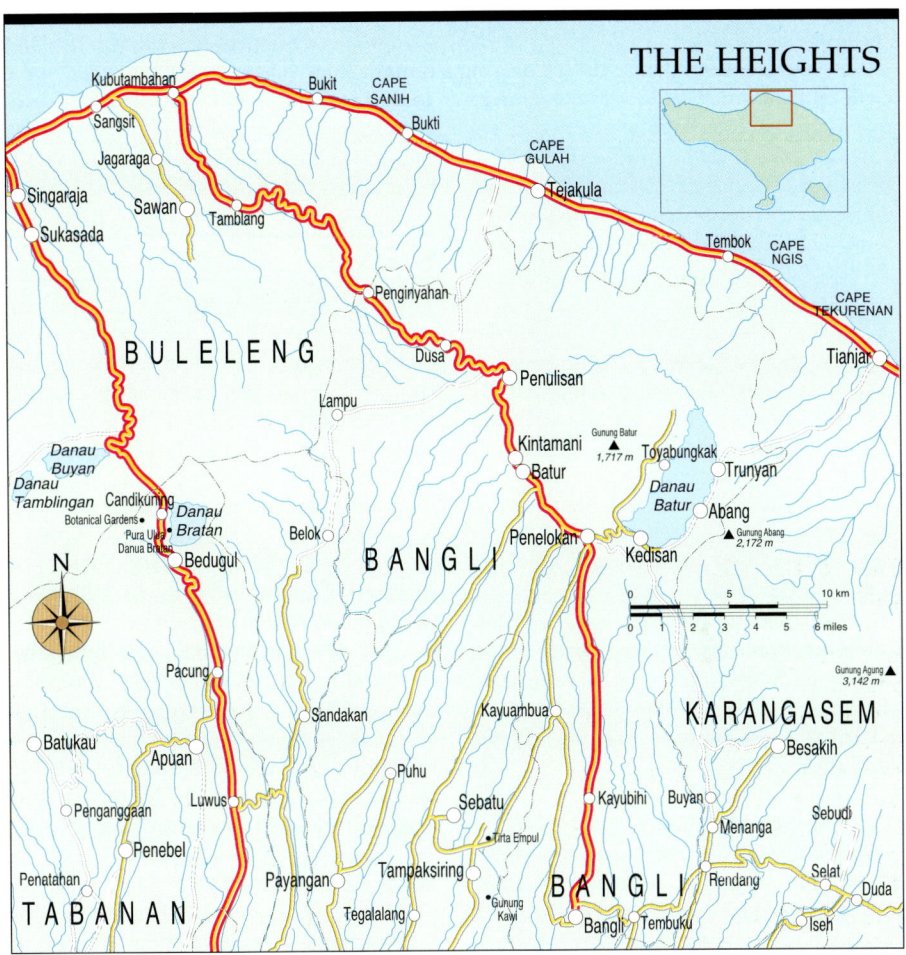

From this crater rim, you are looking at a vast caldera, 11 km (seven miles) across: the hollowed-out remains of a gigantic volcano that in prehistoric times exploded, blowing away its cone and leaving only the bony, saucer-shaped rim on which you're sitting. The lake below fills the heart of the crater, and where you now see clouds, once there was a mountain, holy to the gods.

The effect is even greater if you arrive in the early morning, or even stay overnight and catch it at dawn, as it is in the morning when the brooding presence of Gunung Agung is visible, looking over it all. In the afternoon, too often, Bali's highest peak is obscured.

Mount Batur, whose broken crest rises 1,717 m (5,633 ft) above sea level, is low enough to stay, generally, clear of clouds. Its slopes are scarred with lava flows, and all around is a scene of lonely splendor and dramatic desolation. Magnificent though the mountain is, it is the product of several more recent and smaller eruptions and its summit is actually only 328 m (1,066 ft) higher than the outer crater rim at Penelokan.

The volcano is not to be underestimated, however. Its last major eruption in 1926 completely destroyed the village of Batur, situated at that time on the western shore of the lake. It was never rebuilt, but its important temple was relocated on the outer crater rim, between Penelokan and Kintamani; this site is what is meant nowadays when Batur Village is spoken of.

To your right lies **Lake Batur**, 492 m (1,600 ft) below. It is eight kilometers (five miles) long and three kilometers (two miles) wide and fills almost a third of the area of the caldera. The cliffs that fall abruptly down to the lake's eastern edge rise to their maximum height in the summit of Mount Abang, 2,172 m (7,126 ft), and in a direct line between Batur and Agung.

The right-hand (eastern) shore of the lake appears to press right up against these cliffs, but long ago some Bali Aga remnants, retreating in the face of invaders, found a flat piece of land and established the village of Trunyan, where few would be interested in following them. The village is clearly visible, a prominent patch of red in an otherwise pastel landscape played over by the changing shadows of the clouds.

At your feet the road zigzags down from Penelokan, branching right to Kedisan on the lake's edge immediately below you and continuing across the lava flows to the hot springs of Air Panas, about halfway along the left-hand shore.

Where to Stay and Eat

Accommodation at Penelokan is available at the **Lakeview Restaurant and Hotel** ✆/FAX (0366) 51464, Penelokan (moderate). The hotel has recently been renovated and upgraded, the view is wonderful, the restaurant good but the accommodation overpriced. Like most hotels around here it organizes treks to see the sunrise from the crater of Mount Batur, departing at 3 PM and returning to the hotel at 10 PM. It's not hard to find places to eat here: the crater rim is lined with them. However most shut after the daylight-dependent day-trippers have gone. Penelokan is only a 15-minute drive from Air Panas, or the nearby village of Kedisan on the shores of the lake. These are better places to stay if you plan to climb Batur, notably Kedisan, although it doesn't share Penelokan's marvelous view.

How to Get There

Most visitors to Penelokan arrive by tour buses or minivans booked through tour operators or the National Tourist Board. Otherwise it can be reached by *bemo* from Denpasar, or by road. Drivers will find the road through Bangli better, but not as spectacular, as the route through Ubud: either way Penelokan is a sensible place to break a journey across the island between the southern resorts and the northern coast.

KEDISAN

The view from Penelokan, surveyed by countless pagoda-style restaurants, is a bit distant for some. The road that dives off into the view is very steep: don't attempt it unless your rental car is in good shape. The route down will test brakes and steering, and the climb will examine your engine and clutch for wear. There are always one or two local cars, blocked up on rocks, stuck on the road and few move the rocks after they've been repaired. This is, however, the only way down to the village of Kedisan.

This village is on the shores of the lake, next to the lava flows that rubbed out the village of Batur. It can make a pleasant stop. The main activities here are boat trips over to Trunyan Island, expeditions across the northern lava field, or, more usually, the hour and a half walk up to the peak of Ulung Batur.

Where to Stay and Eat

There are two main hotels here and a scattering of home-stays. By far the most dynamic is the **Hotel Surya** ✆ (0366) 51138, Box 1006, Kintamani, whose touts include the very policemen charging travelers for visiting the crater rim and almost everyone else who spoke to me during my most recent visit. Their rooms are nothing special but good value for the price (budget).

Next door the **Hotel Segara** ✆ (0366) 51136 FAX (0366) 51212, Kintamani, tries less hard and offers courtyard detached homes overlooking the lake (budget). Don't expect hot water at either. They both have restaurants, and the local lake-fish are so fresh you can often see them being brought in, dangling on the end of fishing lines in the hands of local women.

How to Get There

The best way to get to Kedisan is by using the free transfers from Ubud or the half-price shuttles from Kuta, Denpasar or the Ngurah Rai Airport offered by the Surya Hotel. If driving a rental vehicle, think before driving down to Kedisan from Penelokan. The steep drive down will, perhaps fatally, test for faults in your braking system, and the return journey uphill will ferret out any possible problems with your motor. Don't attempt it if you have any concerns about the car's mechanical condition. In any case, drive carefully: the road is littered with stones, left behind after serving as emergency handbrakes for vehicles in trouble, and often scattered with the broken glass of some recent bingle (Australian for minor traffic accident).

EXCURSIONS FROM KEDISAN

Despite being at lake level in one of the largest craters of central Bali, Kedisan is, by virtue of its energetic hotels, one of the best bases to explore the hot springs of Air Panas, the outdoor graveyard at Trunyan. Kedisan is also an ideal base for climbing Ulung Batur.

Toyah Bungkah and the Hot Springs

The road from Keidan to Toyah Bungkah and the hot springs at Air Panas is now one of the best in the country, looping crazily over the new, barely vegetated lava flow that wiped out the village of Batur. The springs themselves consist merely of a communal bathing pool where the hot water runs into the lake. You can sit in the water at sunset in the company of 50-odd villagers, some of them scrubbing their washing on the side. It's nicer, though, to swim in the lake itself which the waters of the spring make warm at this point. A charge of Rp4,000 is levied for entrance into the village, plus another Rp1,000 for a vehicle.

The big new hotel here is the **Hotel Puri Bening** ((0366) 51234 FAX (0361) 730285 (moderate). Few people were staying there when we visited, and it is possible the place will become something of a white elephant. At present, anyway, Air Panas is mostly visited by backpackers keen to hike in the cool upland air, but the medicinal claims of the sulfurous waters might not convince those same backpackers to stop over. In any case most visitors at present choose to stay at they **Under the Volcano Homestay** ((0366) 51166 (budget). You are most likely to arrive at the upper of the place's two sites (10 rooms and a restaurant) close to the road;

A meditating figure along the wayside.

there are an additional 14 rooms down by the lakeside.

There are several other *losmens* here, all inexpensive. If you want somewhere a little more comfortable, but less expensive than the Puri Bening, you could try the **Puri Wisata Pualam** (inexpensive).

The road continues beyond Air Panas to **Songan** where there is an attractively situated temple up a track to your left in the center of the village.

THE ASCENT OF MOUNT BATUR

There's no need for a guide in order to climb Mount Batur, unless you plan to set off in the early morning to see the sun rise; in this case you will need to start at 3:30 AM and can easily find a guide by asking around at Air Panas/Toyah Bungkah, which is where you'll start even if your climb has been organized in Kedisan, Penelokan or even further afield.

A small *warung* has been established right on the crater rim, staffed whenever there are likely to be walkers arriving in urgent need of refreshment.

Even for those who are not going up to watch the sunrise, an early start is advisable, not because of the distance but because of the heat later in the day. From Air Panas, take the lane that leads toward the mountain from the center of the village. Anyone will point it out to you if you say, "Batur — jalan jalan" (meaning "Mount Batur on foot"). It curves gently round to the left until, after about a kilometer (just over half a mile), you reach a temple. Pass the temple, continuing on the clear track, and follow it as it winds across the now cindery scrubland around the base of the mountain. After crossing the second of two (usually dry) riverbeds, the path turns upwards, heading directly for the peak.

Next comes a steep, dusty bit where the assistance of handholds is provided by some small pine trees. At the top is an orange refuse bin that marks the junction of the track with another coming up from the left. From here the path crosses a level stretch and then diverges into several subsidiaries, all making for the ridge on the right. Once you have achieved this, the path becomes unified again and runs clearly ahead of you toward the summit. Views back over the lake are superb.

As you climb, Agung begins to appear behind you above the rim of the outer crater to the east.

Around the Crater Rim

After a time, the path divides, one branch carrying on straight ahead, the other leading off to the left. Take the left-hand branch for the gentler ascent. This will lead you to a low point on Batur's crater rim, and with any luck you will encounter local boys offering cold drinks. Considering the distance they have come and the weight they have had to carry, it's only charitable to buy one, and for only a little less than the price they ask.

From here, the around-the-crater path rises steeply to the right. The ground is sandy and loose and most comfortably negotiated barefoot. The wind sings in the tough grass. Make for the two small pines.

Finally you arrive at the high point of the volcano's crater rim, the pinnacle that has been ahead of you throughout most of the ascent; and here there are two orange refuse bins to prove it. You are here standing on the top of the high crest that rises so impressively on the right of the volcano when viewed from Penelokan.

The around-the-crater route is narrow but well trodden. It is not, however, for the fainthearted. At least at one point the track crosses a narrow ridge with steep cliffs on either side and steam issuing out of the rocks just below. Anyone with a fear of heights will not need to be told to keep away.

The descent on the route toward Kedisan begins a little way further around to the left from where you first attained the crater coming up from the springs, at the next refuge bin, in fact. The path descends steeply and unpleasantly in a continuous incline to the plain. This is a common ascent route but inferior to the one from Air Panas because its steepness is unrelieved, and also because this way you miss the chance of a hot-spring bath on your descent. At Kedisan you are rewarded instead, on arrival at level ground, by a small *warung* where you can buy soft drinks and small cakes; sometimes the *warung* is unmanned and you are invited to leave the money due in a box. The owner is said to be a trained *leyak*, or witch, and well aware when his dues have not been paid, and by whom!

ACROSS LAKE BATUR TO TRUNYAN

The Bali Aga village of Trunyan, best known for its local practice of not cremating bodies, instead just leaving them to decompose in the open air, is reached only by boat, most easily found at Kedisan.

Arranging your crossing to Trunyan on one of the colorful wooden boats, like so much else in Bali, involves negotiation. There are official rates, advertised at an official booking office on the southern shores of the lake, but the ferries depart when they are full. Consequently passengers must either charter a boat (in practice this means negotiating a price with the skipper) or wait for a group planning to charter a boat to come along and then make arrangements to join them.

Up in Penelokan, you will hear preposterous prices quoted for chartering a boat; at the lakeside they are reasonable — if you negotiate with determination and if you're prepared to wait. The official rates are Rp75,000 per boat, assuming eight passengers per boat, or rather more if you charter the whole boat. This fee should include both a visit to the cemetery at Kuban (a short distance from Trunyan, but accessible only by

OPPOSITE: Trunyan cemetery, where the village dead are laid out to decompose. These skulls have been placed at the cemetery entrance to elicit donations from tourists. ABOVE: Mount Batur from the crater rim. The volcano erupted in 1917 and then again in 1926, on the second occasion destroying the ancient village of Batur on the shore of the lake.

boat). Check whether or not a visit to the hot springs at Air Panas is included in the price.

Trunyan

The trip across the lake takes approximately half an hour. Initially you'll have to pay for a seat in an eight-person boat, but the smaller donations that are the theme of any visit to the Bali Aga village of Trunyan begin at the quay. As you pull up at the little beach serving the cemetery, a reception committee of two solicits the first donation and presents you with a register for signature.

The place of the dead is on the right. In Trunyan, the custom is neither to cremate nor bury the dead but to lay them out to decay in the open air and be picked clean by the elements of nature. Consequently visitors often enter the designated territory with some trepidation. It's not clear exactly what horrors the tourist might be allowed to see in periods shortly following a death. When I was there, there were merely seven or eight wicker tents containing, in some cases, a skull, more often simply bones and scraps of clothing, plus some funeral gifts such as a Sprite bottle or a few hundred rupiah coins.

A small group of skulls placed on a ledge near the entrance marks the spot where a further donation is requested. In the same way that the donation register you sign on the beach — like almost all such registers in Bali — shows only previous donations of several thousands of rupiah, so, any small notes you donate as you enter the cemetery itself have been removed (for setting a bad example) by the time you leave.

Back to Kedisan

It used to be claimed that boatmen on the lake were in the habit of stopping in the middle and demanding an increase in the fare. The existence now of an official ticketing office seems to have curbed this custom for the most part, and simple requests for more as you approach the landing stage back at Kedisan should be treated on their merits. The appeals may sound slightly threatening;

Washing cattle in Lake Batur. K'tut Tantri's book *Revolt in Paradise* contains a description of cattle being drowned as ritual sacrifices in this lake. The upland central area of the island is much cooler than the coastal region; it's frequently in cloud and experiences heavy rainfall.

THE VOLCANIC PEAKS ROUTE

but it is very unlikely they are not meant to sound that way. The only relevant English phrase the boatmen may know is likely to be a blunt-sounding, "More money." Don't be taken aback. He's only requesting a tip.

CLIMBING MOUNT ABANG

Gunung Batur is not the only volcano you can climb: there's also the peak of Mount Abang to taunt climbers. Follow the road from Penelokan east (as if you were going back to Bangli), and take the second turn on the left immediately after the road begins to drop down from the ridge (the first left leads to a restaurant). It's only a few meters down, and there's a shop on the corner, but no sign. This road quickly leads back onto the outer crater rim, but this time running east. After four kilometers (two and a half miles), the main section of the road peels off to the right and descends, eventually to Besakih. The road along the rim continues for another kilometer or so, passes a couple of *warung*, skirts to the right of a small temple, descends a hill, then turns right. There is a house nearby. From this point on you have to walk. The path is well defined but slippery, and it's about two hours to the summit, which is marked by a temple. (There is another temple about halfway up the ascent.)

BATUR AND KINTAMANI

Going west along the rim of the caldera from Penelokan, you pass several restaurants: the **Puri Selera**, the **Suling Bali**, the **Puri Dewata** (all inexpensive), and the smartest of them, **Restaurant Gunawan** ((0366) 51050 (moderate). Since these restaurants do their entire business serving tourists visiting the crater rim during the day, they are only open at lunch time.

The **Temple of Ulu Danu** at Batur dates from 1926 when its predecessor down on the shore of the lake was destroyed. Like all temples in Bali, it faces the mountains, in this case the one that was responsible for its destruction. Its situation is magnificent, and to watch the gorgeously clad celebrants processing around the outside of its walls on its festival days, the wild country of mountain and lake contrastingly pale in the background, is to see something both wonderful and sad — humans struggling to placate the insensibility of Nature — and very much of the essence of Bali.

The best place to stay in the region of Kintamani is the **Lakeview Restaurant and Hotel** (/FAX (0366) 51464 (moderate) at Penelokan, though there are also a scatter of home-stays in the area.

PENULISAN

After Kintamani the road continues to Penulisan. This is one of the loveliest routes in the island, temperate in vegetation now on account of the altitude, and luxuriant on account of the heavy rainfall. It's like an English country road in summer, but forever in leaf. The tarmac is smooth, traffic light, and passage all the way is downhill.

The temple at Penulisan, **Pura Tegeh Koripan**, is the tallest in Bali. Three hundred and thirty-three steps lead from the road up to this easily achieved viewpoint. Few people visit the temple, and there is no commercialization whatsoever. The atmosphere at the top is secluded and quiet, as mossy and crumbling as a Victorian churchyard. The air is scented from the various bushes that sprout on all sides and obscure the view — which is spectacular to the north, with the coast and the blue sea lying far below you almost at your feet, and extensive but less well defined to the south. The air is fresh, and the highland fogs usually well behind.

For all Kintamani's scruffy ambiance, and Penelokan's deserved reputation for excessive hustling, these crater rim villages ending in Penulisan are remarkable places, perched on a narrow volcanic ridge with barely room for more than the one main street. They haunt the imagination when many a more pretentious settlement has long been forgotten.

THE EASTERN HIGHLANDS

The Eastern Highlands and the slopes of Bali's highest mountain, Gunung Agung, are dominated in importance by the temple of Besakih, where you'll find a Tourist Office (no phone), which is open daily 8 AM to 6 PM, in the parking lot by the temple.

Besakih and Mount Agung

The **Mother Temple of Besakih** is the oldest and the largest in Bali. It is very important to the Balinese, and visitors to the island will often be asked if they have visited this temple and their commitment to investigating Balinese culture judged accordingly. Thousands of pilgrims visit Besakih every day of the year, and in former times the old kings made annual pilgrimages with their courts to the temple. Admission to the site is Rp10,000, and beware of "guides" who attach themselves to you and attempt to avoid discussing the fee they propose to charge. This always ends in tears, so establish the rate in advance. If you're wearing beach gear a sash and a sarong will be needed to enter the temple at all, and in any case non-Hindus are not allowed into the temples within the complex.

There is still plenty to see: it's the largest and the most dramatically sited temple on all Bali. It is constructed over a mass of terraces that ascend what are in fact the lower slopes of Mount Agung. This is, of course the Mother Temple because Mount Agung is Bali's highest mountain. The various courtyards and enclosures are connected by flights of steps, and it is these, together with the tall, multistory *meru* that, with Agung rising steeply immediately behind the central enclosures, make the prospect of Besakih so impressive.

The day-to-day business of the temple is run by the *pemangku*, easily identifiable by their white clothes. They receive the offerings, sprinkle the pilgrims three times with holy water as they offer up flowers, also three times, and place clusters of wet rice grains on each temple and on the brow in such a way that they remain there for some time.

The Brahmanic *pedanda*, or high priests, only appear for the great ceremonies, though they can regularly be seen at cremations sitting in their high lofts chanting their mantras and wafting incense to the gods.

The main temple complex, or Pura Panataran, at Besakih (there are other, subsidiary ones, especially away to the right) consists of six walled courts, each higher up the mountain than the last. Before you reach the first of these there is a small walled shrine containing a seven-tiered *meru* on your right — this is the original shrine of the temple.

The Mother Temple at Besakih, the island's premier place of worship, situated on the lower slopes of Mount Agung, Bali's highest summit.

The wide central staircase, flanked on each side by seven rising stone platforms each carrying six carved figures, leads to the first large court. It contains the usual pavilions for offerings, for *gamelan* orchestras and the like. The second court is similar but contains three ceremonial chairs situated on a high stone platform known as a *padmasana*, or world shrine, intended for the three major manifestations of God — Siwa, Wisnu and Brahma. The other courts follow on up fewer steps and contain many of the thatched *meru* that are so characteristic of the temple.

oranges grow everywhere, and there is a sense of relaxed peacefulness in this cooler, wooded enviroment, overlooking the coastal plains.

As is so often the case in Asia, the presence of items from modern life — cigarettes, radios broadcasting advertisements for hair conditioner — act as authenticating devices for religious observances. There is no trace of the idea, common in the West, that antiquity and sanctity go hand in hand, no trace of the idea that the modern is faintly vulgar.

The Mother Temple, badly damaged at the time of Agung's 1963 eruption, has been entirely rebuilt. The eruption occurred just as the most extensive and important of all Bali's many rituals, the once-in-a-hundred-years Dasa Rudra, was about to be performed, and resulted in confusion and doubt about the intentions of the gods at that time. What exactly did they mean by rejecting these devotions in this cataclysmically dramatic way? Had the Balinese somehow incurred the wrath of the gods, and how? Details of the events at that traumatic time in Balinese history can be found in Anna Mathews' *The Night of Purnama* (1965).

The countryside all around the Mother Temple is especially beautiful. Mandarin

The Ascent of Mount Agung
Besakih is a popular place from which to begin the attempt on Mount Agung. Note that "attempt" is the operative word — the ascent is not easy. Though some have claimed that the climb there and back can be done in a single day if a very early start is made, it is far wiser to go prepared to spend a night on the volcano.

A guide is essential as the early part of the route winds through fields, but more importantly because, if an accident were to occur, it is vital to have someone capable of going back quickly and organizing help. It is fairly easy to find a guide in Besakih — **Wayan Pasak**, Dalam Puri, Besakih, took me up and can be recommended. He is the owner of a *warung* at a parking lot on the left of the upper (left-hand) road leading to Besakih, about a kilometer (just over half a mile) before the temple. A reasonable fee is Rp50,000.

For the climb you will need a flashlight and adequate food and water; also required are stout boots and a hat.

The trail climbs right through the center of the Mother Temple itself, ascending 34 steps and then turning right and going up the broad lane between the central complex and the large one immediately to its right.

After initial meandering (not apparent until you see it in daylight) the path begins to climb. It rises, virtually straight now, along the crest of a long spur, through lush temperate forest. It's earthy underfoot, and on the steeper sections it can be slippery. Handholds are often needed, and some well-placed branches have become worn smooth by frequent use; at other times there are only thorny briars, which you should do your best to avoid. For predawn ascents the temperature is moderate, and there is little problem with insects, but you should choose a date when there is a full, or three-quarter moon.

First light comes shortly before 5 AM and is marked by the instantaneous eruption of bird song. This wonderful moment is followed half hour later by sunlight appearing on the plains behind you, with the triangular shadow of the mountain lying dramatically across the landscape. This shadow shortens as the early morning advances and, soon after, the trail itself is sunlit.

The wooded ravines falling away precipitously on either side of you, only dimly discernible in moonlight, are now brilliantly and breathtakingly illuminated.

The spot where the ridge of the trail joins onto the central stock of the volcano is called the **Door of Agung**. At the point of contact there is a steep area of loose black ash where progress is difficult, but it doesn't last long. Another short ridge takes you to the Door, on the right.

At the Door of Agung, large slabs of rock overlook some broad ledges where it is possible to camp (though there is no water), and indeed various useful items such as cooking pans are often left there. There are also shrines and the remains of offerings. The rock faces themselves have been painted with the names of innumerable visitors, many of whom attempted the ascent no further than this elevated point. The view over southern

---

Mount Agung — OPPOSITE: The first rays of dawn strike the mountain. ABOVE: A hiker above treeline in the grayness of first light.

and western Bali is extensive, though the lack of any other mountains close by makes it less than spectacular. Clouds frequently drift by beneath you.

From here to the summit is another two to three hours' climb across terrain that is partly firm, partly ash. The peak you reach is actually the highest point on the mountain, but you cannot see the crater itself from there as it lies across unstable and dangerous terrain further to the east.

The descent is hardly easier than the ascent. The steep and earthy track makes going down, grasping for dear life at trees while your feet shoot away from under you, both tiring and agony for the toes. You'll not want to linger long on the summit if you hope to be back in Besakih before dark (5:45 PM).

From Sebudi

If your aim is to see into the crater of Agung, it is far better to make the ascent from Sebudi, rather than Besakih. Take the road to Selat, east of Rendang, and ask from there. Again, hiring a guide is advised as the path is not well marked. Sebudi is a small village, so it might be more practical to engage a guide in advance of your visit.

Where to Stay and Eat

As most visitors visit on day-trips, there are very few good places to stay. Two kilometers (just over a mile) before the temple there is the **Arca Valley Homestay and Restaurant** on the road to Menanga (no phone, budget) and you'll get someone to put you up if you ask around the market that springs up daily. The only people who stay at Basakih are those planning to climb the mountain. Spoiled by a steady stream of day-trip visitors, the restaurants don't have to try too hard here — and they don't.

How to Get There

Besakih is almost always reached through tours booked from the tourist office or arranged privately from the southern resort areas. If driving yourself, head for Bangli or Hanjarangkan to Menanga, where you take the turning for Besakih (six kilometers or four miles). After a descent of about a kilometer (just over half a mile), the road traverses a wooden bridge over the River Yehunda; the bridge replaced one that was destroyed by the 1963 eruption of Agung.

From here on, the road ascends steadily toward Besakih. As you approach, a slip road leads off uphill to the left. If you take this road you will arrive nearer the central area of the temple than if you go straight on to the official entrance, though the latter approach is the more spectacular, being a processional avenue along the temple's major alignment. Taking the left-hand route, you arrive at a parking lot on your left (where you must leave your car) followed by a mass of food and souvenir stalls as wall as permanent shops. Beyond these is the temple.

It is also possible to cross over to Besakih from Penelokan. From Penelokan the views are magnificent, down to the left through the trees to the lake and volcano below. After the turnoff to the right it becomes steeper and potholed. The road descends along a giant spur, affording wonderful views, in good weather, of Mount Agung to the left.

Rendang to Klungkung

From Rendang, south of Besakih, a most attractive road runs east then south through Selat and Sidemen to Klungkung.

Not far out of Rendang, on the right side of the road, there is a high, tapering barn-like building used for drying tobacco.

Iseh has had its share of resident artists and writers, but is itself of little interest. The attraction of this area of Bali is the countryside itself, rice terraces with forest above them and Mount Agung on the skyline. This steeply hilly countryside is reminiscent of the Massif Central of France, or mid-Wales.

At **Sidemen** there is a modern dam across the river, several new out-of-town houses, children who ask for money and the feeling that the idyll has come to an end. But the road continues down via **Sukat** through pleasant country, until the gradient lessens and you find yourself entering the ancient provincial capital of Klungkung.

The mountainous village of Penelokan is dominated by Mount Agung's symmetrical vocanic peak — Bali's highest mountain, it is usually shrouded in clouds by midday.

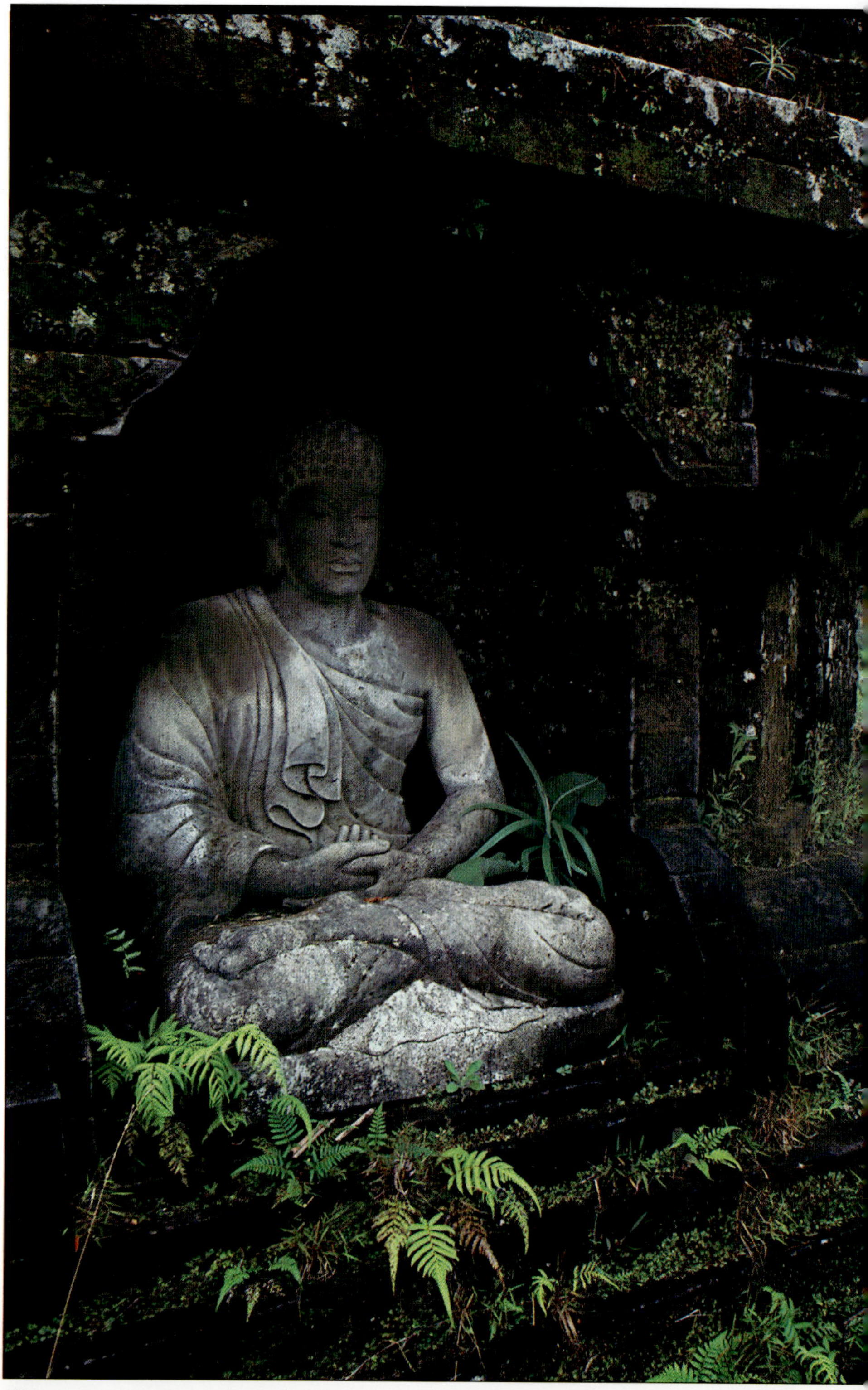

East Bali

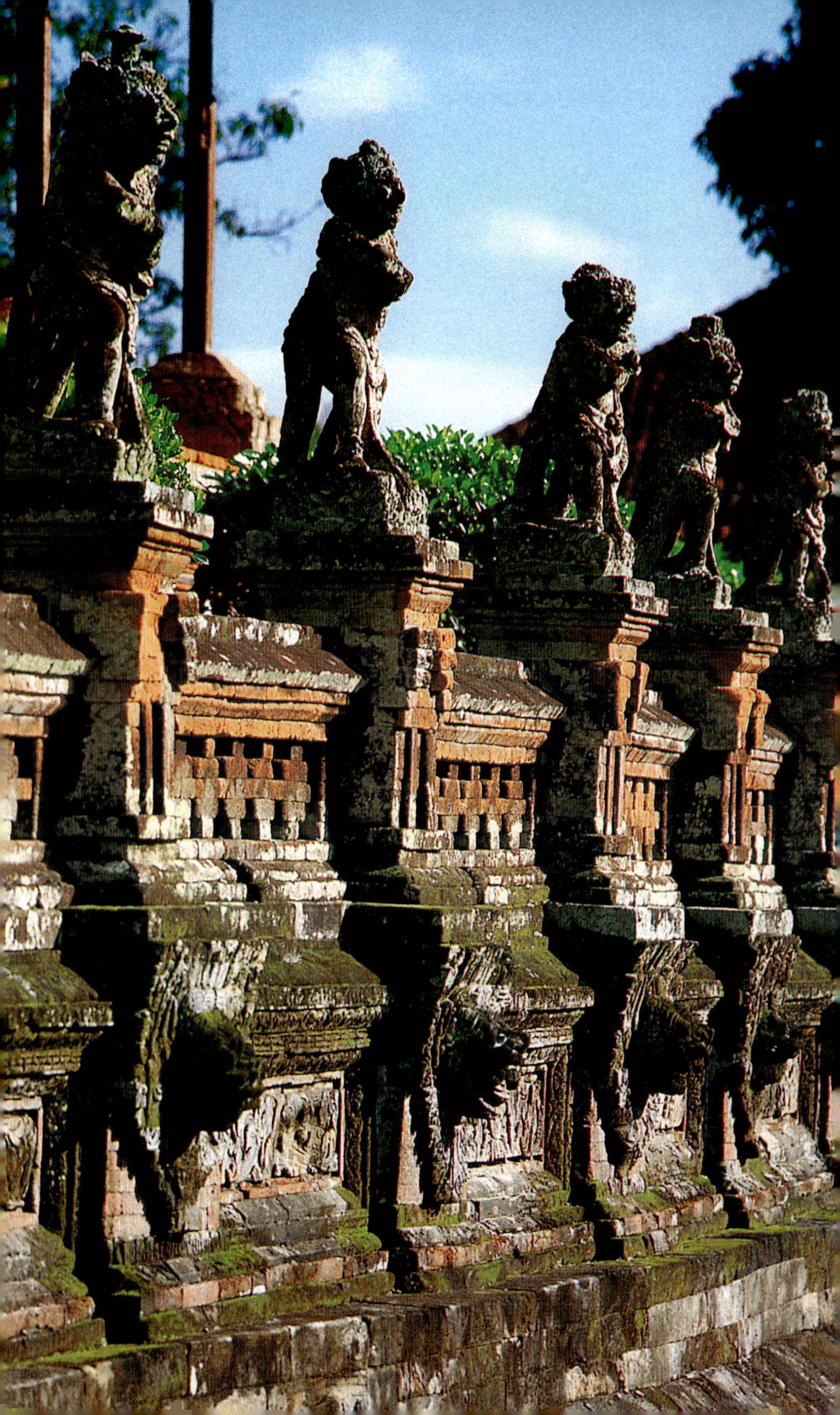

EASTERN BALI, THE LOWER SLOPES OF THE GREAT volcanoes that make up the central highlands, shelters some of the most atmospheric and authentic towns on the island, some notable water palaces and beautiful unspoiled rice terraces, as well as little-known coastal resorts where tourism is still in its early stages, not yet impacting on traditional ways of life.

Spin northeast off the Jalan Ngurah Rai (Bypass), head through Klungkung and drop down to the coast at Padangbai. For Indonesians, this is an important transit town on the tortuous ferry links that join the islands into a single country. For travelers, it is an atmospheric town and beach resort with few formal facilities. It is easy to stay for a while and get to know the locals in the low-key scatter of small-scale developments. Further east and Candi Dasa is a beach resort whose beach has washed away. This actually makes it a rather welcoming place, as the residents make up for their natural disadvantages by making even more effort to keep visitors happy. Hotel rates are lower than the main resorts, it is a good dive center, and there are a few patches of sand for sunbathing. This is the beach resort favored by many expatriates.

Continuing north from here, the roads pass through the regional center of Amlapura (Karangasem), where very few tourists stay (though they can), and on through some of the most spectacular rice terracing in Bali. Tirtagangga is a good base to explore the agrarian landscape, as well as water palaces dating back to the era of Balinese kingdom-states. Dropping back to the northern coast the road heads on to Amed, one of the most remote of all recent developments. A few small hotels are set on or over a looping sequence of beaches, some with black sand and others white, lined with the countless outrigger canoes of fishermen commuting from Java. This is a part of the island where villagers labor to drain salt from the sea, survive on a diet of fish, and the few hotels and lodges represent the last high watermark of tourism to the island.

From this turning point the main coast road heads west, back to Tulamben and more established tourism. But for many visitors these small eastern settlements contain all the charm of an unspoiled Bali while still being reasonably close to the main southern resorts.

KLUNGKUNG

Thirty-nine kilometers (24 miles) east of Denpasar lies the former royal capital of Klungkung, sometimes known by its original name of Semarapura. Klungkung itself is a combination of a quiet country town and an Oriental market. Marigolds piled by their thousands on blue tarpaulins, groups of girls skinning tiny mauve-colored onions, *bemo*s arriving from all parts, patented scorpion medicines being sold at the curbside, the harsh glare of kerosene lamps as corn cobs are toasted and yesterday's hits from Jakarta jangle out from a mobile jukebox, a post-cremation *angklung* (processional *gamelan*) in the intensely hot afternoon. Klungkung may have only the one monument, but it is attractive in a way Denpasar no longer is, its atmosphere little diluted by the impulse to cater to the foreign needs and tastes of tourists.

The town is quiet and tidy. There is a market, some shops, one passable hotel (see below), and a famous monument, **Kertha Gosa**, the courthouse of the old kingdom of Klungkung. It consists of two buildings, an elegant little "floating palace" — a raised and much-decorated pavilion set in the middle of a wide moat and originally used

Klungkung — OPPOSITE: Part of the "floating palace," at Kertha Gosa. Klungkung has the charm of an Indonesian country town little touched by the tourist influx that has inundated nearby locations. ABOVE: Handpainted movie posters.

East Bali

as a retreat for the judges — and the actual court, raised high on your right as you enter.

The dreadful punishments said to be reserved for sinners in another life are vividly illustrated on the roof of the little court — mothers who refused to suckle their young being forced to give the breast to a poisonous fish, confirmed bachelors being savaged by a wild boar, and so on. These pictures are in fact 40-year-old copies, made on asbestos, of the originals.

Everything is very delicate, not least the worn red-brick floor, and the only pity is that the compact complex, so restful in design, is situated so very close to Klungkung's main intersection. This was, however, the intention of is builders: The open-sided court was not only raised up high but set at the very center of the town, open, public and for all to see. A quieter place among the water lilies was set aside for the judges — high priests (*pedanda*) from the Brahmana caste — to consider their judgments.

Both buildings are intricately carved; the stone animals supporting the pillars in the courthouse are particularly noteworthy. Entrance is Rp10,000; Rp5,000 for children. The monument is open from 6 AM to 6 PM daily.

The **market** has recently been relocated one kilometer (just over half a mile) out of town and is over by early afternoon.

WHERE TO STAY

The only hotel in Klungkung that is remotely satisfactory is the **Logi Ramayana Palace Hotel** ((0366) 21044, Jalan Diponegoro 152 (budget). The owner, Nyoman Gede, speaks excellent English, and there is a large temple attached, reached down a few steps from the restaurant. If this is full, cross the street to **Cahaya Pusaka** ((0366) 22119, Jalan Diponegoro 135 (budget).

HOW TO GET THERE

Klungkung is an important link in the public-transportation system around the east of Bali. You can transfer here for a *bemo* to Besakih in the north and for Padangbai, Candi Dasa and Amlapura to the east. Klungkung is 57 km (36 miles) from Kuta, 47 km (29 miles) from Denpasar and 27 km (17 miles) from Candi Dasa.

ABOVE and OPPOSITE: The terrors that await evildoers in the afterlife, and the glee with which their tormentors go about their work, are vividly depicted on the walls of the Kertha Gosa (the ancient courthouse) in Klungkung.

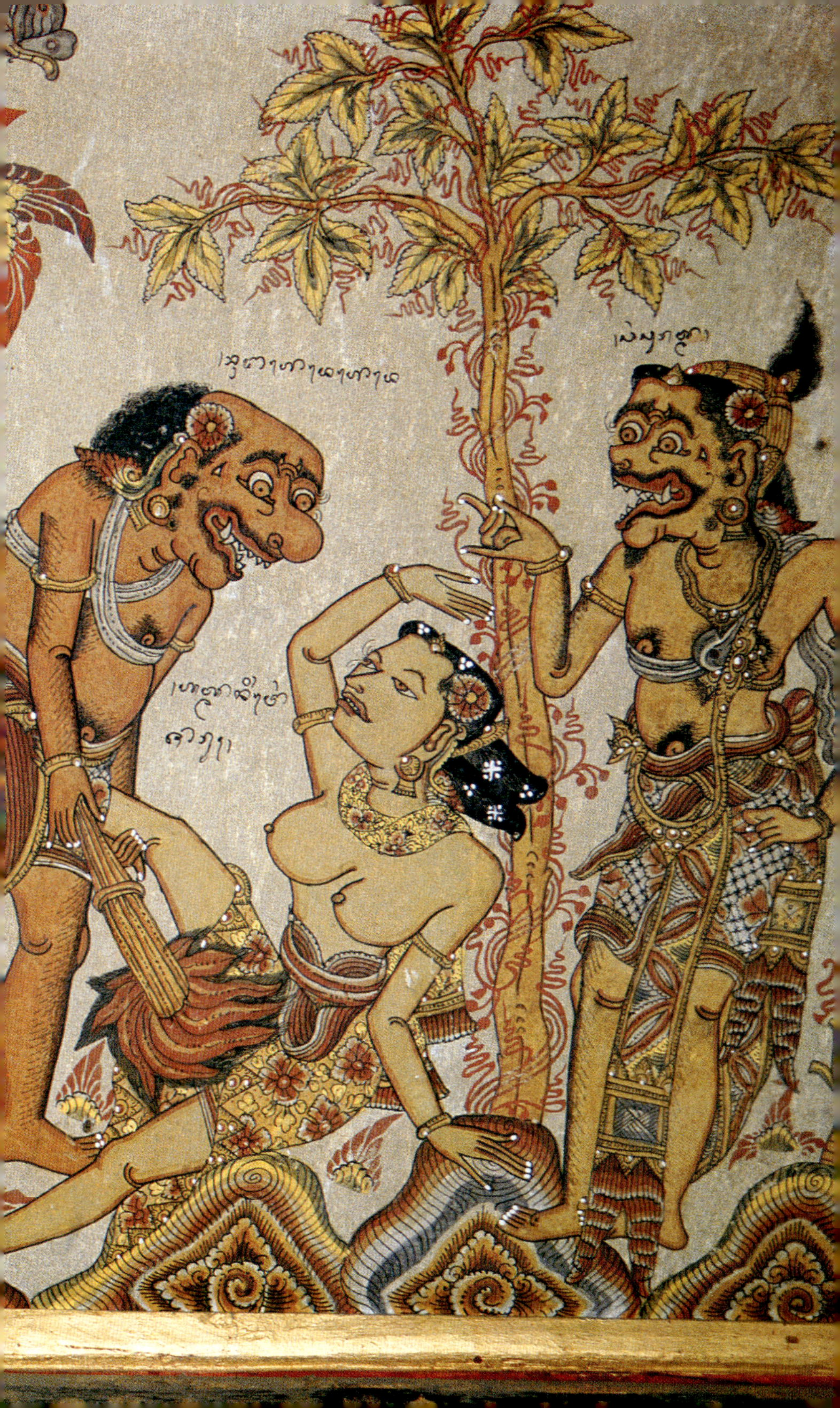

Kusamba's main street. This is the small market and fishing village from which boats leave for **Nusa Penida** and **Nusa Lembongan**. To reach the sea, turn right in the middle of the village. A lane runs straight to the beach past a mosque. Ask at the last *warung* on the right about boats to the islands. Don't, however, expect to be able to leave any later than early afternoon: Waves tend to build up in the Badung Strait during the day and by mid-afternoon landing on the beach at Kusamba — there is no jetty — becomes dangerous. The one way fare in a wooden motorized *prahu* is about Rp75,000, and the trip takes an hour. As usual you will have to wait for enough passengers to turn up to justify the crossing. If you want to go on your own and at once it will cost you in the region of Rp150,000. Boats will also take you to Nusa Lembongan.

Bat Cave

A couple of kilometers east of Kusamba is the extraordinary **Goa Lawah**. It's only a relatively small opening in the limestone cliff, but it is the home of what appear to be hundreds of thousands of semi-nocturnal bats. A temple has been built immediately in front of the caves entrance, and it's necessary to pay a donation of Rp10,000 in return for the loan of a scarf.

It isn't possible to enter the cave as the low roof is completely covered in bats and the floor coated in a thick layer of guano. Several shrines stand just inside the cave, also guano-crowned. But there's no need to go in to see the bats at close quarters — they crowd together over large areas of the outside walls, and it is easy to get within half a meter of them. Hanging upside down in full daylight, they twist their necks and peer at onlookers as they approach, preparing themselves no doubt for flight. With the massed creatures, they're squeaking, the crowds of kneeling devotees, the incense, the priests' prayers and the flashing of tourists' cameras — it's at one and the same time grotesque, comic and wonderful.

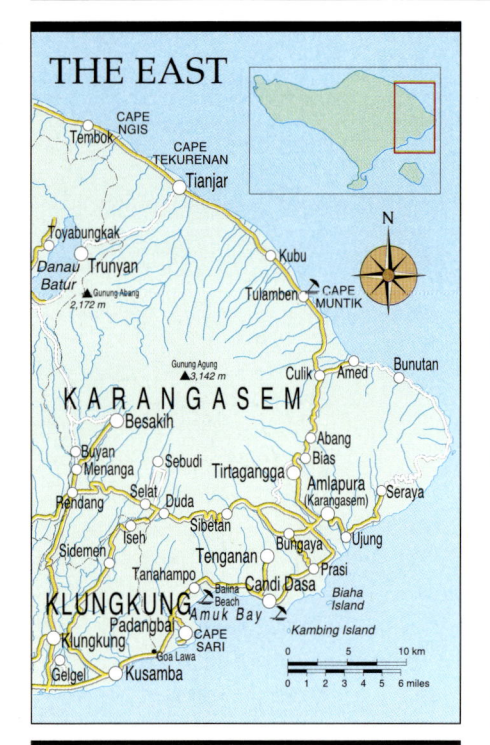

Excursions from Klungkung

Directly to the south of Klungkung, leaving the town by Jalan Puputan, are the villages of **Gelgel** and **Kamasan**. Gelgel is the old, pre-eighteenth century capital of the area and, though it was ravaged by lava in 1963, the old **Royal Temple** still stands. Pottery making can also be seen here. Kamasan is the center for a traditional style of painting.

A worthwhile excursion from Klungkung is to the fields of lava left by the eruption of Mount Agung in 1963. Set out from town on Jalan Diponegoro, passing the Logi Ramayana Hotel on your right, on the road to Karangasem, then crossing the River Unda by way of a high bridge. The extensive lava fields can be seen to the right of the road. The lava flowed seawards in two arms, this one to the west and another, following the valleys of the rivers Buhu, Banka and Njuling, to the east. Both Amlapura, which stands on the banks of the Njuling, and Klungkung were thus lucky to escape serious damage.

This is also the route to the nearest port to the islands of Nusa Penida and Nusa Lembongan. Seven kilometers (four miles) from Klungkung, the road runs through

Goa Lawah — the sacred Bat Cave. Home to hundreds of thousands of fruit bats, a temple has been built here, and throughout the day a stream of devotees arrive, many bearing offerings. The temple is as interesting as the bats, and the juxtaposition of the two is astonishing.

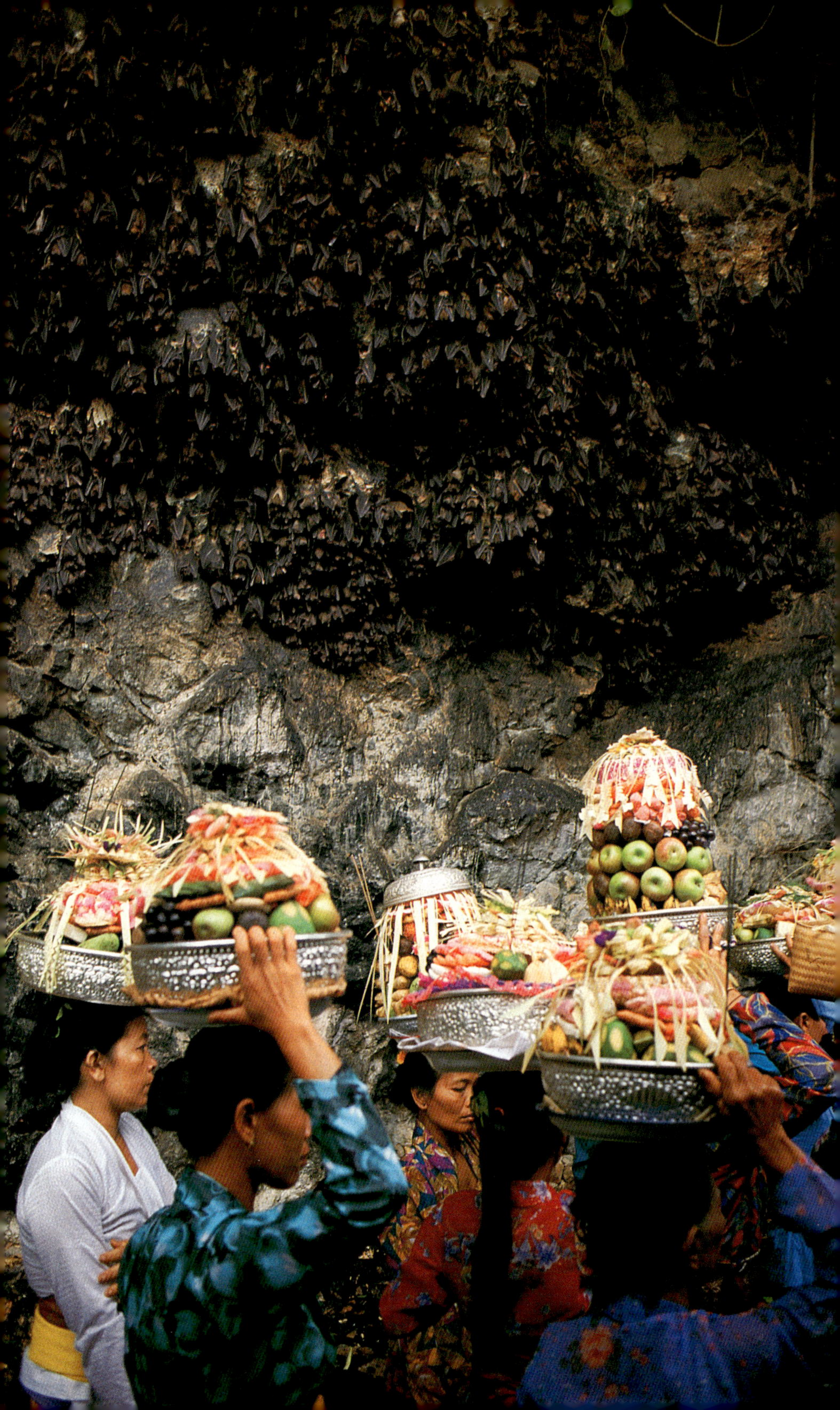

The cave is situated directly on the main road and no one should drive past without sparing a few minutes for a look, however pressed they are for time, or however anxious to get on to the comforts and consolations of Candi Dasa.

Salt from the Sea

Directly over the road from the bat temple, on the black sand beach, is a primitive salt factory, where salt is procured from sea water. Under a thatched roof water drips down bamboo pipes and a solitary worker displays a bowl of gleaming salt crystals for your admiration. Nusa Penida shimmers along the horizon.

The salt-making process is as follows: Wet sand is spread out on the beach and when partly dry is placed in a container inside one of the huts. Eventually a salty liquid begins to drip out, and this is transferred to long wooden troughs where the last of the water evaporates. It's an interesting process to observe, and like the bats of Goa Lawah, at once wholly natural and surprising: another place to see this activity is around Amed.

PADANGBAI

Eighteen kilometers (11 miles) from Klungkung is Padangbai, the terminal for the ferries to Lombok and a center for maritime links with the other islands. The village consists of a single street running inland from the harbor, and tourist accommodation plus some fishermen's huts on the left.

Padangbai has the attraction of being a fishing village away from the main tourist centers. The sandy beach is home to many colorful *prahu*, and the sale of the night's catch in the early morning alongside the boats is a colorful spectacle. Also, many of Padangbai's inhabitants are Moslems, and to stand on a hillside above the bay at sunset and hear the muezzin's song from the mosque — while a bird orchestra circles the valley as if in harmony with the words of the Prophet — is to experience something of the Old East preserved almost intact. Meanwhile there are enough Hindus here to keep temples lively with the usual Balinese pageants and festivities.

What to See and Do

The appeal of Padangbai isn't in any of its overwhelming sights, but in the quiet experience of a fishing port not yet overwhelmed by tourism. There is no official tourist information office, but if you have questions the best person to ask is the well-traveled Balinese manager, Do Deck, of the **Café Papa John (** (0812) 392-3114 (cell), The Waterfront, who is a mine of information. For flight reconfirmation, tours and lodging in Lombok there is a privately run **Tourist Information Office (** (0363) 41502 facing the harbor.

The main beach in Padangbai is usually chock-a-block with brightly painted outrigger canoes, so for swimming it's worth crossing a headland to one of the neighboring coves. To the east is the Blue Lagoon, known locally as Baong Penyu, which is good for snorkeling in the morning. To the west is Little Beach (Bias Tugel to the locals) which is, once again, calmest in the morning. Hike across another headland and you'll reach Black Sand Beach (Pantai Mimba) which is a favorite for meditators, who go there to think. Some of Bali's finest dives are found in the area, and a good local operator is **Geko Dive (** (0363) 41516 FAX (0363) 41790 E-MAIL geko dive@indosat.net.id, Jalan Silayukti, Padangbai.

Where to Stay

The most luxurious place to stay in the area is a few kilometers east of town, in the **Amankila (** (0363) 41333 FAX (0363) 41555 E-MAIL amanres@indosat.net.id, Manggis, (expensive). This sublimely designed and managed haven of comfort is slightly spoiled by the constant stream of tankers heading across the bay from a newly built refinery. Within Padangbai itself there are a number of places to stay, all offering excellent value for money. The best place to stay in Padangbai is the biggest, the **Puri Rai (** (0363) 41385 FAX (0363) 41386, Jalan Silayukti 3 (inexpensive). It has both air-conditioned rooms priced in United States' dollars and cheaper fan-cooled rooms priced in rupiah. It is well-kept and has a clean, cheerful restaurant under separate management that serves just about every kind of food, including Indonesian, Chinese and Western. A good alternative is the **Padang Bai Beach Inn** ((0363) 4147, Jalan Silayukti (budget to inexpensive), with very comfortable two-floor thatched longhouses, ideal for families, as well as basic chalet accommodation for backpackers. There is no restaurant here but they serve very good breakfasts.

In the immediate area are a number of small *losmens* with rock-bottom prices, especially off-season. There are also a few restaurants and bars, most specializing in seafood fresh from the fishing boats, including the **Pandan Restaurant**, a few yards away from the Puri Rai.

There are many *losmens* nearby offering ultra-cheap rooms, and for inexpensive but good food there is the **Depot Segara**.

Padangbai is small — all of the places listed are within 200 m (about 220 yards) of each other.

How to Get There

As a major jumping-off point for ferries to Lombok and boats to the other islands, Padangbai is well-served by local *bemos* as well as shuttle buses catering to tourists. Ferries for Lombok leave Padangbai every hour and a half, 24 hours a day. Fares are Rp9,500 for economy class and Rp16,000 first class. The fee for automobiles is Rp170,000: the crossing takes between three and five hours, depending on the weather. For further information the Harbor Office ((0363) 41840. Padangbai is 18 km (11 miles) from Klungkung

CANDI DASA

Candi Dasa (pronounced "chandi dasa") is a compact resort 13 km (eight miles) southwest of Amlapura, and is the main resort development on this stretch of coast. The name probably means Ten Tombs and refers to some ancient monuments near the village of **Bug Bug** (pronounced "boog boog"), two kilometers (one and a quarter miles) to the east.

Candi Dasa's tragedy is that because of ecological mismanagement, it no longer has a beach. It used to: its protective offshore reef was mined for lime in the 1980s and what beach there had been was swept away by ocean currents. Concrete groins have been constructed to prevent further erosion, and

More arid than the southern regions of the island, the eastern strip of lowland, behind Candi Dasa, is also devoted to rice cultivation.

their rectangular patterns now dominate what's left of the shore, acquiring, as planned, small patches of sand to try to replace the lost beach, but most of the hotels, rather forlornly, give onto a rocky shore.

Even so, there is considerable peace and quiet, and at a lower cost than that at Sanur, for example. Candi Dasa originated in the rage to find a quieter alternative to Kuta in the lower price bracket, and though the unspoiled ambiance of the early 1980s is now gone, the place does remain relatively tranquil. A local bylaw restricts wandering vendors and all forms of street-trading and another one makes it difficult or impossible to establish noisy outlets such as discotheques so residents here perfect their suntans in their hotel garden or along the sea wall with the minimum of interruptions, and for those who regard a sandy beach as essential to their well-being there are plenty to be found up and down the coast.

General Information

There is a **Tourist Office** ((0363) 41204, Lila Arnawa, Candi Dasa, open 8 AM to 2 PM daily, where it is possible to arrange transport. One local operator is **Safari Rent a Car** ((0812) 392-1475 (cell). There is no private health clinic here and any serious injury should be referred over to the **government clinic** ((0361) 22188 in Prasi or, rather better, to the main hospital in Denpasar.

What to See and Do

Established first as a beach destination, back when there was a beach, for its major attractions Candi Dasa still looks out to sea. It's a major center for snorkeling and diving, with three tiny offshore islands, Gili Tepekong, Gili Biaha and Gili Mimpang, the last being little more than a rock. Underwater there are drop-offs and chasms, and it's a good place to spot big pelagics. Boat owners will take snorkelers out for about Rp75,000 but make sure masks and flippers are included in the price, and watch out for currents, which can be fierce. Meanwhile there are also trails that hike into the **foothills** of Gunung Agung immediately inland. After all that exertion, relax with a skilled massage at the **Dewi Spa and Salon** ((0363) 41982, Jalan Raya Candi Dasa.

Where to Stay

The most exclusive place to stay in the area is not in Candi Dasa but a few minutes' drive to the west in an exclusive enclave known, postally at least, as Manggis. **Amankila** ((0363) 41333 FAX (0363) 41555, Manggis, Candi Dasa, is perched on a hillside with an views across to Nusa Penida and Lombok. Each room is a self-contained villa and a road winds down to what is essentially a private beach, but since the construction of a refinery in the Amuk Bay the view is not as idyllic as it once was. Rates start from US$550 for a regular suite and prices heading up from there. A slightly less expensive alternative is the **Serai** ((0363) 41011 FAX (0363) 41015 E-MAIL seraimanggis@ghmhotels.com, Desa Buitan, Manggis (expensive), which is secluded. Less expensive again is the **Balina Beach** ((0363) 41002 FAX (0363) 41001, Desa Bunutan, Manggis, with a range of designer bungalows which vary in price, and a good restaurant (moderate).

In Candi Dasa proper the **Puri Bagus Beach Hotel** ((0363) 41291 FAX (0363) 41290, Jalan Raya Candi Dasa, is one of the best hotels (expensive). It is situated at the end of a drive at the far eastern end of the beach, and though there is no beach as such, both the site and the swimming are good. The only hotel in Candi Dasa with a beach is the moderately priced **Candi Beach Cottage** ((0363) 41234 FAX (0363) 41111, Desa Senkidu, Kecamatan, Manggis, situated about a kilometer (half a mile) before you reach the village center when coming from Klungkung. It has a swimming pool and a lush garden, together with an excellent restaurant. Other good hotels with moderate rates include the **Candi Dasa Beach Hotel** ((0363) 41126 FAX (0363) 41537 E-MAIL arbhuana @indo.net.id, Jalan Raya Candi Dasa, and the **Ida Beach Village** ((0363) 41118 FAX (0363) 41041, Desa Samuh, built in the style of a traditional Balinese village with air-conditioned cottages and traditional *lumbungs* or rice barns, thatched and fan-cooled, ideal for families.

Candi Dasa has some smart new accommodation offering luxurious villas in garden settings. The two to consider first are the **Kubu Bali** ((0363) 41532 FAX (0363) 41531, Jalan Raya Candi Dasa (moderate), and the slightly more expensive **Hotel Taman Air**—also known as **The Watergarden** ((0363) 41540 FAX (0363) 41164, Jalan Raya Candi Dasa, which has 12 villas, five with air-conditioning set among waterfalls and elegant gardens (moderate). Both of these hostelries are a few meters up the gentle hill on the left of the main road when arriving from Klungkung.

For simple accommodation on the eastern side of town try the **Hotel Genggong** ((0363) 41105 (budget).

To the west of town are some *losmens* offering very inexpensive accommodation. Of these, the **Pelangi Homestay** ((0363) 41270, Jalan Raya Candi Dasa (budget), is clean and friendly and can be recommended, not least for the gentle sounds of *gamelan* played by the owner at nightfall, or the **Pandawa Bungalows** ((0363) 41929, Jalan Raya Candi Dasa, which has 10 bamboo bungalows on the beach (budget).

WHERE TO EAT AND NIGHTLIFE

As for food, a superior place to eat in Candi Dasa is the **Lotus Seaview** ((0363) 41257, an offshoot of the famous Café Lotus in Ubud. It's expensive, but they serve only first-class fare.

Other good dining spots are the restaurant belonging to the **Kubu Bali**, on the main road and below the hotel itself which is famous for its seafood, and **TJ's**, up against the Hotel Taman Air and sharing the same phone number. The latter serves good Western meals and stuffed baked potatoes, etc. For Indonesian cuisine try **Warung Ibu Rusimi**, Jalan Raya Candi Dasa, for inexpensive but well-prepared traditional dishes.

Once strangely quiet, Candi Dasa has finally decided to allow dance venues. There is live music every night at **Ciao Pub'n Ristorante Italiano** ((0363) 41278, Jalan Raya Candi Dasa from about 9 PM. Also along Jalan Raya Candi Dasa you'll find **Go-Go's**, popular with the young, and the **Beer Garden Disco**, which stays open even later.

HOW TO GET THERE

Tourist shuttle buses link Candi Dasa with Ubud, Sanur and Kuta, while public transport uses Denpasar's Batubulan Terminal. It is 72 km (45 miles) northwest of Denpasar.

The beach at Candi Dasa is lined with small hotels along all but this unusually solitary stretch.

Excursions from Candi Dasa: Tenganan

Immediately to the west of Candi Dasa a road leads off to the left running four kilometers (two and a half miles) to Tenganan. Motorbikes wait to take those with no other means of transportation.

Tenganan is Bali's foremost example of the social organization of the Bali Aga, whose other main village is at Trunyan (see page 178), but Tenganan is as neat, tidy and prosperous as Trunyan is grubby and impoverished. Fortunately the village has not yet been spoiled by rows of stalls selling cheap mass-produced clothes and souvenirs to tourists.

The prime feature of Tenganan life is that everything is held communally; membership in the community is as a result strictly controlled. As the village is a major landowner in the area, its privileged three hundred or so inhabitants do little menial work and are free to devote their time to weaving, writing on *lontar* leaves, or simply admiring one another's fighting cocks, some of which are dyed pink. Styles and forms of dance (the *rejang*), ritual fighting (*pandan*), instrumental music (*gamelan selunding*) and *ikat* cloth (*gringsing*) are found here that occur nowhere else in Bali. Full details can be found in Madi Kertonegoro's *The Spirit Journey to Bali Aga, Tenganan Pegringsingan*, a whimsical and informative book that depicts well the genial spirit of the village.

The village looks utterly unlike any other in Bali. The family compounds are arranged in long lines on either side of the north–south concourses which rise in successive terraces as they move uphill. Because the compounds each have a pavilion with an overhanging roof immediately inside the external wall, the appearance is of a street of houses with thatched roofs in, perhaps, the west of England. At the far end is a communal meeting place, the *bale paruman desa*, while the village temple is near the entrance from the road, surrounded by frangipani trees.

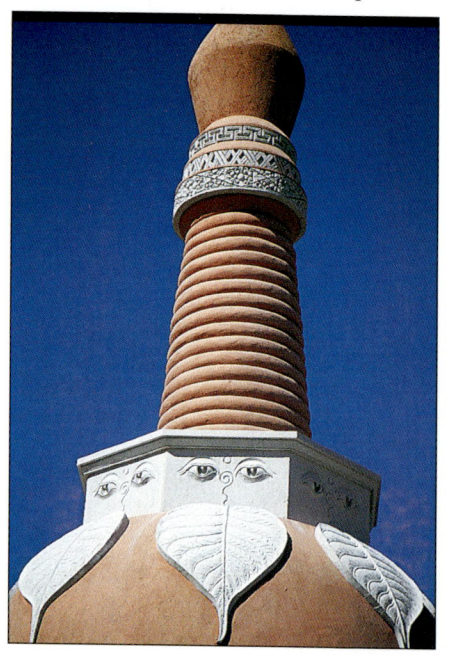

The section of the village away to the right (east) is reserved for villagers who have in some way forfeited full membership of the community. It is known as **Banjar Pande**. Here small windmills (*pinengan*, meaning wings) can be seen above the houses, serving no practical purpose but constructed just for pleasure. Up the hill behind Banjar Pande is the cemetery; the Bali Aga here do not expose their dead like their cousins in Trunyan but bury them in the ground in accordance with the practice of the Indra sect of Hinduism.

At first sight it looks as if Tenganan is mostly tourist shops. All the sales activity, however, is concentrated in the first street you come to; in the parallel street to the right there is none at all. All the shops are part of people's houses. In the **Indra Art Shop**, for example, you can take a coffee while the owner, I Wayan Gelgel, inscribes a motto for you on a *lontar*. First he cuts in the words with a pointed knife, then rubs in a black oil from the burnt *kemiri* nut. He has a collection of old *lontar* books, leaves threaded on a string with bamboo covers. The words are inscribed on one side, illustrations on the other. The texts are old stories from the *Ramayana*. The books are fastened closed with an old Chinese coin, Bali's first money, used now only for ceremonial purposes. The *lontar* leaves have been first boiled in salty rice water to strengthen and preserve them.

The craft shop of I Nyoman K. Nurati is in the house where the Swiss writer Urs Ramseyer stayed while writing his *Art and Culture of Bali* — he now runs a hotel in Sidemen.

AMLAPURA (KARANGASEM)

The Balinese usually refer to their main towns by the name of the districts, or *kabupaten*. Denpasar is Badung; Singaraja, Buleleng; and Amlapura, Karangasem. This last substitution is so common that occasionally, even when the name Amlapura is being used, it is listed in alphabetical indexes under the letter "k." The name Amlapura was only officially adopted in 1963, and Karangasem is still the name on the lips of every *bemo* conductor in the streets of Klungkung touting for passengers heading east. There is a **Tourist Information Office** ((0363) 21196, open mornings, Monday to Saturday.

THE PALACE

There is only one site deserving of a visit in the town: the palace (entrance: Rp10,000). It's setting, however, is the real draw, for which you don't need an entrance fee.

OPPOSITE LEFT : The Buddhist temple at Banjar. RIGHT: Buddhism coexists with the dominant Hinduism — there are, for example, Buddhist *pedanda* (high priests) as well as Hindu ones. ABOVE LEFT: As in this example from Amlapura, erotic dalliance is in no way alien to Hindu art, while at Candi Dasa RIGHT a different aesthetic is enforced.

AMLAPURA (KARANGASEM)

The various *puri* are part of one and the same complex and together originally constituted the living quarters of the family of the rajah of Karangasem. Some — the Madhura, for instance — are now virtually taken over by humbler residences that continue, however, to have the air of being within the domain of a palace.

The Puri Amsterdam, with its "floating" pavilion (i.e., a pavilion set in the middle of a lake), is still largely intact. Unfortunately you can not go inside the main building. Karangasem was one of the old Balinese kingdoms that made an accommodation with the Dutch, and as a result the rajah's family was allowed to retain its former status, at least outwardly. The portraits and other items that can be seen on the verandah of the main building suggest, in their combination of Dutch and Balinese styles, that the interior must have been a stately place indeed. Now cocks crow in their cages, and only the click of the rare tourist's camera and the rustle of the wind in the trees break the silence.

From here you can go down through the triple-tiered, red brick gateway and across the road to inspect more royal outhouses. In this area the problem of knowing whether or not you are actually in someone's house or an ancient monument becomes acute. The problem is easily solved by engaging some of the children who will gather around you as guides; wherever they take you, consider yourself invited. The area is extensive, on both sides of the road, and exceptionally delightful because it is quiet, lived in and — with its trees and muted elegance — human and touching.

WHERE TO STAY

Not many people stay in Amlapura, and there are correspondingly few places catering to travelers. One is the budget **Losmen Lahar Mas** ((0363) 21345, Jalan Garot Subroto 1, is a traditional Balinese *losmen*. Eating here is likely to be local food and roadside stalls, inexpensive everywhere. It is generally more convenient to explore the town as a day-trip from Candi Dasa or further afield.

HOW TO GET THERE

As it's rather off the tourist route, most public transportation is designed for the local market. There are two *bemo* stations in Amlapura, a small one for Ujung and a big one for all other destinations. Alternatively, Amlapura is well within taxi distance, and an easy drive, from Candi Dasa: a distance of about eight kilometers (five miles).

EXCURSIONS FROM AMLAPURA

Three kilometers (two miles) to the south of Amlapura is **Ujung**, and the site of the most atmospheric of the water palaces built by the last ruler of Amlapura, Anuk Agung Anglurah. The site is almost wholly in ruins, but the concept is so magnificent, and the crumbling remains now given over to agriculture so picturesque, that the complex leaves an indelible impression on the mind.

Ujung was built with Dutch aid in 1921 but severely damaged by volcanic activity in 1963. It was in the process of being restored (by two Australians who began work in 1974) when it was finally destroyed by an earthquake in 1979. The present descendants of the rajah have agreed with the government on a restoration program, and work has begun on a small scale, but to date little has been completed.

A member of the rajah's family living on the site might act as your guide and also show you a tattered photograph of the area taken a year before the earthquake. It's quite evocative in its present ruined condition.

Frangipani (*kamboja*) and palms sprout from among the fallen pillars and make artlessly elegant compositions with the grazing cattle and the one remaining dome. Above the white masonry and its flowering vegetation rise tier after tier of terraces, once gardens, topped at the skyline with further ornamental structures. A walk up steps and then away to the right will lead you to a magnificent carved head from which gushes water, against the background of the foothills of Mount Agung.

That dereliction can have its own distinctive beauty is nowhere in Bali more evident than in the ruined water palace at Ujung.

Bemos charge a mere Rp500, and a motorbike rider will charge you around Rp1,500 each way, with perhaps another Rp1,000 if they wait for you before bringing you back.

TIRTAGANGGA

Five kilometers (three miles) to the north of Amlapura is the village of Tirtagangga, a small settlement set in spectacular rice paddies that is near to the best preserved of Bali's famous water palaces. This was built by Anuk Agung Anglurah, the last raja of the Amlapura, in 1947 as part of his grand fascination with the beauty and potential of water. The village of Tirtagangga, whose name actually means "Ganges Water," was a logical place to site his water palace, but it was extensively damaged by the eruption of Gunung Agung in 1963 and, although more recent than the Water Palace at Ujung, feels far older than its years and is also in working order. The palace itself is five kilometers (three miles) to the north of Tirtagangga and, though damaged, it is still in working order. It's a charming place, little known to tourists, where fountains play and lotus flowers beam with transcendental serenity, and visitors can swim in the pools or even stay overnight. Opening hours are 7 AM to 6 PM daily; Rp1,100 is charged to go in, with another Rp2,000 if you want to swim; children pay half-price.

Where to Stay and Eat

It is possible to stay in the grounds of the Water Palace itself at the budget to inexpensive **Tirta Ayu Restaurant and Homestay** ((0363) 21697, Taman Tirtagangga, Dasa Ababi, Kecamatan Abang, owned by descendants of the raja. Alternatively, there is a range of accommodation offering better value — and better food — in the spectacular landscapes of terraced paddies to the north of Tirtagangga. A good example is the **Puri Prima** (/FAX (0363) 21316, Tirtagangga, with a range of rooms overlooking the paddies and with some of the best Balinese cooking I've found on the island. On a budget, drop a few hundred meters to the south of the Puri Prima and try the inexpensive **Kusuma Jaya Inn** ((0363) 21250, Tirtagangga, where you'll still get wonderful views.

How to Get There

The easiest way to get to Tirtagangga is with your own vehicle: it is an easy drive four kilometers (two and a half miles) north of

OPPOSITE: The palace gate at Amlapura (Kerangasem). ABOVE: Frangipani, often found in cemeteries, perfumes the air with its strong fragrance.

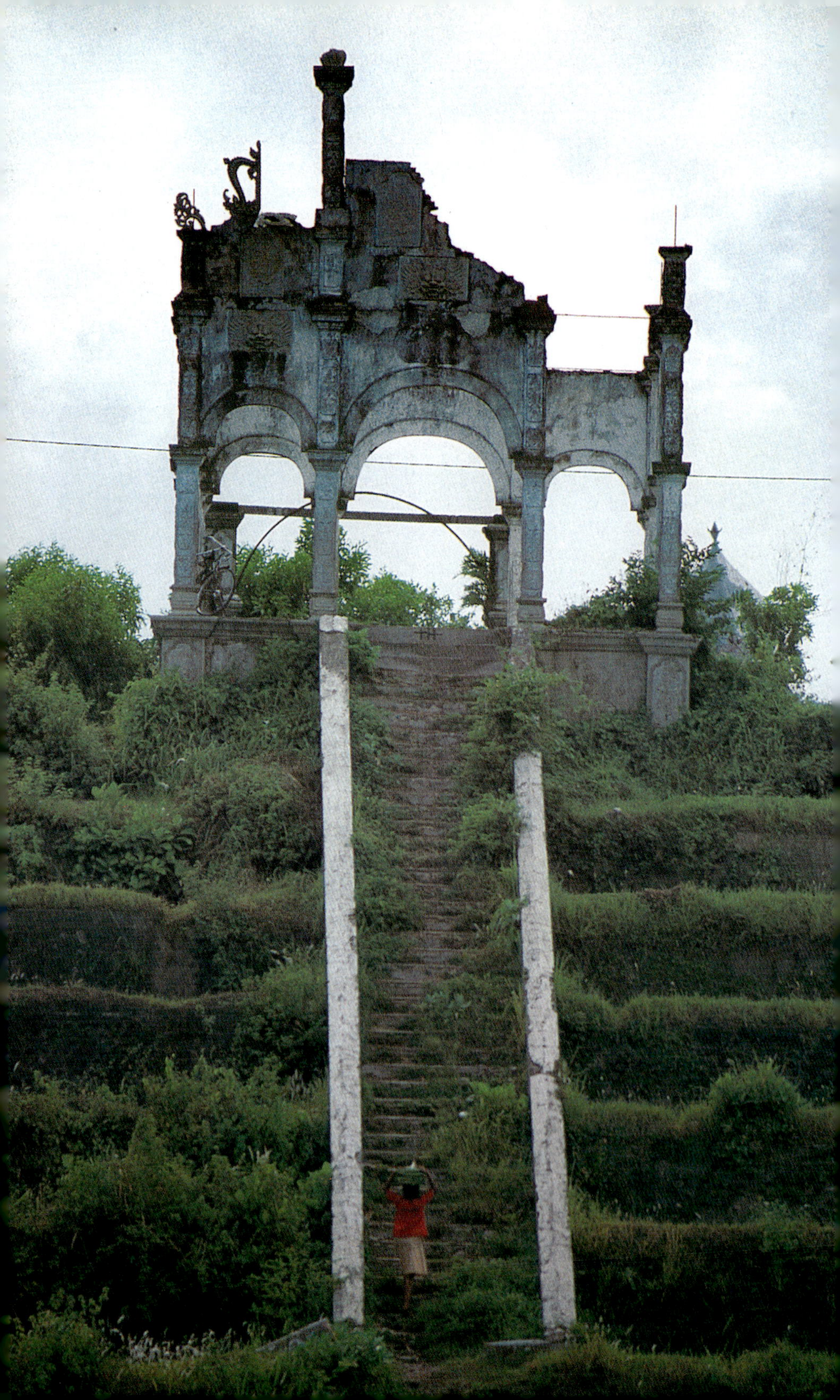

Amlapura. Alternatively the village is on the main route from Amlapura to Culik, so there are plenty of *bemos*. However the Water Palace is a fair trek from the village, unless you want to use a local motorcycle taxi, so without your own transport it is better to arrange a special tour or charter a taxi.

AMED

Amed, marked as a small village on the map, is generally taken to refer to the string of small fishing villages — and the beaches where they store their boats — in the extreme northeastern corner of the island. This is one of the least developed but most promising areas of Bali's coastline, where a few basic hotels and home-stays have grown up over recent years. The area was brought to the attention of travelers coming here for the diving, which is good, but a good part of its appeal is because it is so unspoiled. The land is poor and dry, so instead of farming, the Balinese here look out to sea for their salvation. The coast to the west of Amed is given over to salt production, one of the island's most laborious and lowest-paid occupations. Seawater is hauled inland in buckets and spread to dry by evaporation in flat, terraced pools crafted out of mud. The residue is loaded into hollowed-out palms and washed with seawater to produce a supersaturated brine. Drained down a piece of string from bamboo baskets the final solution dries into stalactites of pure(ish) salt, ready for sale.

As a career move, this has little to recommend it, and most of the locals hope for more luck from harvesting the sea. Every beach here is lined with canoes, insect-like with their upswept outriggers and painted every color of the rainbow, pulled up on the beach as neatly — and parked as closely — as any inner-city line of scooters. And if, lined up on the beach, they are a spectacular sight, that is nothing to the transformation that takes place at dawn. In the darkness men stream down to the coast, sharing cigarettes and singing low songs of praise and of prayer. Then they shoulder their craft, helping each other launch into the light morning swell. In minutes several thousand lateen-rigged fishing boats take to the water in one of the island's greatest regattas, their multicolored slashes of sail dotting the horizon as they sail out to fish the waters of the Straits of Lombok. Unsurprisingly, a new career in tourism can't fail to appeal and there are a number of homestays and bungalow developments under construction along the coast.

WHAT TO SEE AND DO

This is one of the least developed, but also one of the loveliest, parts of Bali, so don't expect any official tourist information offices, phones are a rarity and many places still survive without electricity. However there are signs of change: there is new sidewalk on the first 10 kilometers (seven miles) of coast road from Amed village heading east, and on my last visit workers were hauling up pylons to bring power to the region. It is hoped that progress doesn't spoil the area, and it has to be said that the locals welcome the new links with the outside world, along with increased chances to sell their fish.

The activities here center on diving and snorkeling. The diving operator most in evidence on Amed Beach is the **Nusantara Bahari Explorer Diving Club (** (0361) 431273

OPPOSITE: A section of the ruins of the water palace at Ujung. ABOVE: Brightly-painted fishing canoes line the beaches along Cape Jambela.

FAX (0363) 21044, and another based at the Divers Café at Amed Beach, Jemeluk. For those with their own equipment, or who just want to lie on the beach, they can almost — once they've cleared a space of boats — guarantee the place to themselves. The waters are generally calm — although there can be currents, and the sand here can be either white or a gravelly gray.

There's no nightlife to speak of and little happens even by day. This is a place to slow down to the natural speed of the changing tides and glacial speed of drying salt. Many people love it and stay much longer than they first intend.

Where to Stay and Eat

A thin collection of fairly basic accommodation is scattered along the road. One of the first you'll find is the budget **Congkang 3 Brothers** (no phone), Amed, Karangasem, whose waterside bungalows, like many in this area, take advantage of the low rainfall by having bathrooms open to the skies. Two other budget options, also on the beach, include the **Good Karma** (no phone) FAX (0363) 22244, Dusun Selang, Amed, and the **Amed Cottages** (no phone), with a dive center.

Further along the coast into the village of Jemeluk, diving becomes more central to most operators. The budget **Diver's Café** (no phone) can help with equipment and advice. Continuing east there more upmarket accommodation options which have been built into the rugged coastline of cliffs and coves. Best, perhaps, is the expensive **Indra Udhyana** ((0361) 241107 FAX (0361) 234903, Amed Beach, Bunutan, which has dance performances, diving facilities, air-conditioning and 33 gorgeous rooms. Less expensive are the **Hidden Paradise Cottages** (/FAX (0363) 431273, Lipah, Bunutan, Abang with pool and water sports facilities (moderate).

An idiosyncratic option is the **Coral View Villas** ((0361) 431273 FAX (0363) 22958 E-MAIL hpc@dps.centrin.net.id, Lipah, Bunutan, Abang (moderate). The crazy sculptures that flank the lobby are just a hint of the crazy sculptures inside the hotel itself that make this an entertaining as well as a comfortable refuge. At the other end of the scale is the best-advertised of all the lodges, with signs placed every kilometer along the road: this is the inexpensive **Meditasi** (no phone) FAX (0363) 22244, Aas Beach, Amed, which makes a great point of having no electricity. This isn't all it lacks really, as they don't even buy any food for their guests unless they are absolutely full — and maybe not even then. Still, the thatch and stone cottages are well-built in imitation of far more expensive resort hotels and it's right on a fishing beach so is a good place to watch the dawn chorus of sailing *jukung* boats. It's an acquired taste but will suit those who like their lives very simple. All of these places are situated right on the sea, facing small sandy coves with excellent snorkeling, and diving by arrangement.

How to Get There

The easiest way to get here is, again, by your own transport: from the north coast, drive east from Singaraja and turn left at Culik, for the last five kilometers (three and a half miles) into Amed. From the south drive up through Tirtagangga and turn right at Culik to drive along the same road. Amed is beginning to feature on some shuttle bus timetables but otherwise you'll have to stop off at Culik, which is on *bemo* routes from Amlapura, and then hire an *ojek* for the final few kilometers (about Rp3,000 to one of the nearer lodges). You'll have trouble persuading an *ojek* rider to take you much beyond Meditasi as the road continues to deteriorate as it rounds Mount Seraya and if you want to travel on to Ujung near Amlapura and make a circuit you'll need your own (sturdy) car or even a motorbike, which is better at skirting potholes. Whatever the vehicle, fill up with gas and leave plenty of time.

From Amed it's a 15-minute drive to the other important diving location in northeastern Bali, Tulamben.

TULAMBEN

From the road, Tulamben appears dramatic yet uninviting — dramatic, if you look left and see the flank of Agung descending in one long sweep from the volcano's summit into the sea — uninviting, because the coast here is stony and treeless. But no matter, the great attraction of Tulamben is under water.

Five hundred meters (550 yards) from the shore lies the wreck of an American World War II ship sunk by the Japanese. It's 150 m (500 ft) long and has attracted such a wealth of tropical fish and other marine life that it is today one of Bali's premier diving sites (see WRECK-DIVE A NEW REEF, page 12 in TOP SPOTS). Most of the hotels and homestays here arrange their own diving, though some of the better schools include the **Tulamben Dive Center** ((0363) 41032, **Mega Dive** ((0361) 288192 at the Mimpi Resort, and **Dive Paradise Tulamben** ((363) 41052 at the Bali Sorga; without notice." The hotel takes tour groups and is the only full-feature, resort-type hotel I've found on this stretch of coast.

Most of the accommodation options, however, are to the west of the village and nearer the *Liberty* wreck itself, which provides the region's focus. The best option is the expensive **Mimpi Resort** (/FAX (0363) 21642 in Tulamben, which has well-laid-out bungalows, almost all air-conditioned, and its own dive center. A less expensive option is the **Ganda Mayu Bungalow and Restaurant** ((0361) 730200 FAX (0361) 730385, Tulamben, the latter's Japanese manager is Emiko Shibuya, and she lives on the premises.

WHERE TO STAY AND EAT

Accommodation here tends to be rather expensive for what it is. The best reason to stay here is to dive in peace: between about 11 AM and 4 PM the wreck can get very crowded, with up to 100 divers a day going down, and it is worth diving early in the morning, or taking a night-dive, in which case staying overnight is the only option. At Tulamben you can stay at the large **Emerald Tulamben Beach Hotel** ((0361) 462673 FAX (0361) 462407 WEB SITE www.iijnet.or.jp/inc/bali/, whose rates are expensive and "subject to change whose rates run budget to inexpensive for 10 beachfront bungalows and a dive center very near the wreck entry point.

HOW TO GET THERE

Most visitors arrive in shuttle buses organized by diver operators based in the southern resorts, and dive the *Liberty* as a day-trip, albeit with three or four hours drive each way. Public *bemos* run here from either Singaraja or Amlapura. With your own transport, Tulamben is easy to find, on the northern coast road 10 km (seven and a half miles) west of Culik.

Myriad wooden outriggers in full sail off the coast of Amed.

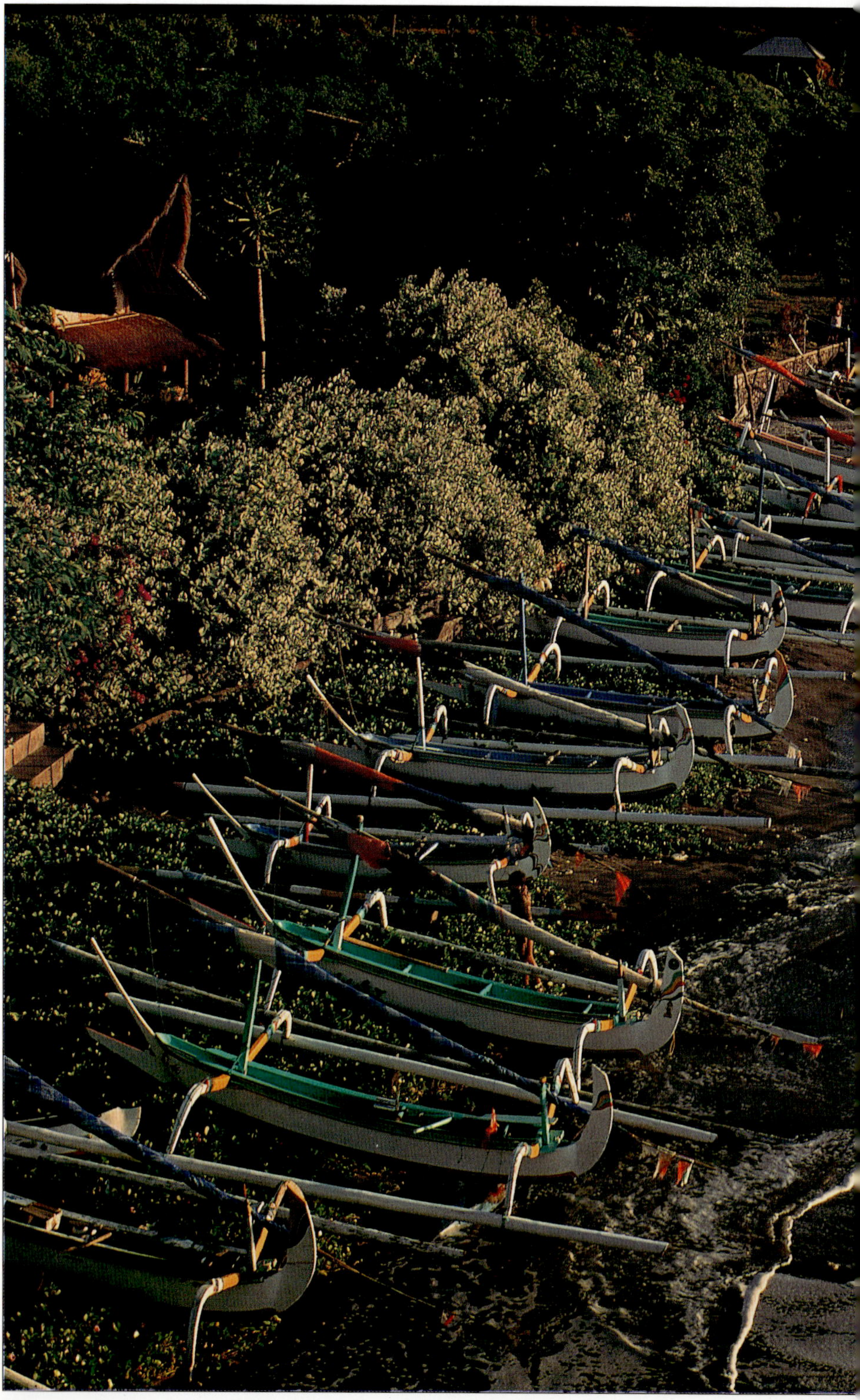

The Northern Coast

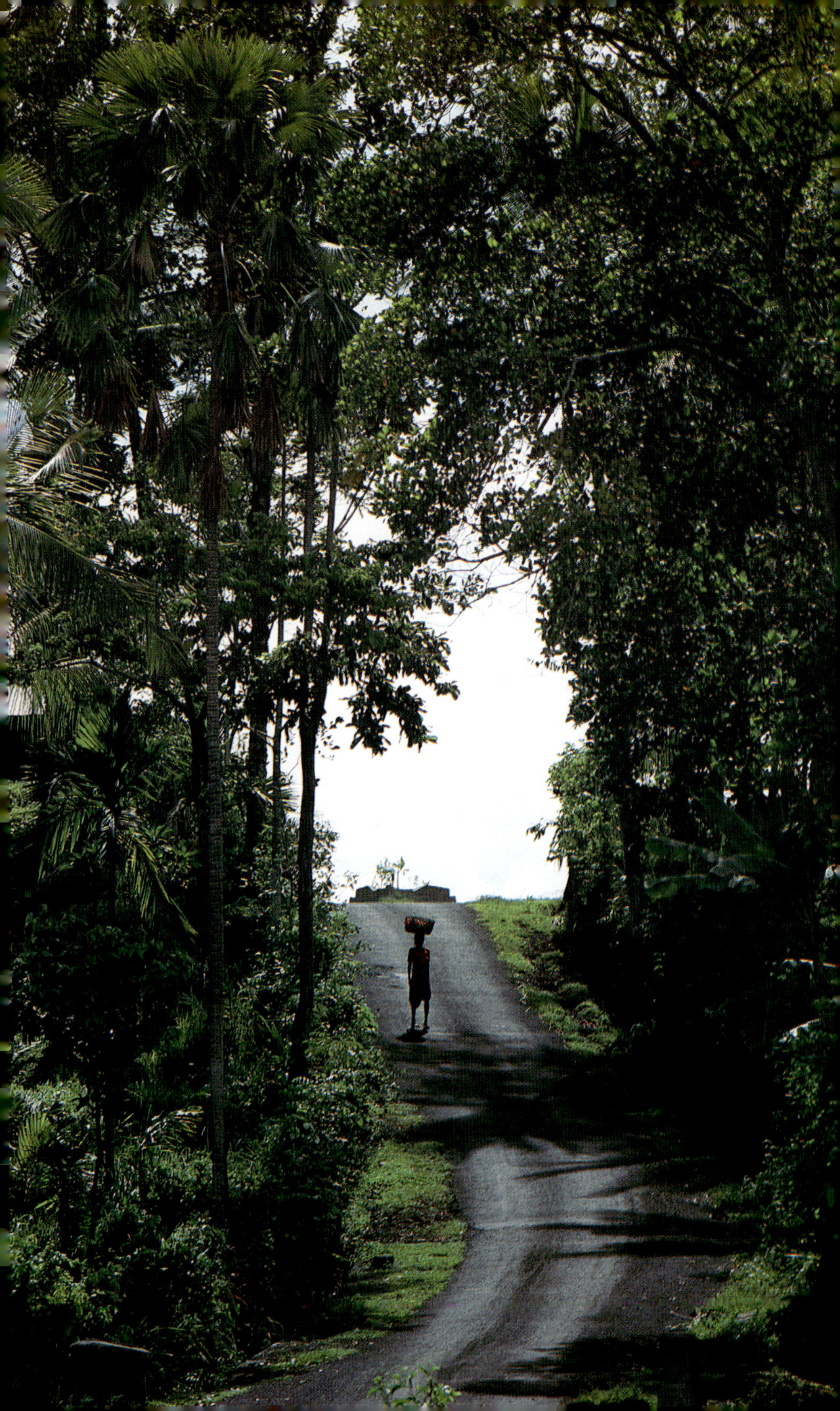

NOT SO LONG AGO NORTHERN BALI WAS REGARDED AS THE CENTER OF THE ISLAND. It was here that the colonial Dutch set up their power-base at Singaraja, which was Bali's best port. International liners used to dock here (now they make land at Benoa) and this was the main port of arrival for foreign tourists.

K'tut Tantri, the American expatriate who first established her glamorous and quickly famous international hotel at Kuta in the 1930s, landed here but chose to settle in the south as it was as far as she could get from the center of the colonial Dutch operations, and the tourist industry has followed. Singaraja, once the power base and capital, largely faded into obscurity.

The north is in many ways distinct from the rest of the island. Whereas to the south the land falls away from the central mountains gently, creating the extensive fertile plains where most of the island's population lives, to the north the land drops more steeply to the coast, affording little easily cultivable ground. Temperatures, too, are slightly higher than in the south and the rainfall approximately half that of the southern plains.

Nevertheless, the very fact that the area is somewhat different from the rest of the island is in itself an attraction. The abrupt descent of the land to the sea provides excellent views northward from temples perched on projecting spurs of land, the drier climate allows the cultivation of grapes and the seven-kilometer (four-and-a-third-mile) beach resort strip of Lovina immediately to the west of Singaraja provides fine snorkeling and a peaceful ambiance that is very much to some people's taste.

And while southern Bali gets most of the tourists' attention and Denpasar is now the island's administrative center, there are constant rumors of a new airport, and already Lovina has become a significant beach resort. As laid-back backpackers find Kuta too frenetic they are, increasingly heading to the calmer waters that wash the northern coast. There are some expensive hotels up here now, but where Lovina really wins is with it's selection of cheap accommodation, the chance to meet dolphins every morning, and the low-stress, not-quite yellow sand of its long beach.

SINGARAJA

Historically, Singaraja was once the most important city in Bali. Because it was such an important center of the Balinese administration, when the Dutch first moved into the island in 1846 they used it as their starting point and capital. The Japanese too, when they took over Bali in World War II, used Singaraja as their base. This was their major port and Singaraja assumed great importance as they worked to destabilize the remaining kingdoms in the island.

Not a lot remains of the great city. Although it is capital of Buleleng Regency this is not a wealthy area of Bali and there are few signs of past or present glory. It is chiefly interesting for its sizeable Muslim community, breaking the Hindu orthodoxy that prevails elsewhere, and can seem an attractive enough place on a sunny morning, particularly from its upper streets, which command views to the sea. But Bali is not a place that excels in its urban environments, and there is very little to see in the town. The library, **Gedong Kirtya**, is said to contain a collection of Balinese manuscripts, sacred and other texts inscribed on palm leaves (*lontar*), but no one I know has ever found the place open. The **Tourist Information Bureau (** (0362) 25141, Jalan Veteran, next door to the library, seems a superfluous institution but is open most mornings.

The town is at its best by night when the **Night Market** provides a dimly lit spectacle and adds a touch of glamour to a town that has little to offer in the way of sightseeing through the day. When electricity is available, the market operates from 6 PM to 10 PM. On the frequent occasions when they have to make do with kerosene lamps, it tends to end earlier. Many fruit sellers who set up at night along the main streets stay in business until midnight, however. The market operates seven days a week, the annual holiday Nyepi being the only exception.

Virtually no foreign visitors stay in Singaraja as the attractive beachside *losmens*

North Bali is remote from the rest of the island — poorer, hotter and quieter, with fewer tourists and a laid-back ambiance.

and hotels of Lovina, only a 15-minute *bemo* ride away, are so much more inviting. Anyone intent on spending a night in the northern capital, however, might try the **Wijaya Hotel** ((0362) 21915 FAX (0362) 25817, Jalan Sudirman 74. Alternatively an upmarket option is to stay at the **Kalaspa Health Retreat** ((0361) 419606, Br. Asahapanji, Ds. Wanagiri Suksada, Bululeng, where, presumably, you can get illnesses cured (expensive).

There are three *bemo* stations in Singaraja — **Sanket** for Denpasar, **Penarukan** for eastern destinations such as Air Saneh and Amed as far as Amlapura and **Banyuasri** for western destinations such as Banjar and Pulaki as far as Gilimanuk. Singaraja is 78 km (49 miles) north of Denpasar.

LOVINA

Lovina was launched onto the world as a new name in the 1960s, when the last rajah of Buleleng built a resort out here amid a chain of six villages on the northern coast, 14 km (nine miles) east of Singaraja. From west to east, the main villages are named Temukus, Kalibukbuk and Anturan. Of these the middle settlement, Kalibukbuk, is the most developed, with the government tourist office and the most comprehensive facilities. The western village of Temukus is quieter and more backpacker-oriented, while the eastern village of Anturan is home to more upmarket hotels and guests.

Now usurped by the general name Lovina, these villages have grown into each other along the beach that extends for several kilometers along the coast. The sand is not actually black, but just a rather darker shade of beige than is admissible under some ill-defined definition of brochure-writing etiquette. In a spirited show of defiance, the local authorities call their sand black and newcomers, when they see it, are generally pleasantly surprised.

Lovina has continued to expand, albeit at nothing like the pace of Kuta or Sanur, and more organically many of the other tourist destinations on the island. While Nusa Dua was planted on a forgotten shore of swampline and arrived, fully formed, in just a few years, Lovina still retains a quiet, though no longer quite forgotten, air. In many ways it is reminiscent of what Sanur must have been like a couple of generations ago, with a selection of small *losmens* growing into medium-sized hotels and the gaps in between being filled with cybercafés and dive schools. Yet while many of the smaller homestays still have no phone, several new luxury hotels

THE NORTHERN COAST

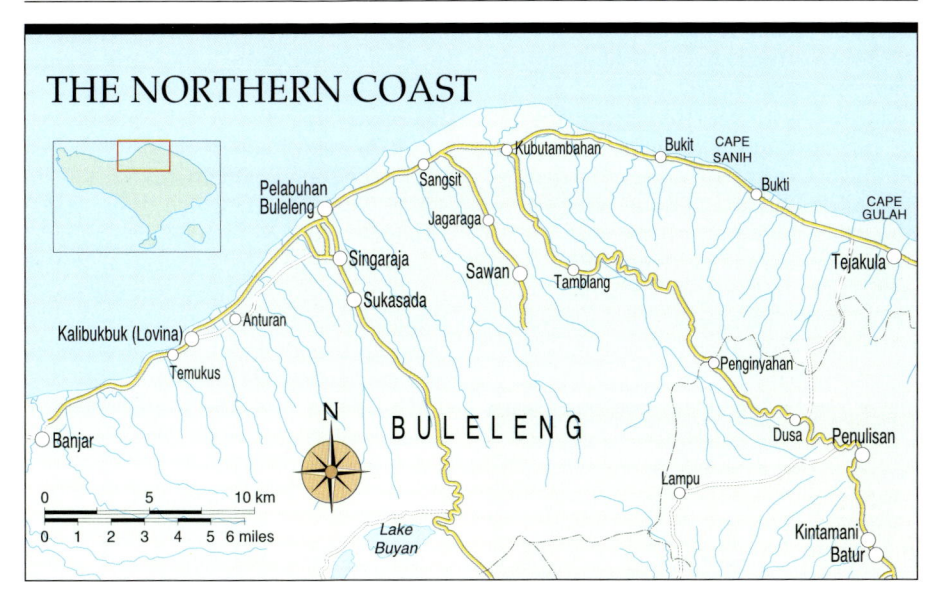

have opened, especially to the east toward Singaraja, standing incongruously among the rice paddies, and regular visitors complain that their favorite hideaway is no longer a secret, especially during the peak months of August and December.

Despite these changes, the charm of Lovina for the moment still remains. A transfer time of five hours or so from Ngurah Rai Airport keeps the riff-raff out, and in a pleasant area of tranquility calm sea-waters, a snorkelable offshore reef and the daily dawn display of dolphins offshore make this one of the best places in Bali to settle down and relax awhile.

GENERAL INFORMATION

Lovina is relatively spread out along a series of roads that turn right off the main coast road, about 14 km (nine miles) west of Singaraja. Nothing is too hard to find though, with most of the important facilities on the main road, which is called Jalan Siririt. This is where you'll find the **Tourist Office** ((0362) 91910, Jalan Siririt, which is open from 8 AM to 8 PM, daily, though they only take telephone calls in the mornings. Rather oddly, presumably, in the afternoon they just let it ring even though three members of staff are usually there.

Should you need medical attention here call the Private Hospital, **Anak Aung Udayana** ((0362) 41459, Jalan Siririt. There is an ATM in sight of the Tourist Office, undermining what, historically, was Lovina's reputation for offering poor exchange rates: now they are comparable with the rest of the island. There's no shortage of ways to get around. Every visitor who tries to walk anywhere will be constantly accosted with the cry "Transport?" If, however, you need to rent a car or a motorcycle one place offering this service is **Perama** ((0362) 21161, Jalan Siririt, Kalibukbuk, and chauffeur-drive on car or motorcycle can be arranged through **Marga Sakti Transport** ((0362) 41061 or (0362) 411570; ask for K'tut Sutarwan.

WHAT TO SEE AND DO

Dolphins and Diving

You will have no problem seeing the dolphins in Lovina. Everywhere and all day long boatmen will ask you if you'd like to go with them the next morning to see these magnificent creatures (see WATCH DOLPHINS AT PLAY, page 21 in TOP SPOTS for a full description of this not-to-be-missed experience). All you have to do is get up early in the morning which, unfortunately, is not something that Lovina encourages.

As for diving, there are several operators spread around Lovina. One is **Malibu Dive**

The lonely coast of North Bali — black sand, fishing nets; the shoreline serves as a major footpath.

Centre ((0362) 41225 E-MAIL mailbox@singarja.wasantara.net.id, Kalibukbuk, but there are more: just ask around. The coast road gives fast access from here to the best diving in the north, included Menjangan Island, one and a half hours to the east and Tulamben, for the famous wreck dive, about the same distance to the west. There's also interesting marine life on Lovina's own reef, especially convenient for a night-dive. See SPORTING SPREE, page 29 in YOUR CHOICE, for details on diving in these and other regions in Bali.

Siririt. A new hotel, offering good facilities at a reasonable price is the **Celik Agung** ((0362) 41309 FAX (0362) 41379, Jalan Siririt (inexpensive).

Of the many budget-category places on offer, a good option is the **Manik Sari** ((0362) 41089, Jalan Siririt, which offers clean, straightforward accommodation, a bar, a restaurant, and warm welcome for a very reasonable price (budget). **Palestis Beach Cottages** ((0362) 41035, Jalan Binaria, is outstanding, friendly and clean and has a brand new swimming pool (budget).

These last three are in the center of Kalibukbuk village, where a large statue of a dolphin now dominates the shoreline. Unsurprisingly, this is now known as "Dolphin Square," and there is now a guard who charges Rp500 to park near it.

Note that accommodation in Lovina tends to be cheaper than in Kuta or Legian, and spacious fan-cooled rooms with attached bathrooms can easily be found for US$4.

WHERE TO EAT

An excellent restaurant is the **Sea Breeze Café** ((0362) 41138, on the beach, offering such unexpected delicacies such as cauliflower cheese, lemon meringue pie and mango crumble. Many visitors from Singaraja consider it the best eating place in Lovina — informal but comfortable and offering a varied and imaginative cuisine. Well-patronized by visitors and also offering good, reasonably priced meals is the **Warung Kopi Bali** ((0362) 41361, Jalan Siririt, in the center of the village and often full at dinner time. Also popular, the Bali **Apik Bar and Restaurant** ((0362) 41050 is known for its wide range of drinks and hearty pizzas.

WHERE TO STAY

The eastern end of Lovina remains largely upmarket. Best is the **Puri Bagus** ((0362) 21430 FAX (0362) 22627, Jalan Siririt, where luxury rooms cost from US$200 per night. Less expensive and sharing the same stretch of beach, is the **Sol Lovina** ((0362) 41775 FAX (0362) 41659, Jalan Siririt (moderate), and the **Hotel Aneka Lovina** ((0362) 41121 FAX (0362) 41827, Jalan Siririt (moderate). The former offers a tennis court, and both hotels have swimming pools. Less expensive, but nevertheless aimed at the better-off visitor and still at the eastern end of the beach, is the inexpensive **Banyualit Beach Inn** ((0362) 41789 FAX (0362) 41563, Jalan

NIGHTLIFE

There's a certain amount of nightlife here, but it's of the quiet variety and tends to function around the hotel bars, all of which have restaurants. After the hotels have faded out the **Poco Bar** on the street leading from the main road to Dolphin Square (probably called Dolphin Street by now) has a six-piece band that plays cover versions of west coast sounds and stays open until about midnight.

After that the town is taken over by small herds of motorcyclists bleating, hopefully, "Transport?"

HOW TO GET THERE

Shuttle buses run to Denpasar, departing at 10 AM and 2 PM and at 10 PM leave for just about everywhere else in Bali as well. The fare to Kuta, for example, is Rp25,000. Long-distance buses leave for Jogyakarta (Yogjakarta) at 1 PM and for Surabaya at 7 PM. There's little point taking a *bemo* as this ends up costing as much as a shuttle bus but with far less comfort or convenience. Lovina is 89 km (56 miles) from Denpasar.

EXCURSIONS FROM LOVINA

North Bali has several attractions in addition to the beach — where the choices are limited, anyway, to the pleasures of snorkeling, swimming and dolphin watching.

THE HOT SPRINGS AT BANJAR

The Hot Springs at Banjar is one of the nicest places in the north. Whereas before 1985 there were only muddy pools fed by water falling through bamboo pipes, now there is a modern complex worthy, albeit on a small scale, of Budapest or Baden-Baden. There are now two tiled pools, one set above the other, into which a warm and slightly sulfurous stream of water gushes through magnificent dragon (*naga*) mouths. There is a restaurant up above, and the ambiance, with its flowering shrubs and terraced garden overlooking the baths, is utterly delightful. It's like coming across the Emperor Nero's private retreat right in the middle of a tropical jungle.

To get there, ask the *bemo* driver for Air Panas at Banjar. You will be put down at a road junction where several horse-drawn traps (*dokar*) will be waiting to take you the two-kilometer (one-and-a-quarter-mile) drive up to the nearby village, from where you'll have to walk; or you can go on the back of one of the many motorbikes waiting at the junction all the way from the main road.

There's a hotel at Banjar, too, a couple of hundred meters from the pools. It's the **Pondok Wisata Grya Sari** ((0362) 92903 FAX (0362) 92966, Banjar (moderate).

A privately negotiated ride on the back of a bike is also the best way to get from the springs to the **Buddhist Temple**, Banjar's

ABOVE: Twentieth-century life recorded in stone and OPPOSITE in the temple at Kubutambahan.

other attraction and something not to be missed. It's a walk of under a kilometer (around half a mile) through jungle but it's possible to lose your way; the motorbikes go by the road the long way round.

The temple is a beautiful mixture of Buddhist and Balinese Hindu elements. Set on a steep hill overlooking the sea, it contains a lily pond, a yellow Buddha and numerous red-tiled roofs at different levels that make a most attractive combination. It's an easy walk back down to the coast road.

The falls at **Labuanhaji** are of less interest. A river forces its way through a cleft in the rocks and falls some six meters (20 ft) into a murky pool. There is another fall and pool above, accessible by a slippery path.

It's certain that after heavy rain these waterfalls would be more impressive, nevertheless, given their modest scale and the lack of any facilities (in contrast to Banjar), they are barely worth the one-kilometer (just-over-half-a-mile) trudge from the road. If you do go, boys will press their services on you as "guides," in effect showing you where to turn off the lane and take the short brick path beside the paddy.

How to Get There

Banjar is 18 km (just over 11 miles) west of Singaraja. The hot springs are most often reached on excursions, best from Lovina as it is a long way from the southern resorts.

PURA BEJI'S UNHEARD MELODIES

The celebrated Pura Beji at Sangsit is one of the most elaborately crafted temples in all Bali. Here carved wings stand right out, all but free from the mother stone.

In the clammy silence, the smiling faces of the men and gods gaze out in voluptuous ease, caught forever in a moment of serene resignation. The peace and infinite generosity of Balinese Hinduism is wonderfully expressed here in this gorgeous place. "Heard melodies are sweet," wrote the English poet Keats, "but those unheard are sweeter." Here at Pura Beji the most sublime cosmic harmonies have become modulated into beautifully wrought shapes of pink stone.

The temple is not difficult to find. Sangsit itself is eight kilometers (five miles) east of Singaraja, and a small sign points the way downhill off Sangsit's main street, but anyone will show you the way — it's the only place in this little agricultural market any visitor ever goes to.

SAWAN'S GONGS

Sawan, another nine kilometers (five and a half miles) east, is an attractive village. It's known as the place where gongs for *gamelan* orchestras are fired — just say "gong" and any child will lead you up a lane and through a barn door, and there you will discover a couple of men and a woman hammering, polishing and working bellows for the fire.

The primary charm, however, lies in simply wandering through this restful place, taking lunch at a street-side *warung* and watching the easy, tranquil village life go by. Sawan is reached by *bemo* from the main road between Sangsit and Kubutambahan, passing the village of **Jagaraga** on the way up.

The **temple** at **Kubutambahan** is at the junction of the road from Kintamani and the coast road. Most visitors give the place only a couple of minutes — time enough to photograph the carving of a man on a flowery bicycle: The guardian will show you where it is once you have signed the visitors' book and made your donation.

YEH SANIH

At Yeh Sanih, another six kilometers (four miles) east, freshwater springs have been diverted to create bathing pools between the road and the sea. There's an accompanying restaurant and accommodation, **Bungalow Puri Sanih** (inexpensive). Frogs croak, mosquitoes bite and boys flop into the cool water.

The coast, as elsewhere in northern Bali, has a bleak appearance, but it's certainly peaceful, and there's a place to stay right on the beach called the **Air Sanih Seaside Cottages** ((0362) 23357 (budget). There's also a small temple up a short path on the other side of the road. You might be lucky enough when you visit it to hear a strange and beautiful whistling and tinkling in the air — a few members of a local bird orchestra out for a quick run through of a small part of their repertoire.

The intricate carvings at Pura Beji Temple in Sangsit, east of Singaraja.

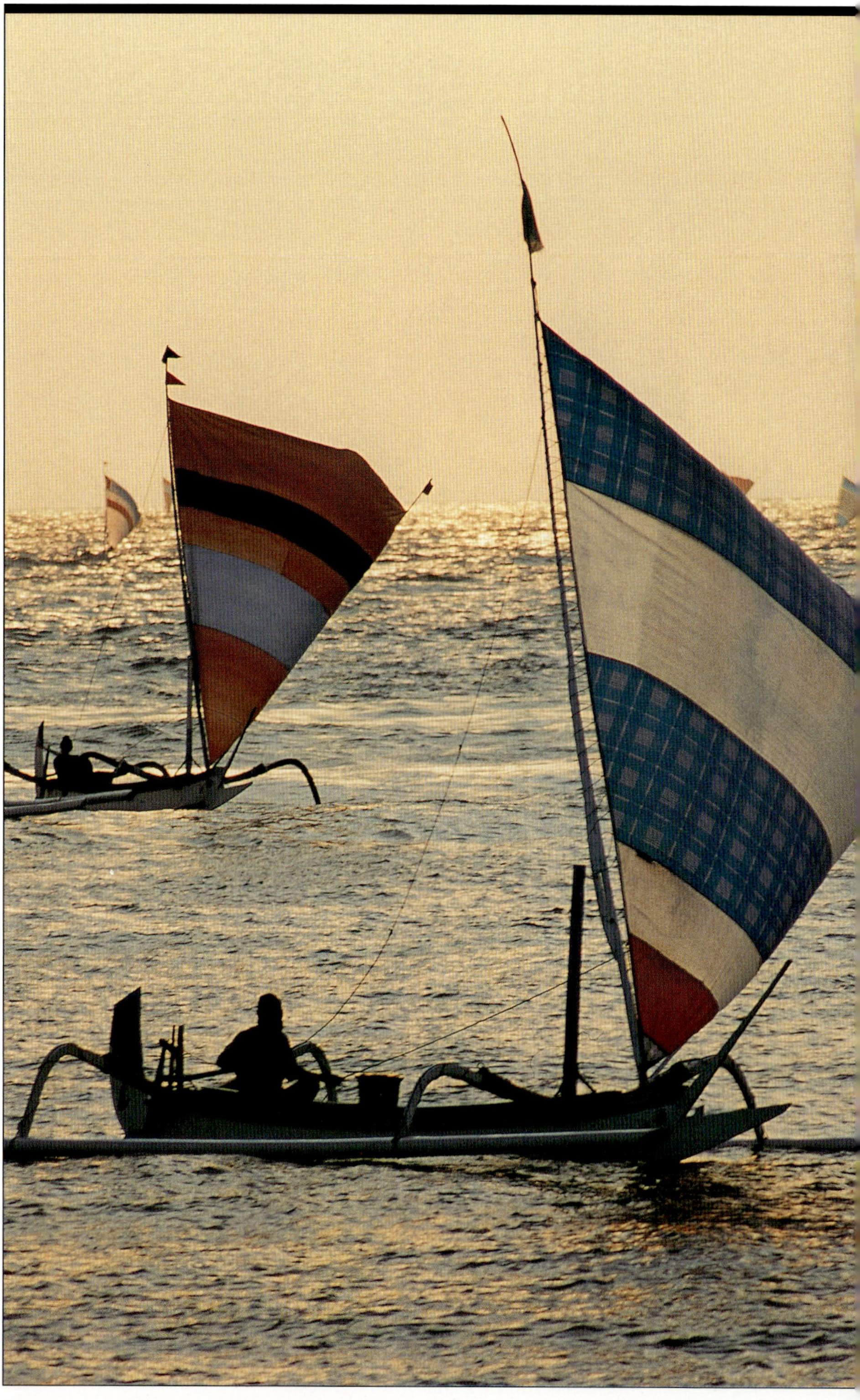

West Bali and the Bali Barat National Park

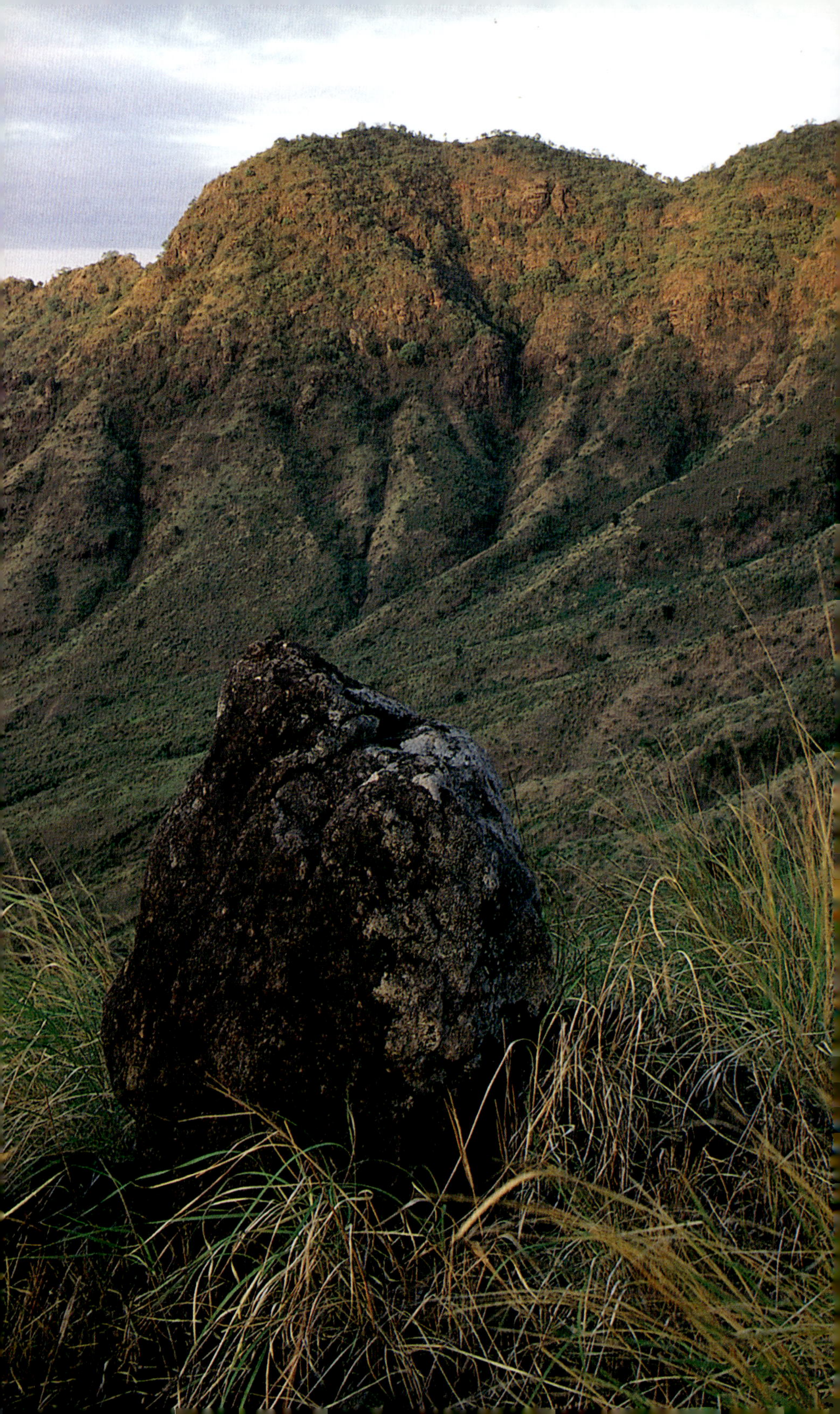

WEST BALI

Bali's western corner, approaching the neighboring island of Java, has always tended to be overlooked by the tourist industry. While there are notable coral reefs — including the best in the country, around Menjangan Island — and a number of perfectly acceptable beaches, there is simply not enough of interest to retain visitors' interest for long. Not enough, at any rate, to persuade most travelers to undertake the long drive from the spectacular east.

What should be the solution is, to a certain extent, the problem. The Bali Barat National Park, which developed more as an easy solution to the problem of what to do with a rugged and not very fertile interior rising sheer above the coastal flatlands, is mostly closed to the public. The reasoning is essential to conserve the area's flora and fauna, but there appear to be plenty of cut logs easing out onto the southern highway despite these measures. The lack of public access might well be making the task of the illegal loggers even easier.

For most visitors the experience of western Bali will be limited to the road that runs around the perimeter: fast and relaxing on the northern shore, crowded and frequently alarming on the south, heading back toward Bali's resort districts with its traffic swelled with trucks and buses heading from Java.

The most worthwhile tourist attractions are on the northern coast, but as visitors can approach west Bali from along the northern or southern coastline it seems sensible to structure this chapter around it's furthest point: Gilimanuk, the most westerly town in Bali and the ferry port for Java.

GILIMANUK

Standing at the ferry terminal in Gilimanuk, the Java coast looks tantalizingly near. It is. Barely three kilometers (two miles) across the Bali Straits. And although in the Pleistocene epoch Bali was, in fact joined to the Java mainland, it certainly isn't now. Without the new generation of powerful, stable ferries it would be impassable. The sea floor here is barely 60 m (about 200 ft) in depth. Not only are the straits prone to currents that flow between two separate seas, but they also, because of their shallow depth, throw up waves that are exceptionally high.

This doesn't mean that crossing the straits is difficult these days. A constant chain of ferries operate, transporting trucks, buses and cars 24 hours a day to and from Java. Even if your rental agent specified his vehicle wasn't to leave Bali, the people at the ferry terminal certainly won't stop you. The crossing takes anything from 30 minutes to an hour, depending on the sea conditions, and to give an idea of price, a motorcycle with rider pays Rp5,000 for the crossing — less than a dollar.

Since a 24-hour ferry service has been launched, Gilimanuk has rather struggled to find a reason for tourists to pause. The main road is lined, near the port, with stalls catering to bus-loads of Indonesian tourists, generally trying to sell them a surprisingly homogeneous selection of batik fabrics made, in the first place, in the Javanese city of Solojakarta. To the south is a quiet grid of residential streets. In an attempt to increase it's appeal there is now a **Tourist Office** on Jalan Muhara, and there are rumors that a museum is opening, devoted to archaeological finds in the area. Even so, there's no obvious advantage to staying overnight here, but if you need a place for the night the most appealing prospect (and it's not very inviting) is the **Hotel Sari** ((0365) 61264 FAX (0365) 61265, Jalan Pogot 333, which has two-story bamboo chalets, in some of which your car can sleep en-suite (budget). The best place to eat here, by quite a long way, is **Wayan Sudana** ((0365) 61067, on the main road into town just west of the huge, triumphal civic arch marking the start of town. It's a simple place, but very good for genuine Indonesian food, well-prepared and inexpensive.

Bemos for Gilimanuk leave from the Ubung terminal in Denpasar: it's 134 km (83 miles) so be prepared for a somewhat long ride. Driving independently is, along the busy southern road, alarming, with very slow trucks and pushy Javanese buses knocking

---

Remote (by Bali standards), the Bali Barat National Park is a haven for bird life and flora. Its drier conditions suit a different range of species than the rest of the island.

the pleasure out of spectacular terrace and coast views. The route via Pengastulan and along the northern coast is much longer, but much more spectacular and relaxed.

THE FAR WEST

Immediately to the east of the Civic Arch of Gilimanuk, two things happen. First there is a turning to the left heading off through the Bali Barat National Park along the northeastern coast, while a few meters further along the road to Denpasar, on the right, are the National Park Headquarters. Report here to get permission to visit the park, and to take aboard a park guide. In my experience the guides are of little practical use, and invariably ill-informed, but you do need to retain their expensive services and perhaps you'll have more luck with the guide you get than I ever have.

THE BALI BARAT NATIONAL PARK

Greatly expanded from the small national reserve established by the Dutch, the Bali Barat National Park, also known as the West Bali National Park was gazetted in 1983 in an area of low rainfall far from any permanent water supply. Trails link the major features of the mainland section of the West Bali Park. The few who use them are for the most part amateur naturalists on the lookout for the rare species thought to be present in the area, for example, the white starling, the cattle-like *banteng* and the Balinese tiger. It is now so long since a sighting of the latter was reported that it is thought to be, tragically, extinct. Often sighted are Munkjak deer — small animals which, surprisingly for a deer, bark when aroused — and the much smaller mouse deer. Either are likely to be seen in full flight, as long experience has told them they risk ending up on satay sticks if they let humans get too close. You're also very likely to see gray and black monkeys, but anyone who's visited the various quasi-religious monkey sanctuaries scattered around Bali is unlikely to be too impressed by this.

Nonetheless, visitors to the park do require permits and guides, and these can be arranged at the park headquarters, known as the **Directorate General of Forest Protection and Nature Conservation (** (0365) 61060 or (0365) 61173, east of Gilimanuk. Here it is possible to arrange treks that thread through certain authorized areas of the national park. There's also an office at Labuhan Lalang, 12 km (seven and a half miles) east of Cekik, on the northern side of the park. Although The park authorities has another office south of Denpasar at Jalan Suwung 40 (PO Box 320), this isn't very useful as you'll still need to pick up a ranger.

Treks last up to seven hours, but the only time you're likely to see birds or animals is in the early morning, so you're better off doing a short trek, early, than pounding about through hours of the midday heat seeing nothing. Four-hour treks cost Rp95,000, with seven hours costing Rp207,000. Most people just opt to see the breeding program that is trying to save the Bali starling. Even that costs Rp65,000, plus donation, if you've transport that has space to give the guide a lift to the breeding station in the reserve.

From the main park headquarters, you take the road heading north through the park for five kilometers (three miles), then head down a track for two further kilometers (just over a mile) to find the breeding center.

The **Bali starling**, also known as **Rothschild's myna**, is only found on the arid slopes of Prapat Agung, the most westerly of all Bali's volcanoes. Pure white, with blue patches round the eyes, these beautiful birds are endemic to this area, and are mainly threatened by habitat loss and being caught for sale as domestic songbirds. When it was still legal to sell them, Bali starlings were fetching more than US$1,000 each. It's the provincial symbol of Bali and it's only endemic species. Which makes it particularly galling that they should be so rapidly becoming extinct. In 1985 there were still thought to be 150 in the park, but now numbers are down to just 50. In conservation terms, this is not a large enough population to maintain a healthy gene pool.

The rather desperate solution was to establish the **Pre-release Breeding Program** within the Bali Barat Park. Birds kept in captivity in Surabaya and Jakarta in Java have been relocated here, to breed with other birds caught in the wild. In a small compound, fortified like a small prison compound,

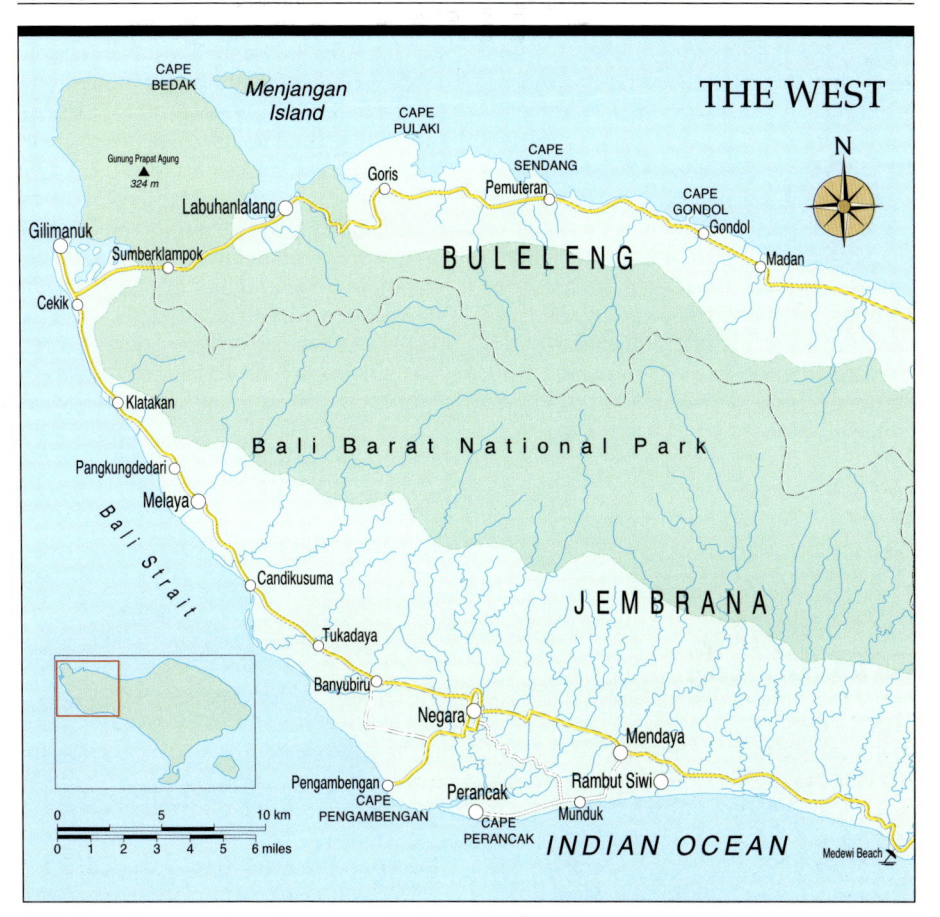

35 Bali starlings are breeding away, laying two or three eggs up to three times a year. The fledglings, when they are old enough to fend for themselves, are released into the wild.

THE BALI BARAT MARINE PARK AND THE NORTHWEST COAST

The most rewarding attraction in the national park is underwater. **Labuhan Lalang** is the site of the jetty for boats to **Menjangan Island**, which has some of the finest fish and coral populations throughout Bali, though there is little more than a parking lot and a couple of *warungs* at the point where the boats take off. While much of the rest of the north coast's coral has been dynamited by fishermen from Java, this section of the national park has, so far, been preserved. Both snorkeling and diving are possible here, and most dive operators will arrange park entry on their clients' behalf.

WHERE TO STAY AND EAT

Although there is basic accommodation available in Gilimanuk, and a few hotels catering for passing trade on the busy southern coast road, the best base for exploring both the park and the marine park is around the village of Pemuteran (see below) on the northern coast, which is convenient for diving, even if the trek to the park board headquarters takes 45 minutes. For most visitors, who only visit the park headquarters once and then regret it, this is a manageable drawback.

HOW TO GET THERE

The Bali Barat National Park takes up much of the inland mountainous area of western Bali, but if you want to stray from the coast road you are required to hire a guide, either from the National Park Headquarters in

Cekik or at their checkpoint at Labuhan Lalang. The Marine Park protects the offshore reefs that ring Mount Prapat Agung and Menjangan Island that form Bali's northwestern bulge. There are various tours to the Bali Barat National Park and to the Marine Park advertised in the southern resorts, and on these your park entry will be arranged on your behalf, but with four hours traveling — at least — in each direction it can hardly be recommended to do this, as suggested, in a day-trip, especially as it would take several dives to do any justice to Menjangan Island.

Best to rent a car and drive there yourself: by far the better route from the southern resorts is the spectacular drive that threads through the mountains from Antosari to Pengastulan and then along the little-used north coast road. The southern route is dangerous with a lot of heavy traffic.

PEMUTERAN

There is little happening in the roadside settlement of Pemuteran, but it is placed inland from a long and little-developed beach, sometimes with white sand and sometimes with black, that is where some of the most relaxed and isolated hotels and resorts give the best desert-island experience on the island.

Four kilometers (two and a half miles) to the east is the **Pulaki Monkey Temple**. Situated on the road overlooking the sea, it is the home for hundreds of monkeys. Don't imagine, though, that you're doing them a special favor when you buy them nuts from the ever-ready vendors — every local farm vehicle that passes empties out onto the road sacks full of fruit leftovers for them, an operation that makes the temple an inevitable slowing-down point for all traffic. It's in the nature of a religious offering, just as when *bemo* drivers pull up at shrines — no one is getting off, but the conductor jumps down and places a tiny wicker tray of flowers and food there. The monkeys of Pulaki, sitting as often as not all over the road eating grapes and pineapple, are happy beings on the receiving end of the same pious devotion.

Offshore the snorkeling is good, where dynamite and cyanide fishermen from Java haven't entirely killed the reef. Most of the activities in this area are based at **Reef Seen Aquatics** (/FAX (0362) 92339 E-MAIL reefseen@ denpasara.wasantara.net.id, Desa Pemuteran, Gerokgak, Singaraja, on the beach next to the Taman Sari Hotel, who arrange horse-riding, diving and the chance to play your part in freeing a local turtle (see TAKE CARE OF A TURTLE, page 11 in TOP SPOTS).

WHERE TO STAY AND EAT

The most luxurious accomodation option is the German-owned **Matahari Hotel** ((0362) 92312 FAX (0362), Pemuteran, which offers 32 private air-conditioned villas, drooping with bougainvillea (expensive). Although it gives its address as Lovina, (perhaps they are trying to bluff down their transfer times from the airport) and is well-located for Menjangan. There's also an exclusive four-villa development called the **Puri Ganesha Villas** ((0362) 93433 WEB SITE www.puri ganeshabali.com, Desa Pemuteran, Gerokgak, Singaraja, which offers an upmarket home-stay that makes the most of contact with the English owner's family-in-law (very expensive). The nearest hotel to Menjangan is the large and comfortable, but rather soulless, **Mimpi Menjangan Boutique Resort** ((0361) 701070 FAX (0361) 701074 E-MAIL sales@mimpi.com WEB SITE www.mimpi.com, Kawasan Bukit Permai, Jimbaran (expensive).

Expats escaping the busy urban south of the island tend to go for the mid-priced comforts of the air-conditioned villas of the **Taman Sari Bali Cottages** (/FAX (0362) 93264 E-MAIL tamanri@indosat.net.id, Desa Pemuteran, Singaraja (moderate), which is also right next door to the turtle release project. This is also the best place to drop into for a mid-priced seafood meal.

You don't have to spend that much to stay on this patch of shore: three kilometers (two miles) to the east of the Matahari **Segara Bukit Beach Cottages** ((0828) 365231 (cell) FAX (0362) 22471, Banyopoh, known locally as "Soggy Biscuits" (inexpensive). The village of Banyopoh is too small to appear on most maps, but their local temple is Pulaki (see above).

HOW TO GET THERE

Pemuteran is 65 km (40 miles) west of Singaraja on the coast road to Gilimanuk. It is four and a half hours from the southern resorts: three and a half from Ubud. *Bemos* pass traveling between Singaraja and Gilimanuk.

THE SOUTHWEST COAST

The long coast road on the southern shore doesn't offer enough of interest to justify risking your life amidst the very heavy traffic.

OPPOSITE: The coast of West Bali is almost entirely devoid of foreign travelers. In the absence of a tourist trade, Balinese toil away to make a living from the sea. ABOVE: Pura Pulaki, Pemuteran, West Bali. Every village, however small, has its village temple.

Trucks, scooters and cars compete for the better stretches of pavement on this main artery that links Denpasar with Java. Tiredness, here can kill: take a break if it all starts getting too much. What towns there are offer little of interest to travelers, although they are unusual, for Bali, in the way they blend influences. There are a couple of notable Christian settlements and a number of Muslims here, as well as a scattering of Balinese relocated after the 1963 eruption of Gunung Agung.

Negara

The first major town heading east from Gilimanuk is Negara, the capital city of Jembrana Regency. It is not a rich regency and it isn't a rich capital either. The **Tourist Office** ((0365) 41060, Pecangakan Civic Center, Jalan Setia Budhi 1, is open in the mornings, and if you need medical attention address yourself to the **RSU** ((0365) 41006, Jalan Aminanui 6. For anything more serious, however, it would be wise to head east to Denpasar for medical or other services.

What puts Negara on the tourist map are its **Water Buffalo Races**, that take place here twice a year, in August and in October, although the exact date isn't fixed too far in advance. Two carts compete at a time, each pulled by two buffaloes. Because the 11.5-km (seven-mile) track isn't wide enough for passing, there are separate start and finishing lines for each competitor, and the one that crosses its own finishing line first stands a good chance of being declared the winner. Nothing is certain, however, as "strength, color and style" as well as speed are taken into account by the judges. These races are in fact a further sign of the influence of immigrants to this region: the idea was bought over from Madura, where such races are a regular feature.

Thanks to the tourist industry they are a regular feature now in Negara as well. Every second Thursday (usually) there are buffalo races organized in the afternoon, for tourists. But while the real races attract crowds of locals and frenzied betting, the tourist races don't attract much beyond a crowd of Westerners who've paid substantial amounts to allow farm-workers to supplement their income.

The date of the races varies from year to year, so consult the **Badung Government Tourist Office** ((0361) 234569 or (0361)-223602, Merdeka Building, Jalan Surapati 7, Denpasar, to see if a race day coincides with your visit.

Where to Stay and Eat

The one outstanding place to stay here is **Cahaya Matahari Bungalows** ((0365) 82218 FAX (0365) 40632, Banjar Anyar, Batuagung, (budget). Just six bungalows here are set on the outskirts of town among the rice paddies, and there are guides available if you want to go trekking. To stay nearer the center, try the **Wira Pada Hotel** ((0365) 41161, Jalan Ngurah Rai 107, near to where the *bemos* stop to pick up passengers (inexpensive).

How to Get There

From Denpasar, *bemos* leave from the Ubung terminal, traveling along the crowded and dangerous coast road. Negara is 96 km (60 miles) west of Denpasar. Allow close to three hours.

MEDEWI BEACH

Medewi Beach, 24 km (15 miles) east of Negara and 72 km (45 miles) from Denpasar, is a useful hideaway for surfers. The waves here are famously reliable, and the fishing-village atmosphere, which it still retains, appeals to those who are well tired of Kuta's razzmatazz. Also, as there's precious little beach to speak of, you don't get swimmers or sunbathers interrupting your breaks.

Most of the accommodation is aimed at surfers: **Medewi Beach Cottages** ((0365) 40029 FAX (0365) 41555, Medewi Beach, Pekutatan, with prices ranging from budget to inexpensive, has sophisticated facilities for its location, while **Jinjaya Bungalows** ((0365) 42945, Medewi Beach, Pekutatan, is a smaller, bamboo *losmen* nearby (budget). On Sundays the Medewi Beach Cottages put on a performance of the local *jogged bumbung* dance. The beach is just a short stroll down a paved road from the main Denpasar/Negara highway: simply ask the driver to let you off at Medewi.

While Kuta is known for its sunsets, the northen coast has its share also.

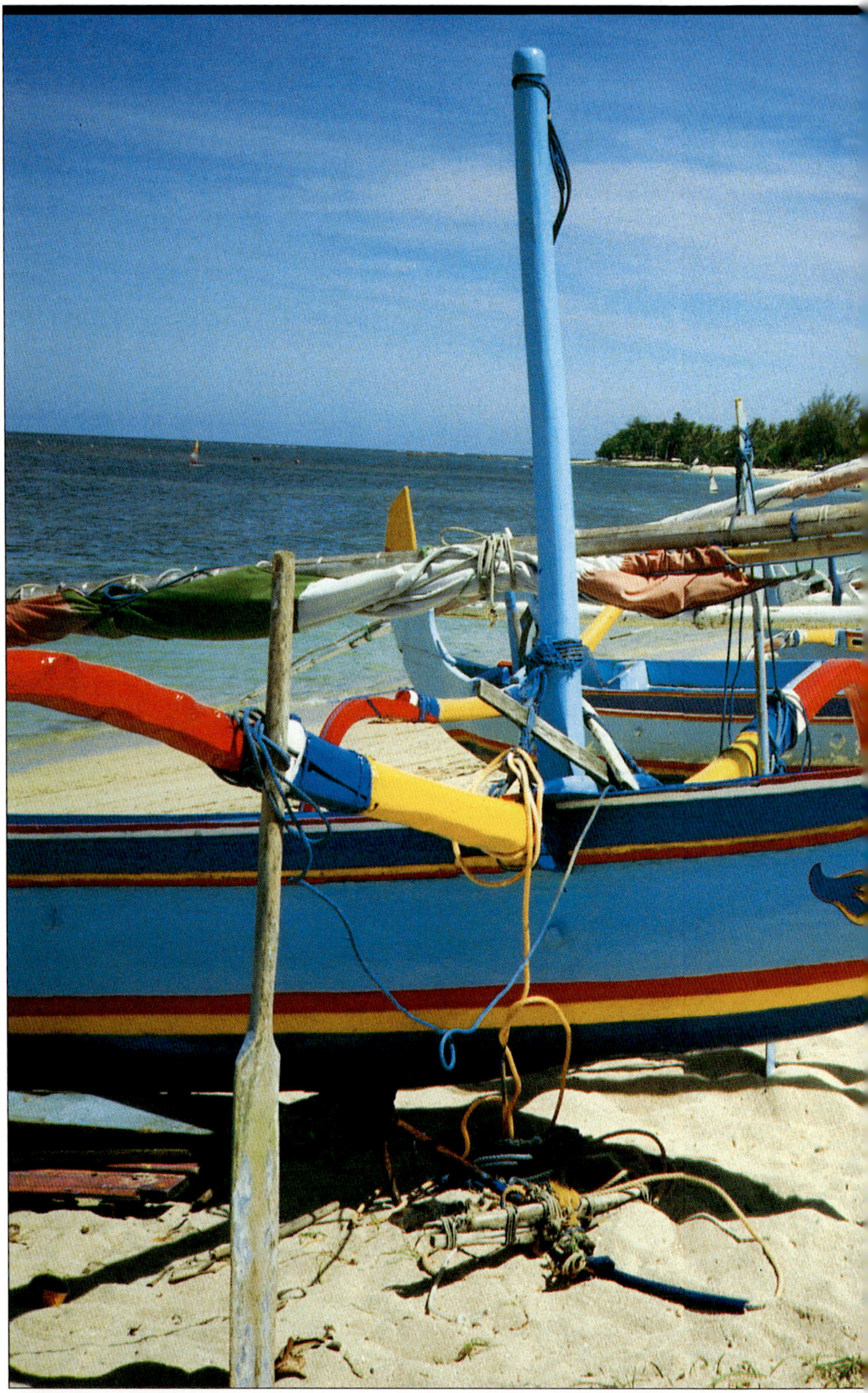

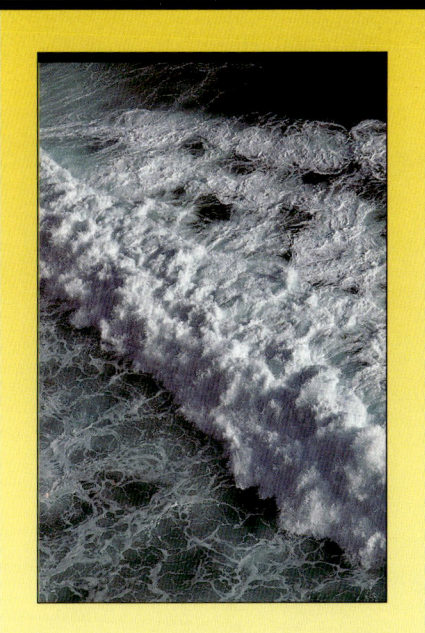

The Offshore Islands

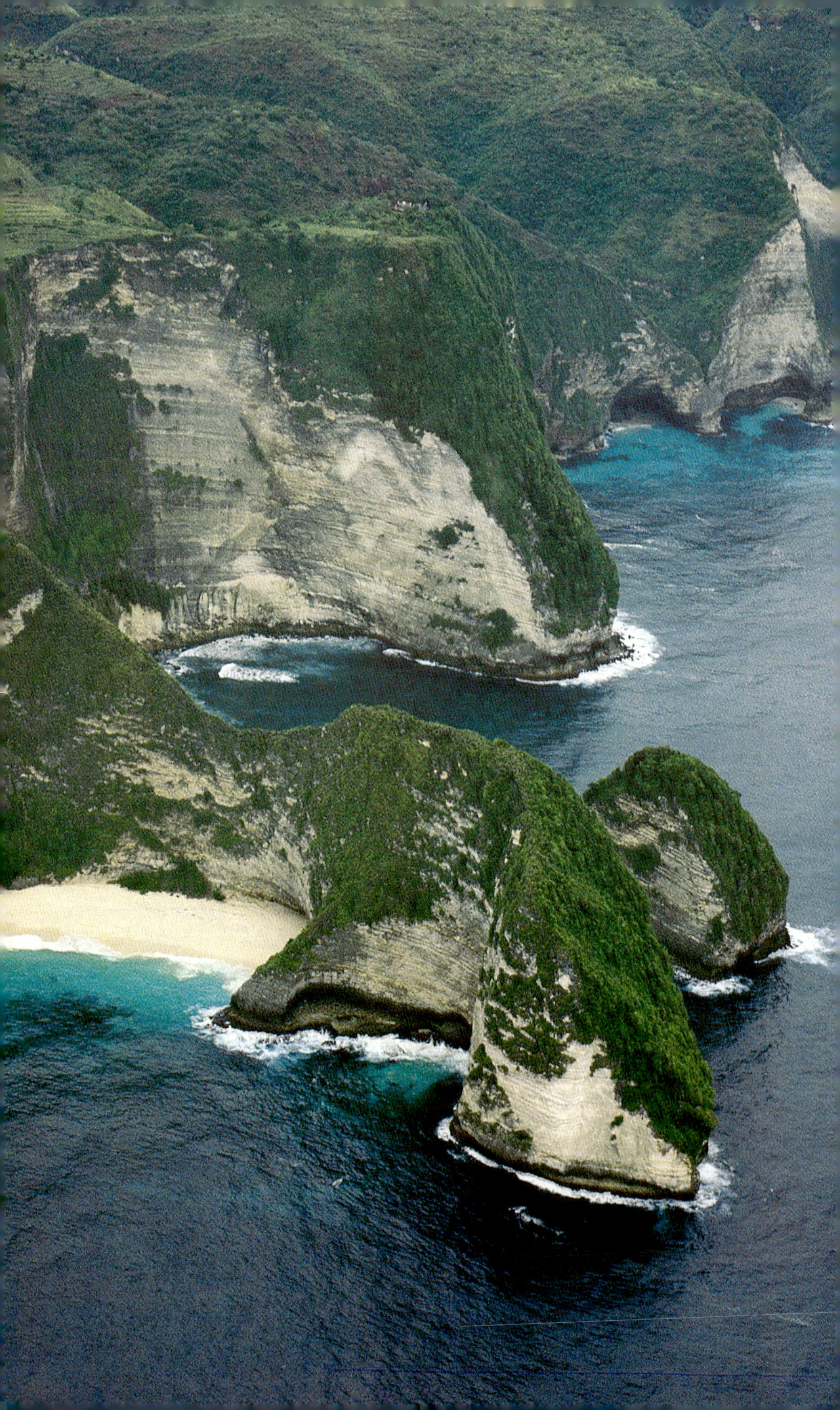

THE THREE ISLANDS OFF BALI'S SOUTHEASTERN COAST, Nusa Lembongan, Nusa Penida and Nusa Ceningan rank among the least visited parts of Bali. Nusa Lembongan is most often visited by travelers on dollar-priced day-trips out of Sanur, Benoa or Kusamba. The smaller island of Nusa Ceningan is close to Nusa Lembongan and has little happening on land but can be a rewarding dive destination. Meanwhile the largest of the islands, Nusa Penida, doesn't see many visitors at all. However it is possible to travel here independently and explore the islands properly, with a range of accommodation available, though most tends to be fairly basic. There is even a network of transportation options geared to the local market. The southern coast is spectacular and the best way to explore, for confident drivers, is by scooter. It's not a well-traveled route but for this very reason it can be rewarding for the adventurous with time on their hands.

From the coast of Bali the islands blend into a single landmass, and look deceptively close. Access is not, however, that easy, except in high-powered and expensive boats priced for tourists. The Badung Strait can be very dangerous. Smaller boats, particularly, cross early in the day as sea conditions commonly worsen as the weather heats up. Independent travelers are best advised to overnight at their chosen mainland departure points so they can make an early start.

NUSA LEMBONGAN AND NUSA CENINGAN

The small island of Nusa Lembongan, a strip of land barely four kilometers (two and a half miles) in length, and its even smaller neighbor island of Nusa Ceningan have recently become a popular spot for surfers and divers. Together the two islands constitute a worthwhile expedition which can be undertaken in comfort on a tourist boat with full diving facilities and an onboard bar, or independently, sharing space in a wooden *jukung* outrigger boat with the local Balinese.

The southern end of the island manages to attain a few meters in height. From then on it descends to the long sandy northern spit where accommodation, in the form of hotels and *losmens*, are situated.

Essentially, Lembongan's tourist facilities are divided between two beaches: **Jungutbatu** and **Mushroom Beach** (not a psychedelic haven, but named after some mushroom-shaped rocks nearby). Jungutbatu is rough and ready, with a sandy beach offering snorkeling and scuba diving. Beyond the reef there is surfing as well. A wreck to the right, its prow rising from the water like a giant shark's fin, is a prominent feature of the seascape.

Mushroom Beach is cleaner and more developed, rather busy through the day with day-tripping visitors from the southern resorts. The daily Bali Hai day-cruise ships from Benoa bring their passengers for lunch to Mushroom Beach, and they maintain a restaurant, small pool and beachside chairs for their exclusive use.

WHERE TO STAY AND EAT

The **Nusa Lembongan Resort (** (0361) 725864 FAX (0361) 725866 E-MAIL sales@nusalembongan.com WEB SITE www.nusalembongan.com, Box 3846, Denpasar has the best in upmarket accommodation available on Mushroom Beach (expensive); and, in addition, there are two hotels. The smart one is the **Waka Nusa Resort (** (0361) 261130 or (0361) 723629 MAINLAND FAX (0361) 722077, which has a swimming pool, restaurant and facilities for sailing, snorkeling and picnics (expensive). On the low cliff at the other end of the short beach stands the **Mushroom Beach Bungalows** (budget) with 10 fan-cooled rooms. If your funds are running low there is a scattering of *losmens*, generally without telephone or address.

In Jungutbatu the only completely satisfactory place to stay is the moderately priced **Puri Nusa (**/FAX (0361) 298613 at the far end of the beach — even this is relatively simple. Young divers and surfers perfect their suntans on the terrace and strum guitars in the evening. If you're looking for the quiet life and are content with early nights, Puri Nusa might be the place for you.

The other places are very inexpensive and cater to backpackers who don't have many rupiah left in their pockets. The most popular

The spectacularly precipitous south coast of Nusa Penida.

of them are the brightly painted **Agung's** (15 rooms, some with fan) which shows videos in the evenings and **Mainski ₵** (0811) 94426 (cell), which is, perhaps, the liveliest. The others, **Tarci Bungalows** (20 rooms), **Ketut Losmen** (six rooms), **Nusa Indah** (seven rooms), **Bunga Lombongan** (eight rooms) and, in the village itself, **Bungalow No. 7** (nine rooms) have little to recommend them other than the low price which gets a lot lower if, after the last boat has left, they still have no guests.

How to Get There

Most people these days arrive at Nusa Lembongan with one of the big tour companies, on one of Bali Hai's catamarans, their high-speed surf boat. (**Bali Hai ₵** (0361) 720331 FAX 720334 E-MAIL balihai@indosat.net.id WEB SITE www.bali-paradise.com/balihai, Benoa Harbor.) Their surfboats take about 30 people and power through the waves on two-hour morning trips (7:30 AM to 9:30 AM) for US$49, for dolphin spotting (see them disappear at speed, probably) and three-island day cruise for US$64 including snorkeling, lunch and Bali Hai beach club. Children under 12 and those with bad backs or hearts are urged not to attend. Alternatively, Aristocat (same owners as Bali Hai) is a luxurious 20-m (64-ft) catamaran doing rather calmer day-trips for US$90. Children over eight get a reduced price. Another operator with a range of boats, from sailing yachts taking two and a half hours to hydrofoils that skim across in only 40 minutes, contact **PT Island Explorer Cruises ₵** (0361) 728088 FAX (0361) 728098 E-MAIL explorer@ denpasar.wasantara.net.id WEB SITE www.8mspace.net/islandexplorer. The sailing cruise, lasting all day, costs US$65, while their "QuickCat" charges US$23 one way. Boats leave from Benoa Harbor, a short distance from Sanur. Alternatively, you can approach a *jukung* skipper on Sanur beach (to the left of Bali Beach Hotel) and engage him to take you across. You should leave Sanur early as the trip by these small boats takes three hours and the fishermen don't like to be out on the Badung Strait after mid-afternoon because of the increased swell.

NUSA PENIDA

Nusa Penida is altogether a more substantial island. It is a limestone plateau, 20 km by 16 (12 miles by 10) and rising to a height of 530 m (1,735 ft). Being limestone, the relief is rocky and dry, the rainfall sinking straight into the ground and forming inaccessible underground caverns. This lack of usable water for irrigation has kept the island historically very poor. In Balinese religion, the island is considered malign, and in earlier times convicts from the kingdom of Klungkung were banished there. Few Balinese voluntarily visit and though the diving and surfing is good, the sea here can be dangerous and lifeguards a rather distant dream.

Nevertheless, today it supports a population of approximately 45,000. Agriculture has improved following government assistance in building cisterns to catch the rainwater, and seaweed farming — evidence of which can be seen all along the northern coast — seems promising. A jetty recently completed at Toyapakeh should boost the economy by allowing large vessels to dock and carry away seaweed and rock which are the island's main products.

Despite the changes taking place, Nusa Penida retains an air of remoteness. Foreign visitors are immediately surrounded by crowds of children — and sometimes adults — crying "Turis! Turis!" (tourist), and inland the roads are very rough. Few islanders speak even rudimentary English. Nevertheless, the cliffs on the south side of the island are worth the hard traveling, and there are a couple of other rewarding sites to visit in the north.

General Information

Sampalan is the main village on the island, but it has little to show the visitor other than a market. The coast road forms its main and only street worthy of the name. Nonetheless, the village is attractive. On a bright morning, its narrow, tree-lined road shades crowds of country people going about their daily round of tasks — evoking parts of eastern Indonesia more than it does mainland Bali. There is no official tourist information office

THE OFFSHORE ISLANDS

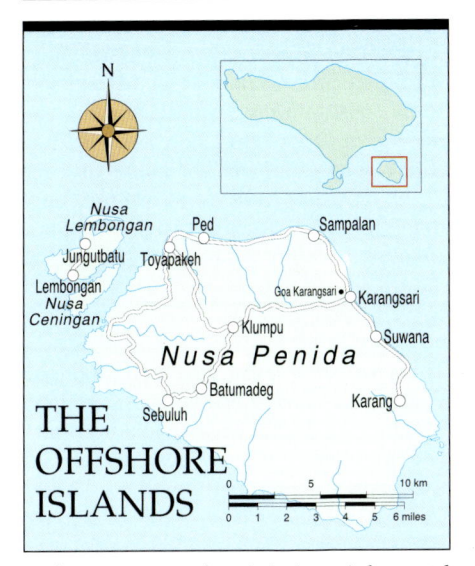

and transport, such as it is, is mainly rental motorbikes — though this can be scary as the roads are often sheer. A round-trip of the island takes at least a day and covers about 70 km (45 miles).

WHAT TO SEE AND DO

Nusa Penida's sights, such as they are, are generally incidental to the adventure of getting to them and the experience of traveling some of Bali's most remote regions. If you take the coast road eastwards from Sampalan — your transport will probably be a truck loaded with goods as well as passengers — you will, after about 20 minutes, reach a large cave, **Goa Karangsari**. Just say "goa" (cave), and your fellow passengers will tell you when you've arrived.

It isn't strictly necessary to have a guide, but a light of some sort is essential. The odds are you'll hire the two together at the *warung* where the truck will put you down. Nusa Penida has little experience of tourism, but the word has got round that foreigners are rich. Thus the few visitors who do appear are treated as manna from heaven and prices quoted can be laughably high. You will probably spend Rp4,000 to be shown around the cave by a guide bearing a powerful kerosene lamp. This is atmospheric, but a flashlight would show you considerably more.

Entrance to the cave is through a narrow gap in the rocky hillside. Inside it's spacious, with a high roof and a level, sandy floor. It extends for some 300 m (325 yards), and at the far end you emerge on another hillside overlooking an inland valley supporting only scrub and with few signs of habitation. About halfway through the cave you pass beneath a colony of bats, and a little further on there is a place where water drips down from the roof and a small shrine has been constructed. There are various side passages, but for the most part they peter out without leading to further major features. If, on the other hand, you take the coast road west from Sampalan you will arrive after 10 minutes at the celebrated temple at **Ped** (also sometimes spelled "Peed"). It stands on the right side of the road in the village of the same name and is the home of Bali's sourest deity, Ratu Gede Macaling. (The word "macaling" derives from a Balinese word meaning "fang.")

According to the tenets of Balinese religion, malign forces must be placated as much as benign ones worshipped, so the temple is crowded with visitors from all over Bali on its *odalan* (anniversary feast day). The place itself is large but not especially beautiful. The shrine to Ratu Gede Macaling is in an extension to the northwest of the temple.

Cross-country

The greatest attraction of Nusa Penida is the dramatic southern coastline. Access, however, is difficult. There is no public transportation here, so it's necessary to rent a scooter, possibly with driver, or try to find a four-wheel-drive vehicle or charter a *bemo*.

The road south branches off the coast road two kilometers (one and a quarter miles) west of Sampalan and rises steeply and circuitously to **Klumpu**. Thus far the road is tarred and in good condition. It's after Klumpu that the going gets difficult. The track rises and falls over rough ground, and there are frequent rocky outcrops that have to be negotiated — there are half a dozen places where a pillion rider has to get off and walk. Though generally well drained, there are patches that are slippery after rain.

Bear right at **Batumadeg**, avoiding the road left which leads via Batukandik to the east of the island. The road now is even rougher than before. On both sides are terraces of manioc, corn and occasionally tobacco, wherever the terrain allows cultivation. The high hills that form the island's center rise to the left. The entire drive, from Sampalan to **Sebuluh**, takes about a good hour and a half.

From Sebuluh, a village of thatched houses set in a hollow, it is necessary to walk. A child — who will be surprised to receive payment — can easily be found to take you. Something in the region of Rp500 should be offered. You descend into a dry valley, and then up again to the cliff edge, a walk of twenty minutes. Monkeys play in the trees en route. The path arrives at the cliff via a most spectacular and terrifying path. The highest point on this coast, 228 m (750 ft) above sea level, is in this area, and this extraordinary aerial stairway descends almost the entire distance, running diagonally down across the cliff face. It is constructed of bamboo and wood, and though it makes use here and there of natural ledges in the cliff it is elsewhere supported only on trees growing out from the cliff face.

The purpose of this exposed stairway (which no one with the slightest vertigo should consider negotiating) is give the villagers of nearby Sebuluh access to a place where fresh water gushes out in great profusion a few meters above sea level. In earlier times this was an invaluable source of drinking water during periods of drought. The women would ascend the horrendous route carrying giant buckets of water on their heads, while the men carried two containers apiece slung on either end of a pole. The villagers still go down every 210 days for the *odalan* of the temple below on the rocks at the sea's edge.

The best place to see the whole structure lies 15 minutes' walk to the west. You follow the track down over some terraces to where a left-hand turnoff leads along a deep and grand valley, heavily wooded on the far side, and onto a spur jutting out into the sea and culminating in a small temple. From here you can see the extent of the stairway, the water pouring out over a large rock, and the impressive coast to the east.

There are three other such stairways on the south coast of Nusa Penida, known as **Seganing**, **Anceng** and **Swean**. But the one at Sebuluh is the longest.

It is a peculiar feature of the island that its supply of fresh water, otherwise in such short supply, is situated here at the inaccessible south coast rather than in the north where most of the population lives. The resulting cliff routes are immensely dramatic and one of the most impressive and extraordinary things to be seen anywhere in Bali—yet they are almost wholly unknown to travelers.

WHERE TO STAY

There are a few *losmens* on the island, and your host is likely to be your first point of contact for local information and transport. In Sampalan the best accommodation is at the government-run **Bungalows Pemda** (budget) at the east end of the village, designed for local officials, or the very friendly **Losmen Made** on the main beach.

There is no restaurant, but a couple of *warung* on the main street; don't count on them being open after 8 PM. Elsewhere on the island you have to leave time to return to Sampalan though local residents will often offer informal hospitality.

HOW TO GET THERE

The most comfortable way to reach Nusa Penida is to use the modern and expensive tourist links to get first to Nusa Lembongan (see travel details above), and then cross over the short distance over generally calm waters to the larger island of Nusa Penida. The inhabitants of Nusa Penida, however, and most of those from Nusa Lembongan as well, use public transportation direct from the mainland, via Kusamba or Padangbai.

Motorized *jukung* from Kusamba leave from two places on the beach about a kilometer (just over half a mile) apart. Crossings both ways take place in the morning as the surf at Kusamba tends to get bigger as the day progresses and can make landing and departing difficult, if not dangerous. The fare is around Rp5,000 for locals, and you may be able to travel for this amount too, though it is normal to charge foreigners about 50% more, and it is not advisable to argue when the fare is so very low to begin with. Boats leave when they are full, so how quickly you get away is entirely a matter of chance.

As the crossing takes between two and three hours, you may prefer to take the speedboat service from Padangbai, which leaves several times during the morning, beginning at around 7 AM. There is one boat which is moored at Nusa Penida overnight; consequently, you wait on the beach at Padangbai until it arrives on its first trip of the day from the island. Wait for it immediately to the left (east) of the jetty. The crossing takes 40 minutes. Crossings later in the morning cannot be relied on to happen, so the best plan is to spend the night in Padangbai if getting there in the early morning is likely to pose difficulties.

The crossing is 14 km (nine miles) from Kusamba, marginally further from Padangai.

Most of the boats from Kusamba arrive on Nusa Penida at Toyapakeh, whereas the speedboat from Padangbai arrives at Buyuk, close to Sampalan, the capital. But it makes little difference which one you arrive at as there are regular *bemo* services along the coast road, and the trip from Toyapakeh to Sampalan only takes about 15 minutes.

Sailing on sunset-tinged waters off Nusa Penida's often inaccessible coastline.

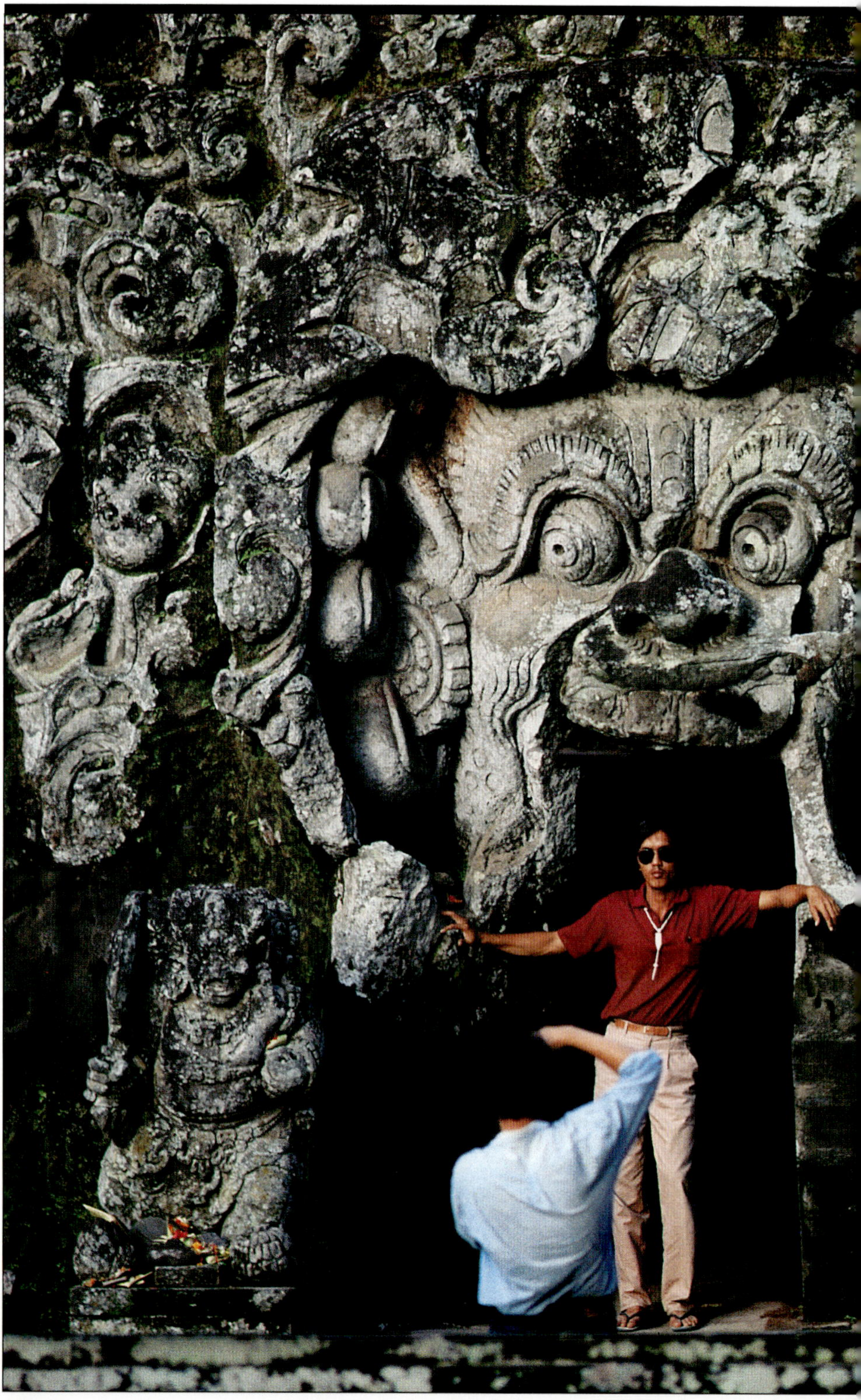

Travelers' Tips

GETTING THERE

Most people arrive in Bali by air. The island is well-served by flights from most points in Asia, Australia and Western Europe, with many airlines stopping off in the busy far eastern airports of Singapore or Hong Kong before flying down to land at Ngurah Rai International Airport (DPS). There are also direct flights to Bali from the west coast of the United States.

The airport receives a large volume of flights from other Indonesian cities and smaller towns in the Indonesian archipelago.

For the adventurous — and for those who have the time — there are plenty of long-distance buses that travel between Java and Bali. Indeed there are some travel companies (see BEYOND BALI, page 240) who run special coaches from Bali as far as the northern tip of Sumatra, or vice versa.

In this seafaring culture there are plenty of ferries that carry individual foot passengers as well as cars, motorcycles and trucks from island to island. From Gilimanuk, ferries leave for Java every hour and a half, 24 hours a day; other ferries from Padangbai travel on to Lombok. These ferries are fast and inexpensive. The neighboring islands look close — Java seems within swimming distance from Gilimanuk. It isn't though. Resist the temptation to hire a local fishing boat to make the crossing: both straits have serious currents and should be treated with respect.

ARRIVING

group against the Dutch in 1946. There's a statue of him at the junction at the end of the airport road, where you turn left for Sanur or right for Nusa Dua. The airport is often just referred to as Tuban, after the village nearby. The airport is very close to all the major resorts in southern Bali.

Taxis are available at the point where arriving travelers emerge from the airport onto the forecourt. The rates are somewhat inflated but fixed, so at least travelers are spared the difficulties of bargaining for the first hour or so of their stay. It is possible to rent cars at the airport but their rates are slightly higher than similar companies in the southern resorts, with Kuta offering the best deals.

Those on their way to Kuta who want to economize can catch a *bemo* (daylight hours only), by leaving the international terminal through the parking lot, passing the domestic terminal on the right and continuing on until a road leads in from the left. Stand at the junction and the *bemos* (blue transit vans) coming out of the side road will find you. The fare to Kuta is around Rp500.

ARRIVING

VISAS AND RED TAPE

Passports must be valid for six months from the date of entry into Indonesia.

You do not need to acquire a visa in advance if you are a passport holder of one of the following countries: Argentina, Australia, Austria, Belgium, Brazil, Brunei, Canada, Chile, Denmark, Egypt, Finland, France, Germany, Greece, Iceland, Ireland, Italy, Japan, Kuwait, Luxembourg, Malaysia, Malta, Morocco, Mexico, the Netherlands, New Zealand, Norway, the Philippines, Singapore, South Korea, Spain, Sweden, Switzerland, Saudi Arabia, Taiwan, Thailand, Turkey, the United Kingdom, the United States of America, the United Arab Emirates and Venezuela.

For all of the above, passports will be stamped allowing a maximum stay of 60 days

Some boats go further. PELNI, one of the national shipping lines, has regular services between Bali and Java, Sulawesi and the Moluccas. There are plenty of small boats, ferries and other marine transport to and from Lombok. Any visitor coming from Lombok (or even Sumbawa) will find a range of options to suit even the most modest of budgets.

At the luxury end of the scale, a number of cruise ships now visit Bali as part of their regular schedules, landing at Tanjung Benoa. But the time allotted to visitors, is minimal.

FROM THE AIRPORT

Ngurah Rai is the official name of Denpasar airport, after the hero who led a resistance

An adventerous drive around the Gunung Bisbis volcano takes you to the ruined "floating" temple at Ujung, where lillies and flowering trees adorn its shores.

on arrival in Indonesia. These visas cannot be renewed. At press time, these visas were free of charge, although rumors suggest the government plans to institute fees up to US$50. You must be in possession of a ticket out of the country (though "purchase of a ticket is also accepted"), and entry must be through one of the following. By air: Jakarta, Medan, Manado, Ambon, Bali, Biak, Surabaya and Batam, or by sea: Semarang, Jakarta, Bali, Pontianiac, Balikpapan, Tanjung Pinang and Kupang. For entry or exit through other places a special visa is required.

Nationals of all other countries must obtain their visas in advance. Because of the situation in East Timor, holders of Portuguese passports are, at the time of writing, likely to have trouble applying for Indonesian visas.

It is common practice for foreigners living in Bali to fly from Bali to Singapore and then back again on the same day, in order to obtain another 60-day stamp in their passport.

If you do hold a renewable visa and need to renew it in Bali, the **Immigration Office (Kantor Imigrasi)** ((0361) 227828 is at Renon Complex, Niti Mandala in Denpasar, with another on your right immediately before you enter the ceremonial arch into the airport ((0361) 751038, Jalan Ngurah Rai, Kuta. They are open Monday to Thursday from 7 AM to 1 PM, Friday from 7 AM to 11 PM and Saturday from 7 AM to noon; closed Sunday.

CUSTOMS ALLOWANCES

Indonesian customs regulations allow a maximum of two liters of alcoholic beverages, 200 cigarettes or 50 cigars or 100 grams (three and a half ounces) of tobacco, and a "reasonable" amount of perfume per adult. Cars, photographic equipment, typewriters and tape-recorders must be declared on arrival and must be taken out again with you. Television sets, radios, narcotics, weapons and ammunition, printed matter in Chinese characters and Chinese medicines are strictly prohibited.

Advance approval must be acquired for carrying transceivers, and all movie films and video cassettes must be controlled by the Film Censor Board. Fresh fruit, plants and animals must have quarantine permits.

LEAVING

It is worth noting that Bali is a source for inexpensive air tickets. A number of outlets in Kuta (in particular) offer attractive fares to destinations worldwide. For the tourist who might be interested in either cut-price business class and first class air tickets, or a multi-leg vacation, great savings can be made buy purchasing tickets here.

DEPARTURE TAX

There is a departure tax of Rp50,000 on international flights and R25,000 on domestic flights.

AIRLINE OFFICES

Most airlines require travelers to reconfirm their outbound flights 24 hours before departure. Any travel agent in Bali will do this for you, at a small charge, or you can do it yourself using the following contact details.

The national carrier is **Garuda Indonesia** ((0361) 227825 FAX (0361) 226298, Jalan

ABOVE: The charm of Bali is the charm of its people. OPPOSITE: Along the north coast, near Lovina, there are some relaxing hot springs.

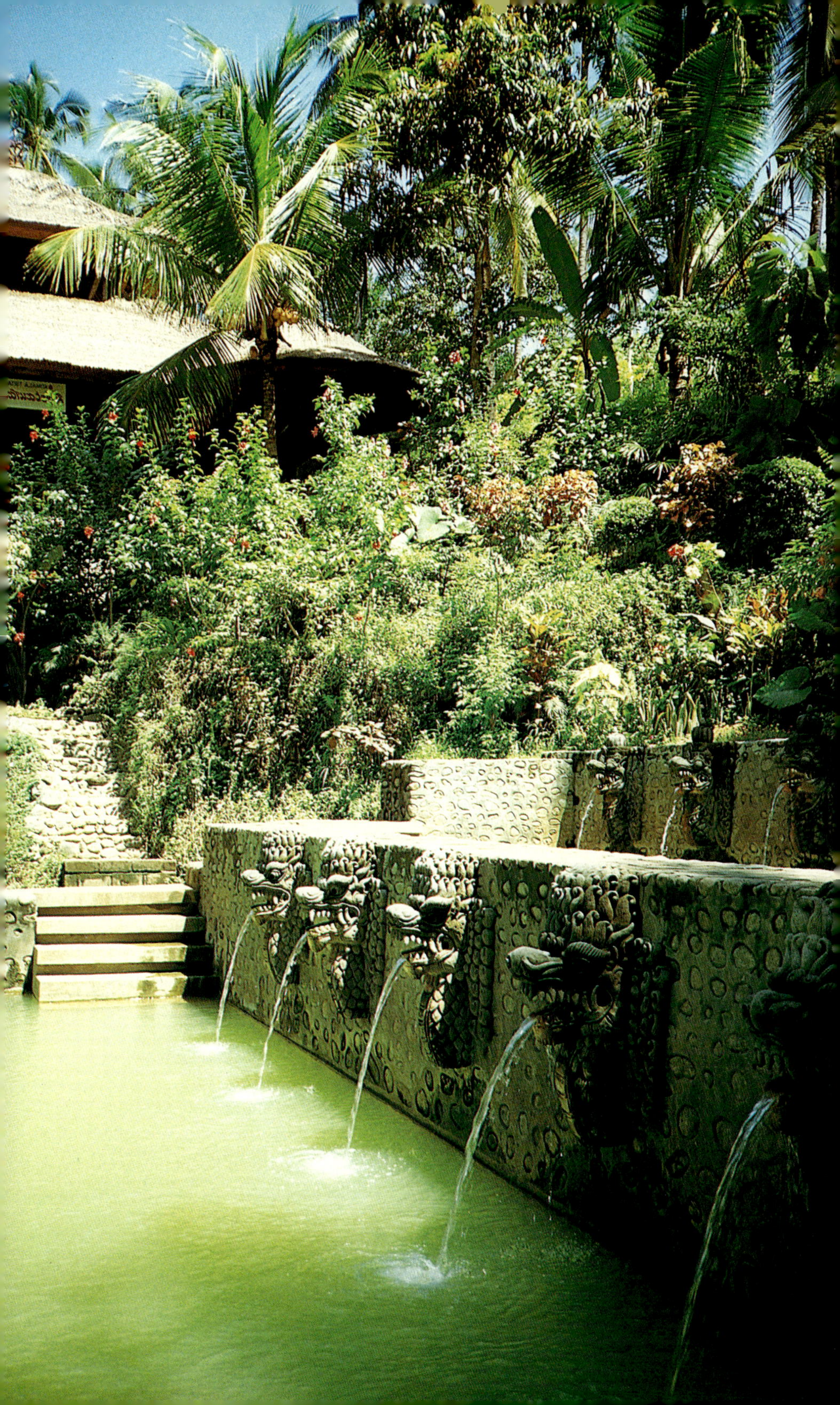

Melati No. 61, Denpasar, with offices at the following locations: **Natour Kuta Beach Hotel** ((0361) 751179; Bali **Beach Hotel** ((0361) 288511; **Sanur Beach Hotel** ((0361) 288011; **Nusa Indah Hotel** ((0361) 771906.

Telephone numbers for the other airlines are as follows:

International
Air France ((0361) 287734
Air New Zealand ((0361) 756170
Ansett Australia ((0361) 289637
Cathay Pacific ((0361) 286001
Continental ((0361) 287774
Eva Air ((0361) 751011
Japan Airlines ((0361) 287576
KLM ((0361) 756124
Korean Air ((0361) 289402
Lufthansa ((0361) 287069
Malaysian Airlines ((0361) 285071
Qantas ((0361) 751472
Singapore Airlines ((0361) 261666
Thai Airways ((0361) 288141

Domestic
Bouraq ((0361) 223564
Merpati Nusantara ((0361) 228842
Sempati Air ((0361) 754218

BEYOND BALI

Numerous bus companies operate on the Denpasar–Surabaya route, usually traveling overnight. Any place offering bookings for the shuttle bus can book you onto one. The fare includes the short ferry crossing from Gilimanuk to Banyuwangi, and a free meal at one of the stops. The air-conditioned buses are much more comfortable than the non-air-conditioned variety. Videos are screened on these buses during the first part of the journey.

There is no railway on Bali, but a fast and modern rail service runs to Jakarta from Banyuwangi, on the tip of Java. The best Indonesian trains are luxurious and a pleasure to travel on, and the express train to Jakarta is sometimes one of these. Local trains are a different matter, however, though extraordinarily cheap. Information about connections to Surabaya and Jogyakarta, as well as the special train to Jakarta, can be obtained locally at the railway's office at Jalan Diponegoro No. 172, in Denpasar.

To go to Lombok, the Mabua company-run jet-powered sea shuttles depart from Benoa Harbor (not to be confused with Tanjung Benoa), and you can even go there for the day. Spice Island Cruises offer three- and four-night excursions by sea to Sumbawa (Badas); Komodo is included on the four-night trip. For trips to Sulawesi, contact the **Ujung Tourist Office** ((0411) 320616.

CONSULATES AND EMBASSIES

Several countries maintain consulates, consular agencies, representatives or honorary consuls in Bali. They are:
Australia (also serving the United Kingdom, New Zealand, Canada and Papua New Guinea) ((0361) 235092 FAX (0361) 235 146, Jalan Prof. Moch Yamin 51, Renon, Denpasar.
France (Honorary) ((0361) 280227 or (0361) 280227 FAX (0361) 287303, Smailing Tours, Jalan Ngurah Rai (Bypass) 88X, Sanur.
Germany (Honorary) ((0361) 288535 FAX (0361) 288826, Jalan Pantai Karang No. 17, Sanur.
Italy (Honorary) ((0361) 701001, Lotus Tours, Jalan Ngurah Rai (Bypass), Jimbaran.
Japan ((0361) 234808 FAX (0361) 231308, Jalan Raya Puputan, Renon, Denpasar.
Netherlands (Honorary) ((0361) 751517 FAX (0361) 752777, KCP Travel, Jalan Raya Kuta 127, Kuta.
Norway and Denmark ((0361) 235098 FAX (0361) 234834, Jalan Jaya Giri VIII No. 10, Renon, Denpasar.
Sweden and Finland ((0361) 288407 ℅ Segara Village Hotel, Sanur.
Switzerland and Austria (Honorary) ((0361) 751735 FAX (0361) 754457 ℅ Swiss Restaurant, Jalan Pura Bagus Taruna, Legian, Kuta.
United States ((0361) 233605 FAX (0361) 222426, Jalan Hayam Wuruk 188, Denpasar.

Other nationals may be able to get advice from one of the above, or they can contact their embassy in Jakarta.

EMBASSIES AND CONSULATES IN JAKARTA

The following are the phone numbers of the various embassies in Jakarta. (The city code for Jakarta is 021.)
Australia (522-7111
Canada (525-0790

CONSULATES AND EMBASSIES

France (314-2897
Germany (384-9547
Great Britain (310-4229
Italy (337440
Japan (324308
Netherlands (511515
New Zealand (330680
Spain (314-2355
United States (360360

Selected Indonesian Missions Abroad

Australia Canberra ((02) 6250-8600
Canada Ottawa ((613) 236-7403
France Paris ((01) 45 03 07 60
Germany Bonn ((0228) 382990
Great Britain London ((020) 7499-7661
Hong Kong (2890-4421
Italy Rome ((06) 482-5951
Japan Tokyo ((03) 441-4201
New Zealand Wellington ((04) 475-8697
Singapore (737-7422
South Korea Seoul ((02) 783-5675
Spain Madrid ((01) 413-0294
United States Washington, DC ((0202) 775-5200

TOURIST INFORMATION

Indonesia's foreign embassies are quite good places to start researching information on Bali, although they are unlikely to offer any-

---

A Balinese painting from a private collection. The rural scene, and the crowding of the canvas with largely decorative detail, is very typical of the traditional Balinese school of painting.

thing that is not contained in this book. Within the country itself there are tourist offices in all the towns regularly visited by foreigners, always open in the mornings and usually in the afternoons as well. Their contact details are listed in the text. Generally they are very helpful and do their impartial best to give advice and information.

The same is not necessarily true of the vultures who will always be found circling the tourist office, nor of the many travel agents who try to look official with prominent "Tourist Information" signs. They are more likely to be interested in getting commissions from tickets for tours or travel. Don't be too suspicious, however, as many operators are genuine and genuinely keen to help you make the most of Bali.

GETTING AROUND

Looked at on a world map, Bali looks so tiny that many visitors arrive with the expectation they'll be able to walk around it in a few hours. Not so. Even the smaller towns can be quite large enough to get comprehensively lost in, and thanks to the traffic any journey within the island can take a long time.

DRIVING IN BALI

It's true, the driving in Bali is terrible. If the car in front stops, the driver behind is more likely to try to pass than to slow down. Blinkers are used rarely, or not at all, or misleadingly. Lights often don't work, work badly, or are set incorrectly.

And there are the roads. Even the main roads are narrow and filled with huge buses clearly not adapted to the island's road system. Traffic circles are beginning to appear, especially in the southern resort areas and by general rule the driver on the traffic circle gives way to people coming on, but as this is Bali most people just edge out until someone else is forced to give way. The Balinese believe road junctions are home to evil spirits, and after seeing them drive over them I'm tempted to think they're right.

Generally the road surface is poor, but it's sometimes terrible. Most stretches are mined with gaping chasms, rough unfilled potholes, piles of gravel for some future road-building project, broken or parked vehicles. Then there's the constant risk the driver in front will stop for a chat, or, turning to wave at a friend just spotted by the road, crash. Don't laugh: it happens.

Of course it's always likely you'll either be lost, or looking for a small unmarked turning that, though it looks like an ox-track, is actually the hidden start of one of the island's major roads. Street signs are a rarity, grudgingly issued perhaps from a buried ministerial bunker where the policy is to confuse potential invaders by withholding any route-finding information. You've got more chance of navigating successfully around Bali by taking a line of sight from the sun than relying on street signs.

Add the simple fact that there is a lot of traffic, and you have a recipe for disaster. It's not just the Balinese, of course. Western drivers, often unused to the conditions and sometimes unused to driving on the left, play their own part. Very quickly they become infected with all the local bad driving habits and then add a few of their own.

There is a plus side. The cost, for a start. Gas prices have recently gone up — to Rp1,200 (about 15 cents) a liter. Suzuki Vitaras rent out for as little as US$10 per day for periods of more than a week, though they start off at twice that for a single day and stay expensive from international car-rental companies. Small but effective scooters can be found for as little as US$3 if you're taking them for 10 days or more, though single days cost about twice that.

The advantage with scooters is that you don't need so much space to shelter from oncoming traffic and it is easier to turn round when you inevitably take the wrong turn. The disadvantage is that if there is a crumple zone on a scooter, it's usually you, and the dogs that hang around in the middle of the road become more of a serious driving hazard. There are tourist casualties every month from motorcycle accidents, especially on the major roads.

In the event of an accident, try to get off the road and sort matters out without involving the police. The other driver will certainly want to do this as well. Involving the police is a last resort as they can, with forms and interviews, complicate matters enormously.

Drivers will require valid international drivers licenses. Otherwise life get complicated. If you don't have a full international driving license you'll have to go into Denpasar for a **Tourist Driving License** ((0361) 243939, Jalan Cok Agung Tresna 14, Renon, Denpasar, Monday-Thursday, Saturday 8:30 PM to 2:30 PM, Friday 8:30 AM to 1 PM. If you have a license from your home country you will need to provide a photocopy of your passport (photo and identification page) and a copy of your valid home driving license. If you don't even have this you'll have to take a driving test: it's quick and easy and the person renting the car will invariably take you there in person, and probably help ensure you pass. Car and motorcycle licenses are valid for a month and cost Rp75,000.

Because Bali is so compact there are maps of it reproduced on every hand. The free advertising magazine, the Bali *Echo*, for example, always has one as its center double-page spread. The best map for driving is the **Berndtson and Berndtson** 1:200,000 road map, Rp52,000, which is handily encapsulated in plastic to avoid tearing or going soggy in rain and also has detailed maps of the major areas of interest to visitors. There are others. My personal favorite for general travel in Bali is the idiosyncratic **Bali Pathfinder Guide** produced by Murni's studio ((0361) 976453 E-MAIL baliartmurni@baliartmurni.com

OPPOSITE: Fishing *prahu* on the beach at Sanur. They will even take you across the Badung Strait to Jungutbatu on Nusa Lembongan — a trip that seems frighteningly far for such simple craft. ABOVE: Creating its own Balinese paradise, the Grand Hyatt Hotel.

WEB SITE www.baliartmurni.com, Jalan Pengosekan ke Nyuhkuning, which should be available in good Balinese bookshops, Rp35,000. This is part-map, part-art and part-guide, and is especially good when you're trying to get orientated in an unfamiliar town, although strangely it overlooks Sanur.

CAR RENTAL

Renting a car is a good way of getting around Bali for those with the confidence to drive here. Prices are keen, and many Balinese rent cars as needed, rather than owning their own. The two-door Suzuki Vitara, handy for the rougher roads, is a particularly popular option for couples or individuals, but the rear bench seats aren't too comfortable for full-sized adults. Families and groups may want to go for the larger Toyota Kijang jeeps.

Insurance, which the renter will try to persuade you to take out, can be worthwhile for covering damage to the vehicle, but watch out for large excesses, which you have to pay in the event of any damage. Also, most importantly, test-drive the vehicle before agreeing to the rental, as you'll probably be responsible for any repairs too. Any problems on the road are liable to become the problem of the driver, rather than the rental company. Daily rentals are usually for 12 hours, so if you want to drive at night (not, generally, a very good idea) you'll have to rent for a minimum of two days.

Local rental companies are listed through the text in the touring chapters, and some further companies include **CV Ardisa Rent Car** ((0361) 224064, Jalan Jempiring 1, Denpasar; **Singa Mandawa Car Rental** ((0361) 231168, Jalan Noja 1/16, Denpasar; and **Wirasana Rent Car** ((0361) 286066, Jalan Ngurah Rai (Bypass) 545X, Sanur. Single-day rental is generally taken to mean a 12-hour period, so if you want to use the car after dark you'll often need to rent for more than one day. Rates are negotiable, and drop for longer rental periods. Insurance is optional and usually offered by the rental agency. Alternatively contact **PT Asuransi Aken Raharja** ((0361) 224027, Jalan WR Suprataman 117X, Tohpati, Denpasar, who provide an independent insurance service. This is recommended.

MOTORBIKE RENTAL

Thousands of visitors a year rent motorbikes while on Bali. It's an excellent way to see the island, and especially good for getting away from the main tourist trail. Bikes are easy to park and easy to turn when you miss a junction. It's also easier, on a scooter, to ask for directions from pedestrians. Take extra care on the main roads, however, where the traffic in recent years has become very heavy.

Motorcycle rental is very established here, and most of the car rental companies will also supply motorbikes if asked. There are also plenty of specialists, who can be spotted simply by lines of motorcycles by the side of the road. The best are the ubiquitous 100cc Japanese scooters, which are fast enough for the road conditions and can carry heavy luggage between seat and handlebars. Larger trial bikes look very impressive but you don't see the locals riding them often: they're just that little bit wide for threading through traffic and are likely to be harder to fix in event of mechanical problems, punctures etc. They're also more expensive to rent.

There are police checks, and they will want to see your driving license and the vehicle registration document. These should be carried at all times. Helmets are compulsory but there are no minimum standards. Rental agencies generally supply construction worker's hard hats, which pass the legal test but wouldn't be much good in an accident. It's best to bring your own helmet, or, considering the heat and humidity of Bali, a bicycle helmet. Big-bike fans will find their happiness complete when they find **Bali Big Bike Tour and Rental** ((0361) 773391 E-MAIL orimotor@indo.net.id WEB SITE www.full speed.to/ogimotor, Jalan Ngurah Rai (Bypass) 27X, Kuta, who run self-ride and escorted tours on big Harley-Davidsons. To rent a Hog of your own, however, gets quite expensive, with daily charges at about US$100, but it is a very dignified way to deal with Bali's traffic.

If you don't have an international driver's license validated for motorcycle use, you will have to get a special permit to ride a motorbike in Bali. For this, you'll go to the **Denpasar Police Office** ((0361) 227711, Jalan Seruni,

GETTING AROUND

Denpasar (your rental company will take you), and undergo a written test. (The unconfirmed legend is that someone always makes sure you put down the right answers.)

BICYCLE RENTAL

Inexpensive and convenient, bicycle rental seems to skirt the licensing problems of renting motorized transport. Bikes, usually quite rugged mountain machines, can be easily rented in tourist centers. Bear in mind however that Bali is very hot and humid, and also that other road users don't make many concessions to cyclists, wobbling along the edge of the road, coping with potholes and roadworks. Bicycle rental is only really advisable for minor roads without much traffic.

BEMO CULTURE

Although there are a number of taxis, operating mainly between large hotels and the airport, many travelers prefer to use *bemos*. Their pleasure is not always shared: the Balinese are naturally slight, and a Westerner crushing in to already crowded transport — with a huge backpack as well — can stretch limited facilities. Sometimes it is the only way to travel, especially if you find yourself stranded between towns on a busy road, in which case you don't want to risk walking. You might well complete your journey in the company of sacks of rice, chickens and even a couple of pigs.

Fares are fixed, and everyone except the tourist knows them. It isn't a bargaining situation. Nevertheless (as it seems eminently reasonable to take from a foreigner money he seems to want to throw away), larger amounts than necessary are usually accepted if you don't keep your wits about you. The best plan, if you don't know the correct fare, is to watch what the locals hand over, and to keep a stock of small coins so that you can offer the exact fare, or what you judge might well be the right fare. This avoids leaving it up to the conductor to decide whether or not to give you any change. There are no tickets.

Nor are there timetables. The *bemo* drivers rent their vehicles on a day-to-day basis and consequently have to do their best to recuperate the rental charge and make what profit they can. *Bemos* leave when they're full, rarely before. They can't be relied on to run after dark, except on the Denpasar to Kuta route. In some places, such as the mountain villages of Penelokan and Kintamani, or in

Young women proceed to a purification ceremony on Kuta Beach.

the country around Ubud, the last *bemos* of the day tend to leave well before five. Inquire on your outward journey, so as not to take a chance on getting stranded.

You can sit in the front alongside the driver if you like; there's no extra charge (i.e., it isn't "first class.") You pay the conductor (*kernet*) for the distance you've traveled when you get off. There are no fixed stops, other than at each end of the route. When you want to get out, shout "Stopa!" or "Stop!" To get on, wave one down — you won't have any trouble as they're always on permanent lookout for customers, with the *kernet* calling out the *bemo*'s destination to pedestrians as the vehicle passes. If you aren't sure if the *bemo* you are about to hail is going where you want to go, just ask. No one will mind if it turns out you stopped the *bemo* for nothing — they're as hungry for travelers as bees for nectar. Crowd in wherever you can: No *bemo* is ever too full to refuse taking on another passenger.

You won't have been using *bemo*s long before a driver suggests you charter one. This means you decide where the vehicle goes, just as if it were a taxi; the driver is an independent operator and is under no obligation to ply any particular route. It's a good way to get off the beaten track fast, but it is more expensive, and the driver will hope you're not going to mind if he picks up extra passengers in the normal way as well.

With the low state of the rupiah, traveling by *bemo* is slightly masochistic, as most travelers can perfectly well afford to charter a vehicle of their own, but outside the tourist areas the *bemo* station is the best, and often the only, place for long-distance transport.

ACCOMMODATION

There is every possible type of accommodation available in Bali. Most of the international-standard hotels are in the southern resorts, but over the years most parts of the country have seen a steady flow of visitors and a good range of hotels have been set up in their wake. Even in the most improbable places there are still basic hotels. Fortunately they've developed from the basic home-stay concept on traditional lines. Balinese houses are traditionally designed in pavilions, and their guest pavilions were traditionally self-contained, with en-suite facilities, even if the bathroom amounted to just a toilet and a *mandi*, filled with cold water for washing. As they have grown in sophistication self-contained accommodation with en-suite facilities are still normal even in very inexpensive places.

Most of the glossy hotels are found in Nusa Dua, Sanur or Kuta. Nusa Dua has a whole area of nothing but five-star hotels; Sanur has a reasonable range, but little in the rock-bottom bracket; while Kuta, Legian and Seminyak offer the complete range of accommodation.

Like everything else in Indonesia, accommodation is excellent value when you're bringing in major foreign currencies, though the now-usual habit of quoting rates in United States dollars in the more expensive hotels fails to disguise a major rate hike there in recent years.

Prices are also flexible. At the top end of the range you won't be able to bargain the rates down at the reception desk, but book through tour operators, at home or in Indonesia, and there are discounts to be had. Mid-priced hotels will often drop their rates drastically if they're not full, outside the high season months of July to September or the

Christmas period. At the least expensive end of the scale, a cheap room in a *losmen*, or homestay, will almost invariably be clean, have an overhead fan and look out onto a central garden. It will have a cold water shower and breakfast (tea or coffee with toast and fruit) is usually included in the price. Sometimes the bathroom will be a *mandi*, which is a large tiled cistern that contains cold water, with a ladle for washing. **Do not**, under any circumstances, get soap in this water supply, or — worse still — climb in it to wash. Many places in Bali find it hard to get water and the contents of the *mandi* need to be kept clean for the next guest — as the last left it for you.

Once you leave the tourist belt, however, it is unlikely that you will have much choice in lodging.

There are *losmens* almost everywhere, and even where there are none the friendly local people will be only too eager to adjust the family arrangements in order to provide you with a room for the night and themselves with some additional income.

There are, of course, subsidiary tourist enclaves, such as at Lovina in the north and Candi Dasa in the east, where there are good quality small hotels. In Denpasar there is one reasonable hotel and others that are far from prepossessing. At Ubud there is again a very wide range to choose from, many very expensive, though less expensive ones can be found.

Tax complicates the hotel rates. The government tax is 10%, and is charged even at the least expensive hotels. However this is the first thing to be discounted in the bargaining process. The more expensive hotels add 21% to the bill, including an arbitrary 11% for service which rarely gets anywhere near the hotel staff.

The **rates** in the body of the text are based on the price of the average double room. Most hotels have a range of rooms to suit different budges: some might be fan-cooled, others air-conditioned; some might have hot water, others cold; size and facilities vary. Add the fact that the room rate is also almost certainly negotiable as well this guidebook could clearly be filled with price details that aren't especially helpful or reliable. For this reason the hotel prices in the text have been divided into broad bands. These are:

budget	under Rp100,000 (US$12)
inexpensive	Rp100,000 to 250,000 (US$12 to 30)
moderate	Rp250,000 to 700,000 (US$30 to 80)
expensive	over Rp700,000 (US$80).

Note that Bali's high seasons are July to August and from 20 December to approximately 20 January. Higher prices can be expected at these times.

EATING OUT

In areas that see large numbers of travelers, Indonesian food approaches rarity; it's sometimes easier to get a Mexican, German or Italian meal than a Balinese one. You certainly never need eat non-Western food if you don't want to. Unfortunately, what Indonesian food is available is de-spiced for Western palates, and Balinese food, without spices, often tastes stodgy. Even at small roadside *warungs*, or small semi-mobile eateries, the food will often be toned down, which doesn't do it any favors. "Pedas" means spicy in Indonesian, or "lalah" in Balinese, if you want to liven up your meal.

Elsewhere on the island you'll have to put up with what you find. In all the places tourists frequent, attempts will be made to offer Western-style food, but these will not differ greatly from the local fare. There are eating places here and there, however, that are delights to discover.

Note that prices for alcoholic beverages generally approach Western levels, and a couple more drinks can quickly double the price of any meal.

It is important to remember that prices at the budget end of the scale are very low. It is possible to eat a simple meal for around Rp8,500 (about US$1) at an outdoor food cart and to find a room in a *losmen* for Rp50,000 (US$4) almost anywhere in Bali, including the southern tourist belt. Proper restaurants are also very reasonable, with meals costing about US$3, where the waiters will almost certainly speak English and the tablecloths will be clean. Expect to pay a little more in air-conditioned restaurants. Imported wines are rarely available and very expensive, and

The *wayung kulit*: the puppeteer, both magician and priest, jester and guardian of an ancient tradition.

BASICS

even the two domestic wines will more than double your eventual bill. A further saving is that tipping is not generally expected in restaurants.

The exception to this is in the expensive, international hotels, where restaurants do often now expect to be tipped, and prices, designed to make the most out of guests made captive by their own inertia, are often much higher. In the better hotels meals costing more than US$20 per head can be found although this usually (but not always) reflects a higher standard of cuisine.

BASICS

TIME

Bali is one hour ahead of Java, eight hours ahead of Greenwich Mean Time and three hours behind Australian Eastern Standard Time. It is 13 hours ahead of New York, 16 hours ahead of California, and two hours behind Sydney, Australia.

WATER

The water in Bali is generally not drinkable. Upper-caste Balinese drink bottled water, and so should visitors. Ice is usually safe, as it comes from government-approved ice factories, although bear in mind that it may have become contaminated by the time it reaches remote establishments.

WEIGHTS AND MEASURES

Bali uses the metric system of weights and measures. Fish are sold in kilos and distances measured in kilometers.

CURRENCY AND BANKING

You can bring unlimited amounts of foreign currency into Indonesia, but only up to Rp50,000 in Indonesian money, which must be declared on entry.

There's very little reason for acquiring rupiah before you arrive in Bali. The exchange kiosk at the airport stays open until after the last flight of the day has arrived, and rates are virtually identical to those offered by the banks and the moneychangers in Kuta, Sanur,

etc. In addition, exchange rates for the rupiah are often not particularly advantageous outside Indonesia.

Rupiah come in 25-, 50-, 100-, 500- and 1,000-rupiah coins and 100-, 500-, 1,000-, 5,000-, 10,000-, 20,000- and 50,000-rupiah notes. The small denomination coins are very rarely seen nowadays. (At the time of writing 25 rupiah bought just US$0.027. There isn't much you can buy for that, even in Indonesia.) Note that in the supermarkets you will often be given sweets (candies) instead of small change.

Money changing facilities are found everywhere in the tourist areas of southern Bali, and few charge commission. The exchange bureaus are infamous for shortchanging you if they think they can get away with it, something that isn't so hard, as newcomers get lost among the many zeros on the notes. Two places in Legian that offer a good rate and take no commission are PT, in Central Kuta opposite Goa 2002, and the Kodak Film outlet directly opposite the entrance to the Legian Beach Hotel on Jalan Melasti in Legian.

ATM machines have been installed throughout the island, and can be found in all the resort areas. Using the interbank exchange rate, these are by far the easiest way to get money, although it is sometimes necessary to try a few machines before you find one that works. Be aware that although crime is rare in Bali, the area around an ATM is a logical place for thieves to lurk.

When receiving money transfers from abroad, it's a good idea to have the sender send you a copy of the transfer notice to an address other than the bank, just to be on the safe side.

When traveling to villages upcountry, make sure you have plenty of small change, as vendors away from the tourist areas may not have change for large notes.

Rate of Exchange

At the time of writing, exchange rates were as follows:
US$1 = 9,350 rupiah
1 euro = 8,764 rupiah
Can$1 = 6,201 rupiah
Aus$1 = 5,212 rupiah

COMMUNICATIONS AND MEDIA

Telephone

Telephone service used be one of Bali's weaknesses. Subscribers told stories of "secret sharers" who occupied their line and pushed up their bill even when they were temporarily disconnected for nonpayment, and you would as a matter of course have to try 20 or 30 times before getting a line.

The situation is much better now. There are phones taking phone cards from which you can make **international calls**. Much cheaper, however, are the now numerous **Wartel** offices; they're virtually everywhere, and foreign residents without private phones use them for all their international calls.

You will soon realize that there are two different **access codes for international calls**: 001 and 008. The first is for calls via the official telecommunications organization, the second via a private company. Charges are the same, but 008 is generally considered the more efficient, with a shorter waiting time.

You'll often see the word "hunting" after a phone number. This means is that there are several lines to the one number.

The **area code** for southern Bali, including Kuta, Sanur, Nusa Dua, Ubud and Denpasar, is 0361. For northern Bali it's 0362; it's 0363 for Candi Dasa and the northeastern beaches at Tulamben and Amed, and for the central heights—Kintamani, Penelokan, Kedisan and Air Panas—it's 0366. The full numbers (including area code) are shown throughout this book. When dialing within area codes omit the first four numbers.

The following numbers may be useful:
Operator (100
Fire (113
Police (110
Ambulance (118 or (26305
International operator (102
Time (103
International inquiries (106
Directory inquiries (108
Complaints (117
Search and Rescue (111

Mail

To find the post office, ask for "kantor pos." In **Kuta** the main office is near the Night Market, with a very efficient branch in Jalan Bakung Sari, close to the junction with the main Denpasar to Tuban road. In **Sanur**, it's across Jalan Ngurah Rai (Bypass) on Jalan Segara. The **Denpasar** post office is inconveniently located on the road to Sanur, away from the town center. Opening hours, generally, are Monday to Thursday 8 AM to 2 PM, Friday and Saturday 8 AM to noon.

As in many Asian countries, it is advisable to make certain the mail clerk cancels your stamps. Relative money values are such that the postage on a heavy letter overseas can equal a day's pay for an Indonesian worker; consequently, the temptation to remove your stamps might occasionally be irresistible.

Many postal agents will sell stamps, accept your mail and post it for you; they are generally quite reliable. Register any important or valuable mail.

Express mail is quite inexpensive and should save a couple of days.

At the time of writing, postal rates were as follows: For sending an **airmail postcard**

A simple grass roof provides an oasis of shade among rice terraces.

to Australia and Asia Rp4,000, to Europe Rp6,000, to the United States Rp7,500; for **airmail letters** to Australia and Asia Rp4,000, to Europe Rp6,000 to the United States Rp7,500.

If you've bought some larger purchases — which is a tempting option in Bali, with fine products for sale, low prices and (most significantly perhaps) some very convincing salespeople, you might find yourself wishing to take the weight off your luggage by sending packages home. This is easy and quick at a post office, most of which have a wrapping service and will also perform a customs check on your package as they wrap it up. Airmail is recommended for lighter packages. Sample rates for **parcels** up to one kilogram, traveling airmail are: to Australia Rp125,792, to Europe (UK) Rp200,200, to the United States Rp191,737. Larger purchases might have to go by surface mail, taking two months or so. To send 10 kg (22 lbs) to Australia would cost Rp221,949; to the United Kingdom Rp367,003, and to the United States Rp334,880.

Posting things to Bali is complicated by the fact that addresses often don't include street numbers. It is quite common for hotels and individuals to give their address, unnumbered, on a street that might be a mile or more long. This is partly because Bali's growth has proceeded so fast that there just aren't enough numbers to cope with later developments, and partly because the community is so tight-knit that individuals within it don't feel the need to identify their location this precisely. If, as users of this book, readers find themselves floundering to locate an unnumbered street address, I can only apologize. This will usually be because their stationary didn't give a street number, and asking for one produced but a blank stare. Find the street, I'm afraid, is the best advice, and then ask for the establishment by name.

PRESS AND RADIO

There are two English-language papers published in Jakarta, *The Indonesia Times* and *The Jakarta Post*. They are usually on sale in southern Bali from about mid-morning on the day of issue. Neither contain much news about Bali. The *Bali Post* is not translated into English, sadly, and conspiracy theorists suspect this is to protect visitors from hearing too much about the real issues that exist in the island.

Bali has an abundance of free publications paid for by the often useful advertisements they carry. The best of them is *Bali Plus*, published monthly. It's pocket-sized and there isn't room for many articles, but its "What's on in Bali" has no equal.

Then there's the full-color broadsheet *Bali Kini*, the similar *Bali Now* and *Hello Bali*, the government tourist office's *Tourist Indonesia*, and the *Bali Advertiser*, "advertising for the expatriate community." There's even a magazine devoted to surfing in Bali, which (usefully) lists tide tables. All can be found in hotel lobbies and cafés.

ETIQUETTE

The Balinese are a polite people and visitors should try to follow suit. A few simple points will see you a long way toward fitting in with the local environment.

- Give and take everything with the right hand; the left is considered unclean.

- Never touch anyone on the head, even a child.

- Don't photograph people bathing in rivers, and in other circumstances ask first, if only with a smile and a gesture.

- Don't beckon someone toward you with your index finger as it's very rude.

- Wear a sash around your waist whenever you go into a temple, and at a ceremony such as a cremation don't wear shorts, flip-flops or a skimpy T-shirt. No one will be the slightest bit amused if you wear a sarong; they will be delighted, and many people will compliment you on your taste.

- Pointing at people or standing with your arms folded is widely considered vulgar. Standing with your hands on your hips, a very normal Western pose, is seen as a sign of aggression, and you can see the Balinese flinch.

Dance is arguably the finest flower of Balinese art. The Sword *(kris)* Dance demonstrated at a show for tourists.

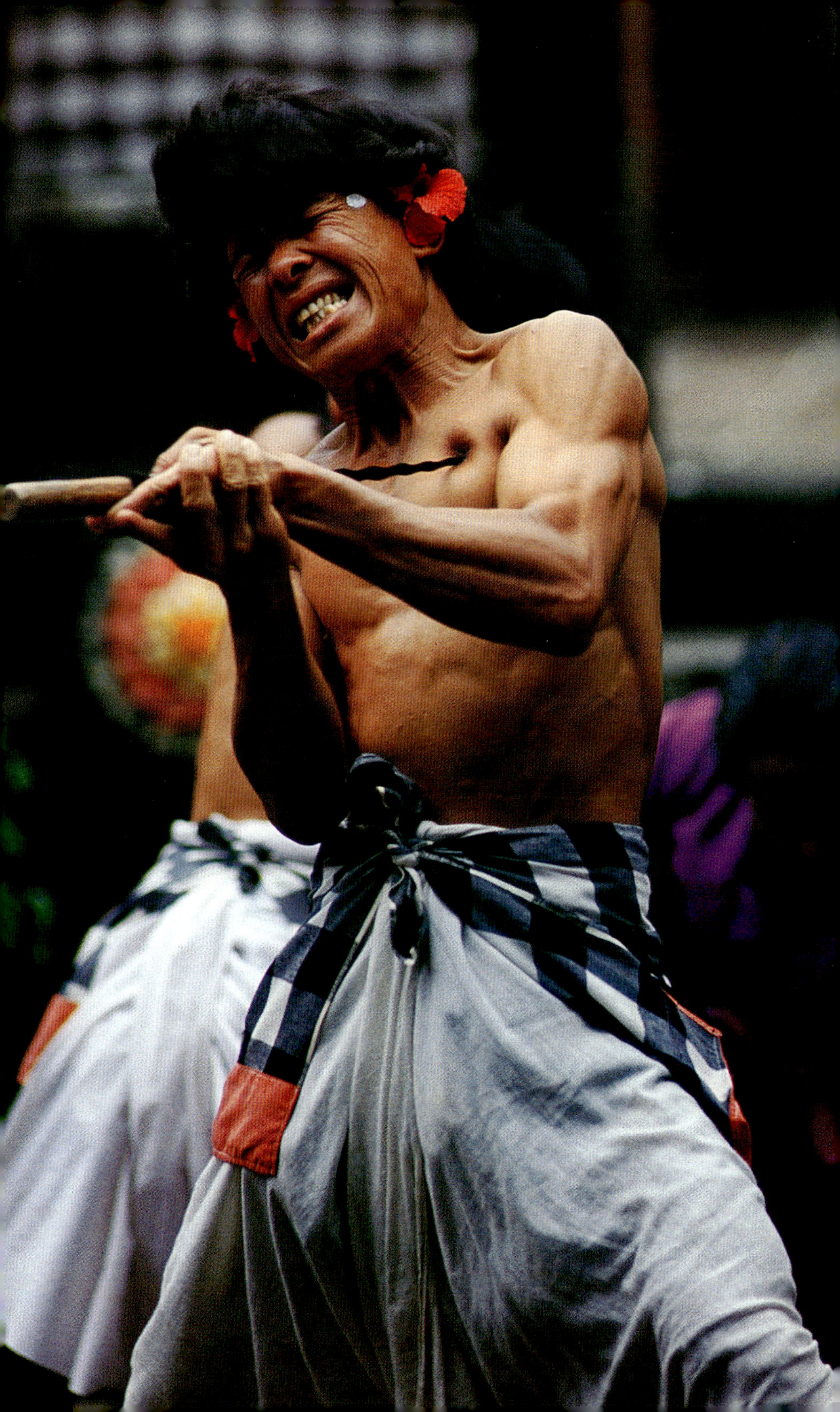

ETIQUETTE

The Balinese, incidentally, rarely say "thank you" in the normal run of things on receipt of a gift. If they do so, it will be because they have been trained to do it by the hotel where they work. Similarly, it's impolite to call someone simply by his first name, but hotel workers have been trained to accept this slight along with other imported barbarisms.

WHAT TO WEAR

The Indonesian government used to issue a poster detailing undesirable and preferred modes of dress. Its essential message was that tourists should remember that this is someone else's country and local conventions should be adhered to. The beach and adjacent streets are one thing, but the rest of the island is very much another.

It's particularly important to wear reasonably formal dress when visiting government offices. This may differ from what's considered formal back home. Simply observe what the better-off Indonesians wear to get an idea of expectations. Short sleeves, for instance, are perfectly acceptable for men, and ties are rare. But long trousers, shoes as opposed to sandals or flip-flops, and above all a neat, pressed, generally tidy appearance are essential ingredients in such situations.

For women, modesty is the keynote. Remember that it's going to be hot, sometimes very hot, and that loose-fitting clothes are much cooler than close-fitting ones. Cotton is also cooler than synthetic fabrics.

To enter a Balinese temple, one must wear a sarong and a sash. Most temples will rent these for a small fee, but it is simpler to buy them for a few thousand rupiah and carry them with you.

A moment's thought is worth pages of advice. You would never dream of turning up at a funeral at home in beachwear, but it's astonishing how many tourists turn up in shorts and a T-shirt to a Balinese cremation.

BARGAINING

Be prepared to bargain for most things in Bali. It's the most natural, and surely the most ancient, system in the world. If you want to buy, and the shopkeeper wants to sell, why should anything as rigid as a fixed price come between you?

You can even bargain for your hotel room, along the lines of "What price will you give me if I stay a week?" or "What's the discount, seeing as it is low season?" It may turn out to be inappropriate, but it's necessary to understand the Balinese will never be surprised — to them, it is fixed prices that are unnatural, the foreign importation.

The secret of successful bargaining is to get your offer in first. Once the vendor has named a price, it would involve loss of face to accept anything much less than 60% of it. Nevertheless, for you to make the first offer, and then go on to describe it immediately as your last price, is to go against the spirit of the business, and is guaranteed to remove the smile off any Indonesian face. You've simply broken the rules, and been very rude in the bargain because you've left no room to maneuver.

There are places where you don't bargain — restaurants and the larger shops, for instance. The Balinese don't haggle over *bemo* fares, though you might find yourself having to if you haven't managed to find out the correct fare in advance. But wherever you're dealing with those who are master of their own business, whether it's a girl hawking T-shirts on the beach or a boy offering to drive you around on the back of his motorbike, bargaining is the accepted, and expected, way to go about things.

In Bali, sellers frequently approach tourists with their wares. This often annoys visitors — on Kuta Beach for example — but remember that any answer, even "No thanks," or simply making eye contact, can be taken as an indication of some degree of interest. A silent shake of the head — and a smile — will usually see you aren't disturbed any longer.

TIPPING

Tipping isn't customary on Bali, but this shouldn't prevent you from rewarding someone who has provided you with a useful service. You might, for example, tip room service after an extended stay but not after a short one, and the polite way to do this is to leave a bank note in an envelope

HEALTH

There are no obligatory vaccinations for entry into Indonesia, other than for yellow fever if you have been in an infected area during the previous six days. It's prudent, though, to consult your doctor and perhaps have an anti-tetanus vaccination before leaving home.

Malaria exists all over Indonesia, though the risk in Bali is negligible. The medical authorities no longer recommend taking anti-malaria pills for vacationers visiting the island. Many doctors believe that long trousers and long-sleeved shirts provide more protection than medical prophylactics. You should therefore play it safe and cover up as evening approaches and mosquitoes become active. Put on repellent and light antimosquito coils where appropriate. Taking vitamin B complex is reputed to help repel mosquitoes, too.

Dengue fever has been reported on Bali. Protecting yourself from mosquito bites is again the best precaution — and note that the mosquitoes that cause dengue fever bite at all times of the day. But the risk is small. The main symptom of dengue fever is dizziness, with aching bones, headache and fever as secondary symptoms. It is a serious, but very rarely life-threatening illness, but as there is no effective treatment for the illness there's little to be done but suffer through it. Mosquito bites do tend to become septic, almost as a matter of course. It's wise to carry some antiseptic ointment for use on these and more serious cuts and abrasions.

Because of the risk of hepatitis, beware of food sold from roadside stalls or carts, and drink only bottled water and soft drinks, or water that has been properly boiled.

A significant enemy is probably the sun. Get into the habit of wearing a hat, avoid sunbathing in the middle of the day, and only lie on the beach for short periods during your first few days. Suntan lotions with a high protection factor will help. Take care to find your own tolerance levels, and don't expect to look like a sun-kissed surfer after your first afternoon.

If you become ill, there are local health clinics known as *puskesmas*, but tourists are not expected to use them and you could find yourself being charged distinctly non-

Making the most of the last rays of sun at Legian Beach.

HEALTH

local rates for very elementary treatment. It's better to go to one of the Western doctors — associated with the **Hyatt**, **Bali Beach**, **Club Méditerranée** or **Nusa Dua hotels** — who will usually see patients, even if they're not guests of the hotel or resort; or visit one of the private clinics listed in the touring chapters.

At the time of writing Bali was rabies-free.

For dental treatment you can contact the **NDC**(/FAX (0361) 771324, Jalan Pratama 81, Nusa Dua.

The greatest risk, however, is undoubtedly the traffic. Take great care crossing the road, let alone driving, in Bali.

In case of **serious illness or injury**, it is best to leave Bali as soon as possible for treatment in Singapore or Australia. Local hospitals and clinics are not well equipped.

WATER SAFETY

Lives are lost every year on Bali's beaches — as recently as 1992, 29 people drowned in these waters. This is a major threat to health here, and one there's not much the best doctors can do anything about. Beaches are most dangerous when the surf is up, so watch out for riptides. Never go more than waist deep unless you are a very strong swimmer. If a current is pulling you out to sea, don't try to swim against it, but rather paddle sideways out of the current. If in distress of any kind, raise a hand above your head — it's the international signal for help and represents your best chance of being rescued.

Swimming pools see their share of accidents too. In less expensive establishments they rarely have depth marks, so don't just dive in head-first.

SEX

Male visitors may be offered prostitutes in Bali, especially in Kuta. Men are sure to hear the whispered words, "Balinese girl, very young," on some dark night. The prostitutes, incidentally, will almost certainly be from one of the other islands, as the well-developed Javanese sex industry is bound to spill over to a certain extent. Reflect that the girls are indeed likely to be very young, almost certainly circumcised, and absolutely certainly not acting of their own free will, and act accordingly.

There is also an obvious gigolo scene, especially in Kuta. Some Balinese, both male and female, actively seek relationships with visitors. Usually this is not for direct payment, although you certainly won't see them rushing to pick up a restaurant or hotel bill. Generally these relationships don't seem to travel well.

In Kuta there is an established transvestite tradition, with "Sucky Sucky Girls" patrolling the road along Kuta beach after dark.

Their approach is sparky but alarmingly direct.

There's an **AIDS Center** ((0361) 239191, on Jalan Sudirman, Denpasar, dealing with all aspects of the illness. Rates of infection in Bali are not known, but are suspected to be high.

DRUGS

Getting caught with drugs in Bali is bad for your health and disastrous for your lifestyle. Don't be tempted to import or use drugs in Bali.

Under the Indonesian Narcotic Drugs Law of 1976, it is an offense for anyone to have knowledge of drug use and not pass it on to the police. As for actual possession, amounts are irrelevant, and it is in no way the case that having a small amount constitutes only a minor offense. There have been recent cases of police raids on houses in the Ubud area in which, once drugs have been found, not only the owner of the drugs but everyone present has been arrested and given blood tests. A positive result is sufficient proof for conviction. It seems to be acceptable for foreigners to buy their way out of situations like this, but these days this doesn't come cheap and may well exceed US$100,000.

If you can't afford this, you've got a shock coming. Maximum penalties are as follows. For possessing cannabis or cocaine: six years' imprisonment, with a fine of Rp10 million; for possessing "other narcotic drugs": 10 years and Rp15 million. Selling or importing drugs is punishable by a 21-year sentence, or life, while the death penalty is given for the second category of substances (though to date this has not been imposed in a drugs case anywhere in Indonesia).

The southern Bali prison is at Kerobokan, just north of Kuta. There are always a number of foreigners incarcerated here, serving sentences for drug offenses.

There was a time when Bali was considered a paradise for psychedelic experiences. It is emphatically not so now. Visitors should neither import nor use any narcotic substances here — you may never know who informed on you, as informers are protected by Indonesian law from identification in court. Be warned.

SECURITY

Bali is refreshingly free of violent crime. Previously unknown, there have been reports of muggings in Kuta, especially after dark, but it is still rare and not comparable with crime rates in Europe, let alone America.

This isn't to say that things never get stolen. In a country where visitors are clearly much richer than almost all of the people this is, perhaps, only to be expected. Theft is almost never confrontational — the first the victim usually notices is when they go to use the camera/video camera/pair of sunglasses/mobile phone and find it gone.

Balinese often get very upset to hear of any such outrage being perpetrated in their town. The *banjar* system means they often have a very good idea who should be, and is, in the area. Their punishment of thieves is likely to be vigorous and direct. Report the theft to the police for your insurance, but there's less help to be expected from this quarter.

WHEN TO GO

Bali enjoys a benign climate. Situated on the southern edge of the equatorial belt, it does not experience the yearlong rainfall that produces the rainforests of the Amazon or the Congo. Instead, Bali has a long dry season, roughly from April to October, and a short wet season, November to March. Thus April to October is the high season, though the period from July to September is most crowded, thanks to the Australian and European school holidays, when hotels are full and rates increase. In fact, global warming seems to be changing Bali's climate, so the rigidity of the climate can no longer be guaranteed. The island also fills up at Christmas, even though that is in the middle of the wet season. Traditional "Rain Stoppers" perform complicated ceremonies to move rain away from important outdoor events, and around Christmas the Balinese joke that all the rain from the resort areas seems to be shifted to fall over Denpasar.

These seasons are caused by the relative heating and cooling of the great continents to the south and north of Indonesia. In the Australian summer that continent becomes hotter than its surrounding seas. Hot air rises, and so winds are ultimately drawn in from the cooling continent of Asia to the north. Deflected sideways by the rotation of the earth, these winds, wet because they have crossed the seas to the north of Indonesia, become Bali's wet-season northwest monsoon. By contrast, in the Australian winter, winds blow northward from the cooling continent and, coming from so dry a place across a relatively narrow ocean, become the southeasterlies of Bali's dry season.

Traditional life goes on even in the midst of the tourist invasion — a purification ceremony at Kuta.

Records show that the south of the island receives annually 78% of the maximum possible sunlight (and 63% even in January, the wettest month). As a result, skies are often clear for days on end, even during the rainy season. Although temperatures never equal the heights they can reach, for example, during a Greek or North African summer, high humidity, which averages 75%, can make the heat sapping. The average monthly temperature does not exceed 31°C (89°F), or drop below 24°C (78°F). Day and night, wet season and dry, the temperature varies between warm and hot on the coast. In the mountainous regions nights are much cooler, and only here will a sweater be needed.

WHAT TO TAKE

As little as possible. Unless you're planning to spend a night or two in the volcanic center, even a sweater won't be needed. The usual rule is to take twice as much money and half as much luggage. Thanks to the incredible sinking rupiah you won't need too much cash, and thanks to the industrious and creative Balinese craftsmen what you don't bring, you can buy. There are only a few things worth bringing with you.

Take medicaments and prescription drugs, as these might not be available in Bali.

Take glasses or contact lenses, as the Balinese opticians don't seem to match the speed or versatility of their Javanese compatriots.

Take reading matter, as English-language books, in Bali, are expensive, though many less expensive hotels and *losmens* keep shelves of books to swap.

Take lightweight T-shirts. Strangely, even though T-shirt vendors line the approaches to every half-decent attraction in the island, they are all of fairly thick fabric. High-quality fine material is better for the sapping heat, but this is rarely found.

PHOTOGRAPHY

Heat and humidity are the greatest challenges to photographers. The heat is quite capable of damaging color film, especially if left baking in a car through the day. Humidity can affect photographic equipment: lower-priced SLRs seem particularly vulnerable. Air-conditioning can cause condensation problems when photographers take their cameras, chilled from their air-conditioned hotel room or vehicle, out to take a photograph: in seconds the lens and viewfinder will mist over. There's no point trying to wipe this off — the lens just smears and of course you risk damage — the only answer is to put the camera in the sun until it warms up. This can be infuriating, especially as that perfect photograph takes off up the road.

The tropical sun isn't just hot: it's also bright. Try to take photographs early in the morning and in the late afternoon. In the day it is very hard to balance out sunlight and deep shade: consider using a flash to even out the light.

Photographic film is widely available and not expensive. However these films may not have been stored correctly and serious photographers will probably want to bring their own. Slide film is less readily available, although you will find Fuji and Kodak transparency film in Kuta.

In general the Balinese quite enjoy being photographed. Exceptions include cockfights (as this is technically illegal) and people bathing in rivers (which is equivalent to being snapped in the shower back home)

LANGUAGE

Bali has its own language, Balinese. Though part of the Malayo-Polynesian family of languages, it is as distinct from Malay (Indonesian) as English is from German. It exists in three forms: High, Middle and Low. Lower-ranking people use High Balinese when speaking to their superiors; high-ranking people speak Low Balinese among themselves or when speaking to inferiors, except in formal situations. Middle Balinese is used in delicate social circumstances.

The ancient Javanese tongue of Kawi is used by priests; it is the language of the gods in the shadow puppet dramas.

The language generally known as Bahasa Indonesia ("the Indonesian language"), the official language of Indonesia, is virtually indistinguishable from Malay. It is taught in all schools as part of Indonesian government policy. Most young Balinese can speak it when necessary. It is also the easiest for the visitor to master. Try to learn at least a few phrases of. There are no articles, no plurals, and no tenses, and the verb "to be" isn't used (e.g., Bali *bagus* means "Bali is beautiful").

Pronunciation is easy and straightforward: The important point is that Indonesian is easy to *hear*. Most Westerners can pick up the sounds and general intonation almost at once. In this, Indonesian contrasts strongly with most other Asian languages which, with their complex systems of tones, are very difficult for speakers of European languages.

Because the language is so easy, it's immense fun to try. It's also very poetic. Start off with some of the following:
Good Morning.   *Selamat pagi*. ("May your action be blessed this morning.")
How are you?   *Apa khabar*? ("What's the news?")
I'm fine.   *Khabar baik*. ("The news is good.")
Thank you.   *Terima kasih*.
It's a pleasure.   *Kembali*.
Good-bye (when you are leaving).   *Permisi*. (The reply to this is *Mari*.)
What is your name?   *Siapa namamu*?
My name is…   *Nama saya*…
Please speak slowly.   *Tolong bicara pelanpelan*.
I'll come back later.   *Saya akan kembali nanti*.
May I come in?   *Boleh saya masuk*?
This is good!   *Ini bagus*!
Is it safe to swim here?   *Anam berenang disini*?
How much is this?   *Berapa haga ini*?
About…   *Kira kira*…
1, 2, 3, 4, 5…   *Satu, dua, tiga, empat, lima*…
…6, 7, 8, 9, 10.   …*enam, tujuh, delapan, sembilan, sepuluh*.
11, 12, 13…   *sebelas, dua belas, tiga belas* (*belas* = ten)
20, 30…   *dua puluh, tiga puluh* (*puluh* = tens)
100   *seratus*
200, 300…   *dua ratus, tiga ratus* (*ratus* = hundreds)
1,000   *seribu*
2,000, 3,000…   *dua ribu, tiga ribu* (*ribu* = thousands)
100,000   *seratus ribu*

In answer to the eternal question "Where are you going?" try *"Makan angin"* ("To eat the wind").

A helpful little booklet is John Barker's *Practical Indonesian*, available all over Bali. If you're lucky enough to be staying in a smart hotel with in-house movies, these will usually have subtitles in Indonesian. As pronunciation is so straightforward this is a good way of picking up the language, even if you end up talking like a fourth-rate Hollywood actor.

WEB SITES

The official site of **Indonesia Tourism**: www.tourismindonesia.com is a worthy overview of the attractions of Bali and the rest of Indonesia.

Bali and Beyond www.baliandbeyond.com is a monthly newsletter run by one of the island's leading tour operators. There are plenty of trade stories and a list of what's on for the month ahead.

Want to Know Bali? www.baliclick.com is a beautiful site. Just sit and watch the images on the front page for a virtual tour of the island or click through to hotels and restaurants.

Bali Paradise online www.bali-paradise.com is a comprehensive site that covers every aspect of travel in Bali. It is especially useful for its timetable of festivals around the island.

Bali Travel Net www.bali-travel.net is a travel guide run by Panorama Travel, an Indonesian tour operator.

Bali Insiders Guide www.balivillas.com/guide.html contains a highly informative set of links to press cuttings on travel to Bali, even though they seem to have stolen a guidebook title.

Images of Bali www.rossuk.simplenet.com/Bali/Bali.htm is a collection of 237, often sensationally good, pictures of Bali to whet your appetite for travel.

Bali Online www.halo-bali.com is a tradey sort of site that gets straight into the business of booking hotels and tours. Most of this can be done at other sites that leaven their sell with a little more peripheral information.

Bali Travel Forum www.balivillas.com/baliforum is a highly informative chatroom, with loads of FAQs about Bali and specific hotels and tours.

Access Bali Online www.baliwww.com/bali is a straightforward site with plenty of interesting information.

Welcome to Bali www.pande-bali.com is a soft-sell web site run by a Bali-based tour operator.

Recommended Reading

BAUM, VICKI. *A Tale from Bali*. 1937, Charles E. Tuttle Co., 2000. Translated from German, this novel is set between 1904 and 1906, when the Dutch were extending their control over the island.

BELO, JANE. *Trance in Bali*. Westport: Greenwood Press, 1960. This 1930s account by Jane Belo, one of the more important early tourists, tells of Balinese rituals and lifestyles discovered by the first visitors.

COVARRUBIAS, MIGUEL. *The Island of Bali*. 1937; Periplus Editions, 1999. This classic systematically surveys Balinese life and culture, interspersing personal recollections from this Mexican painter who made two extended visits to the island.

EISEMAN, FRED B., ET AL. *Bali, Sekala and Niskala*. Periplus Editions, 1989. The leading authority on everything Balinese, Eiseman covers a vast range of information from Balinese scripts to the manufacture of concrete telephone poles on the Bukit. Breathtaking.

EISEMAN, MARGARET AND FRED. *Flowers of Bali*. 1987; Periplus Editions, 1994. An identification aid to some of the more common flowers of the island, with color photographs.

HOLT, ANGELA. *Art in Indonesia: Continuities and Change*. Cornell University Press, 1967. The arts of Bali put in an Indonesian context.

KERTONEGORO, MADI. *The Spirit Journey to Bali Aga, Tenganan Pegringsingan*. Bali: Harkat Foundation, 1986. A whimsical, eccentric but amusing account of legends from the Candi Dasa/Tenganan area.

KOCH, C.J. *The Year of Living Dangerously*. 1978; Penguin, 1995. This imaginative and sympathetic novel, set in Jakarta at the time of the fall of Sukarno in 1965, provides enormously interesting insight into Indonesian life and politics.

LEURAS, LEONARD AND IAN R. LLOYD. *Bali, the Ultimate Island*. St. Martins Press, 1987. The ultimate Bali picture book, with additional photographs by Cartier Bresson and other old masters.

MCPHEE, COLIN. *A House in Bali*. 1947; Charles E. Tuttle Co., 2000. McPhee was an American composer who went to Bali to study the *gamelan* (which he describes as "a shining rain of silver.") The first Westerner to build a house at Kuta, his book is sensitive and intelligent.

MCPHEE, COLIN. *Music in Bali. A study in Form and Instrumental Organization in Balinese Orchestral Music*. De Capo Press, 1976. This is still the most comprehensive study of Balinese music and is essential reading for musical students.

ROBINSON, GEOFFREY. *Bali, the Dark Side of Paradise*. Cornell University Press, 1998. An essential glimpse behind the tourist image of Bali that charts the class tensions, ethnic divisions and violence that underlie its twentieth-century history.

SCHULTE NORDHOLT, HENK. *State, Village and Ritual in Bali: A Historical Perspective*. Amsterdam: VU University Press, 1991. This book examines how Bali's cultural strengths of social organization and religious feelings have been harnessed by the colonial forces and, later, the national government.

TANTRI, K'TUT. *Revolt in Paradise*. 1960; Gramedia Paperbacks, 1990. A high-spirited account of the adventures of a young American woman who went to Bali alone in the 1930s, helped set up Kuta's first hotel, was imprisoned by the Japanese, and became famous throughout the region as "Surabaya Sue," freedom fighter with the Indonesians.

VON HOLZEN, HEINZ. *The Food of Indonesia: Bali and the Spice Islands*. Tuttle Publishing, 1995. The classic book on Balinese cuisine by a chef who still runs cooking courses in Nusa Dua. A classic and the best.

VICKERS, ADRIAN. *Bali, a Paradise Created*. 1990; Charles E. Tuttle Co., 1997. A very informative and refreshing analysis of Bali, the Balinese and the forces that have shaped the country. Highly recommended.

WIKAN, UNNI. *Managing Turbulent Hearts: A Balinese Formula for Living*. University of Chicago Press, 1990. A revealing examination of how the Balinese emphasize grace and dignity and use ceremony to cope with bereavement, fear and ambition.

Quick Reference A–Z Guide to Places and Topics of Interest with Listed Accommodation, Restaurants and Useful Telephone Numbers

The symbols Ⓕ FAX, Ⓣ TOLL-FREE, Ⓔ E-MAIL, Ⓦ WEB-SITE refer to additional contact information found in the chapter listings.

A accommodation
  bargaining 252
  camping 27
  exceptional hotels 37, 39
  general information 52, 53, 120, 126, 130, 135, 138, 246
  government tax 247
  losmens (home-stays) 27, 62, 112, 247
  room rates 246, 247
  tipping 252
Agung River 154
Air Panas 36, 174, 175, 176, 177, 178, 213, 249
  accommodation
    Hotel Puri Bening ((0366) 51234 Ⓕ 175
    Puri Wisata Pualam 176
    Under the Volcano Homestay
      ((0366) 51166 175
  attractions
    hot springs 175, 178
Air Sanih 27, 34
  attractions
    natural pool 34
  sports
    hiking 27
airlines
  domestic carriers 240
  international carriers 238
Amed 29, 31, 34, 54, 189, 194, 203, 210, 249
  access 204
  accommodation. See under Lipah
    Amed Cottages 204
    Congkang 3 Brothers 204
    Coral View Villas ((0361) 431273 Ⓕ 204
    Good Karma Ⓕ 204
    Hidden Paradise Cottages
      (/FAX (0361) 431273 204
    Indra Udhyana ((0361) 241107 Ⓕ 204
    Meditasi Ⓕ 204
  attractions
    lateen-rigged fishing boats 203
    salt production 203
  general information 203
    Diver's Café 204
  sports
    diving and snorkeling 31, 203, 204
Amlapura 13, 35, 36, 80, 110, 189, 190, 192, 195, 199, 201, 203, 204, 205, 210
  access 200
  accommodation
    Homestay Balakiran 36
    Losmen Lahar Mas ((0363) 21345 200
  attractions
    Palace 199, 200
    Puri Amsterdam 200
    Puri Madhura 200

  environs and excursions
    Ujung 200
  general information
    bemo stations 200
    Tourist Information Office ((0363) 21196 199
  history 80, 200
Amuk Bay 29
Antosari 222
Anturan 210
Arung River 161

B backpacking
  accommodation 36, 139
  general information 36–37
  transportation 36
Badung River 109
Badung Strait 192, 229, 230
Bali Aga 27, 50, 80, 86, 174, 177, 178, 198
Bali Barat National Park See West Bali National Park
Bali Straits 219
Balina Beach 29
Balinese names 90
Bangli 34, 80, 164, 165, 170, 172, 174, 180, 184
  access 165
  accommodation and restaurants
    Artha Sastra Inn ((0366) 91179 164
  attractions
    old palace (Artha Sastra Inn) 164
    Pura Dalem Pengungekan 164
    Pura Kehen 164
    Pura Penyimpenan 164
  history 80
Banjar 34, 210, 213, 214
  access 213, 214
  accommodation
    Pondok Wisata Grya Sari
      ((0362) 92903 Ⓕ 213
  attractions
    Buddhist Temple 213
    Hot Springs 34, 213
Banka River 192
Banyopoh 223
  attractions
    Pulaki Monkey Temple 223
Banyuwangi 240
bargaining 51, 252
Batubulan 16, 18, 50
  attractions
    barong dance 16, 18, 50
  shopping
    stone carvings 50
Batukandik 231
Batumadeg 231
Batur 174, 180
  attractions
    Temple of Ulu Danu 180

259

Bedugul 33, 61, 166, 170, 172
  access 172
  accommodation and restaurants 172
    Bedugul Hotel and Restaurant 172
  attractions
    Botanical Gardens 61, 170, 172
  general information 33, 172
  sports
    golf 33, 172
    water-skiing and parasailing 172
Benoa 31, 106, 110, 136, 209, 229, 230, 240
  general information
    Bali Hai ((0361) 720331 Ⓕ Ⓔ Ⓦ 31, 66, 230
Besakih 14, 26, 35, 80, 102, 171, 180, 184, 185, 190
  access 184
  accommodation
    Arca Valley Homestay and Restaurant 184
  attractions
    Mother Temple 35, 80, 171, 181, 182
    Pura Panataran 181
    temple meru 102, 181
  general information
    Tourist Office (no phone) 180
    Wayan Pasak (Agung guide) 182
  sports
    climbing Mount Agung 26, 182
bird orchestras 102, 194, 215
Bona 151
  attractions
    Balinese dances 151
Bug Bug 195
  attractions
    ancient monuments 195
Buhu River 192
Bukit Peninsula 14, 29, 52, 79, 106, 118, 134, 141, 145
  attractions
    Ulu Watu 14, 141, 145
Bunutan 204
Buyuk 233

C
Campuhan 48, 156, 157, 159
Candi Dasa 29, 30, 31, 38, 52, 53, 189, 190, 194, 195, 198, 200, 247, 249
  access 197
  accommodation
    Amankila ((0363) 41333 Ⓕ Ⓔ 38, 197
    Balina Beach ((0363) 41002 Ⓕ 197
    Candi Beach Cottage ((0363) 41234 Ⓕ 197
    Candi Dasa Beach Hotel
      ((0363) 41126 Ⓕ 197
    Genggong ((0363) 41105 197
    Ida Beach Village ((0363) 41118 Ⓕ 197
    Kubu Bali ((0363) 41532 Ⓕ 197
    Pandawa Bungalows ((0363) 41929 197
    Pelangi Homestay ((0363) 41270 197
    Puri Bagus Beach Hotel
      ((0363) 41291 Ⓕ 197
    Serai ((0363) 41011 Ⓕ Ⓔ 197
    Taman Air (or Watergarden)
      ((0363) 41540 Ⓕ 197
  attractions 196
    Dewi Spa and Salon ((0363) 41982 196
  environs and excursions
    Tenganan 198
  general information
    Safari Rent a Car ((0812) 392-1475 196
    Tourist Office ((0363) 41204 196

  nightlife
    Beer Garden Disco 197
    Ciao Pub'n Ristorante Italiano
      ((0363) 41278 197
    Go-Go's 197
  restaurants
    Kubu Bali ((0363) 41532 197
    Lotus Seaview ((0363) 41257 197
    TJ's ((0363) 41540 197
    Warung Ibu Rusimi 197
  sports
    diving and snorkeling 30, 31, 189, 196
    hiking 196
Candikuning 172
  attractions
    Pura Ulu Danu 172
Canggu 30, 122
  accommodation
    Legong Keraton Beach Cottages
      ((0361) 730280 Ⓕ 122
caste system 89, 90, 95, 98
Cekik 26, 61, 220, 222
Celik 205
Celuk 51, 133
  shopping
    silverware 51
children, traveling with
  accommodation 40–42, 139
  attractions 40–42
  general information 40
climate 26, 29, 30, 39, 128, 161, 209, 255, 256
cockfighting 72, 96, 101, 102, 198, 256
cremation ceremonies 12, 14, 16, 87, 90, 95, 96, 111, 121, 166, 181, 250, 252
cuisine 57, 58
Culik 203, 204
culture 41-43, 57, 61, 72, 80, 86, 89, 90, 93, 136, 148, 151
currency 248, 249
customs 238

D
dance 16, 18, 41–46, 49, 50, 52, 55, 72, 79, 101, 102, 107, 109, 120, 132, 136, 141, 151, 152, 161, 166, 198, 225
  barong 16, 18, 45, 50, 102, 151
  calonarang 151
  gabor 151
  jogged bumbung 225
  kecak 43, 109, 136, 141, 150, 151, 166
  kris dance 151
  legong 44, 150, 151
  rejang 198
  sanghyang jaran 45
Denpasar 13, 16, 18, 26, 30, 31, 33, 36, 50, 51, 54, 55, 61, 74, 83, 84, 89, 106, 110, 112, 115, 124, 126, 133, 141, 142, 148, 151, 161, 164, 165, 166, 172, 174, 175, 189, 190, 196, 197, 199, 209, 210, 213, 219, 220, 224, 225, 238, 240, 244, 249, 255
  access 109
  accommodation
    Darmawisata ((0361) 484186 109
    Natour Bali ((0361) 225681 Ⓕ 109
    Pemecutan Palace ((0361) 423491 109
  attractions
    Bali Museum ((0361) 222680 107
    Bird Market 109
    Cinema ((0361) 423023 109
    Flora Bali Orchid Farm
      ((0361) 225847 Ⓕ 109

D

kecak dances *109*
National Art Center *109*
Pura Jagatnatha *108*
Tanah Lapang Puputan Badung *107*
Werdi Budaya Arts Center *109*
festivals and special events
  Bali Arts Festival, mid-June to end of July *109*
  Nyepi (Balinese New Year), March/April *54, 89, 109*
general information 16, 18, 55, 107, 115
  Academy of Dance Indonesia
    (dance courses) *109*
  Ayung River Rafting ((0361) 238759 (F) *30*
  Bali Origin (/FAX (0361) 238504 (E) *65*
  Bali Taxi ((0361) 701111 *107*
  Baruna ((0361) 753820 (F) *31*
  Batubulan bemo station *109, 165*
  Conservatory of Performing Arts
    (dance courses) *109*
  CV Ardisa Rent Car ((0361) 224064 *244*
  Ena Dive Center (0361) 287945 *31*
  Forestry Department ((0361) 235679 *26*
  Garuda Indonesia ((0361) 227825 (F) *238*
  I Made Rajeg ((0361) 224121 (F) (E) *61*
  Immigration Office
    ((0361) 227828 *107, 238*
  Jans Tours ((0361) 232660 (F) *65*
  Kereneng bemo station *114*
  Post Office *249*
  Praja ((0361) 289090 *107*
  PT Asuransi Aken Raharja
    ((0361) 224027 *244*
  Sanglah General Hospital ((0361) 227911, 227915 *107*
  Singa Mandawa Car Rental
    ((0361) 231168 *244*
  Tegal bemo station *109*
  Tourist Driving License ((0361) 243939 *243*
  Ubung bemo station *109, 172, 219, 225*
history 83, 107
restaurants
  Ayam Bakar Tallwang ((0361) 241537 *109*
  Bundo Kanduang ((0361) 228551 *109*
  Natour Bali ((0361) 225681 *109*
shopping
  Cloth Market *109*
  Flora Bali Orchid Farm
    ((0361) 225847 (F) *109*
  gold jewelry *51*
  Jewelry Market *109*
  Pasar Badung *109*
  Sanggraha Kriya Asta *109*
departure tax *238*
drugs *254, 255*

E

East Timor *238*
eating and drinking
  beverages 59, 60, 247
  festive dishes 57
  rice 57, 148
  rijsttafel 58
  satay 58
  tropical fruits 58, 59
embassies and consulates
  consulates in Bali 240
  embassies in Jakarta 240
  Indonesian embassies abroad 241
etiquette *14, 18, 36, 247, 250, 252*

F

family life *90, 93*
festivals and special events *18, 54, 55, 98, 101, 102*
  Galungan, every 210-days 55
  Kuningan, every 210-days 55
  Nyepi (Balinese New Year), March/April 54, 89, 115

G

gamelan *14, 18, 20, 35, 46, 47, 62, 101, 152, 161, 189, 197, 198, 214*
Gelgel *110, 192*
attractions
  Royal Temple *192*
history 110
shopping
  pottery *192*
geography *79, 170, 209*
getting around
  by bemo 36, 109, 110, 245, 246
  by bicycle 245
  by car or motorcycle 242, 243, 244, 245
    accidents *243*
    Bali maps *243*
    car rental *244*
    driving licences *243, 244*
    general information *33, 242, 243*
    motorbike rental *244, 245*
    routes *33, 34, 35*
getting to Bali
  by ferry 236
  by long-distance bus 236, 240
  by plane 236
Gianyar *50, 51, 80, 83, 133, 161, 162, 163*
history 80, 83
Gilimanuk *26, 35, 61, 110, 210, 219, 220, 221, 223, 224, 236, 240*
access 219
accommodation
  Hotel Sari ((0365) 61264 (F) *219*
attractions
  Java Ferry Terminal *219*
general information
  Tourist Office *219*
restaurants
  Wayan Sudana ((0365) 61067 *219*
shopping
  batik fabrics *219*
Goa Gajah *164*
attractions
  statues and stone carvings *164*
Goa Lawah *192, 194*
Gunung Bisbis *34*
Gunung Kawi *162, 163*

H

Hanjarangkan *184*
health *59, 248, 253, 254*
  clinics 253
  dangerous beaches 254
  sun 253
  water 59, 248, 253
history
  Balinese kingdoms 80
  Drake, Sir Francis 110
  Dutch colonialism 72, 80, 83, 84, 110, 148, 209
  early traders 79
  Hinduism 79, 80, 89
  Indonesia today 86
  Islam 80
  prehistoric period 79
  Prince Diponegoro 83
  purge of communists 85

slavery 83, 110
Suharto 70, 85
Sukarno 85
Western artists 84, 126, 128, 148, 153
I Internet 113
Iseh 185
attractions
 rice terraces 185
J **Jagaraga** 35, 215
Jakarta 86, 220, 240, 250
Java 25, 50, 70, 79, 80, 84, 91, 98, 110, 126, 189, 219, 220, 224, 236, 240, 248
Jemeluk 204
Jimbaran 27, 38, 130, 135, 141, 143
 access 145
 accommodation 145
 Bali InterContinental
  ((0361) 701888 Ⓕ Ⓔ 145
 Jimbaran Bay ((0361) 701010 Ⓕ Ⓦ 38, 40, 143
 Keraton Bali Cottages
  ((0361) 701961 Ⓕ Ⓔ 143
 Pansea Puri Bali (701605 Ⓕ 143
 Puri Bamboo ((0361) 701377 Ⓕ Ⓔ 145
 Puri Indraprasta ((0361) 701552 145
 Ritz-Carlton ((0361) 702222 Ⓕ Ⓦ 143
 attractions
  boat building 143
  camel riding 27
  Fish Market 143
 general information 58
  Jimbaran Clinic ((0361) 701467 142
  motorcycle taxis 142
 restaurants
  Antar Café ((0361) 703382 145
  Bali Edelweis (772094 145
  beachfront warungs 142, 145
  Café Latino ((0361) 701880 145
  Jimbaran Bay ((0361) 701010 145
  Netayan Jimbaran Restaurant
   (/FAX (0361) 702253 145
  Ramayana ((0361) 702859 145
Jimbaran Bay 29, 40, 58, 106, 141, 143
Jogyakarta 213, 240
Jungutbatu 229
 accommodation
  Puri Nusa (/FAX (0361) 298613 229
K **Kalibukbuk** 36, 210
Kalimantan 49
Kamasan 48, 192
 shopping
  paintings in traditional style 48, 192
Karangasem *See* Amlapura
Kedaton 41
 attractions
  giant fruit bats 41
  Monkey Forest 41
Kediri 126
Kedisan 26, 174, 176, 177, 178, 249
 access 174
 accommodation and restaurants
  Segara ((0366) 51136 Ⓕ 174
  Surya ((0366) 51138 174
 attractions
  lava fields 174
  Trunyan Island 174
 general information
  Surya Hotel ((0366) 51378 26

Keidan 175
Kerobokan 255
Kintamani 26, 34, 110, 172, 180, 249
 general information
  Jero Wijaya Lakeside Cottage
   ((0366) 51249 26
Klumpu 231
Klungkung 35, 48, 80, 83, 110, 185, 189, 194, 195, 197, 199, 230
 access 190
 accommodation
  Cahaya Pusaka ((0366) 22119 190
  Logi Ramayana Palace Hotel
   ((0366) 21044 190
 attractions
  Kertha Gosa 189
  Town Market 190
 environs and excursions
  lava fields 192
 history 80, 83, 230
Komodo 128, 240
Kuban 177
Kubutambahan 35, 171, 215
 attractions
  Temple 215
Kusamba 80, 192, 229, 232
 environs and excursions
  Goa Lawah 192, 194
  Nusa Penida and Nusa Lembongan 192
  salt factory 194
 general information
  Nusa Penida crossings 232
Kuta 14, 28, 29, 30, 31, 33, 35, 36, 38, 40, 51, 52, 55, 64, 74, 89, 106, 107, 110, 111, 112, 113, 114, 119, 120, 121, 122, 123, 124, 126, 128, 130, 133, 142, 145, 150, 161, 175, 190, 196, 197, 209, 210, 212, 213, 237, 244, 246, 248, 249, 252, 254, 255
 access 124, 237
 accommodation
  Agung Cottages ((0361) 757427 Ⓕ 120
  Hard Rock Hotel ((0361) 761869 Ⓕ Ⓔ 120
  Holiday Inn Bali Hai ((0361) 753035 Ⓕ 120
  Komala Indah 1 120
  Losmen Arthawan ((0361) 752913 120
  Naga Sari Beach Club ((0361) 751960 120
  Natour Kuta Beach ((0361) 751361 120
  Poppies Cottages
   ((0361) 751059 Ⓕ Ⓔ Ⓦ 120
 attractions
  Adrenalin Park ((0361) 757841 118
  Bemo Corner 38, 114, 116
  Kuta Beach 111, 112, 114, 115, 116
  Kuta Square 35
  massages 118
  Night Market 116, 120
  Waterbom ((0361) 755676 Ⓕ Ⓔ 40, 116
 general information 55, 113
  Adrenalin Park (bungee jumping)
   ((0361) 757841 118
  airport taxis 124
  Bali Bahagia Rent Car ((0361) 751954 112
  Bali Big Bike Tour and Rental
   ((0361) 773391 244
  Bali Bungee Co. (/FAX (0361) 752658 118
  Bali Clinic ((0361) 733301 Ⓕ 112
  Garuda Indonesia ((0361) 751179 240
  Hotel Sahid Bali (massages)
   ((0361) 753855 118

Impian Nusa (cybercafé)
  ℓ/FAX (0361) 761326 Ⓔ *113*
KCB Tours and Travel
  ℓ (0361) 75157 Ⓕ Ⓔ *64, 65*
Krakatoa (cybercafé)
  ℓ (0361) 730849 Ⓕ Ⓔ *113*
Kuta Surf Rescue ℓ (0361) 234569, 223602 *115*
post offices *113, 249*
PT Shop (money changing) *248*
taxi *112*
Tourist Information ℓ (0361) 751419 *112*
Toyota Rent Car ℓ (0361) 751356 *112*
Waka Louka ℓ (0361) 426792 Ⓕ *65, 67*
Wayan Kantra (motorcycle rental)
  ℓ (0361) 487889 *113*
history 110
nightlife
  All Stars Surf Cafe ℓ (0361) 761869 *124*
  Apache Raggae Bar ℓ (0361) 761869 *124*
  Bounty Ship 1 ℓ (0361) 761869 *124*
  Hard Rock Café ℓ (0361) 761869 *120, 124*
  Peanuts *123*
  Sari Bar ℓ (0361) 761869 *124*
  Tubes ℓ (0361) 761869 *124*
restaurants
  Depot Kuta ℓ (0361) 51155 *123*
  Kin Khao Thai Restaurant
    ℓ (0361) 732153 *123*
  Made's Warung *122*
  Made's Warung II ℓ (0361) 732130 *122*
  Poppies ℓ (0361) 751059 *38, 122*
  TJ's ℓ (0361) 751093 *122*
  Un's ℓ (0361) 752607 *122*
shopping
  Aloha Surf Station ℓ (0361) 758286 *119*
  Bali Plaza *51, 120*
  Bali Shopping World *51*
  cheap cassettes and CDs *119*
  Dreamland ℓ (0361) 755159 *119*
  Kertai Bookshop *119*
  Kuta Square *120*
  Matahari *35, 120*
  Miko Opals ℓ (0361) 761231 *119*
  Night Market *120*
  Nona ℓ (0361) 755919 *119*
  Setya Budi Art ℓ (0361) 730560 *120*
  Sol ℓ (0361) 755072 *119*
  Suarti Designer Collection ℓ (0361) 754252 *119*
  textiles *51*
  Tidore ℓ (0361) 730934 *119*
  Toko Kaca Taman Sari ℓ (0361) 730424 *119*
  Uluwatu ℓ (0361) 753428 *51, 119*
sports
  boogie boarding *30*
  bungee jumping *116*
  horseback riding *28*
  surfing *30*
Kuta Reef *30*

L Labuanhaji *214*
attractions
  waterfalls *214*
Labuhan Lalang *26, 220, 221, 222*
Lake Batur *23, 35, 174*
Lake Bratan *170, 172*
Lake Buyan *172*
Lake Tambingan *172*
language *58, 61, 79, 256*
  Bahasa Indonesia 256

Balinese *256*
basic restaurant terms *58, 247*
Indonesian words and expressions *257*
language courses *61*
Legian *28, 29, 30, 36, 38, 40, 52, 74, 106, 111, 112, 113, 114, 121, 122, 123, 124, 212, 246, 248.*
See also under Kuta
accommodation
  Blue Ocean ℓ (0361) 730289 Ⓕ *121*
  Legian Garden Cottage
    ℓ (0361) 751876 Ⓕ *121*
  Sri Ratu Cottages ℓ (0361) 751566 *121*
  Suri Wathi Beach House
    ℓ (0361) 753162 Ⓕ Ⓔ *121*
general information
  A.J. Hacket Bungee ℓ (0361) 730666 Ⓕ *116*
  Bali Jaran-Jaran Keneka
    ℓ (0361) 751672 Ⓕ *28*
  Kodak Film Shop (money changing) *248*
  Surf@Soda Club ℓ (0361) 756735 *118*
nightlife
  A Bar *124*
  Buddha Bar *124*
  Café Luna ℓ (0361) 730805 *124*
  Double Six *38, 124*
  Goa 2002 *38, 124*
  Jaya Pub *124*
  Villas Club *124*
restaurants
  Café Luna ℓ (0361) 730805 *38, 123*
  Fabios ℓ (0361) 730562 *123*
  Hana Restaurant (no phone) *123*
  Kin Khao Thai Restaurant
    ℓ (0361) 732153 *123*
  Ryoshi ℓ (0361) 731377 *123*
  Surya Café ℓ (0361) 757381 *123*
  Swiss Restaurant ℓ (0361) 751735 *38, 122*
  Topi Kopi ℓ (0361) 754243 *122*
  Warung Kopi ℓ (0361) 753602 *123*
  Yashi ℓ (0361) 751161 *123*
  Zanzibar ℓ (0361) 733527 *123*
sports
  bungee jumping *116*
  horseback riding *28*
  surfing *30*
Lombok *13, 80, 194, 195, 236, 237, 240*
Lovina *21, 22, 29, 31, 32, 33, 34, 36, 40, 53, 74, 110, 209, 210, 214, 247*
access 211, 213
accommodation
  Aneka Lovina ℓ (0362) 41121 Ⓕ *212*
  Banyualit Beach Inn ℓ (0362) 41789 Ⓕ *212*
  Celik Agung ℓ (0362) 41309 Ⓕ *212*
  Manik Sari ℓ (0362) 41089 *212*
  Palestis Beach Cottages ℓ (0362) 41035 *212*
  Puri Bagus ℓ (0362) 21430 Ⓕ *212*
  Sol Lovina ℓ (0362) 41775 Ⓕ *212*
attractions
  Dolphin Square *212*
  dolphin-watching *21, 22, 32, 40, 209, 211*
  Lovina Beach *21, 210*
general information
  Anak Aung Udayana ℓ (0362) 41459 *211*
  Malibu Dive Centre ℓ (0362) 41225 Ⓔ *212*
  Marga Sakti Transport ℓ (0362) 41061, 411570 *211*
  Perama ℓ (0362) 21161 *211*
  Tourist Office ℓ (0362) 91910 *211*

L

nightlife
  Poco Bar *212*
restaurants
  Bali Apik Bar and Restaurant
    ℃ (0362) 41050 *212*
  Sea Breeze Café ℃ (0362) 41138 *212*
  Warung Kopi Bali ℃ (0362) 41361 *212*
sports
  diving *211*
  snorkeling *32, 209, 211*
luggage *256*

M

mail *250*
  general information 249
  parcels 250
  postal rates 249
Manggis *194, 197*
Mas *48, 50*
  shopping
    masks *50*
    woodcarvings *48*
Medewi Beach *29, 30, 225*
  accommodation
    Jinjaya Bungalows ℃ (0365) 42945 *225*
    Medewi Beach Cottages
      ℃ (0365) 40029 Ⓕ *225*
  attractions
    jogged bumbung dance *225*
Menanga *184*
Mengwi *35, 102, 166, 171*
  attractions
    Taman Ayun *35, 166*
    temple meru *102, 166*
Menjangan Island *13, 26, 30, 212, 219, 221, 222, 223*
  sports
    diving *13, 31, 221*
    snorkeling *221*
Mewang *151*
  attractions
    Balinese dances *151*
Moluccas *80, 237*
money *248, 249*
Mount Abang *26, 36, 171, 174, 180*
  sports
    climbing *26, 180*
Mount Agung *12, 13, 23, 25, 26, 35, 54, 141, 166, 170, 173, 174, 176, 180, 181, 182, 184, 185, 192, 196, 201, 204, 224*
  attractions
    Door of Agung *183*
  sports
    climbing *23, 26, 182, 184*
Mount Batur *23, 25, 26, 36, 125, 155, 170, 171, 173, 174, 175, 176, 177, 180*
  attractions
    Ulung Batur *174, 175*
  sports
    climbing *23, 26, 176, 177*
Mount Prapat Agung *220, 222*
Mount Seraya *204*

N

Negara *224, 225*
  access 225
  accommodation
    Cahaya Matahari Bungalows
      ℃ (0365) 82218 Ⓕ *224*
  Wira Pada Hotel ℃ (0365) 41161 *224*
  festivals and special events
    Water Buffalo Races, August and October *224*
  general information 224
    RSU (clinic) ℃ (0365) 41006 *224*
    Tourist Office ℃ (0365) 41060 *224*
newspapers and magazines *250*
Ngurah Rai Airport *29, 38, 51, 52, 53, 110, 112, 113, 124, 145, 175, 211, 236, 237*
  general information
    airport taxis *237*
    departure tax *238*
    Immigration Office ℃ (0361) 751038 *238*
Njuling River *192*
Nusa Ceningan *229*
  sports
    diving and surfing *229*
Nusa Dua *14, 27, 29, 30, 31, 32, 33, 36, 38, 39, 40, 41, 51, 52, 74, 106, 110, 116, 119, 126, 128, 130, 134, 210, 237, 246, 249, 254*
  access 141
  accommodation
    Amanusa ℃ (0361) 772333 Ⓕ *38, 140*
    Bali Club Méditerranée
      ℃ (0361) 771520 Ⓕ *41, 135, 139*
    Grand Hyatt Bali ℃ (0361) 771234 Ⓕ *135, 139*
    Hotel Bualu ℃ (0361) 771310 Ⓕ *140*
    Melia Bali Sol Hotel
      ℃ (0361) 771510 Ⓕ Ⓔ *139*
    Nikko Bali ℃ (0361) 773377 Ⓕ *27, 140*
    Nusa Dua Beach Hotel
      ℃ (0361) 771210 Ⓕ *39, 139*
    Putri Bali ℃ (0361) 771020, 771420 *139*
    Tamen Sari Suite Hotel
      ℃ (0361) 773953 Ⓕ Ⓔ *140*
  attractions
    Balinese dances *136*
    beaches *135*
    Mandara Spa ℃ (0361) 771791 Ⓕ *137*
    Sri Agung Spa ℃ (0361) 772828 *137*
  environs and excursions
    Ulu Watu Temple *141*
  general information *27, 32, 135, 137*
    ATMs *138*
    Bali Taxi ℃ (0361) 701111 Ⓕ *136*
    CV Nusa Dua Internet ℃ (0361) 775496 Ⓔ *136*
    Galleria Shopping Center *135*
    Garuda Indonesia ℃ (0361) 771906 *240*
    Made Latra ℃ (0361) 773763 *136*
    NDC (clinic/dentist)
      ℃/FAX (0361) 771324 *135, 254*
    Waka Land Cruise
      ℃ (0361) 426972 Ⓕ Ⓔ Ⓦ *133*
  restaurants
    Bola Bali ℃ (0361) 775490 *141*
    Galih ℃ (0361) 775740 *140*
    Galleria Shopping Center *52*
    Matsuri Japanese Restaurant
      ℃ (0361) 772267 *140*
    Sendok ℃ (0361) 772850 *140*
    Taman Sari Thai Restaurang
      ℃ (0361) 773953 *141*
    Warung Bali ℃ (0361) 775523 *141*
  shopping
    Galleria Shopping Center *135, 136, 137, 138*
    Tragia Supermarket *138*
    Uluwatu ℃ (0361) 751933 *51*
    Yakkum Craft ℃ (0274) 895386 Ⓔ Ⓦ *138*

sports
    diving *31*
    golf *32, 33, 137*
    sailing and windsurfing *30*
Nusa Lembongan *13, 31, 36, 128, 192, 229, 232*
  access 230, 232
  accommodation
    Agung's *230*
    Bunga Lombongan *230*
    Bungalow No. 7 *230*
    Ketut Losmen *230*
    Mainski ((0811) 94426 *230*
    Mushroom Beach Bungalows *229*
    Nusa Indah *230*
    Nusa Lembongan Resort
      ((0361) 725864 Ⓕ Ⓔ Ⓦ *229*
    Puri Nusa (/FAX (0361) 298613 *229*
    Tarci Bungalows *230*
    Waka Nusa Resort ((0361) 261130,
      723629 Ⓕ *229*
  attractions
    Jungutbatu Beach *229*
    Mushroom Beach *229*
  general information 230
    Bali Hai ((0361) 720331 Ⓕ Ⓔ Ⓦ *229, 230*
  sports
    diving *13, 31, 128, 229*
    snorkeling *31, 229*
    surfing *229*
Nusa Penida *31, 79, 128, 134, 136, 137, 192, 229, 230*
  access 232
  accommodation 232
  attractions
    Anceng, Seganing, and Swean Stairways *232*
    cliff routes *232*
    Goa Karangsari *231*
    Ped *231*
    Sebuluh Stairway *232*
  sports
    diving *31, 128, 230*
    surfing *230*

P **Padang Padang** *29*
  sports
    surfing *29*
Padangbai *37, 39, 80, 110, 189, 190, 194, 232,*
  233, 236
  access 195
  accommodation
    Amankila ((0363) 41333 Ⓕ Ⓔ *38, 194*
    Padang Bai Beach Inn ((0363) 4147 *195*
    Puri Rai ((0363) 41385 Ⓕ *194*
  attractions
    bird orchestra *194*
    Blue Lagoon *194*
    colorful prahu *194*
    Little Beach and Black Sand Beach *194*
    Mosque *194*
  general information
    Café Papa John ((0812) 392-3114 *194*
    Geko Dive ((0363) 41516 Ⓕ *194*
    Harbor Office ((0363) 41840 *195*
    Nusa Penida crossings *233*
    Tourist Information Office ((0363) 41502 *194*
  restaurants
    Depot Segara *195*
    Pandan Restaurant *195*
    Puri Rai ((0363) 41385 *194*

sports
    diving *194*
    snorkeling *194*
painters and paintings *48–49, 57, 128, 153, 192*
Pakrisan River *162*
Payangan *153, 157, 172*
Ped *231*
  attractions
    Ped Temple *231*
    Ratu Gede Macaling Shrine *231*
Pejeng *163*
  attractions
    Archaeological Museum *163*
    Moon Face Drum *163*
    Pura Kebo Edan *163*
    Pura Panataram Sasih *163*
Peliatan *151*
  attractions
    Balinese dances *151*
Pemuteran *11, 28, 29, 53, 221, 222*
  access 223
  accommodation 223
    Matahari Hotel ((0362) 92312 Ⓕ *223*
    Puri Ganesha Villas ((0362) 93433 Ⓦ *223*
    Segara Bukit Beach Cottages
      ((0828) 365231 Ⓕ *223*
    Taman Sari Bali Cottages
      (/FAX (0362) 93264 *223*
  attractions
    Pulaki Monkey Temple *222*
    turtles *11*
  general information
    Reef Seen Aquatics
      (/FAX (0362) 92339 Ⓔ *11, 28, 222*
  sports
    horseback riding *28*
    snorkeling *222*
Penelokan *26, 170, 172, 174, 175, 176, 177, 180, 184,*
  249
  access 174
  accommodation and restaurants
    Lakeview Restaurant and Hotel
      (/FAX (0366) 51464 *174, 180*
  attractions
    caldera views *173*
  general information
    Lakeview ((0366) 51464 *26*
  restaurants
    Puri Dewata *180*
    Puri Selera *180*
    Restaurant Gunawan ((0366) 51050 *180*
    Suling Bali *180*
Penestanan *48*
Pengastulan *220, 222*
Penulisan *35, 180*
  attractions
    Pura Tegeh Koripan *180*
Pesanggaran *30*
  general information
    Bali Adventure Tours
      ((0361) 721480 Ⓕ Ⓔ Ⓦ *30*
photography *256*
population *70, 79, 89, 224, 230*
Prancak River *25*
Prasi *196*
  general information
    Government Clinic ((0361) 22188 *196*

Pujung *49, 162*
  shopping
    banana tree carvings *49, 162*
Pulaki *34, 41, 210*
  attractions
    Monkey Temple *34, 41*
Pulau Serangan *128, 134, 136*
  attractions
    Pura Sakenan *134*
  festivals and special events
    Kuningan, every 210-days *134*
Pura Yati *26*
  sports
    climbing Mount Batur *26*

R rafting *See* whitewater rafting
religion *18, 41, 57, 59, 70, 79, 86, 89, 96, 101, 102, 181, 209, 214, 222, 230, 231*
Rendang *184, 185*
restaurants
  exceptional restaurants 38
  general information 57, 132, 247
  ordering, basic terms 58, 247
  prices 247, 248
  tipping 253
  warungs 57, 247

S safety *38, 135, 255*
Sampalan *230, 231, 232, 233*
  accommodation
    Bungalows Pemda *232*
    Losmen Made *232*
  attractions
    market *230*
  restaurants
    warungs *232*
Sangeh *35, 40, 166*
  attractions
    Monkey Forest *35, 40, 166*
    trees and flowers *166*
Sangsit *34, 35, 214, 215*
  attractions
    Pura Beji *34, 214*
Sanur *14, 22, 29-31, 33, 36, 39-40, 51-52, 64-65, 74, 83-84, 106-107, 110, 116, 119, 126, 133-134, 141, 145, 161, 196-197, 210, 229-230, 237, 244, 246, 248-249*
  access 127, 133
  accommodation
    Ananda Hotel ((0361) 288327 *131*
    Bali Hyatt ((0361) 288271 Ⓕ Ⓔ *39, 130*
    Bali Senia Hotel ((0361) 289358 Ⓕ Ⓔ *132*
    Bali Warma ((0361) 285618 Ⓕ *131*
    Baruna Beach ((0361) 288546 Ⓕ *131*
    Diwangkara ((0361) 288577 *130*
    Grand Bali Beach
      ((0361) 288511 Ⓕ *126, 127, 130*
    Ida's Homestay ((0811) 387211 Ⓕ *131*
    Natour Sindhu Beach
      ((0361) 288351 Ⓕ Ⓔ *131*
    Puri Suar ((0361) 285572 *132*
    Raddin ((0361) 288833 Ⓕ Ⓔ Ⓦ *130*
    Radisson Bali ((0361) 281781 Ⓕ Ⓔ Ⓦ *130*
    Santai (/FAX (0361) 281684 Ⓔ *131*
    Santrian Beach Resort ((0361) 288009 Ⓕ *131*
    Sanur Beach Hotel ((0361) 288011 Ⓕ Ⓔ *130*
    Segara Village Hotel
      ((0361) 288407 Ⓕ Ⓔ *130*
    Tandjung Sari ((0361) 288341 Ⓕ Ⓔ *39, 130*
    Yulia Homestay ((0361) 288089 *131*
  attractions
    Batujimbar *127*
    beach massages *129*
    Museum Le Mayeur *128*
    Peruna Beauty Line Salon ((0361) 289536 *129*
    Sanur Beach *126*
    Sehatku ((0361) 287880 *129*
    Semawang *128*
    Sindhu *127*
  environs and excursions 133
    Pulau Serangan *128, 134*
  general information
    airport taxis *127*
    Aquapro ((0361) 270791 Ⓕ Ⓔ *128*
    Atlantis ((0361) 283676 Ⓔ *128*
    Bali Adventure Rafting ((0361) 721480 *30*
    Bali Car Rental ((0361) 288550 *127*
    Bali Diving Perdana ((0361) 286493 *22*
    Bali Indonesia ((0361) 288271 *64*
    Bali International Rafting
      ((0361) 281408 Ⓕ *30*
    Bali Safari Dive ((0361) 282656 Ⓔ *128*
    Citra Bali Dive Center ((0361) 286788 Ⓕ *31*
    Garuda Indonesia ((0361) 288011, *288511 240*
    Grand Bali Beach Golf Course
      ((0361) 288511 Ⓕ *33, 128*
    Grand Komodo Tours ((0361) 287166 Ⓕ *128*
    Legian Clinic ((0361) 758503 *127*
    Ocha Internet Café ((0361) 264186 Ⓔ *127*
    Pacto ((0361) 288247 *64*
    Post Office *249*
    Praja Taxi Company ((0361) 289191 *127*
    Santai Internet Café (/FAX (0361) 281684 Ⓔ *131*
    Sobek ((0361) 287059 Ⓕ Ⓔ *30*
    Wirasana Rent Car ((0361) 286066 *244*
  history 83
  nightlife
    Grantang Bar ((0361) 288271 *133*
    Jazz Bar and Grill ((0361) 285892 *133*
    Jazz Warung ((0361) 287761 *133*
    Kafe Wayang ((0361) 287591 *133*
    Lazer & Sport Bar ((0361) 288807 *133*
    Legong ((0361) 288066 *132*
    Mango Café ((0361) 288411 *133*
    Planet Sanur Café ((0361) 287597 *133*
  restaurants
    Bali Hyatt ((0361) 288271 *130*
    Chong Gi-Wa (/FAX (0361) 287084 *132*
    Kita ((0361) 288453 *132*
    Krui Puti ((0361) 288212 *132*
    Kul Kul Restaurant ((0361) 288038 *132*
    Night Market *132*
    Ryoshi ((0361) 288473 *132*
    Tandjung Sari ((0361) 288441 *132*
    Telaga Naga ((0361) 281234,
      extension 8080 *132*
    Trattoria Da Marco's ((0361) 288996 *132*
  shopping
    Earth and Fire *129*
    Lama Gallery ((0361) 286809 Ⓕ *129*
    Mama & Leon Boutique
      ((0361) 288044 Ⓕ *129*
    Miralin Collection (/FAX (0361) 286061 *129*
    Nogo Ikat Center ((0361) 288765 *129*
    Rafflesia ((0361) 288528 *129*
    Suarti Designer Collection
      ((0361) 298914 *129*
    Uluwatu ((0361) 288977 *51, 129*

sports
    diving *30, 31*
    golf *33, 128*
    sailing *30*
    surfing and windsurfing *30, 128*
Sawan *35, 214*
    attractions
        gongs for gamelan orchestras *214*
Sayan *38, 58, 156, 157*
Sebatu *162*
    attractions
        public baths *162*
Sebudi *26, 184*
    sports
        climbing Mount Agung *26, 184*
Sebuluh *232*
    attractions
        aerial stairway *232*
    festivals and special events
        Temple Festival, every 210 days *232*
Selat *184, 185*
Seminyak *36, 38, 40, 52, 74, 106, 110, 111, 112, 113, 114, 118, 119, 121, 122, 123, 124, 145, 246*
    accommodation
        Legian ((0361) 730622 Ⓕ Ⓔ Ⓦ *38, 39, 121*
        Oberoi Bali ((0361) 730361 Ⓕ Ⓔ Ⓦ *38, 39, 110, 114, 115, 121*
        Puri Bunga Cottages
            ((0361) 730939 Ⓕ Ⓔ Ⓦ *122*
    general information
        horse stables ((0361) 730401 *118*
    restaurants
        Gateway of India ((0361) 732940 *123*
        Kafe Warisan ((0361) 731175 *38, 122*
        La Lucciola ((0361) 730838 *38, 123*
        Soda Club ((0812) 380-8846 *123*
        Tivoli *123*
        Warung Batavia ((0361) 243769 *123*
    shopping 38, 119, 120
        Ⓔ Ekstra ((0811) 398685 *120*
        Irie Collection (/FAX (0361) 754732 *119*
        Titien Collection (/FAX (0361) 730448 *119*
        Warisan ((0361) 730710 *120*
    sports
        horseback riding *118*
        surfing *118*
    shopping
        bargaining 51, 252
        general information 48, 138
        gold and silver 51
        masks 50
        paintings 48–49
        stone carvings 50
        textiles 51
        woodcarvings 49–50
Sidemen *185, 199*
Singapadu *40, 50, 51, 60, 133*
    attractions 40, 60, 133
        Bali Reptile Park *40*
    shopping
        masks *50*
        silverware *51*
Singaraja *28, 29, 33, 34, 36, 80, 83, 84, 110, 170, 199, 204, 205, 209, 211, 214, 223*
    accommodation
        Kalaspa Health Retreat
            ((0361) 419606 *210*
        Wijaya Hotel ((0362) 21915 Ⓕ *210*

attractions
    Gedong Kirtya *209*
    Night Market *209*
general information
    bemo stations *210*
    Tourist Information Bureau
        ((0362) 25141 *209*
    history 80, 83, 209
Soka Beach *29*
Songan *176*
    attractions
        temple *176*
Straits of Lombok *203*
Sukat *185*
Sukawati *161*
Sulawesi *49, 80, 237, 240*
Sumatra *28, 58, 79, 236*
Sumbawa *237, 240*
Surabaya *84, 213, 220, 240*

T **Tabanan** *61, 80*
    attractions
        Bali Butterfly Park ((0361) 814282 Ⓕ *61*
    history 80
Taman Burung Bali Bird Park *40, 60, 133*
    attractions
        king bird of paradise *60, 133*
        Komodo Dragon *40*
    general information
        Park Information
            ((0361) 299352 Ⓕ Ⓔ Ⓦ *40, 60, 133*
Tampaksiring *162, 172*
    attractions
        Sukarno Palace *162*
        Tirta Empul *162*
Tanah Lot *14, 28, 33, 124*
    access 126
    accommodation
        Dewi Sinta ((0361) 812933 Ⓕ *126*
        Mutiara Tanah Lot Bungalows
            ((0361) 225457 Ⓕ *126*
    attractions
        temple shrines *125*
    general information
        Bali Nirvana Resort Golf Course
            ((0361) 815960 *33, 126*
    sports
        golf *33, 126*
Tanjung Benoa *53, 58, 128, 134, 135, 136, 137, 139, 140, 237, 240*
    accommodation
        Grand Mirage ((0361) 771888 Ⓕ Ⓔ *140*
        Pondok Agung ((0361) 771143 *140*
        Rasa Dua Homestay ((0361) 772726 *140*
        Rasa Sayang ((0361) 771643 *140*
    attractions
        Aroma Talk (/FAX (0361) 771458 *138*
        Beluga Marina ((0361) 771997 Ⓕ *136*
        Chinese temple *137*
        kecak dances *136*
        Thalasso Bali ((0361) 771888 Ⓕ Ⓔ *137*
    general information 58, 138
        Beluga Marina ((0361) 771997 Ⓕ *136*
        Lingga Sempurna ((0361) 774761 *136*
        Quicksilver Tours ((0361) 771997 Ⓕ *66*
        Waterworld ((0361) 772781 Ⓕ Ⓔ *136*
    restaurants
        Grand Mirage Club ((0361) 772147 *140*

sports
  diving, parasailing and windsurfing 136
Taro 27
  attractions
    elephant rides 27
  general information
    Elephant Trekking ✆ (0361) 286072 27
Tegalalang 162
  shopping
    softwood carvings 162
Teges 151, 164
  attractions
    Balinese dances 151
telephone 249
  Bali area codes 249
  international calls 249
  useful numbers 249
temple architecture 101, 102
Temukus 210
Tenganan 50, 198, 199
  attractions
    Bali Aga architecture and lifestyle 198, 199
    Banjar Pande 198
    cemetery 198
  shopping
    I. Nyoman K. Nurati Craft Shop 199
    ikat weavings 50
    Indra Art Shop 199
time 248
tipping 252
Tirta Empul 162
Tirtagangga 189, 201, 204
  access 201
  accommodation and restaurants
    Kusuma Jaya Inn ✆ (0363) 21250 201
    Puri Prima ✆/FAX (0363) 21316 201
    Tirta Ayu Restaurant and Homestay
      ✆ (0363) 21697 201
  attractions
    rice terraces 189
    water palace 189, 201
Tjampuhan 60, 155
tooth-filing rituals 93, 95, 108
tourist information 241
tours
  Australian tour operators
    Bali Travel Service ✆ (02) 9264 5895 63
    San Michele Travel ✆ (02) 9299 1111 63
    Trailfinders ✆ (07) 3229 0887 63
    Tymtro Travel ✆ (02) 9223 2211 63
  Balinese tour operators
    Bali Hai ✆ (0361) 720331 ⒻⒺⓌ 66
    Bali Indonesia ✆ (0361) 288271 64
    Bali Origin ✆/FAX (0361) 238504 Ⓔ 65
    Golden Wings Bali Avia
      ✆ (0361) 751257 ⒻⒺ 66
    Jans Tours ✆ (0361) 232660 Ⓕ 65
    KCB Tours and Travel
      ✆ (0361) 75157 ⒻⒺ 64, 65
    Lembongan Express ✆ (0361) 724545 67
    Pacto ✆ (0361) 288247 64
    Quicksilver Tours ✆ (0361) 771397 Ⓕ 66
    Satriavi ✆ (0361) 287074 Ⓕ 65
    Waka Louka ✆ (0361) 426792 Ⓕ 65, 67
  New Zealand tour operators
    Budget Travel ✆ (09) 366 0061 63

UK tour operators
  Abercrombie & Kent
    ✆ (020) 7730 9600 ⒻⓌ 62
  Bridge the World ✆ (020) 7911 0900 63
  Flightbookers ✆ (020) 7757 2444 63
  Imaginative Traveller
    ✆ (020) 8742 8612 ⒻⓌ 62
  Travellers' Choice ✆ (0870) 905 6000 ⒻⓌ 63
  Tropical Places ✆ (01342) 330740 ⒻⓌ 63
US tour operators 62
  Himalayan Travel
    TOLL-FREE (800) 225-2380 Ⓦ 62
  STA Travel ✆ (212) 627-3111 Ⓣ 62
  Travel Avenue TOLL-FREE (800) 333-3355 62
Toyah Bungkah 26, 175, 176
  sports
    climbing Mount Batur 26
Toyapakeh 230, 233
travel papers 237, 238
Trunyan 27, 171, 174, 175, 177, 178, 198
  access 177
  attractions
    Bali Aga cemetery 175, 177, 178
  sports
    hiking 27
Tuban 38, 112, 120, 237
Tulamben 12, 13, 30, 34, 189, 204, 212, 249
  access 205
  accommodation 205
    Emerald Tulamben Beach Hotel
      ✆ (0361) 462673 Ⓕ 205
    Mimpi Resort ✆/FAX (0363) 21642 205
  general information
    Dive Paradise Tulamben ✆ (363) 41052 205
    Ena Dive Center ✆ (0361) 287945 Ⓕ 13
    Ganda Mayu Bungalow
      ✆ (0361) 730200 Ⓕ 13
    Mega Dive ✆ (0361) 288192 205
    Tulamben Dive Center
      ✆ (0361) 41032 13, 205
  sports
    snorkeling 13
    wreck-diving 12, 13, 30, 34, 205
Turtle Island *See* Pulau Serangan (Turtle Island)

Ⓤ **Ubud** 21, 35-36, 38-39, 43, 48, 51-52, 58, 60, 61, 74,
  84, 110, 148, 161, 163-165, 172, 174, 197, 223, 247, 249, 255
  access 161
  accommodation
    Agung Rai ✆ (0361) 976659 Ⓦ 153
    Alit House ✆ (0361) 973284 158
    Amandari ✆ (0361) 975333 ⒻⒺ 157
    Brata 1 ✆ (0361) 975598 158
    Bucu View ✆ (0361) 975976 Ⓕ 158
    Chedi ✆ (0361) 975963 ⒻⒺⓌ 39, 157
    Four Seasons Sayan
      ✆ (0361) 977577 ⒻⓌ 38, 156
    Gherhana Sari Art Shop ✆ (0361) 975392 158
    Han Snel's Siti Bungalows
      ✆ (0361) 975699 Ⓕ 158
    Kupu Kupu Barong
      ✆ (0361) 975476 Ⓕ 39, 157
    Menara Café ✆ (0361) 975142 158
    Pita ✆ (0361) 975368 Ⓕ 157
    Tjamphuan ✆ (0361) 975368 Ⓕ 157
    Ubud Inn ✆ (0361) 975071 Ⓕ 158
    Vera ✆ (0361) 975960 158
    Wayan Family 158

attractions
  Agung Rai Museum of Art
    ((0361) 976659 Ⓦ 152
  Antonio Blanco's House 153
  Balinese dances 43, 52, 151, 152
  Birdwatching and Herb Walks 60, 155
  Gusti Lempad's Gallery 154
  Hotel Tjampuhan 153
  Neka Art Museum ((0361) 975074 Ⓕ 152
  Pura Pamerajaan Sari Cokorda Agung 154
  Puri Lukisan Museum ((0361) 975136 48, 152
  Sacred Monkey Forest Sanctuary 154
  Seniwati Gallery ((0361) 975485 Ⓦ 153
  Ubud Palace 151, 152, 154
  wayang kulit 21
environs and excursions 162, 165, 166
general information 58, 161
  Bakor Motor ((0361) 973405 151
  Bali 3000 Internet Café 152
  Bali Bintang Tour ((0361) 975992 155
  Balinese arts courses 61
  Beggar's Bush ((0361) 975009 60, 155
  Café Bukit Bamboo ((0818) 550725 Ⓕ 155
  Casa Luna cooking courses
    ((0361) 977409 152
  Darma Tourist Service ((0361) 978410 151
  Dhyana Putri Adventures
    ((0361) 975180 Ⓕ Ⓔ 62
  Downhill Mountain Bike Tours
    ((0361) 975557 155
  Dwi Bhumi culture courses
    ((0818) 351393 152
  Ganesha Bookshop music courses
    ((0361) 976339 152
  Herb Walk ((0361) 975051 155
  mountain bike rental 151
  Nirwana Batik courses 152
  Perama ((0361) 974772 161
  schedule for dance performances 151, 152
  Sobek ((0361) 287059 Ⓔ 155
  Spirit of Adventure ((0361) 973405 155
  Ubud Clinic ((0361) 974911 Ⓕ Ⓔ Ⓦ 151
  Ubud Tourist Office
    ((0361) 973285 150, 152, 161
health and beauty
  Daya Putih School ((0361) 975467 154
  Meditation Shop 154
  Mentari Massage Centre ((0361) 974001 154
  Nirvana ((0812) 394-6702 154
  Nur Salon ((0361) 975352 154
  Sri Jane ((0812) 398-5048 Ⓔ 154
  Tri Nadi Health Center ((0361) 977934 154
  Ubud Sari Health Resort ((0361) 974393 154
history 148
nightlife
  Café Bukit Bamboo ((0818) 550725 161
  Exiles ((0361) 974842 161
  Funky Monkey 161
  Jazz Café ((0361) 976594 161
  Nuri's Warung 161
  Putra Bar ((0361) 975570 161
restaurants
  Agung Rai ((0361) 976659 153
  Ary's Warung ((0361) 975063 159
  Café Lotus ((0361) 975660 159

  Café Wayan ((0361) 975447 161
  Casa Luna ((0361) 977409 159
  Four Seasons Sayan ((0361) 977577 159
  Gayatri 159
  Han Snel's Siti Bungalows ((0361) 975699 158
  Indus 159
  Lotus Lane ((0361) 975357 159
  Menara Café ((0361) 975142 158
  Murni's Warung ((0361) 975233 159
  Nomad Wine Bar and Restaurant 159
  Thai Restaurant and Bar ((0361) 977484 159
  Tutmak Warung Kopi ((0361) 975754 159
shopping
  Agung Rai Fine Art Gallery
    ((0361) 976659 Ⓦ 48, 153, 156
  Archipelago 156
  Ida Bagus Tilem 49
  Monkey Forest Road 156
  Munut's Gallery 156
  Murni's Warung ((0361) 975233 159
  Neka Gallery 48, 156
  paintings 48
  Puri Lukisan Museum ((0361) 975136 152
  Seni Echo 156
  Seniwati Gallery ((0361) 975485 Ⓦ 153
  Tugen ((0361) 973361 156
  Ubud Market 156
  Uluwatu ((0361) 751933 51
sports
  mountain biking 155
  whitewater rafting 154
Ujung 34, 200, 201, 204
  access 201
  attractions
    water palace 34, 200, 201
Ulu Watu 13, 22, 29, 41, 110, 126, 135, 141, 145
  access 14
  attractions
    dolphin-watching 22
    kecak fire-dance 141
    monkeys 14, 41
    Ulu Watu Surfing Beach 141
  sports
    surfing 29, 135, 141
Unda River 192

Ⓥ visas 237, 238
  volcanoes 12, 23, 26, 34, 52, 65, 70, 79, 96, 170, 172, 176, 182, 185, 189, 204, 220

Ⓦ water 248, 253
  wayang kulit 20, 21, 43, 46, 61, 151, 161
  web sites 55, 257
    Bali information www.baliwww.com/bali 258
    hotel and tour bookings www.halo-bali.com 257
    hotels, restaurants, attractions
      www.baliclick.com 257
    monthly newsletter www.baliandbeyond.com 257
    soft-sell site www.pande-bali.com 258
    tourism information
      www.tourismindonesia.com 257
    travel and festival informations
      bali-paradise.com 257
    travel guide www.bali-travel.net 257

weights and measures 248
West Bali National Park 25, 26, 31, 61, 219, 220, 222
  access 221
  accommodation 221
  attractions
    Bali Barat Marine Park 221, 222
    Menjangan Island 221
    Pre-release Breeding Program 220
    Rothschild's myna 25, 60, 220
  general information 220
    Forestry Department ((0361) 235679 26
  sports
    hiking 26, 220

Y Yeh Gangga Beach 28
  general information
    Bali Horse Riding ((0361) 224603 28
  sports
    horseback riding 28
Yeh Pulu 163
Yeh Sanih 215
  accommodation
    Air Sanih Seaside Cottages ((0362) 23357 215
    Bungalow Puri Sanih 215
  attractions
    bathing pools 215
    temple with bird orchestra 215
  restaurants
    Bungalow Puri Sanih 215
Yehunda River 184

Picture Credits

All photographs were taken by **Nik Wheeler** with the exception of the following:
Alain Evrard: pages 6 *right*, 28, 34 *top*, 37 *top*, 46, 61, 67, 85, 121, 122, 133, 152, 153, 168, 171, 185, 202, 205, 207, 233, and 253; back cover: second and fourth from top.
Rio Helmi: pages 64, 137, and 158.
Jack Barker: pages 11, 40, 122, 131, 140, and 216.
Leonard Lueras: pages 3, 50, 63, 69, 78, 81, 82, 90, 94, 100, 139, 162, 175, 182, 183, 186, 187, 215, 222, 228, 238, and 241.
Martin Westlake: pages 6 *left*, 10, 12, 24, 27, 31, 32, 38, 42 *top and bottom*, 44, 49, 63, 84, 88, 195, 201, 218, 225, and 236.
Bradley Winterton: pages 25, 53, 68, 116, 117, 142, 226, 239, and 243.
Minassio/Globe Press: pages 10, 34 *bottom*, 55, 59, 146, 147, 205, 217, and 248; back cover: top and third and fifth from top.